The COMPLETE ENCYCLICALS, BULLS, and APOSTOLIC EXHORTATIONS

VOLUME I

"Pope Francis is a revolutionary. The revolution he proposes, however, is not a matter of economic or political prescription but a revolution in the self-understanding of the Catholic Church: a re-energizing return to the pentecostal fervor and evangelical passion from which the Church was born two millennia ago and a summons to mission that accelerates the great historical transition from institutional-maintenance Catholicism to the Church of the New Evangelization."

George Weigel

"Pope Francis's groundbreaking new document *Amoris Laetitia* (*The Joy of Love*) asks the Church to meet people where they are, to consider the complexities of people's lives, and to respect people's consciences when it comes to moral decisions. The apostolic exhortation is mainly a document that reflects on family life and encourages families. But it is also the pope's reminder that the Church should avoid simply judging people and imposing rules on them without considering their struggles."

Rev. James Martin, S.J.

"*Laudato Si'* seems destined to go down as a major turning point, the moment when environmentalism claimed pride of place on par with the dignity of human life and economic justice as a cornerstone of Catholic social teaching. It also immediately makes the Catholic Church arguably the leading moral voice in the press to combat global warming and the consequences of climate change."

John L. Allen Jr.

POPE FRANCIS

The COMPLETE ENCYCLICALS, BULLS, and APOSTOLIC EXHORTATIONS

VOLUME I

AVE MARIA PRESS AVE Notre Dame, Indiana

Founded in 1865, Ave Maria Press is a ministry of the United States Province of Holy Cross.

www.avemariapress.com

Paperback: ISBN-13 978-1-59471-739-0

E-book: ISBN-13 978-1-59471-740-6

Cover and text design by K. H. Bonelli and David Scholtes.

Printed and bound in the United States of America.

Contents

Publisher's Note

For the first time, the encyclicals, bulls, and apostolic exhortations—all the major writings—of Pope Francis, the 266th and current pope of the Roman Catholic Church, are gathered together in one volume.

Encyclical comes from the Latin word *encyclius*, meaning "circular." In the ancient Church, encyclicals were actual circulating letters. Today, encyclicals are book-length reflections by the Holy Father on significant issues—usually matters of faith or morals—of vital importance to the worldwide Church and beyond. Papal bulls are also formal declarations, usually much shorter, by the pope. In this context, *bull* also comes from a Latin word, *bulla*, the traditional leaden "seal" on the document. Lastly, apostolic exhortations are occasions for a pope to urge certain activity, often after consultation with a synod of bishops.

Each of the five works collected here is a book unto itself. Each was written by Pope Francis for the Catholic faithful but also with the intention of communicating essential contemporary wisdom for all Christians and all people. This volume presents them in the order in which they were promulgated:

Lumen Fidei (*The Light of Faith*), an encyclical written four months into Pope Francis's papacy, focuses on the centrality of faith, the relationship between reason and faith, the Church's role in the transmission of faith, and how faith results in redeeming the world.

Evangelii Gaudium (*The Joy of the Gospel*) is the apostolic exhortation from later in 2013 and has been called Pope Francis's manifesto. It challenges all Christians to approach evangelization anew and to overcome complacency in order to fulfill Christ's great mission.

Misericordiae Vultus (*The Face of Mercy*), the papal bull for the Extraordinary Jubilee of Mercy in 2015, explains why "we need constantly to contemplate the mystery of mercy."

Laudato Si' (*Praise Be to You*) is the landmark encyclical from 2015 in which Pope Francis issued a clarion call to the Church and the world on climate change, human responsibility, the role of faith in how we live among God's entire creation, and the future of the planet.

Amoris Laetitia (*The Joy of Love*) is an exhortation published in March 2016 after the Synods on the Family, in which Pope Francis ranges in his quotations on and examples of love in the family from St. Thomas Aquinas to Dr. Martin Luther King Jr. to the film *Babette's Feast*.

Abbreviations

The following abbreviations for texts referenced in the documents appear in the endnotes. They are listed below for the convenience of readers who desire to explore the pope's ideas in greater detail.

AAS *Acta Apostolicae Sedis*: Latin for "Acts of the Apostolic See." An official journal of the Holy See first established by Pope Pius X in 1908.

PG *Patrologia Graeca,* edited by J. P. Migne. One hundred sixty-one volumes of patrology (the study of early Christian writers) in Greek, published in Paris between 1857 and 1866.

PL *Patrologia Latina,* edited by J. P. Migne. Two hundred seventeen volumes of patrology in Latin, plus additional indices, published in Paris between 1878 and 1890.

SC *Sacrosanctum Concilium*: Constitution on the Sacred Liturgy. A constitution of the Second Vatican Council, first promulgated by Pope Paul VI in 1963.

Lumen Fidei
The Light of Faith
June 29, 2013

ENCYCLICAL LETTER
LUMEN FIDEI
OF THE SUPREME PONTIFF
FRANCIS
TO THE BISHOPS, PRIESTS, DEACONS, CONSECRATED PERSONS, AND THE LAY FAITHFUL ON FAITH

1. The light of Faith: this is how the Church's tradition speaks of the great gift brought by Jesus. In John's Gospel, Christ says of himself: "I have come as light into the world, that whoever believes in me may not remain in darkness" (Jn 12:46). Saint Paul uses the same image: "God who said 'Let light shine out of darkness,' has shone in our hearts" (2 Cor 4:6). The pagan world, which hungered for light, had seen the growth of the cult of the sun god, *Sol Invictus*, invoked each day at sunrise. Yet though the sun was born anew each morning, it was clearly incapable of casting its light on all of human existence. The sun does not illumine all reality; its rays cannot penetrate to the shadow of death, the place where men's eyes are closed to its light. "No one"—Saint Justin Martyr writes—"has ever been ready to die for his faith in the sun."[1] Conscious of the immense horizon which their faith opened before them, Christians invoked Jesus as the true sun "whose rays bestow life."[2] To Martha, weeping for the death of her brother Lazarus, Jesus said: "Did I not tell you that if you believed, you would see the glory of God?" (Jn 11:40). Those who believe, see; they see with a light that illumines their entire journey, for it comes from the risen Christ, the morning star which never sets.

An illusory light?

2. Yet in speaking of the light of faith, we can almost hear the objections of many of our contemporaries. In modernity, that light might have been considered sufficient for societies of old, but was felt to be of no use for new times, for a humanity come of age, proud of its rationality and

anxious to explore the future in novel ways. Faith thus appeared to some as an illusory light, preventing mankind from boldly setting out in quest of knowledge. The young Nietzsche encouraged his sister Elisabeth to take risks, to tread "new paths . . . with all the uncertainty of one who must find his own way," adding that "this is where humanity's paths part: if you want peace of soul and happiness, then believe, but if you want to be a follower of truth, then seek."[3] Belief would be incompatible with seeking. From this starting point Nietzsche was to develop his critique of Christianity for diminishing the full meaning of human existence and stripping life of novelty and adventure. Faith would thus be the illusion of light, an illusion which blocks the path of a liberated humanity to its future.

3. In the process, faith came to be associated with darkness. There were those who tried to save faith by making room for it alongside the light of reason. Such room would open up wherever the light of reason could not penetrate, wherever certainty was no longer possible. Faith was thus understood either as a leap in the dark, to be taken in the absence of light, driven by blind emotion, or as a subjective light, capable perhaps of warming the heart and bringing personal consolation, but not something which could be proposed to others as an objective and shared light which points the way. Slowly but surely, however, it would become evident that the light of autonomous reason is not enough to illumine the future; ultimately the future remains shadowy and fraught with fear of the unknown. As a result, humanity renounced the search for a great light, Truth itself, in order to be content with smaller lights which illumine the fleeting moment yet prove incapable of showing the way. Yet in the absence of light everything becomes confused; it is impossible to tell good from evil, or the road to our destination from other roads which take us in endless circles, going nowhere.

A light to be recovered

4. There is an urgent need, then, to see once again that faith is a light, for once the flame of faith dies out, all other lights begin to dim. The light of faith is unique, since it is capable of illuminating *every aspect* of human

existence. A light this powerful cannot come from ourselves but from a more primordial source: in a word, it must come from God. Faith is born of an encounter with the living God who calls us and reveals his love, a love which precedes us and upon which we can lean for security and for building our lives. Transformed by this love, we gain fresh vision, new eyes to see; we realize that it contains a great promise of fulfillment, and that a vision of the future opens up before us. Faith, received from God as a supernatural gift, becomes a light for our way, guiding our journey through time. On the one hand, it is a light coming from the past, the light of the foundational memory of the life of Jesus which revealed his perfectly trustworthy love, a love capable of triumphing over death. Yet since Christ has risen and draws us beyond death, faith is also a light coming from the future and opening before us vast horizons which guide us beyond our isolated selves toward the breadth of communion. We come to see that faith does not dwell in shadow and gloom; it is a light for our darkness. Dante, in the *Divine Comedy*, after professing his faith to Saint Peter, describes that light as a "spark, which then becomes a burning flame and like a heavenly star within me glimmers."[4] It is this light of faith that I would now like to consider, so that it can grow and enlighten the present, becoming a star to brighten the horizon of our journey at a time when mankind is particularly in need of light.

5. Christ, on the eve of his passion, assured Peter: "I have prayed for you that your faith may not fail" (Lk 22:32). He then told him to strengthen his brothers and sisters in that same faith. Conscious of the duty entrusted to the Successor of Peter, Benedict XVI proclaimed the present Year of Faith, a time of grace which is helping us to sense the great joy of believing and to renew our wonder at the vast horizons which faith opens up, so as then to profess that faith in its unity and integrity, faithful to the memory of the Lord and sustained by his presence and by the working of the Holy Spirit. The conviction born of a faith which brings grandeur and fulfillment to life, a faith centered on Christ and on the power of his grace, inspired the mission of the first Christians. In the Acts of the Martyrs, we read the following dialogue between the Roman prefect Rusticus and a Christian named Hierax: "'Where are your parents?' the

judge asked the martyr. He replied: 'Our true father is Christ, and our mother is faith in him.'"[5] For those early Christians, faith, as an encounter with the living God revealed in Christ, was indeed a "mother," for it had brought them to the light and given birth within them to divine life, a new experience and a luminous vision of existence for which they were prepared to bear public witness to the end.

6. The Year of Faith was inaugurated on the fiftieth anniversary of the opening of the Second Vatican Council. This is itself a clear indication that Vatican II was a Council on faith,[6] inasmuch as it asked us to restore the primacy of God in Christ to the center of our lives, both as a Church and as individuals. The Church never takes faith for granted, but knows that this gift of God needs to be nourished and reinforced so that it can continue to guide her pilgrim way. The Second Vatican Council enabled the light of faith to illumine our human experience from within, accompanying the men and women of our time on their journey. It clearly showed how faith enriches life in all its dimensions.

7. These considerations on faith—in continuity with all that the Church's magisterium has pronounced on this theological virtue[7]—are meant to supplement what Benedict XVI had written in his encyclical letters on charity and hope. He himself had almost completed a first draft of an encyclical on faith. For this I am deeply grateful to him, and as his brother in Christ I have taken up his fine work and added a few contributions of my own. The Successor of Peter, yesterday, today, and tomorrow, is always called to strengthen his brothers and sisters in the priceless treasure of that faith which God has given as a light for humanity's path.

In God's gift of faith, a supernatural infused virtue, we realize that a great love has been offered us, a good word has been spoken to us, and that when we welcome that word, Jesus Christ the Word made flesh, the Holy Spirit transforms us, lights up our way to the future, and enables us joyfully to advance along that way on wings of hope. Thus wonderfully interwoven, faith, hope and charity are the driving force of the Christian life as it advances toward full communion with God. But what is it like, this road which faith opens up before us? What is the origin of this powerful light which brightens the journey of a successful and fruitful life?

CHAPTER ONE

WE HAVE BELIEVED IN LOVE
(cf. 1 Jn 4:16)

Abraham, our father in faith

8. Faith opens the way before us and accompanies our steps through time. Hence, if we want to understand what faith is, we need to follow the route it has taken, the path trodden by believers, as witnessed first in the Old Testament. Here a unique place belongs to Abraham, our father in faith. Something disturbing takes place in his life: God speaks to him; he reveals himself as a God who speaks and calls his name. Faith is linked to hearing. Abraham does not see God, but hears his voice. Faith thus takes on a personal aspect. God is not the god of a particular place, or a deity linked to specific sacred time, but the God of a person, the God of Abraham, Isaac, and Jacob, capable of interacting with man and establishing a covenant with him. Faith is our response to a word which engages us personally, to a "Thou" who calls us by name.

9. The word spoken to Abraham contains both a call and a promise. First, it is a call to leave his own land, a summons to a new life, the beginning of an exodus which points him toward an unforeseen future. The sight which faith would give to Abraham would always be linked to the need to take this step forward: faith "sees" to the extent that it journeys, to the extent that it chooses to enter into the horizons opened up by God's word. This word also contains a promise: Your descendants will be great in number, you will be the father of a great nation (cf. Gn 13:16; 15:5; 22:17). As a response to a word which preceded it, Abraham's faith would always be an act of remembrance. Yet this remembrance is not fixed on past events but, as the memory of a promise, it becomes capable of opening up the future, shedding light on the path to be taken. We see how faith, as remembrance of the future, *memoria futuri*, is thus closely bound up with hope.

10. Abraham is asked to entrust himself to this word. Faith understands that something so apparently ephemeral and fleeting as a word, when spoken by the God who is fidelity, becomes absolutely certain and unshakable, guaranteeing the continuity of our journey through history. Faith accepts this word as a solid rock upon which we can build, a straight highway on which we can travel. In the Bible, faith is expressed by the Hebrew word *'emûnāh,* derived from the verb *'amān* whose root means "to uphold." The term *'emûnāh* can signify both God's fidelity and man's faith. The man of faith gains strength by putting himself in the hands of the God who is faithful. Playing on this double meaning of the word—also found in the corresponding terms in Greek (*pistós*) and Latin (*fidelis*)—Saint Cyril of Jerusalem praised the dignity of the Christian who receives God's own name: both are called "faithful."[8] As Saint Augustine explains: "Man is faithful when he believes in God and his promises; God is faithful when he grants to man what he has promised."[9]

11. A final element of the story of Abraham is important for understanding his faith. God's word, while bringing newness and surprise, is not at all alien to Abraham's experience. In the voice which speaks to him, the patriarch recognizes a profound call which was always present at the core of his being. God ties his promise to that aspect of human life which has always appeared most "full of promise," namely, parenthood, the begetting of new life: "Sarah your wife shall bear you a son, and you shall name him Isaac" (Gn 17:19). The God who asks Abraham for complete trust reveals himself to be the source of all life. Faith is thus linked to God's fatherhood, which gives rise to all creation; the God who calls Abraham is the Creator, the one who "calls into existence the things that do not exist" (Rom 4:17), the one who "chose us before the foundation of the world . . . and destined us for adoption as his children" (Eph 1:4–5). For Abraham, faith in God sheds light on the depths of his being, it enables him to acknowledge the wellspring of goodness at the origin of all things and to realize that his life is not the product of non-being or chance, but the fruit of a personal call and a personal love. The mysterious God who called him is no alien deity, but the God who is the origin and mainstay of all that is. The great test of Abraham's faith, the sacrifice

of his son Isaac, would show the extent to which this primordial love is capable of ensuring life even beyond death. The word which could raise up a son to one who was "as good as dead," in "the barrenness" of Sarah's womb (cf. Rom 4:19), can also stand by his promise of a future beyond all threat or danger (cf. Heb 11:19; Rom 4:21).

The faith of Israel

12. The history of the people of Israel in the Book of Exodus follows in the wake of Abraham's faith. Faith once again is born of a primordial gift: Israel trusts in God, who promises to set his people free from their misery. Faith becomes a summons to a lengthy journey leading to worship of the Lord on Sinai and the inheritance of a promised land. God's love is seen to be like that of a father who carries his child along the way (cf. Dt 1:31). Israel's confession of faith takes shape as an account of God's deeds in setting his people free and acting as their guide (cf. Dt 26:5–11), an account passed down from one generation to the next. God's light shines for Israel through the remembrance of the Lord's mighty deeds, recalled and celebrated in worship, and passed down from parents to children. Here we see how the light of faith is linked to concrete life-stories, to the grateful remembrance of God's mighty deeds and the progressive fulfillment of his promises. Gothic architecture gave clear expression to this: in the great cathedrals light comes down from heaven by passing through windows depicting the history of salvation. God's light comes to us through the account of his self-revelation, and thus becomes capable of illuminating our passage through time by recalling his gifts and demonstrating how he fulfills his promises.

13. The history of Israel also shows us the temptation of unbelief to which the people yielded more than once. Here the opposite of faith is shown to be idolatry. While Moses is speaking to God on Sinai, the people cannot bear the mystery of God's hiddenness, they cannot endure the time of waiting to see his face. Faith by its very nature demands renouncing the immediate possession which sight would appear to offer; it is an invitation to turn to the source of the light, while respecting the mystery of a countenance which will unveil itself personally in its own good time.

Martin Buber once cited a definition of idolatry proposed by the rabbi of Kock: idolatry is "when a face addresses a face which is not a face."[10] In place of faith in God, it seems better to worship an idol, into whose face we can look directly and whose origin we know, because it is the work of our own hands. Before an idol, there is no risk that we will be called to abandon our security, for idols "have mouths, but they cannot speak" (Ps 115:5). Idols exist, we begin to see, as a pretext for setting ourselves at the center of reality and worshiping the work of our own hands. Once man has lost the fundamental orientation which unifies his existence, he breaks down into the multiplicity of his desires; in refusing to await the time of promise, his life-story disintegrates into a myriad of unconnected instants. Idolatry, then, is always polytheism, an aimless passing from one lord to another. Idolatry does not offer a journey but rather a plethora of paths leading nowhere and forming a vast labyrinth. Those who choose not to put their trust in God must hear the din of countless idols crying out: "Put your trust in me!" Faith, tied as it is to conversion, is the opposite of idolatry; it breaks with idols to turn to the living God in a personal encounter. Believing means entrusting oneself to a merciful love which always accepts and pardons, which sustains and directs our lives, and which shows its power by its ability to make straight the crooked lines of our history. Faith consists in the willingness to let ourselves be constantly transformed and renewed by God's call. Herein lies the paradox: by constantly turning toward the Lord, we discover a sure path which liberates us from the dissolution imposed upon us by idols.

14. In the faith of Israel we also encounter the figure of Moses, the mediator. The people may not see the face of God; it is Moses who speaks to YHWH on the mountain and then tells the others of the Lord's will. With this presence of a mediator in its midst, Israel learns to journey together in unity. The individual's act of faith finds its place within a community, within the common "we" of the people who, in faith, are like a single person—"my first-born son," as God would describe all of Israel (cf. Ex 4:22). Here mediation is not an obstacle, but an opening: through our encounter with others, our gaze rises to a truth greater than ourselves. Rousseau once lamented that he could not see God for himself: "How

many people stand between God and me!"[11] "Is it really so simple and natural that God would have sought out Moses in order to speak to Jean-Jacques Rousseau?"[12] On the basis of an individualistic and narrow conception of knowledge one cannot appreciate the significance of mediation, this capacity to participate in the vision of another, this shared knowledge which is the knowledge proper to love. Faith is God's free gift, which calls for humility and the courage to trust and to entrust; it enables us to see the luminous path leading to the encounter of God and humanity: the history of salvation.

The fullness of Christian faith

15. "Abraham rejoiced that he would see my day; he saw it and was glad" (Jn 8:56). According to these words of Jesus, Abraham's faith pointed to him; in some sense it foresaw his mystery. So Saint Augustine understood it when he stated that the patriarchs were saved by faith, not faith in Christ who had come but in Christ who was yet to come, a faith pressing toward the future of Jesus.[13] Christian faith is centered on Christ; it is the confession that Jesus is Lord and that God has raised him from the dead (cf. Rom 10:9). All the threads of the Old Testament converge on Christ; he becomes the definitive "Yes" to all the promises, the ultimate basis of our "Amen" to God (cf. 2 Cor 1:20). The history of Jesus is the complete manifestation of God's reliability. If Israel continued to recall God's great acts of love, which formed the core of its confession of faith and broadened its gaze in faith, the life of Jesus now appears as the locus of God's definitive intervention, the supreme manifestation of his love for us. The word which God speaks to us in Jesus is not simply one word among many, but his eternal Word (cf. Heb 1:1–2). God can give no greater guarantee of his love, as Saint Paul reminds us (cf. Rom 8:31–39). Christian faith is thus faith in a perfect love, in its decisive power, in its ability to transform the world and to unfold its history. "We know and believe the love that God has for us" (1 Jn 4:16). In the love of God revealed in Jesus, faith perceives the foundation on which all reality and its final destiny rest.

16. The clearest proof of the reliability of Christ's love is to be found in his dying for our sake. If laying down one's life for one's friends is the greatest proof of love (cf. Jn 15:13), Jesus offered his own life for all, even for his enemies, to transform their hearts. This explains why the evangelists could see the hour of Christ's crucifixion as the culmination of the gaze of faith; in that hour the depth and breadth of God's love shone forth. It was then that Saint John offered his solemn testimony, as together with the Mother of Jesus he gazed upon the pierced one (cf. Jn 19:37): "He who saw this has borne witness, so that you also may believe. His testimony is true, and he knows that he tells the truth" (Jn 19:35). In Dostoevsky's *The Idiot*, Prince Myshkin sees a painting by Hans Holbein the Younger depicting Christ dead in the tomb and says: "Looking at that painting might cause one to lose his faith."[14] The painting is a gruesome portrayal of the destructive effects of death on Christ's body. Yet it is precisely in contemplating Jesus' death that faith grows stronger and receives a dazzling light; then it is revealed as faith in Christ's steadfast love for us, a love capable of embracing death to bring us salvation. This love, which did not recoil before death in order to show its depth, is something I can believe in; Christ's total self-gift overcomes every suspicion and enables me to entrust myself to him completely.

17. Christ's death discloses the utter reliability of God's love above all in the light of his resurrection. As the risen one, Christ is the trustworthy witness, deserving of faith (cf. Rv 1:5; Heb 2:17), and a solid support for our faith. "If Christ has not been raised, your faith is futile," says Saint Paul (1 Cor 15:17). Had the Father's love not caused Jesus to rise from the dead, had it not been able to restore his body to life, then it would not be a completely reliable love, capable of illuminating also the gloom of death. When Saint Paul describes his new life in Christ, he speaks of "faith in the Son of God, who loved me and gave himself for me" (Gal 2:20). Clearly, this "faith in the Son of God" means Paul's faith in Jesus, but it also presumes that Jesus himself is worthy of faith, based not only on his having loved us even unto death but also on his divine sonship. Precisely because Jesus is the Son, because he is absolutely grounded in the Father, he was able to conquer death and make the fullness of life

shine forth. Our culture has lost its sense of God's tangible presence and activity in our world. We think that God is to be found in the beyond, on another level of reality, far removed from our everyday relationships. But if this were the case, if God could not act in the world, his love would not be truly powerful, truly real, and thus not even true, a love incapable of delivering the bliss that it promises. It would make no difference at all whether we believed in him or not. Christians, on the contrary, profess their faith in God's tangible and powerful love which really does act in history and determines its final destiny: a love that can be encountered, a love fully revealed in Christ's passion, death, and resurrection.

18. This fullness which Jesus brings to faith has another decisive aspect. In faith, Christ is not simply the one in whom we believe, the supreme manifestation of God's love; he is also the one with whom we are united precisely in order to believe. Faith does not merely gaze at Jesus, but sees things as Jesus himself sees them, with his own eyes: it is a participation in his way of seeing. In many areas in our lives we trust others who know more than we do. We trust the architect who builds our home, the pharmacist who gives us medicine for healing, the lawyer who defends us in court. We also need someone trustworthy and knowledgeable where God is concerned. Jesus, the Son of God, is the one who makes God known to us (cf. Jn 1:18). Christ's life, his way of knowing the Father and living in complete and constant relationship with him, opens up new and inviting vistas for human experience. Saint John brings out the importance of a personal relationship with Jesus for our faith by using various forms of the verb "to believe." In addition to "believing that" what Jesus tells us is true, John also speaks of "believing" Jesus and "believing in" Jesus. We "believe" Jesus when we accept his word, his testimony, because he is truthful. We "believe in" Jesus when we personally welcome him into our lives and journey toward him, clinging to him in love and following in his footsteps along the way.

To enable us to know, accept, and follow him, the Son of God took on our flesh. In this way he also saw the Father humanly, within the setting of a journey unfolding in time. Christian faith is faith in the incarnation of the Word and his bodily resurrection; it is faith in a God who is so close to us that he entered our human history. Far from divorcing us from reality, our faith in the Son of God made man in Jesus of Nazareth enables us to grasp reality's deepest meaning and to see how much God loves this world and is constantly guiding it toward himself. This leads us, as Christians, to live our lives in this world with ever greater commitment and intensity.

Salvation by faith

19. On the basis of this sharing in Jesus' way of seeing things, Saint Paul has left us a description of the life of faith. In accepting the gift of faith, believers become a new creation; they receive a new being; as God's children, they are now "sons in the Son." The phrase "Abba, Father," so characteristic of Jesus' own experience, now becomes the core of the Christian experience (cf. Rom 8:15). The life of faith, as a filial existence, is the acknowledgment of a primordial and radical gift which upholds our lives. We see this clearly in Saint Paul's question to the Corinthians: "What have you that you did not receive?" (1 Cor 4:7). This was at the very heart of Paul's debate with the Pharisees: the issue of whether salvation is attained by faith or by the works of the law. Paul rejects the attitude of those who would consider themselves justified before God on the basis of their own works. Such people, even when they obey the commandments and do good works, are centered on themselves; they fail to realize that goodness comes from God. Those who live this way, who want to be the source of their own righteousness, find that the latter is soon depleted and that they are unable even to keep the law. They become closed in on themselves and isolated from the Lord and from others; their lives become futile and their works barren, like a tree far from water. Saint Augustine tells us in his usual concise and striking way: *"Ab eo qui fecit te, noli deficere nec ad te,"* "Do not turn away from the one who made you, even to turn toward yourself."[15] Once I think that by turning away from God I will find myself, my life begins to fall apart (cf. Lk 15:11–24). The beginning of salvation is openness to something prior to ourselves, to a primordial gift that affirms life and sustains it in being. Only by being open to and acknowledging this gift can we be

transformed, experience salvation, and bear good fruit. Salvation by faith means recognizing the primacy of God's gift. As Saint Paul puts it: "By grace you have been saved through faith, and this is not your own doing; it is the gift of God" (Eph 2:8).

20. Faith's new way of seeing things is centered on Christ. Faith in Christ brings salvation because in him our lives become radically open to a love that precedes us, a love that transforms us from within, acting in us and through us. This is clearly seen in Saint Paul's exegesis of a text from Deuteronomy, an exegesis consonant with the heart of the Old Testament message. Moses tells the people that God's command is neither too high nor too far away. There is no need to say: "Who will go up for us to heaven and bring it to us?" or "Who will go over the sea for us, and bring it to us?" (Dt 30:11–14). Paul interprets this nearness of God's word in terms of Christ's presence in the Christian. "Do not say in your heart, 'Who will ascend into heaven?' (that is, to bring Christ down), or 'Who will descend into the abyss?' (that is, to bring Christ up from the dead)" (Rom 10:6–7). Christ came down to earth and rose from the dead; by his incarnation and resurrection, the Son of God embraced the whole of human life and history, and now dwells in our hearts through the Holy Spirit. Faith knows that God has drawn close to us, that Christ has been given to us as a great gift which inwardly transforms us, dwells within us and thus bestows on us the light that illumines the origin and the end of life.

21. We come to see the difference, then, which faith makes for us. Those who believe are transformed by the love to which they have opened their hearts in faith. By their openness to this offer of primordial love, their lives are enlarged and expanded. "It is no longer I who live, but Christ who lives in me" (Gal 2:20). "May Christ dwell in your hearts through faith" (Eph 3:17). The self-awareness of the believer now expands because of the presence of another; it now lives in this other and thus, in love, life takes on a whole new breadth. Here we see the Holy Spirit at work. The Christian can see with the eyes of Jesus and share in his mind, his filial disposition, because he or she shares in his love, which is the Spirit. In the love of Jesus, we receive in a certain way his vision. Without being

conformed to him in love, without the presence of the Spirit, it is impossible to confess him as Lord (cf. 1 Cor 12:3).

The ecclesial form of faith

22. In this way, the life of the believer becomes an ecclesial existence, a life lived in the Church. When Saint Paul tells the Christians of Rome that all who believe in Christ make up one body, he urges them not to boast of this; rather, each must think of himself "according to the measure of faith that God has assigned" (Rom 12:3). Those who believe come to see themselves in the light of the faith which they profess: Christ is the mirror in which they find their own image fully realized. And just as Christ gathers to himself all those who believe and makes them his body, so the Christian comes to see himself as a member of this body, in an essential relationship with all other believers. The image of a body does not imply that the believer is simply one part of an anonymous whole, a mere cog in a great machine; rather, it brings out the vital union of Christ with believers and of believers among themselves (cf. Rom 12:4–5). Christians are "one" (cf. Gal 3:28), yet in a way which does not make them lose their individuality; in service to others, they come into their own in the highest degree. This explains why, apart from this body, outside this unity of the Church in Christ, outside this Church which—in the words of Romano Guardini—"is the bearer within history of the plenary gaze of Christ on the world"[16]—faith loses its "measure"; it no longer finds its equilibrium, the space needed to sustain itself. Faith is necessarily ecclesial; it is professed from within the body of Christ as a concrete communion of believers. It is against this ecclesial backdrop that faith opens the individual Christian toward all others. Christ's word, once heard, by virtue of its inner power at work in the heart of the Christian, becomes a response, a spoken word, a profession of faith. As Saint Paul puts it: "one believes with the heart . . . and confesses with the lips" (Rom 10:10). Faith is not a private matter, a completely individualistic notion or a personal opinion: it comes from hearing, and it is meant to find expression in words and to be proclaimed. For "how are they to believe in him of whom they have never heard? And how are they to hear without a preacher?" (Rom 10:14).

Faith becomes operative in the Christian on the basis of the gift received, the love which attracts our hearts to Christ (cf. Gal 5:6) and enables us to become part of the Church's great pilgrimage through history until the end of the world. For those who have been transformed in this way, a new way of seeing opens up, faith becomes light for their eyes.

CHAPTER TWO

UNLESS YOU BELIEVE, YOU WILL NOT UNDERSTAND

(cf. Is 7:9)

Faith and truth

23. Unless you believe, you will not understand (cf. Is 7:9). The Greek version of the Hebrew Bible, the Septuagint translation produced in Alexandria, gives the above rendering of the words spoken by the prophet Isaiah to King Ahaz. In this way, the issue of the knowledge of truth became central to faith. The Hebrew text, though, reads differently; the prophet says to the king: "If you will not believe, you shall not be established." Here there is a play on words, based on two forms of the verb *'amān*: "you will believe" (*ta'amînû*) and "you shall be established" (*tē'āmēnû*). Terrified by the might of his enemies, the king seeks the security that an alliance with the great Assyrian Empire can offer. The prophet tells him instead to trust completely in the solid and steadfast rock which is the God of Israel. Because God is trustworthy, it is reasonable to have faith in him, to stand fast on his word. He is the same God that Isaiah will later call, twice in one verse, the God who is Amen, "the God of truth" (cf. Is 65:16), the enduring foundation of covenant fidelity. It might seem that the Greek version of the Bible, by translating "be established" as "understand," profoundly altered the meaning of the text by moving away from the biblical notion of trust in God toward a Greek notion of intellectual understanding. Yet this translation, while certainly reflecting a dialogue with Hellenistic culture, is not alien to the underlying spirit of the Hebrew text. The firm foundation that Isaiah promises to the king is indeed grounded in an understanding of God's activity and the unity which he gives to human life and to the history of his people. The prophet challenges the king, and us, to understand the Lord's ways, seeing in God's faithfulness the wise plan which governs the ages. Saint Augustine took up this synthesis of the ideas of "understanding" and "being

established" in his *Confessions* when he spoke of the truth on which one may rely in order to stand fast: "Then I shall be cast and set firm in the mold of your truth."[17] From the context we know that Augustine was concerned to show that this trustworthy truth of God is, as the Bible makes clear, his own faithful presence throughout history, his ability to hold together times and ages and to gather into one the scattered strands of our lives.[18]

24. Read in this light, the prophetic text leads to one conclusion: we need knowledge, we need truth, because without these we cannot stand firm, we cannot move forward. Faith without truth does not save, it does not provide a sure footing. It remains a beautiful story, the projection of our deep yearning for happiness, something capable of satisfying us to the extent that we are willing to deceive ourselves. Either that, or it is reduced to a lofty sentiment which brings consolation and cheer, yet remains prey to the vagaries of our spirit and the changing seasons, incapable of sustaining a steady journey through life. If such were faith, King Ahaz would be right not to stake his life and the security of his kingdom on a feeling. But precisely because of its intrinsic link to truth, faith is instead able to offer a new light, superior to the king's calculations, for it sees further into the distance and takes into account the hand of God, who remains faithful to his covenant and his promises.

25. Today more than ever, we need to be reminded of this bond between faith and truth, given the crisis of truth in our age. In contemporary culture, we often tend to consider the only real truth to be that of technology: truth is what we succeed in building and measuring by our scientific know-how; truth is what works and what makes life easier and more comfortable. Nowadays this appears as the only truth that is certain, the only truth that can be shared, the only truth that can serve as a basis for discussion or for common undertakings. Yet at the other end of the scale we are willing to allow for subjective truths of the individual, which consist in fidelity to his or her deepest convictions, yet these are truths valid only for that individual and not capable of being proposed to others in an effort to serve the common good. But Truth itself, the truth which would comprehensively explain our life as individuals and in society, is

regarded with suspicion. Surely this kind of truth—we hear it said—is what was claimed by the great totalitarian movements of the last century, a truth that imposed its own worldview in order to crush the actual lives of individuals. In the end, what we are left with is relativism, in which the question of universal truth—and ultimately this means the question of God—is no longer relevant. It would be logical, from this point of view, to attempt to sever the bond between religion and truth, because it seems to lie at the root of fanaticism, which proves oppressive for anyone who does not share the same beliefs. In this regard, though, we can speak of a massive amnesia in our contemporary world. The question of truth is really a question of memory, deep memory, for it deals with something prior to ourselves and can succeed in uniting us in a way that transcends our petty and limited individual consciousness. It is a question about the origin of all that is, in whose light we can glimpse the goal and thus the meaning of our common path.

Knowledge of the truth and love

26. This being the case, can Christian faith provide a service to the common good with regard to the right way of understanding truth? To answer this question, we need to reflect on the kind of knowledge involved in faith. Here a saying of Saint Paul can help us: "One believes with the heart" (Rom 10:10). In the Bible, the heart is the core of the human person, where all his or her different dimensions intersect: body and spirit, interiority and openness to the world and to others, intellect, will, and affectivity. If the heart is capable of holding all these dimensions together, it is because it is where we become open to truth and love, where we let them touch us and deeply transform us. Faith transforms the whole person precisely to the extent that he or she becomes open to love. Through this blending of faith and love we come to see the kind of knowledge which faith entails, its power to convince and its ability to illumine our steps. Faith knows because it is tied to love, because love itself brings enlightenment. Faith's understanding is born when we receive the immense love of God which transforms us inwardly and enables us to see reality with new eyes.

27. The explanation of the connection between faith and certainty put forward by the philosopher Ludwig Wittgenstein is well known. For Wittgenstein, believing can be compared to the experience of falling in love: it is something subjective which cannot be proposed as a truth valid for everyone.[19] Indeed, most people nowadays would not consider love as related in any way to truth. Love is seen as an experience associated with the world of fleeting emotions, no longer with truth.

But is this an adequate description of love? Love cannot be reduced to an ephemeral emotion. True, it engages our affectivity, but in order to open it to the beloved and thus to blaze a trail leading away from self-centeredness and toward another person, in order to build a lasting relationship; love aims at union with the beloved. Here we begin to see how love requires truth. Only to the extent that love is grounded in truth can it endure over time, can it transcend the passing moment and be sufficiently solid to sustain a shared journey. If love is not tied to truth, it falls prey to fickle emotions and cannot stand the test of time. True love, on the other hand, unifies all the elements of our person and becomes a new light pointing the way to a great and fulfilled life. Without truth, love is incapable of establishing a firm bond; it cannot liberate our isolated ego or redeem it from the fleeting moment in order to create life and bear fruit.

If love needs truth, truth also needs love. Love and truth are inseparable. Without love, truth becomes cold, impersonal, and oppressive for people's day-to-day lives. The truth we seek, the truth that gives meaning to our journey through life, enlightens us whenever we are touched by love. One who loves realizes that love is an experience of truth, that it opens our eyes to see reality in a new way, in union with the beloved. In this sense, Saint Gregory the Great could write that "*amor ipse notitia est,*" love is itself a kind of knowledge possessed of its own logic.[20] It is a relational way of viewing the world, which then becomes a form of shared knowledge, vision through the eyes of another and a shared vision of all that exists. William of Saint-Thierry, in the Middle Ages, follows this tradition when he comments on the verse of the Song of Songs where the lover says to the beloved, "Your eyes are doves" (Sg 1:15).[21] The two eyes, says William, are faith-filled reason and love, which then become one in rising to the contemplation of God, when our understanding becomes "an understanding of enlightened love."[22]

28. This discovery of love as a source of knowledge, which is part of the primordial experience of every man and woman, finds authoritative expression in the biblical understanding of faith. In savoring the love by which God chose them and made them a people, Israel came to understand the overall unity of the divine plan. Faith-knowledge, because it is born of God's covenantal love, is knowledge which lights up a path in history. That is why, in the Bible, truth and fidelity go together: the true God is the God of fidelity who keeps his promises and makes possible, in time, a deeper understanding of his plan. Through the experience of the prophets, in the pain of exile and in the hope of a definitive return to the holy city, Israel came to see that this divine "truth" extended beyond the confines of its own history, to embrace the entire history of the world, beginning with creation. Faith-knowledge sheds light not only on the destiny of one particular people, but the entire history of the created world, from its origins to its consummation.

Faith as hearing and sight

29. Precisely because faith-knowledge is linked to the covenant with a faithful God who enters into a relationship of love with man and speaks his word to him, the Bible presents it as a form of hearing; it is associated with the sense of hearing. Saint Paul would use a formula which became classic: *fides ex auditu*, "faith comes from hearing" (Rom 10:17). Knowledge linked to a word is always personal knowledge; it recognizes the voice of the one speaking, opens up to that person in freedom and follows him or her in obedience. Paul could thus speak of the "obedience of faith" (cf. Rom 1:5; 16:26).[23] Faith is also a knowledge bound to the passage of time, for words take time to be pronounced, and it is a knowledge assimilated only along a journey of discipleship. The experience of hearing can thus help to bring out more clearly the bond between knowledge and love.

At times, where knowledge of the truth is concerned, hearing has been opposed to sight; it has been claimed that an emphasis on sight was characteristic of Greek culture. If light makes possible that contemplation of the whole to which humanity has always aspired, it would also seem to leave no space for freedom, since it comes down from heaven directly to the eye, without calling for a response. It would also seem to call for a kind of static contemplation, far removed from the world of history with its joys and sufferings. From this standpoint, the biblical understanding of knowledge would be antithetical to the Greek understanding, inasmuch as the latter linked knowledge to sight in its attempt to attain a comprehensive understanding of reality.

This alleged antithesis does not, however, correspond to the biblical datum. The Old Testament combined both kinds of knowledge, since hearing God's word is accompanied by the desire to see his face. The ground was thus laid for a dialogue with Hellenistic culture, a dialogue present at the heart of sacred Scripture. Hearing emphasizes personal vocation and obedience and the fact that truth is revealed in time. Sight provides a vision of the entire journey and allows it to be situated within God's overall plan; without this vision, we would be left only with unconnected parts of an unknown whole.

30. The bond between seeing and hearing in faith-knowledge is most clearly evident in John's Gospel. For the Fourth Gospel, to believe is both to hear and to see. Faith's hearing emerges as a form of knowing proper to love: it is a personal hearing, one which recognizes the voice of the Good Shepherd (cf. Jn 10:3–5); it is a hearing which calls for discipleship, as was the case with the first disciples: "Hearing him say these things, they followed Jesus" (Jn 1:37). But faith is also tied to sight. Seeing the signs which Jesus worked leads at times to faith, as in the case of the Jews who, following the raising of Lazarus, "having seen what he did, believed in him" (Jn 11:45). At other times, faith itself leads to deeper vision: "If you believe, you will see the glory of God" (Jn 11:40). In the end, belief and sight intersect: "Whoever believes in me believes in him who sent me. And whoever sees me sees him who sent me" (Jn 12:44–45). Joined to hearing, seeing then becomes a form of following Christ, and

faith appears as a process of gazing, in which our eyes grow accustomed to peering into the depths. Easter morning thus passes from John who, standing in the early morning darkness before the empty tomb, "saw and believed" (Jn 20:8), to Mary Magdalene who, after seeing Jesus (cf. Jn 20:14) and wanting to cling to him, is asked to contemplate him as he ascends to the Father, and finally to her full confession before the disciples: "I have seen the Lord!" (Jn 20:18).

How does one attain this synthesis between hearing and seeing? It becomes possible through the person of Christ himself, who can be seen and heard. He is the Word made flesh, whose glory we have seen (cf. Jn 1:14). The light of faith is the light of a countenance in which the Father is seen. In the Fourth Gospel, the truth which faith attains is the revelation of the Father in the Son, in his flesh and in his earthly deeds, a truth which can be defined as the "light-filled life" of Jesus.[24] This means that faith-knowledge does not direct our gaze to a purely inward truth. The truth which faith discloses to us is a truth centered on an encounter with Christ, on the contemplation of his life and on the awareness of his presence. Saint Thomas Aquinas speaks of the Apostles' *oculata fides*—a faith which sees!—in the presence of the body of the Risen Lord.[25] With their own eyes they saw the risen Jesus and they believed; in a word, they were able to peer into the depths of what they were seeing and to confess their faith in the Son of God, seated at the right hand of the Father.

31. It was only in this way, by taking flesh, by sharing our humanity, that the knowledge proper to love could come to full fruition. For the light of love is born when our hearts are touched and we open ourselves to the interior presence of the beloved, who enables us to recognize his mystery. Thus we can understand why, together with hearing and seeing, Saint John can speak of faith as touch, as he says in his First Letter: "What we have heard, what we have seen with our eyes and touched with our hands, concerning the word of life" (1 Jn 1:1). By his taking flesh and coming among us, Jesus has touched us, and through the sacraments he continues to touch us even today; transforming our hearts, he unceasingly enables us to acknowledge and acclaim him as the Son of God. In faith, we can touch him and receive the power of his grace. Saint

Augustine, commenting on the account of the woman suffering from hemorrhages who touched Jesus and was cured (cf. Lk 8:45–46), says: "To touch him with our hearts: that is what it means to believe."[26] The crowd presses in on Jesus, but they do not reach him with the personal touch of faith, which apprehends the mystery that he is the Son who reveals the Father. Only when we are configured to Jesus do we receive the eyes needed to see him.

The dialogue between faith and reason

32. Christian faith, inasmuch as it proclaims the truth of God's total love and opens us to the power of that love, penetrates to the core of our human experience. Each of us comes to the light because of love, and each of us is called to love in order to remain in the light. Desirous of illumining all reality with the love of God made manifest in Jesus, and seeking to love others with that same love, the first Christians found in the Greek world, with its thirst for truth, an ideal partner in dialogue. The encounter of the Gospel message with the philosophical culture of the ancient world proved a decisive step in the evangelization of all peoples, and stimulated a fruitful interaction between faith and reason which has continued down the centuries to our own times. Blessed John Paul II, in his Encyclical Letter *Fides et Ratio*, showed how faith and reason each strengthen the other.[27] Once we discover the full light of Christ's love, we realize that each of the loves in our own lives had always contained a ray of that light, and we understand its ultimate destination. That fact that our human loves contain that ray of light also helps us to see how all love is meant to share in the complete self-gift of the Son of God for our sake. In this circular movement, the light of faith illumines all our human relationships, which can then be lived in union with the gentle love of Christ.

33. In the life of Saint Augustine we find a significant example of this process whereby reason, with its desire for truth and clarity, was integrated into the horizon of faith and thus gained new understanding. Augustine accepted the Greek philosophy of light, with its insistence on the importance of sight. His encounter with Neoplatonism introduced him

to the paradigm of the light which, descending from on high to illumine all reality, is a symbol of God. Augustine thus came to appreciate God's transcendence and discovered that all things have a certain transparency, that they can reflect God's goodness. This realization liberated him from his earlier Manichaeism, which had led him to think that good and evil were in constant conflict, confused and intertwined. The realization that God is light provided Augustine with a new direction in life and enabled him to acknowledge his sinfulness and to turn toward the good.

All the same, the decisive moment in Augustine's journey of faith, as he tells us in the *Confessions*, was not in the vision of a God above and beyond this world, but in an experience of hearing. In the garden, he heard a voice telling him: "Take and read." He then took up the book containing the epistles of Saint Paul and started to read the thirteenth chapter of the Letter to the Romans.[28] In this way, the personal God of the Bible appeared to him: a God who is able to speak to us, to come down to dwell in our midst and to accompany our journey through history, making himself known in the time of hearing and response.

Yet this encounter with the God who speaks did not lead Augustine to reject light and seeing. He integrated the two perspectives of hearing and seeing, constantly guided by the revelation of God's love in Jesus. Thus Augustine developed a philosophy of light capable of embracing both the reciprocity proper to the word and the freedom born of looking to the light. Just as the word calls for a free response, so the light finds a response in the image which reflects it. Augustine can therefore associate hearing and seeing, and speak of "the word which shines forth within."[29] The light becomes, so to speak, the light of a word, because it is the light of a personal countenance, a light which, even as it enlightens us, calls us and seeks to be reflected on our faces and to shine from within us. Yet our longing for the vision of the whole, and not merely of fragments of history, remains and will be fulfilled in the end, when, as Augustine says, we will see and we will love.[30] Not because we will be able to possess all the light, which will always be inexhaustible, but because we will enter wholly into that light.

34. The light of love proper to faith can illumine the questions of our own time about truth. Truth nowadays is often reduced to the subjective authenticity of the individual, valid only for the life of the individual. A common truth intimidates us, for we identify it with the intransigent demands of totalitarian systems. But if truth is a truth of love, if it is a truth disclosed in personal encounter with the Other and with others, then it can be set free from its enclosure in individuals and become part of the common good. As a truth of love, it is not one that can be imposed by force; it is not a truth that stifles the individual. Since it is born of love, it can penetrate to the heart, to the personal core of each man and woman. Clearly, then, faith is not intransigent, but grows in respectful coexistence with others. One who believes may not be presumptuous; on the contrary, truth leads to humility, since believers know that, rather than ourselves possessing truth, it is truth which embraces and possesses us. Far from making us inflexible, the security of faith sets us on a journey; it enables witness and dialogue with all.

Nor is the light of faith, joined to the truth of love, extraneous to the material world, for love is always lived out in body and spirit; the light of faith is an incarnate light radiating from the luminous life of Jesus. It also illumines the material world, trusts its inherent order, and knows that it calls us to an ever widening path of harmony and understanding. The gaze of science thus benefits from faith: faith encourages the scientist to remain constantly open to reality in all its inexhaustible richness. Faith awakens the critical sense by preventing research from being satisfied with its own formulae and helps it to realize that nature is always greater. By stimulating wonder before the profound mystery of creation, faith broadens the horizons of reason to shed greater light on the world which discloses itself to scientific investigation.

Faith and the search for God

35. The light of faith in Jesus also illumines the path of all those who seek God, and makes a specifically Christian contribution to dialogue with the followers of the different religions. The Letter to the Hebrews speaks of the witness of those just ones who, before the covenant with

Abraham, already sought God in faith. Of Enoch "it was attested that he had pleased God" (Heb 11:5), something impossible apart from faith, for "whoever would approach God must believe that he exists and that he rewards those who seek him" (Heb 11:6). We can see from this that the path of religious man passes through the acknowledgment of a God who cares for us and is not impossible to find. What other reward can God give to those who seek him, if not to let himself be found? Even earlier, we encounter Abel, whose faith was praised and whose gifts, his offering of the firstlings of his flock (cf. Heb 11:4), were therefore pleasing to God. Religious man strives to see signs of God in the daily experiences of life, in the cycle of the seasons, in the fruitfulness of the earth, and in the movement of the cosmos. God is light, and he can be found also by those who seek him with a sincere heart.

An image of this seeking can be seen in the Magi, who were led to Bethlehem by the star (cf. Mt 2:1–12). For them God's light appeared as a journey to be undertaken, a star which led them on a path of discovery. The star is a sign of God's patience with our eyes which need to grow accustomed to his brightness. Religious man is a wayfarer; he must be ready to let himself be led, to come out of himself and to find the God of perpetual surprises. This respect on God's part for our human eyes shows us that when we draw near to God, our human lights are not dissolved in the immensity of his light, as a star is engulfed by the dawn, but shine all the more brightly the closer they approach the primordial fire, like a mirror which reflects light. Christian faith in Jesus, the one Savior of the world, proclaims that all God's light is concentrated in him, in his "luminous life" which discloses the origin and the end of history.[31] There is no human experience, no journey of man to God, which cannot be taken up, illumined and purified by this light. The more Christians immerse themselves in the circle of Christ's light, the more capable they become of understanding and accompanying the path of every man and woman toward God.

Because faith is a way, it also has to do with the lives of those men and women who, though not believers, nonetheless desire to believe and continue to seek. To the extent that they are sincerely open to love and set out with whatever light they can find, they are already, even without knowing it, on the path leading to faith. They strive to act as if God existed, at times because they realize how important he is for finding a sure compass for our life in common or because they experience a desire for light amid darkness, but also because in perceiving life's grandeur and beauty they intuit that the presence of God would make it all the more beautiful. Saint Irenaeus of Lyons tells how Abraham, before hearing God's voice, had already sought him "in the ardent desire of his heart" and "went throughout the whole world, asking himself where God was to be found," until "God had pity on him who, all alone, had sought him in silence."[32] Anyone who sets off on the path of doing good to others is already drawing near to God, is already sustained by his help, for it is characteristic of the divine light to brighten our eyes whenever we walk toward the fullness of love.

Faith and theology

36. Since faith is a light, it draws us into itself, inviting us to explore ever more fully the horizon which it illumines, all the better to know the object of our love. Christian theology is born of this desire. Clearly, theology is impossible without faith; it is part of the very process of faith, which seeks an ever deeper understanding of God's self-disclosure culminating in Christ. It follows that theology is more than simply an effort of human reason to analyze and understand, along the lines of the experimental sciences. God cannot be reduced to an object. He is a subject who makes himself known and perceived in an interpersonal relationship. Right faith orients reason to open itself to the light which comes from God, so that reason, guided by love of the truth, can come to a deeper knowledge of God. The great medieval theologians and teachers rightly held that theology, as a science of faith, is a participation in God's own knowledge of himself. It is not just our discourse about God, but first and foremost the acceptance and the pursuit of a deeper understanding of the word which God speaks to us, the word which God speaks about himself, for he is an eternal dialogue of communion, and he allows us to enter into this dialogue.[33] Theology thus demands the humility to be "touched" by

God, admitting its own limitations before the mystery, while striving to investigate, with the discipline proper to reason, the inexhaustible riches of this mystery.

Theology also shares in the ecclesial form of faith; its light is the light of the believing subject which is the Church. This implies, on the one hand, that theology must be at the service of the faith of Christians, that it must work humbly to protect and deepen the faith of everyone, especially ordinary believers. On the other hand, because it draws its life from faith, theology cannot consider the magisterium of the Pope and the bishops in communion with him as something extrinsic, a limitation of its freedom, but rather as one of its internal, constitutive dimensions, for the magisterium ensures our contact with the primordial source and thus provides the certainty of attaining to the word of Christ in all its integrity.

CHAPTER THREE

I DELIVERED TO YOU WHAT I ALSO RECEIVED

(cf. 1 Cor 15:3)

The Church, mother of our faith

37. Those who have opened their hearts to God's love, heard his voice and received his light, cannot keep this gift to themselves. Since faith is hearing and seeing, it is also handed on as word and light. Addressing the Corinthians, Saint Paul used these two very images. On the one hand he says: "But just as we have the same spirit of faith that is in accordance with scripture—'I believed, and so I spoke'—we also believe, and so we speak" (2 Cor 4:13). The word, once accepted, becomes a response, a confession of faith, which spreads to others and invites them to believe. Paul also uses the image of light: "All of us, with unveiled faces, seeing the glory of the Lord as though reflected in a mirror, are being transformed into the same image" (2 Cor 3:18). It is a light reflected from one face to another, even as Moses himself bore a reflection of God's glory after having spoken with him: "God . . . has shone in our hearts to give the light of the knowledge of the glory of God in the face of Christ" (2 Cor 4:6). The light of Christ shines, as in a mirror, upon the face of Christians; as it spreads, it comes down to us, so that we too can share in that vision and reflect that light to others, in the same way that, in the Easter liturgy, the light of the paschal candle lights countless other candles. Faith is passed on, we might say, by contact, from one person to another, just as one candle is lighted from another. Christians, in their poverty, plant a seed so rich that it becomes a great tree, capable of filling the world with its fruit.

38. The transmission of the faith not only brings light to men and women in every place; it travels through time, passing from one generation to another. Because faith is born of an encounter which takes place in history and lights up our journey through time, it must be passed on in every age. It is through an unbroken chain of witnesses that we come to

see the face of Jesus. But how is this possible? How can we be certain, after all these centuries, that we have encountered the "real Jesus"? Were we merely isolated individuals, were our starting point simply our own individual ego seeking in itself the basis of absolutely sure knowledge, a certainty of this sort would be impossible. I cannot possibly verify for myself something which happened so long ago. But this is not the only way we attain knowledge. Persons always live in relationship. We come from others, we belong to others, and our lives are enlarged by our encounter with others. Even our own knowledge and self-awareness are relational; they are linked to others who have gone before us: in the first place, our parents, who gave us our life and our name. Language itself, the words by which we make sense of our lives and the world around us, comes to us from others, preserved in the living memory of others. Self-knowledge is only possible when we share in a greater memory. The same thing holds true for faith, which brings human understanding to its fullness. Faith's past, that act of Jesus' love which brought new life to the world, comes down to us through the memory of others—witnesses—and is kept alive in that one remembering subject which is the Church. The Church is a Mother who teaches us to speak the language of faith. Saint John brings this out in his Gospel by closely uniting faith and memory and associating both with the working of the Holy Spirit, who, as Jesus says, "will remind you of all that I have said to you" (Jn 14:26). The love which is the Holy Spirit and which dwells in the Church unites every age and makes us contemporaries of Jesus, thus guiding us along our pilgrimage of faith.

39. It is impossible to believe on our own. Faith is not simply an individual decision which takes place in the depths of the believer's heart, nor a completely private relationship between the "I" of the believer and the divine "Thou," between an autonomous subject and God. By its very nature, faith is open to the "We" of the Church; it always takes place within her communion. We are reminded of this by the dialogical format of the creed used in the baptismal liturgy. Our belief is expressed in response to an invitation, to a word which must be heard and which is not my own; it exists as part of a dialogue and cannot be merely a

profession originating in an individual. We can respond in the singular—"I believe"—only because we are part of a greater fellowship, only because we also say "We believe." This openness to the ecclesial "We" reflects the openness of God's own love, which is not only a relationship between the Father and the Son, between an "I" and a "Thou," but is also, in the Spirit, a "We," a communion of persons. Here we see why those who believe are never alone, and why faith tends to spread, as it invites others to share in its joy. Those who receive faith discover that their horizons expand as new and enriching relationships come to life. Tertullian puts this well when he describes the catechumens who, "after the cleansing which gives new birth," are welcomed into the house of their mother and, as part of a new family, pray the Our Father together with their brothers and sisters.[34]

The sacraments and the transmission of faith

40. The Church, like every family, passes on to her children the whole store of her memories. But how does this come about in a way that nothing is lost, but rather everything in the patrimony of faith comes to be more deeply understood? It is through the apostolic Tradition preserved in the Church with the assistance of the Holy Spirit that we enjoy a living contact with the foundational memory. What was handed down by the apostles—as the Second Vatican Council states—"comprises everything that serves to make the people of God live their lives in holiness and increase their faith. In this way the Church, in her doctrine, life and worship, perpetuates and transmits to every generation all that she herself is, all that she believes."[35]

Faith, in fact, needs a setting in which it can be witnessed to and communicated, a means which is suitable and proportionate to what is communicated. For transmitting a purely doctrinal content, an idea might suffice, or perhaps a book, or the repetition of a spoken message. But what is communicated in the Church, what is handed down in her living Tradition, is the new light born of an encounter with the true God, a light which touches us at the core of our being and engages our minds, wills, and emotions, opening us to relationships lived in communion.

There is a special means for passing down this fullness, a means capable of engaging the entire person, body and spirit, interior life and relationships with others. It is the sacraments, celebrated in the Church's liturgy. The sacraments communicate an incarnate memory, linked to the times and places of our lives, linked to all our senses; in them the whole person is engaged as a member of a living subject and part of a network of communitarian relationships. While the sacraments are indeed sacraments of faith,[36] it can also be said that faith itself possesses a sacramental structure. The awakening of faith is linked to the dawning of a new sacramental sense in our lives as human beings and as Christians, in which visible and material realities are seen to point beyond themselves to the mystery of the eternal.

41. The transmission of faith occurs first and foremost in baptism. Some might think that baptism is merely a way of symbolizing the confession of faith, a pedagogical tool for those who require images and signs, while in itself ultimately unnecessary. An observation of Saint Paul about baptism reminds us that this is not the case. Paul states that "we were buried with him by baptism into death, so that, just as Christ was raised from the dead by the glory of the Father, we too might walk in newness of life" (Rom 6:4). In baptism we become a new creation and God's adopted children. The Apostle goes on to say that Christians have been entrusted to a "standard of teaching" (*týpos didachés*), which they now obey from the heart (cf. Rom 6:17). In baptism we receive both a teaching to be professed and a specific way of life which demands the engagement of the whole person and sets us on the path to goodness. Those who are baptized are set in a new context, entrusted to a new environment, a new and shared way of acting, in the Church. Baptism makes us see, then, that faith is not the achievement of isolated individuals; it is not an act which someone can perform on his own, but rather something which must be received by entering into the ecclesial communion which transmits God's gift. No one baptizes himself, just as no one comes into the world by himself. Baptism is something we receive.

42. What are the elements of baptism which introduce us into this new "standard of teaching"? First, the name of the Trinity—the Father, the Son, and the Holy Spirit—is invoked upon the catechumen. Thus, from the outset, a synthesis of the journey of faith is provided. The God who called Abraham and wished to be called his God, the God who revealed his name to Moses, the God who, in giving us his Son, revealed fully the mystery of his Name, now bestows upon the baptized a new filial identity. This is clearly seen in the act of baptism itself: immersion in water. Water is at once a symbol of death, inviting us to pass through self-conversion to a new and greater identity, and a symbol of life, of a womb in which we are reborn by following Christ in his new life. In this way, through immersion in water, baptism speaks to us of the incarnational structure of faith. Christ's work penetrates the depths of our being and transforms us radically, making us adopted children of God and sharers in the divine nature. It thus modifies all our relationships, our place in this world and in the universe, and opens them to God's own life of communion. This change which takes place in baptism helps us to appreciate the singular importance of the catechumenate—whereby growing numbers of adults, even in societies with ancient Christian roots, now approach the sacrament of Baptism—for the new evangelization. It is the road of preparation for baptism, for the transformation of our whole life in Christ.

To appreciate this link between baptism and faith, we can recall a text of the prophet Isaiah, which was associated with baptism in early Christian literature: "Their refuge will be the fortresses of rocks . . . their water assured" (Is 33:16).[37] The baptized, rescued from the waters of death, were now set on a "fortress of rock" because they had found a firm and reliable foundation. The waters of death were thus transformed into waters of life. The Greek text, in speaking of that water which is "assured," uses the word *pistós*, "faithful." The waters of baptism are indeed faithful and trustworthy, for they flow with the power of Christ's love, the source of our assurance in the journey of life.

43. The structure of baptism, its form as a rebirth in which we receive a new name and a new life, helps us to appreciate the meaning and

importance of infant baptism. Children are not capable of accepting the faith by a free act, nor are they yet able to profess that faith on their own; therefore the faith is professed by their parents and godparents in their name. Since faith is a reality lived within the community of the Church, part of a common "We," children can be supported by others, their parents and godparents, and welcomed into their faith, which is the faith of the Church; this is symbolized by the candle which the child's father lights from the paschal candle. The structure of baptism, then, demonstrates the critical importance of cooperation between Church and family in passing on the faith. Parents are called, as Saint Augustine once said, not only to bring children into the world but also to bring them to God, so that through baptism they can be reborn as children of God and receive the gift of faith.[38] Thus, along with life, children are given a fundamental orientation and assured of a good future; this orientation will be further strengthened in the sacrament of Confirmation with the seal of the Holy Spirit.

44. The sacramental character of faith finds its highest expression in the Eucharist. The Eucharist is a precious nourishment for faith: an encounter with Christ truly present in the supreme act of his love, the life-giving gift of himself. In the Eucharist we find the intersection of faith's two dimensions. On the one hand, there is the dimension of history: the Eucharist is an act of remembrance, a making present of the mystery in which the past, as an event of death and resurrection, demonstrates its ability to open up a future, to foreshadow ultimate fulfillment. The liturgy reminds us of this by its repetition of the word *hodie*, the "today" of the mysteries of salvation. On the other hand, we also find the dimension which leads from the visible world to the invisible. In the Eucharist we learn to see the heights and depths of reality. The bread and wine are changed into the body and blood of Christ, who becomes present in his passover to the Father: this movement draws us, body and soul, into the movement of all creation toward its fulfillment in God.

45. In the celebration of the sacraments, the Church hands down her memory especially through the profession of faith. The creed does not only involve giving one's assent to a body of abstract truths; rather, when

it is recited the whole of life is drawn into a journey toward full communion with the living God. We can say that in the creed believers are invited to enter into the mystery which they profess and to be transformed by it. To understand what this means, let us look first at the contents of the creed. It has a Trinitarian structure: the Father and the Son are united in the Spirit of love. The believer thus states that the core of all being, the inmost secret of all reality, is the divine communion. The creed also contains a Christological confession: it takes us through all the mysteries of Christ's life up to his death, resurrection, and ascension into heaven before his final return in glory. It tells us that this God of communion, reciprocal love between the Father and the Son in the Spirit, is capable of embracing all of human history and drawing it into the dynamic unity of the Godhead, which has its source and fulfillment in the Father. The believer who professes his or her faith is taken up, as it were, into the truth being professed. He or she cannot truthfully recite the words of the creed without being changed, without becoming part of that history of love which embraces us and expands our being, making it part of a great fellowship, the ultimate subject which recites the creed, namely, the Church. All the truths in which we believe point to the mystery of the new life of faith as a journey of communion with the living God.

Faith, prayer, and the Decalogue

46. Two other elements are essential in the faithful transmission of the Church's memory. First, the Lord's Prayer, the "Our Father." Here Christians learn to share in Christ's own spiritual experience and to see all things through his eyes. From him who is light from light, the only-begotten Son of the Father, we come to know God and can thus kindle in others the desire to draw near to him.

Similarly important is the link between faith and the Decalogue. Faith, as we have said, takes the form of a journey, a path to be followed, which begins with an encounter with the living God. It is in the light of faith, of complete entrustment to the God who saves, that the Ten Commandments take on their deepest truth, as seen in the words which introduce them: "I am the Lord your God, who brought you out of the land of Egypt" (Ex 20:2). The Decalogue is not a set of negative commands, but concrete directions for emerging from the desert of the selfish and self-enclosed ego in order to enter into dialogue with God, to be embraced by his mercy and then to bring that mercy to others. Faith thus professes the love of God, origin and upholder of all things, and lets itself be guided by this love in order to journey toward the fullness of communion with God. The Decalogue appears as the path of gratitude, the response of love, made possible because in faith we are receptive to the experience of God's transforming love for us. And this path receives new light from Jesus' teaching in the Sermon on the Mount (cf. Mt 5–7).

These, then, are the four elements which comprise the storehouse of memory which the Church hands down: the profession of faith, the celebration of the sacraments, the path of the Ten Commandments, and prayer. The Church's catechesis has traditionally been structured around these four elements; this includes the *Catechism of the Catholic Church*, which is a fundamental aid for that unitary act with which the Church communicates the entire content of her faith: "all that she herself is, and all that she believes."[39]

The unity and integrity of faith

47. The unity of the Church in time and space is linked to the unity of the faith: "there is one body and one Spirit . . . one faith" (Eph 4:4–5). These days we can imagine a group of people being united in a common cause, in mutual affection, in sharing the same destiny and a single purpose. But we find it hard to conceive of a unity in one truth. We tend to think that a unity of this sort is incompatible with freedom of thought and personal autonomy. Yet the experience of love shows us that a common vision is possible, for through love we learn how to see reality through the eyes of others, not as something which impoverishes but instead enriches our vision. Genuine love, after the fashion of God's love, ultimately requires truth, and the shared contemplation of the truth which is Jesus Christ enables love to become deep and enduring. This is also the great joy of

faith: a unity of vision in one body and one spirit. Saint Leo the Great could say: "If faith is not one, then it is not faith."[40]

What is the secret of this unity? Faith is "one," in the first place, because of the oneness of the God who is known and confessed. All the articles of faith speak of God; they are ways to know him and his works. Consequently, their unity is far superior to any possible construct of human reason. They possess a unity which enriches us because it is given to us and makes us one.

Faith is also one because it is directed to the one Lord, to the life of Jesus, to the concrete history which he shares with us. Saint Irenaeus of Lyons made this clear in his struggle against Gnosticism. The Gnostics held that there are two kinds of faith: a crude, imperfect faith suited to the masses, which remained at the level of Jesus' flesh and the contemplation of his mysteries; and a deeper, perfect faith reserved to a small circle of initiates who were intellectually capable of rising above the flesh of Jesus toward the mysteries of the unknown divinity. In opposition to this claim, which even today exerts a certain attraction and has its followers, Saint Irenaeus insisted that there is but one faith, for it is grounded in the concrete event of the incarnation and can never transcend the flesh and history of Christ, inasmuch as God willed to reveal himself fully in that flesh. For this reason, he says, there is no difference in the faith of "those able to discourse of it at length" and "those who speak but little," between the greater and the less: the first cannot increase the faith, nor the second diminish it.[41]

Finally, faith is one because it is shared by the whole Church, which is one body and one Spirit. In the communion of the one subject which is the Church, we receive a common gaze. By professing the same faith, we stand firm on the same rock, we are transformed by the same Spirit of love, we radiate one light, and we have a single insight into reality.

48. Since faith is one, it must be professed in all its purity and integrity. Precisely because all the articles of faith are interconnected, to deny one of them, even of those that seem least important, is tantamount to distorting the whole. Each period of history can find this or that point of faith easier or harder to accept: hence the need for vigilance in ensuring that

the deposit of faith is passed on in its entirety (cf. 1 Tm 6:20) and that all aspects of the profession of faith are duly emphasized. Indeed, inasmuch as the unity of faith is the unity of the Church, to subtract something from the faith is to subtract something from the veracity of communion. The Fathers described faith as a body, the body of truth composed of various members, by analogy with the body of Christ and its prolongation in the Church.[42] The integrity of the faith was also tied to the image of the Church as a virgin and her fidelity in love for Christ her spouse; harming the faith means harming communion with the Lord.[43] The unity of faith, then, is the unity of a living body; this was clearly brought out by Blessed John Henry Newman when he listed among the characteristic notes for distinguishing the continuity of doctrine over time its power to assimilate everything that it meets in the various settings in which it becomes present and in the diverse cultures which it encounters,[44] purifying all things and bringing them to their finest expression. Faith is thus shown to be universal, catholic, because its light expands in order to illumine the entire cosmos and all of history.

49. As a service to the unity of faith and its integral transmission, the Lord gave his Church the gift of apostolic succession. Through this means, the continuity of the Church's memory is ensured and certain access can be had to the wellspring from which faith flows. The assurance of continuity with the origins is thus given by living persons, in a way consonant with the living faith which the Church is called to transmit. She depends on the fidelity of witnesses chosen by the Lord for this task. For this reason, the magisterium always speaks in obedience to the prior word on which faith is based; it is reliable because of its trust in the word which it hears, preserves and expounds.[45] In Saint Paul's farewell discourse to the elders of Ephesus at Miletus, which Saint Luke recounts for us in the Acts of the Apostles, he testifies that he had carried out the task which the Lord had entrusted to him of "declaring the whole counsel of God" (Acts 20:27). Thanks to the Church's magisterium, this counsel can come to us in its integrity, and with it the joy of being able to follow it fully.

CHAPTER FOUR

GOD PREPARES A CITY FOR THEM
(cf. Heb 11:16)

Faith and the common good

50. In presenting the story of the patriarchs and the righteous men and women of the Old Testament, the Letter to the Hebrews highlights an essential aspect of their faith. That faith is not only presented as a journey, but also as a process of building, the preparing of a place in which human beings can dwell together with one another. The first builder was Noah, who saved his family in the ark (Heb 11:7). Then comes Abraham, of whom it is said that by faith he dwelt in tents, as he looked forward to the city with firm foundations (cf. Heb 11:9–10). With faith comes a new reliability, a new firmness, which God alone can give. If the man of faith finds support in the God of fidelity, the God who is Amen (cf. Is 65:16), and thus becomes firm himself, we can now also say that firmness of faith marks the city which God is preparing for mankind. Faith reveals just how firm the bonds between people can be when God is present in their midst. Faith does not merely grant interior firmness, a steadfast conviction on the part of the believer; it also sheds light on every human relationship because it is born of love and reflects God's own love. The God who is himself reliable gives us a city which is reliable.

51. Precisely because it is linked to love (cf. Gal 5:6), the light of faith is concretely placed at the service of justice, law, and peace. Faith is born of an encounter with God's primordial love, wherein the meaning and goodness of our life become evident; our life is illumined to the extent that it enters into the space opened by that love, to the extent that it becomes, in other words, a path and praxis leading to the fullness of love. The light of faith is capable of enhancing the richness of human relations, their ability to endure, to be trustworthy, to enrich our life together. Faith does not draw us away from the world or prove irrelevant to the concrete concerns of the men and women of our time. Without a love which is

trustworthy, nothing could truly keep men and women united. Human unity would be conceivable only on the basis of utility, on a calculus of conflicting interests or on fear, but not on the goodness of living together, not on the joy which the mere presence of others can give. Faith makes us appreciate the architecture of human relationships because it grasps their ultimate foundation and definitive destiny in God, in his love, and thus sheds light on the art of building; as such it becomes a service to the common good. Faith is truly a good for everyone; it is a common good. Its light does not simply brighten the interior of the Church, nor does it serve solely to build an eternal city in the hereafter; it helps us build our societies in such a way that they can journey toward a future of hope. The Letter to the Hebrews offers an example in this regard when it names, among the men and women of faith, Samuel and David, whose faith enabled them to "administer justice" (Heb 11:33). This expression refers to their justice in governance, to that wisdom which brings peace to the people (cf. 1 Sm 12:3–5; 2 Sm 8:15). The hands of faith are raised up to heaven, even as they go about building in charity a city based on relationships in which the love of God is laid as a foundation.

Faith and the family

52. In Abraham's journey toward the future city, the Letter to the Hebrews mentions the blessing which was passed on from fathers to sons (cf. Heb 11:20–21). The first setting in which faith enlightens the human city is the family. I think first and foremost of the stable union of man and woman in marriage. This union is born of their love, as a sign and presence of God's own love, and of the acknowledgment and acceptance of the goodness of sexual differentiation, whereby spouses can become one flesh (cf. Gn 2:24) and are enabled to give birth to a new life, a manifestation of the Creator's goodness, wisdom, and loving plan. Grounded in this love, a man and a woman can promise each other mutual love in a gesture which engages their entire lives and mirrors many features of faith. Promising love forever is possible when we perceive a plan bigger than our own ideas and undertakings, a plan which sustains us and enables us to surrender our future entirely to the one we love. Faith also helps

us to grasp in all its depth and richness the begetting of children, as a sign of the love of the Creator who entrusts us with the mystery of a new person. So it was that Sarah, by faith, became a mother, for she trusted in God's fidelity to his promise (cf. Heb 11:11).

53. In the family, faith accompanies every age of life, beginning with childhood: children learn to trust in the love of their parents. This is why it is so important that within their families parents encourage shared expressions of faith which can help children gradually to mature in their own faith. Young people in particular, who are going through a period in their lives which is so complex, rich, and important for their faith, ought to feel the constant closeness and support of their families and the Church in their journey of faith. We have all seen, during World Youth Days, the joy that young people show in their faith and their desire for an ever more solid and generous life of faith. Young people want to live life to the fullest. Encountering Christ, letting themselves be caught up in and guided by his love, enlarges the horizons of existence, gives it a firm hope which will not disappoint. Faith is no refuge for the faint-hearted, but something which enhances our lives. It makes us aware of a magnificent calling, the vocation of love. It assures us that this love is trustworthy and worth embracing, for it is based on God's faithfulness which is stronger than our every weakness.

A light for life in society

54. Absorbed and deepened in the family, faith becomes a light capable of illumining all our relationships in society. As an experience of the mercy of God the Father, it sets us on the path of brotherhood. Modernity sought to build a universal brotherhood based on equality, yet we gradually came to realize that this brotherhood, lacking a reference to a common Father as its ultimate foundation, cannot endure. We need to return to the true basis of brotherhood. The history of faith has been from the beginning a history of brotherhood, albeit not without conflict. God calls Abraham to go forth from his land and promises to make of him a great nation, a great people on whom the divine blessing rests (cf. Gn 12:1–3). As salvation history progresses, it becomes evident that God

wants to make everyone share as brothers and sisters in that one blessing, which attains its fullness in Jesus, so that all may be one. The boundless love of our Father also comes to us, in Jesus, through our brothers and sisters. Faith teaches us to see that every man and woman represents a blessing for me, that the light of God's face shines on me through the faces of my brothers and sisters.

How many benefits has the gaze of Christian faith brought to the city of men for their common life! Thanks to faith we have come to understand the unique dignity of each person, something which was not clearly seen in antiquity. In the second century the pagan Celsus reproached Christians for an idea that he considered foolishness and delusion: namely, that God created the world for man, setting human beings at the pinnacle of the entire cosmos. "Why claim that [grass] grows for the benefit of man, rather than for that of the most savage of the brute beasts?"[46] "If we look down to Earth from the heights of heaven, would there really be any difference between our activities and those of the ants and bees?"[47] At the heart of biblical faith is God's love, his concrete concern for every person, and his plan of salvation which embraces all of humanity and all creation, culminating in the incarnation, death, and resurrection of Jesus Christ. Without insight into these realities, there is no criterion for discerning what makes human life precious and unique. Man loses his place in the universe, he is cast adrift in nature, either renouncing his proper moral responsibility or else presuming to be a sort of absolute judge, endowed with an unlimited power to manipulate the world around him.

55. Faith, on the other hand, by revealing the love of God the Creator, enables us to respect nature all the more, and to discern in it a grammar written by the hand of God and a dwelling place entrusted to our protection and care. Faith also helps us to devise models of development which are based not simply on utility and profit, but consider creation as a gift for which we are all indebted; it teaches us to create just forms of government, in the realization that authority comes from God and is meant for the service of the common good. Faith likewise offers the possibility of forgiveness, which so often demands time and effort, patience

and commitment. Forgiveness is possible once we discover that goodness is always prior to and more powerful than evil, and that the word with which God affirms our life is deeper than our every denial. From a purely anthropological standpoint, unity is superior to conflict; rather than avoiding conflict, we need to confront it in an effort to resolve and move beyond it, to make it a link in a chain, as part of a progress toward unity.

When faith is weakened, the foundations of life also risk being weakened, as the poet T. S. Eliot warned: "Do you need to be told that even those modest attainments / As you can boast in the way of polite society / Will hardly survive the Faith to which they owe their significance?"[48] If we remove faith in God from our cities, mutual trust would be weakened, we would remain united only by fear and our stability would be threatened. In the Letter to the Hebrews we read that "God is not ashamed to be called their God; indeed, he has prepared a city for them" (Heb 11:16). Here the expression "is not ashamed" is associated with public acknowledgment. The intention is to say that God, by his concrete actions, makes a public avowal that he is present in our midst and that he desires to solidify every human relationship. Could it be the case, instead, that we are the ones who are ashamed to call God our God? That we are the ones who fail to confess him as such in our public life, who fail to propose the grandeur of the life in common which he makes possible? Faith illumines life and society. If it possesses a creative light for each new moment of history, it is because it sets every event in relationship to the origin and destiny of all things in the Father.

Consolation and strength amid suffering

56. Writing to the Christians of Corinth about his sufferings and tribulations, Saint Paul links his faith to his preaching of the Gospel. In himself he sees fulfilled the passage of Scripture which reads: "I believed, and so I spoke" (2 Cor 4:13). The reference is to a verse of Psalm 116, in which the Psalmist exclaims: "I kept my faith, even when I said, 'I am greatly afflicted'" (v. 10). To speak of faith often involves speaking of painful testing, yet it is precisely in such testing that Paul sees the most convincing proclamation of the Gospel, for it is in weakness and suffering

that we discover God's power which triumphs over our weakness and suffering. The apostle himself experienced a dying which would become life for Christians (cf. 2 Cor 4:7–12). In the hour of trial faith brings light, while suffering and weakness make it evident that "we do not proclaim ourselves; we proclaim Jesus Christ as Lord" (2 Cor 4:5). The eleventh chapter of the Letter to the Hebrews concludes with a reference to those who suffered for their faith (cf. Heb 11:35–38); outstanding among these was Moses, who suffered abuse for the Christ (cf. v. 26). Christians know that suffering cannot be eliminated, yet it can have meaning and become an act of love and entrustment into the hands of God who does not abandon us; in this way it can serve as a moment of growth in faith and love. By contemplating Christ's union with the Father even at the height of his sufferings on the cross (cf. Mk 15:34), Christians learn to share in the same gaze of Jesus. Even death is illumined and can be experienced as the ultimate call to faith, the ultimate "Go forth from your land" (Gen 12:1), the ultimate "Come!" spoken by the Father, to whom we abandon ourselves in the confidence that he will keep us steadfast even in our final passage.

57. Nor does the light of faith make us forget the sufferings of this world. How many men and women of faith have found mediators of light in those who suffer! So it was with Saint Francis of Assisi and the leper, or with Blessed Mother Teresa of Calcutta and her poor. They understood the mystery at work in them. In drawing near to the suffering, they were certainly not able to eliminate all their pain or to explain every evil. Faith is not a light which scatters all our darkness, but a lamp which guides our steps in the night and suffices for the journey. To those who suffer, God does not provide arguments which explain everything; rather, his response is that of an accompanying presence, a history of goodness which touches every story of suffering and opens up a ray of light. In Christ, God himself wishes to share this path with us and to offer us his gaze so that we might see the light within it. Christ is the one who, having endured suffering, is "the pioneer and perfecter of our faith" (Heb 12:2).

Suffering reminds us that faith's service to the common good is always one of hope—a hope which looks ever ahead in the knowledge that only from God, from the future which comes from the risen Jesus, can our society find solid and lasting foundations. In this sense faith is linked to hope, for even if our dwelling place here below is wasting away, we have an eternal dwelling place which God has already prepared in Christ, in his body (cf. 2 Cor 4:16–5:5). The dynamic of faith, hope, and charity (cf. 1 Thes 1:3; 1 Cor 13:13) thus leads us to embrace the concerns of all men and women on our journey toward that city "whose architect and builder is God" (Heb 11:10), for "hope does not disappoint" (Rom 5:5).

In union with faith and charity, hope propels us toward a sure future, set against a different horizon with regard to the illusory enticements of the idols of this world yet granting new momentum and strength to our daily lives. Let us refuse to be robbed of hope, or to allow our hope to be dimmed by facile answers and solutions which block our progress, "fragmenting" time and changing it into space. Time is always much greater than space. Space hardens processes, whereas time propels toward the future and encourages us to go forward in hope.

Blessed is she who believed (Lk 1:45)

58. In the parable of the sower, Saint Luke has left us these words of the Lord about the "good soil": "These are the ones who when they hear the word, hold it fast in an honest and good heart, and bear fruit with patient endurance" (Lk 8:15). In the context of Luke's Gospel, this mention of an honest and good heart which hears and keeps the word is an implicit portrayal of the faith of the Virgin Mary. The evangelist himself speaks of Mary's memory, how she treasured in her heart all that she had heard and seen, so that the word could bear fruit in her life. The Mother of the Lord is the perfect icon of faith; as Saint Elizabeth would say: "Blessed is she who believed" (Lk 1:45).

In Mary, the Daughter of Zion, is fulfilled the long history of faith of the Old Testament, with its account of so many faithful women, beginning with Sarah: women who, alongside the patriarchs, were those in whom God's promise was fulfilled and new life flowered. In the fullness of time, God's word was spoken to Mary, and she received that word into her heart, her entire being, so that in her womb it could take flesh and be born as light for humanity. Saint Justin Martyr, in his dialogue with Trypho, uses a striking expression; he tells us that Mary, receiving the message of the angel, conceived "faith and joy."[49] In the Mother of Jesus, faith demonstrated its fruitfulness; when our own spiritual lives bear fruit we become filled with joy, which is the clearest sign of faith's grandeur. In her own life Mary completed the pilgrimage of faith, following in the footsteps of her Son.[50] In her the faith journey of the Old Testament was thus taken up into the following of Christ, transformed by him and entering into the gaze of the incarnate Son of God.

59. We can say that in the Blessed Virgin Mary we find something I mentioned earlier, namely that the believer is completely taken up into his or her confession of faith. Because of her close bond with Jesus, Mary is strictly connected to what we believe. As Virgin and Mother, Mary offers us a clear sign of Christ's divine sonship. The eternal origin of Christ is in the Father. He is the Son in a total and unique sense, and so he is born in time without the intervention of a man. As the Son, Jesus brings to the world a new beginning and a new light, the fullness of God's faithful love bestowed on humanity. But Mary's true motherhood also ensured for the Son of God an authentic human history, true flesh in which he would die on the cross and rise from the dead. Mary would accompany Jesus to the cross (cf. Jn 19:25), whence her motherhood would extend to each of his disciples (cf. Jn 19:26–27). She will also be present in the upper room after Jesus' resurrection and ascension, joining the apostles in imploring the gift of the Spirit (cf. Acts 1:14). The movement of love between Father, Son, and Spirit runs through our history, and Christ draws us to himself in order to save us (cf. Jn 12:32). At the center of our faith is the confession of Jesus, the Son of God, born of a woman, who brings us, through the gift of the Holy Spirit, to adoption as sons and daughters (cf. Gal 4:4).

60. Let us turn in prayer to Mary, Mother of the Church and Mother of our faith.

Mother, help our faith!

Open our ears to hear God's word and to recognize his voice and call.

Awaken in us a desire to follow in his footsteps, to go forth from our own land and to receive his promise.

Help us to be touched by his love, that we may touch him in faith.

Help us to entrust ourselves fully to him and to believe in his love, especially at times of trial, beneath the shadow of the cross, when our faith is called to mature.

Sow in our faith the joy of the Risen One.

Remind us that those who believe are never alone.

Teach us to see all things with the eyes of Jesus, that he may be light for our path. And may this light of faith always increase in us, until the dawn of that undying day which is Christ himself, your Son, our Lord!

Given in Rome, at Saint Peter's, on 29 June, the Solemnity of the Holy Apostles Peter and Paul, in the year 2013, the first of my pontificate.

FRANCISCUS

Notes

1. *Dialogus cum Tryphone Iudaeo*, 121, 2: PG 6, 758.

2. Clement of Alexandria, *Protrepticus*, IX: PG 8, 195.

3. *Brief an Elisabeth Nietzsche* (11 June 1865), in: *Werke in drei Bänden, München*, 1954, 953ff.

4. *Paradiso* XXIV, 145–147.

5. *Acta Sanctorum*, Junii, I, 21.

6. "Though the Council does not expressly deal with faith, it speaks of it on every page, it recognizes its living, supernatural character, it presumes it to be full and strong, and it bases its teachings on it. It is sufficient to recall the Council's statements . . . to see the essential importance which the Council, in line with the doctrinal tradition of the Church, attributes to faith, the true faith, which has its source in Christ, and the magisterium of the Church for its channel" (Paul VI, General Audience [8 March 1967]: *Insegnamenti* V [1967], 705).

7. Cf., for example, First Vatican Ecumenical Council, Dogmatic Constitution on the Catholic Faith *Dei Filius*, Ch. 3: DS 3008–3020; Second Vatican Ecumenical Council, Dogmatic Constitution on Divine Revelation *Dei Verbum*, 5: *Catechism of the Catholic Church*, Nos. 153–165.

8. Cf. *Catechesis* V, 1: PG 33, 505A.

9. *In Psal*. 32, II, s. I, 9: PL 36, 284.

10. M. Buber, *Die Erzählungen der Chassidim*, Zürich, 1949, 793.

11. *Émile*, Paris, 1966, 387.

12. *Lettre à Christophe de Beaumont*, Lausanne, 1993, 110.

13. Cf. *In Ioh. Evang*., 45, 9: PL 35, 1722–1723.

14. Part II, IV.

15. *De Continentia*, 4, 11: PL 40, 356.

16. "*Vom Wesen katholischer Weltanschauung*" (1923), in *Unterscheidung des Christlichen*. *Gesammelte Studien* 1923–1963, Mainz, 1963, 24.

17. XI, 30, 40: PL 32, 825.

18. Cf. ibid., 825–826.

19. Cf. *Vermischte Bemerkungen / Culture and Value*, ed. G. H. von Wright, Oxford, 1991, 32–33, 61–64.

20. *Homiliae in Evangelia*, II, 27, 4: PL 76, 1207.

21. Cf. *Expositio super Cantica Canticorum*, XVIII, 88: CCL, *Continuatio Mediaevalis* 87, 67.

22. Ibid., XIX, 90: CCL, *Continuatio Mediaevalis* 87, 69.

23. "The obedience of faith (Rom 16:26; compare Rom 1:5, 2 Cor 10:5–6) must be our response to the God who reveals. By faith one freely submits oneself entirely to God making the full submission of intellect and will to God who reveals, and willingly assenting to the revelation given by God. For this faith to be accorded, we need the grace of God, anticipating it and assisting it, as well as the interior helps of the Holy Spirit, who moves the heart and converts it to God, and opens the eyes of

the mind and makes it easy for all to accept and believe the truth. The same Holy Spirit constantly perfects faith by his gifts, so that revelation may be more and more deeply understood" (Second Vatican Ecumenical Council, Dogmatic Constitution on Divine Revelation *Dei Verbum*, 5).

24. Cf. H. Schlier, *Meditationen über den Johanneischen Begriff der Wahrheit*, in *Besinnung auf das Neue Testament. Exegetische Aufsätze und Vorträge* 2, Freiburg, Basel, Wien, 1959, 272.

25. Cf. *S. Th.* III, q. 55, a. 2, ad 1.

26. *Sermo* 229 / L (Guelf. 14), 2 (Miscellanea Augustiniana 1, 487 / 488): "*Tangere autem corde, hoc est credere.*"

27. Cf. Encyclical Letter *Fides et Ratio* (14 September 1998), 73: AAS (1999), 61–62.

28. Cf. *Confessiones*, VIII, 12, 29: PL 32, 762.

29. *De Trinitate*, XV, 11, 20: PL 42, 1071: "*verbum quod intus lucet.*"

30. Cf. *De Civitate Dei*, XXII, 30, 5: PL 41, 804.

31. Cf. Congregation for the Doctrine of the Faith, Declaration *Dominus Iesus* (6 August 2000), 15: AAS 92 (2000), 756.

32. *Demonstratio Apostolicae Predicationis*, 24: SC 406, 117.

33. Cf. Bonaventure, *Breviloquium, prol.*: Opera Omnia, V, Quaracchi 1891, 201; *In I Sent., proem*, q. 1, resp.: Opera Omnia, I, Quaracchi 1891, 7; Thomas Aquinas, *S. Th.* I, q. 1.

34. Cf. *De Baptismo*, 20, 5: CCL 1, 295.

35. Dogmatic Constitution on Divine Revelation *Dei Verbum*, 8.

36. Cf. Second Vatican Ecumenical Council, Constitution on the Sacred Liturgy *Sacrosanctum Concilium*, 59.

37. Cf. *Epistula Barnabae*, 11, 5: SC 172, 162.

38. Cf. *De Nuptiis et Concupiscentia* I, 4, 5: PL 44, 413: "*Habent quippe intentionem generandi regenerandos, ut qui ex eis saeculi filii nascuntur in Dei filios renascantur.*"

39. Second Vatican Ecumenical Council, Dogmatic Constitution on Divine Revelation *Dei Verbum*, 8.

40. In *Nativitate Domini Sermo*, 4, 6: SC 22, 110.

41. Cf. Irenaeus, *Adversus Haereses*, I, 10, 2: SC 264, 160.

42. Cf. ibid., II, 27, 1: SC 294, 264.

43. Cf. Augustine, *De Sancta Virginitate*, 48, 48: PL 40, 424–425: "*Servatur et in fide inviolata quaedam castitas virginalis, qua Ecclesia uni viro virgo casta coaptatur.*"

44. Cf. *An Essay on the Development of Christian Doctrine* (Uniform Edition: Longmans, Green and Company, London, 1868–1881), 185–189.

45. Cf. Second Vatican Ecumenical Council, Dogmatic Constitution on Divine Revelation *Dei Verbum*, 10.

46. Origen, *Contra Celsum*, IV, 75: SC 136, 372.

47. Ibid., 85: SC 136, 394.

48. "Choruses from *The Rock*," in *The Collected Poems and Plays 1909–1950*, New York, 1980, 106.

49. Cf. *Dialogus cum Tryphone Iudaeo*, 100, 5: PG 6, 710.

50. Cf. Second Vatican Ecumenical Council, Dogmatic Constitution on the Church *Lumen Gentium*, 58.

Evangelii Gaudium
The Joy of the Gospel
November 24, 2013

APOSTOLIC EXHORTATION
EVANGELII GAUDIUM
OF THE HOLY FATHER
FRANCIS
TO THE BISHOPS, CLERGY, CONSECRATED PERSONS, AND THE LAY FAITHFUL ON THE PROCLAMATION OF THE GOSPEL IN TODAY'S WORLD

1. The joy of the gospel fills the hearts and lives of all who encounter Jesus. Those who accept his offer of salvation are set free from sin, sorrow, inner emptiness, and loneliness. With Christ joy is constantly born anew. In this Exhortation I wish to encourage the Christian faithful to embark upon a new chapter of evangelization marked by this joy, while pointing out new paths for the Church's journey in years to come.

I. A joy ever new, a joy which is shared

2. The great danger in today's world, pervaded as it is by consumerism, is the desolation and anguish born of a complacent yet covetous heart, the feverish pursuit of frivolous pleasures, and a blunted conscience. Whenever our interior life becomes caught up in its own interests and concerns, there is no longer room for others, no place for the poor. God's voice is no longer heard, the quiet joy of his love is no longer felt, and the desire to do good fades. This is a very real danger for believers too. Many fall prey to it, and end up resentful, angry, and listless. That is no way to live a dignified and fulfilled life; it is not God's will for us, nor is it the life in the Spirit which has its source in the heart of the risen Christ.

3. I invite all Christians, everywhere, at this very moment, to a renewed personal encounter with Jesus Christ, or at least an openness to letting him encounter them; I ask all of you to do this unfailingly each day. No one should think that this invitation is not meant for him or her, since

"no one is excluded from the joy brought by the Lord."[1] The Lord does not disappoint those who take this risk; whenever we take a step toward Jesus, we come to realize that he is already there, waiting for us with open arms. Now is the time to say to Jesus: "Lord, I have let myself be deceived; in a thousand ways I have shunned your love, yet here I am once more, to renew my covenant with you. I need you. Save me once again, Lord, take me once more into your redeeming embrace." How good it feels to come back to him whenever we are lost! Let me say this once more: God never tires of forgiving us; we are the ones who tire of seeking his mercy. Christ, who told us to forgive one another "seventy times seven" (Mt 18:22) has given us his example: he has forgiven us seventy times seven. Time and time again he bears us on his shoulders. No one can strip us of the dignity bestowed upon us by this boundless and unfailing love. With a tenderness which never disappoints, but is always capable of restoring our joy, he makes it possible for us to lift up our heads and to start anew. Let us not flee from the resurrection of Jesus, let us never give up, come what will. May nothing inspire more than his life, which impels us onward!

4. The books of the Old Testament predicted that the joy of salvation would abound in messianic times. The prophet Isaiah exultantly salutes the awaited Messiah: "You have multiplied the nation, you have increased its joy" (9:3). He exhorts those who dwell on Zion to go forth to meet him with song: "Shout aloud and sing for joy!" (12:6). The prophet tells those who have already seen him from afar to bring the message to others: "Get you up to a high mountain, O herald of good tidings to Zion; lift up your voice with strength, O herald of good tidings to Jerusalem" (40:9). All creation shares in the joy of salvation: "Sing for joy, O heavens, and exult, O earth! Break forth, O mountains, into singing! For the Lord has comforted his people, and will have compassion on his suffering ones" (49:13).

Zechariah, looking to the day of the Lord, invites the people to acclaim the king who comes "humble and riding on a donkey": "Rejoice greatly, O daughter Zion! Shout aloud, O daughter Jerusalem! Lo, your king comes to you; triumphant and victorious is he" (9:9).

Perhaps the most exciting invitation is that of the prophet Zephaniah, who presents God with his people in the midst of a celebration overflowing with the joy of salvation. I find it thrilling to reread this text: "The Lord your God is in your midst, a warrior who gives you the victory; he will rejoice over you with gladness, he will renew you in his love; he will exult over you with loud singing, as on a day of festival" (3:17).

This is the joy which we experience daily, amid the little things of life, as a response to the loving invitation of God our Father: "My child, treat yourself well, according to your means. . . . Do not deprive yourself of the day's enjoyment" (Sir 14:11, 14). What tender paternal love echoes in these words!

5. The Gospel, radiant with the glory of Christ's cross, constantly invites us to rejoice. A few examples will suffice. "Rejoice!" is the angel's greeting to Mary (Lk 1:28). Mary's visit to Elizabeth makes John leap for joy in his mother's womb (cf. Lk 1:41). In her song of praise, Mary proclaims: "My spirit rejoices in God my Savior" (Lk 1:47). When Jesus begins his ministry, John cries out: "For this reason, my joy has been fulfilled" (Jn 3:29). Jesus himself "rejoiced in the Holy Spirit" (Lk 10:21). His message brings us joy: "I have said these things to you, so that my joy may be in you, and that your joy may be complete" (Jn 15:11). Our Christian joy drinks of the wellspring of his brimming heart. He promises his disciples: "You will be sorrowful, but your sorrow will turn into joy" (Jn 16:20). He then goes on to say: "But I will see you again and your hearts will rejoice, and no one will take your joy from you" (Jn 16:22). The disciples "rejoiced" (Jn 20:20) at the sight of the risen Christ. In the Acts of the Apostles we read that the first Christians "ate their food with glad and generous hearts" (2:46). Wherever the disciples went, "there was great joy" (8:8); even amid persecution they continued to be "filled with joy" (13:52). The newly baptized eunuch "went on his way rejoicing" (8:39), while Paul's jailer "and his entire household rejoiced that he had become a believer in God" (16:34). Why should we not also enter into this great stream of joy?

6. There are Christians whose lives seem like Lent without Easter. I realize of course that joy is not expressed the same way at all times in life, especially at moments of great difficulty. Joy adapts and changes, but it always endures, even as a flicker of light born of our personal certainty that, when everything is said and done, we are infinitely loved. I understand the grief of people who have to endure great suffering, yet slowly but surely we all have to let the joy of faith slowly revive as a quiet yet firm trust, even amid the greatest distress: "My soul is bereft of peace; I have forgotten what happiness is. . . . But this I call to mind, and therefore I have hope: the steadfast love of the Lord never ceases, his mercies never come to an end; they are new every morning. Great is your faithfulness. . . . It is good that one should wait quietly for the salvation of the Lord" (Lam 3:17, 21–23, 26).

7. Sometimes we are tempted to find excuses and complain, acting as if we could only be happy if a thousand conditions were met. To some extent this is because our "technological society has succeeded in multiplying occasions of pleasure, yet has found it very difficult to engender joy."[2] I can say that the most beautiful and natural expressions of joy which I have seen in my life were in poor people who had little to hold on to. I also think of the real joy shown by others who, even amid pressing professional obligations, were able to preserve, in detachment and simplicity, a heart full of faith. In their own way, all these instances of joy flow from the infinite love of God, who has revealed himself to us in Jesus Christ. I never tire of repeating those words of Benedict XVI which take us to the very heart of the Gospel: "Being a Christian is not the result of an ethical choice or a lofty idea, but the encounter with an event, a person, which gives life a new horizon and a decisive direction."[3]

8. Thanks solely to this encounter—or renewed encounter—with God's love, which blossoms into an enriching friendship, we are liberated from our narrowness and self-absorption. We become fully human when we become more than human, when we let God bring us beyond ourselves in order to attain the fullest truth of our being. Here we find the source and inspiration of all our efforts at evangelization. For if we have received

the love which restores meaning to our lives, how can we fail to share that love with others?

II. The delightful and comforting joy of evangelizing

9. Goodness always tends to spread. Every authentic experience of truth and goodness seeks by its very nature to grow within us, and any person who has experienced a profound liberation becomes more sensitive to the needs of others. As it expands, goodness takes root and develops. If we wish to lead a dignified and fulfilling life, we have to reach out to others and seek their good. In this regard, several sayings of Saint Paul will not surprise us: "The love of Christ urges us on" (2 Cor 5:14); "Woe to me if I do not proclaim the Gospel" (1 Cor 9:16).

10. The Gospel offers us the chance to live life on a higher plane, but with no less intensity: "Life grows by being given away, and it weakens in isolation and comfort. Indeed, those who enjoy life most are those who leave security on the shore and become excited by the mission of communicating life to others."[4] When the Church summons Christians to take up the task of evangelization, she is simply pointing to the source of authentic personal fulfillment. For "here we discover a profound law of reality: that life is attained and matures in the measure that it is offered up in order to give life to others. This is certainly what mission means."[5] Consequently, an evangelizer must never look like someone who has just come back from a funeral! Let us recover and deepen our enthusiasm, that "delightful and comforting joy of evangelizing, even when it is in tears that we must sow. . . . And may the world of our time, which is searching, sometimes with anguish, sometimes with hope, be enabled to receive the good news not from evangelizers who are dejected, discouraged, impatient or anxious, but from ministers of the Gospel whose lives glow with fervor, who have first received the joy of Christ."[6]

Eternal newness

11. A renewal of preaching can offer believers, as well as the lukewarm and the non-practicing, new joy in the faith and fruitfulness in the work of evangelization. The heart of its message will always be the same: the

God who revealed his immense love in the crucified and risen Christ. God constantly renews his faithful ones, whatever their age: "They shall mount up with wings like eagles, they shall run and not be weary, they shall walk and not be faint" (Is 40:31). Christ is the "eternal Gospel" (Rv 14:6); he "is the same yesterday and today and forever" (Heb 13:8), yet his riches and beauty are inexhaustible. He is forever young and a constant source of newness. The Church never fails to be amazed at "the depth of the riches and wisdom and knowledge of God" (Rom 11:33). Saint John of the Cross says that "the thicket of God's wisdom and knowledge is so deep and so broad that the soul, however much it has come to know of it, can always penetrate deeper within it."[7] Or as Saint Irenaeus writes: "By his coming, Christ brought with him all newness."[8] With this newness he is always able to renew our lives and our communities, and even if the Christian message has known periods of darkness and ecclesial weakness, it will never grow old. Jesus can also break through the dull categories with which we would enclose him and he constantly amazes us by his divine creativity. Whenever we make the effort to return to the source and to recover the original freshness of the Gospel, new avenues arise, new paths of creativity open up, with different forms of expression, more eloquent signs and words with new meaning for today's world. Every form of authentic evangelization is always "new."

12. Though it is true that this mission demands great generosity on our part, it would be wrong to see it as a heroic individual undertaking, for it is first and foremost the Lord's work, surpassing anything which we can see and understand. Jesus is "the first and greatest evangelizer."[9] In every activity of evangelization, the primacy always belongs to God, who has called us to cooperate with him and who leads us on by the power of his Spirit. The real newness is the newness which God himself mysteriously brings about and inspires, provokes, guides, and accompanies in a thousand ways. The life of the Church should always reveal clearly that God takes the initiative, that "he has loved us first" (1 Jn 4:19) and that he alone "gives the growth" (1 Cor 3:7). This conviction enables us to maintain a spirit of joy in the midst of a task so demanding and

challenging that it engages our entire life. God asks everything of us, yet at the same time he offers everything to us.

13. Nor should we see the newness of this mission as entailing a kind of displacement or forgetfulness of the living history which surrounds us and carries us forward. Memory is a dimension of our faith which we might call "deuteronomic," not unlike the memory of Israel itself. Jesus leaves us the Eucharist as the Church's daily remembrance of, and deeper sharing in, the event of his Passover (cf. Lk 22:19). The joy of evangelizing always arises from grateful remembrance: it is a grace which we constantly need to implore. The apostles never forgot the moment when Jesus touched their hearts: "It was about four o'clock in the afternoon" (Jn 1:39). Together with Jesus, this remembrance makes present to us "a great cloud of witnesses" (Heb 12:1), some of whom, as believers, we recall with great joy: "Remember your leaders, those who spoke to you the word of God" (Heb 13:7). Some of them were ordinary people who were close to us and introduced us to the life of faith: "I am reminded of your sincere faith, a faith that dwelt first in your grandmother Lois and your mother Eunice" (2 Tm 1:5). The believer is essentially "one who remembers."

III. The new evangelization for the transmission of the faith

14. Attentive to the promptings of the Holy Spirit who helps us together to read the signs of the times, the XIII Ordinary General Assembly of the Synod of Bishops gathered from 7–28 October 2012 to discuss the theme: The New Evangelization for the Transmission of the Christian Faith. The Synod reaffirmed that the new evangelization is a summons addressed to all and that it is carried out in three principal settings.[10]

15. In first place, we can mention the area of *ordinary pastoral ministry*, which is "animated by the fire of the Spirit, so as to inflame the hearts of the faithful who regularly take part in community worship and gather on the Lord's day to be nourished by his word and by the bread of eternal life."[11] In this category we can also include those members of the faithful who preserve a deep and sincere faith, expressing it in different ways,

but seldom taking part in worship. Ordinary pastoral ministry seeks to help believers to grow spiritually so that they can respond to God's love ever more fully in their lives.

A second area is that of *"the baptized whose lives do not reflect the demands of Baptism,"*[12] who lack a meaningful relationship to the Church and no longer experience the consolation born of faith. The Church, in her maternal concern, tries to help them experience a conversion which will restore the joy of faith to their hearts and inspire a commitment to the Gospel.

Lastly, we cannot forget that evangelization is first and foremost about preaching the Gospel to *those who do not know Jesus Christ or who have always rejected him*. Many of them are quietly seeking God, led by a yearning to see his face, even in countries of ancient Christian tradition. All of them have a right to receive the Gospel. Christians have the duty to proclaim the Gospel without excluding anyone. Instead of seeming to impose new obligations, they should appear as people who wish to share their joy, who point to a horizon of beauty and who invite others to a delicious banquet. It is not by proselytizing that the Church grows, but "by attraction."[13]

John Paul II asked us to recognize that "there must be no lessening of the impetus to preach the Gospel" to those who are far from Christ, "because this is the first task of the Church."[14] Indeed, "today missionary activity still represents the greatest challenge for the Church"[15] and "the missionary task must remain foremost."[16] What would happen if we were to take these words seriously? We would realize that missionary outreach is *paradigmatic for all the Church's activity*. Along these lines the Latin American bishops stated that we "cannot passively and calmly wait in our church buildings";[17] we need to move "from a pastoral ministry of mere conservation to a decidedly missionary pastoral ministry."[18] This task continues to be a source of immense joy for the Church: "Just so, I tell you, there will be more joy in heaven over one sinner who repents than ninety-nine righteous persons who need no repentance" (Lk 15:7).

The scope and limits of this Exhortation

16. I was happy to take up the request of the Fathers of the Synod to write this Exhortation.[19] In so doing, I am reaping the rich fruits of the Synod's labors. In addition, I have sought advice from a number of people and I intend to express my own concerns about this particular chapter of the Church's work of evangelization. Countless issues involving evangelization today might be discussed here, but I have chosen not to explore these many questions which call for further reflection and study. Nor do I believe that the papal magisterium should be expected to offer a definitive or complete word on every question which affects the Church and the world. It is not advisable for the Pope to take the place of local bishops in the discernment of every issue which arises in their territory. In this sense, I am conscious of the need to promote a sound "decentralization."

17. Here I have chosen to present some guidelines which can encourage and guide the whole Church in a new phase of evangelization, one marked by enthusiasm and vitality. In this context, and on the basis of the teaching of the Dogmatic Constitution *Lumen Gentium*, I have decided, among other themes, to discuss at length the following questions:

a) the reform of the Church in her missionary outreach;
b) the temptations faced by pastoral workers;
c) the Church, understood as the entire People of God which evangelizes;
d) the homily and its preparation;
e) the inclusion of the poor in society;
f) peace and dialogue within society;
g) the spiritual motivations for mission.

18. I have dealt extensively with these topics, with a detail which some may find excessive. But I have done so, not with the intention of providing an exhaustive treatise but simply as a way of showing their important practical implications for the Church's mission today. All of them help give shape to a definite style of evangelization which I ask you to adopt *in every activity which you undertake*. In this way, we can take up, amid

our daily efforts, the biblical exhortation: "Rejoice in the Lord always; again I will say: Rejoice" (Phil 4:4).

CHAPTER ONE

THE CHURCH'S MISSIONARY TRANSFORMATION

19. Evangelization takes place in obedience to the missionary mandate of Jesus: "Go therefore and make disciples of all nations, baptizing them in the name of the Father and of the Son and of the Holy Spirit, teaching them to observe all that I have commanded you" (Mt 28:19–20). In these verses we see how the risen Christ sent his followers to preach the Gospel in every time and place, so that faith in him might spread to every corner of the earth.

I. A Church which goes forth

20. The word of God constantly shows us how God challenges those who believe in him "to go forth." Abraham received the call to set out for a new land (cf. Gn 12:1–3). Moses heard God's call: "Go, I send you" (Ex 3:10) and led the people toward the Promised Land (cf. Ex 3:17). To Jeremiah God says: "To all whom I send you, you shall go" (Jer 1:7). In our day Jesus' command to "go and make disciples" echoes in the changing scenarios and ever new challenges to the Church's mission of evangelization, and all of us are called to take part in this new missionary "going forth." Each Christian and every community must discern the path that the Lord points out, but all of us are asked to obey his call to go forth from our own comfort zone in order to reach all the "peripheries" in need of the light of the Gospel.

21. The Gospel joy which enlivens the community of disciples is a missionary joy. The seventy-two disciples felt it as they returned from their mission (cf. Lk 10:17). Jesus felt it when he rejoiced in the Holy Spirit and praised the Father for revealing himself to the poor and the little ones (cf. Lk 10:21). It was felt by the first converts who marveled to hear the apostles preaching "in the native language of each" (Acts 2:6) on the day of Pentecost. This joy is a sign that the Gospel has been proclaimed and is bearing fruit. Yet the drive to go forth and give, to go out from ourselves,

to keep pressing forward in our sowing of the good seed, remains ever present. The Lord says: "Let us go on to the next towns that I may preach there also, for that is why I came out" (Mk 1:38). Once the seed has been sown in one place, Jesus does not stay behind to explain things or to perform more signs; the Spirit moves him to go forth to other towns.

22. God's word is unpredictable in its power. The Gospel speaks of a seed which, once sown, grows by itself, even as the farmer sleeps (Mk 4:26–29). The Church has to accept this unruly freedom of the word, which accomplishes what it wills in ways that surpass our calculations and ways of thinking.

23. The Church's closeness to Jesus is part of a common journey; "communion and mission are profoundly interconnected."[20] In fidelity to the example of the Master, it is vitally important for the Church today to go forth and preach the Gospel to all: to all places, on all occasions, without hesitation, reluctance, or fear. The joy of the Gospel is for all people: no one can be excluded. That is what the angel proclaimed to the shepherds in Bethlehem: "Be not afraid; for behold, I bring you good news of a great joy which will come to all the people" (Lk 2:10). The Book of Revelation speaks of "an eternal Gospel to proclaim to those who dwell on earth, to every nation and tongue and tribe and people" (Rv 14:6).

Taking the first step, being involved and supportive, bearing fruit and rejoicing

24. The Church which "goes forth" is a community of missionary disciples who take the first step, who are involved and supportive, who bear fruit and rejoice. An evangelizing community knows that the Lord has taken the initiative, he has loved us first (cf. 1 Jn 4:19), and therefore we can move forward, boldly take the initiative, go out to others, seek those who have fallen away, stand at the crossroads, and welcome the outcast. Such a community has an endless desire to show mercy, the fruit of its own experience of the power of the Father's infinite mercy. Let us try a little harder to take the first step and to become involved. Jesus washed the feet of his disciples. The Lord gets involved and he involves his own,

as he kneels to wash their feet. He tells his disciples: "You will be blessed if you do this" (Jn 13:17). An evangelizing community gets involved by word and deed in people's daily lives; it bridges distances, it is willing to abase itself if necessary, and it embraces human life, touching the suffering flesh of Christ in others. Evangelizers thus take on the "smell of the sheep" and the sheep are willing to hear their voice. An evangelizing community is also supportive, standing by people at every step of the way, no matter how difficult or lengthy this may prove to be. It is familiar with patient expectation and apostolic endurance. Evangelization consists mostly of patience and disregard for constraints of time. Faithful to the Lord's gift, it also bears fruit. An evangelizing community is always concerned with fruit, because the Lord wants her to be fruitful. It cares for the grain and does not grow impatient at the weeds. The sower, when he sees weeds sprouting among the grain, does not grumble or overreact. He or she finds a way to let the word take flesh in a particular situation and bear fruits of new life, however imperfect or incomplete these may appear. The disciple is ready to put his or her whole life on the line, even to accepting martyrdom, in bearing witness to Jesus Christ, yet the goal is not to make enemies but to see God's word accepted and its capacity for liberation and renewal revealed. Finally an evangelizing community is filled with joy; it knows how to rejoice always. It celebrates every small victory, every step forward in the work of evangelization. Evangelization with joy becomes beauty in the liturgy, as part of our daily concern to spread goodness. The Church evangelizes and is herself evangelized through the beauty of the liturgy, which is both a celebration of the task of evangelization and the source of her renewed self-giving.

II. Pastoral activity and conversion

25. I am aware that nowadays documents do not arouse the same interest as in the past and that they are quickly forgotten. Nevertheless, I want to emphasize that what I am trying to express here has a programmatic significance and important consequences. I hope that all communities will devote the necessary effort to advancing along the path of a pastoral and missionary conversion which cannot leave things as they presently

are. "Mere administration" can no longer be enough.[21] Throughout the world, let us be "permanently in a state of mission."[22]

26. Paul VI invited us to deepen the call to renewal and to make it clear that renewal does not only concern individuals but the entire Church. Let us return to a memorable text which continues to challenge us. "The Church must look with penetrating eyes within herself, ponder the mystery of her own being. . . . This vivid and lively self-awareness inevitably leads to a comparison between the ideal image of the Church as Christ envisaged her and loved her as his holy and spotless bride (cf. Eph 5:27), and the actual image which the Church presents to the world today. . . . This is the source of the Church's heroic and impatient struggle for renewal: the struggle to correct those flaws introduced by her members which her own self-examination, mirroring her exemplar, Christ, points out to her and condemns."[23] The Second Vatican Council presented ecclesial conversion as openness to a constant self-renewal born of fidelity to Jesus Christ: "Every renewal of the Church essentially consists in an increase of fidelity to her own calling. . . . Christ summons the Church as she goes her pilgrim way . . . to that continual reformation of which she always has need, in so far as she is a human institution here on earth."[24]

There are ecclesial structures which can hamper efforts at evangelization, yet even good structures are only helpful when there is a life constantly driving, sustaining, and assessing them. Without new life and an authentic evangelical spirit, without the Church's "fidelity to her own calling," any new structure will soon prove ineffective.

An ecclesial renewal which cannot be deferred

27. I dream of a "missionary option," that is, a missionary impulse capable of transforming everything, so that the Church's customs, ways of doing things, times and schedules, language and structures can be suitably channeled for the evangelization of today's world rather than for her self-preservation. The renewal of structures demanded by pastoral conversion can only be understood in this light: as part of an effort to make them more mission-oriented, to make ordinary pastoral activity on every level more inclusive and open, to inspire in pastoral workers

a constant desire to go forth and in this way to elicit a positive response from all those whom Jesus summons to friendship with himself. As John Paul II once said to the bishops of Oceania: "All renewal in the Church must have mission as its goal if it is not to fall prey to a kind of ecclesial introversion."[25]

28. The parish is not an outdated institution; precisely because it possesses great flexibility, it can assume quite different contours depending on the openness and missionary creativity of the pastor and the community. While certainly not the only institution which evangelizes, if the parish proves capable of self-renewal and constant adaptivity, it continues to be "the Church living in the midst of the homes of her sons and daughters."[26] This presumes that it really is in contact with the homes and the lives of its people, and does not become a useless structure out of touch with people or a self-absorbed group made up of a chosen few. The parish is the presence of the Church in a given territory, an environment for hearing God's word, for growth in the Christian life, for dialogue, proclamation, charitable outreach, worship, and celebration.[27] In all its activities the parish encourages and trains its members to be evangelizers.[28] It is a community of communities, a sanctuary where the thirsty come to drink in the midst of their journey, and a center of constant missionary outreach. We must admit, though, that the call to review and renew our parishes has not yet sufficed to bring them nearer to people, to make them environments of living communion and participation, and to make them completely mission-oriented.

29. Other Church institutions, basic communities and small communities, movements, and forms of association are a source of enrichment for the Church, raised up by the Spirit for evangelizing different areas and sectors. Frequently they bring a new evangelizing fervor and a new capacity for dialogue with the world whereby the Church is renewed. But it will prove beneficial for them not to lose contact with the rich reality of the local parish and to participate readily in the overall pastoral activity of the particular Church.[29] This kind of integration will prevent them from concentrating only on part of the Gospel or the Church, or becoming nomads without roots.

30. Each particular Church, as a portion of the Catholic Church under the leadership of its bishop, is likewise called to missionary conversion. It is the primary subject of evangelization,[30] since it is the concrete manifestation of the one Church in one specific place, and in it "the one, holy, catholic, and apostolic Church of Christ is truly present and operative."[31] It is the Church incarnate in a certain place, equipped with all the means of salvation bestowed by Christ, but with local features. Its joy in communicating Jesus Christ is expressed both by a concern to preach him to areas in greater need and in constantly going forth to the outskirts of its own territory or toward new sociocultural settings.[32] Wherever the need for the light and the life of the Risen Christ is greatest, it will want to be there.[33] To make this missionary impulse ever more focused, generous, and fruitful, I encourage each particular Church to undertake a resolute process of discernment, purification, and reform.

31. The bishop must always foster this missionary communion in his diocesan Church, following the ideal of the first Christian communities, in which the believers were of one heart and one soul (cf. Acts 4:32). To do so, he will sometimes go before his people, pointing the way and keeping their hope vibrant. At other times, he will simply be in their midst with his unassuming and merciful presence. At yet other times, he will have to walk after them, helping those who lag behind and—above all—allowing the flock to strike out on new paths. In his mission of fostering a dynamic, open, and missionary communion, he will have to encourage and develop the means of participation proposed in the *Code of Canon Law*,[34] and other forms of pastoral dialogue, out of a desire to listen to everyone and not simply to those who would tell him what he would like to hear. Yet the principal aim of these participatory processes should not be ecclesiastical organization but rather the missionary aspiration of reaching everyone.

32. Since I am called to put into practice what I ask of others, I too must think about a conversion of the papacy. It is my duty, as the Bishop of Rome, to be open to suggestions which can help make the exercise of my ministry more faithful to the meaning which Jesus Christ wished to give it and to the present needs of evangelization. Pope John Paul II asked for

help in finding "a way of exercising the primacy which, while in no way renouncing what is essential to its mission, is nonetheless open to a new situation."[35] We have made little progress in this regard. The papacy and the central structures of the universal Church also need to hear the call to pastoral conversion. The Second Vatican Council stated that, like the ancient patriarchal Churches, episcopal conferences are in a position "to contribute in many and fruitful ways to the concrete realization of the collegial spirit."[36] Yet this desire has not been fully realized, since a juridical status of episcopal conferences which would see them as subjects of specific attributions, including genuine doctrinal authority, has not yet been sufficiently elaborated.[37] Excessive centralization, rather than proving helpful, complicates the Church's life and her missionary outreach.

33. Pastoral ministry in a missionary key seeks to abandon the complacent attitude that says: "We have always done it this way." I invite everyone to be bold and creative in this task of rethinking the goals, structures, style, and methods of evangelization in their respective communities. A proposal of goals without an adequate communal search for the means of achieving them will inevitably prove illusory. I encourage everyone to apply the guidelines found in this document generously and courageously, without inhibitions or fear. The important thing is to not walk alone, but to rely on each other as brothers and sisters, and especially under the leadership of the bishops, in a wise and realistic pastoral discernment.

III. From the heart of the Gospel

34. If we attempt to put all things in a missionary key, this will also affect the way we communicate the message. In today's world of instant communication and occasionally biased media coverage, the message we preach runs a greater risk of being distorted or reduced to some of its secondary aspects. In this way certain issues which are part of the Church's moral teaching are taken out of the context which gives them their meaning. The biggest problem is when the message we preach then seems identified with those secondary aspects which, important as they are, do not in and of themselves convey the heart of Christ's message.

We need to be realistic and not assume that our audience understands the full background to what we are saying, or is capable of relating what we say to the very heart of the Gospel which gives it meaning, beauty, and attractiveness.

35. Pastoral ministry in a missionary style is not obsessed with the disjointed transmission of a multitude of doctrines to be insistently imposed. When we adopt a pastoral goal and a missionary style which would actually reach everyone without exception or exclusion, the message has to concentrate on the essentials, on what is most beautiful, most grand, most appealing, and at the same time most necessary. The message is simplified, while losing none of its depth and truth, and thus becomes all the more forceful and convincing.

36. All revealed truths derive from the same divine source and are to be believed with the same faith, yet some of them are more important for giving direct expression to the heart of the Gospel. In this basic core, what shines forth is the beauty of the saving love of God made manifest in Jesus Christ who died and rose from the dead. In this sense, the Second Vatican Council explained, "in Catholic doctrine there exists an order or a 'hierarchy' of truths, since they vary in their relation to the foundation of the Christian faith."[38] This holds true as much for the dogmas of faith as for the whole corpus of the Church's teaching, including her moral teaching.

37. Saint Thomas Aquinas taught that the Church's moral teaching has its own "hierarchy," in the virtues and in the acts which proceed from them.[39] What counts above all else is "faith working through love" (Gal 5:6). Works of love directed to one's neighbor are the most perfect external manifestation of the interior grace of the Spirit: "The foundation of the New Law is in the grace of the Holy Spirit, who is manifested in the faith which works through love."[40] Thomas thus explains that, as far as external works are concerned, mercy is the greatest of all the virtues: "In itself mercy is the greatest of the virtues, since all the others revolve around it and, more than this, it makes up for their deficiencies. This is particular to the superior virtue, and as such it is proper to

God to have mercy, through which his omnipotence is manifested to the greatest degree."[41]

38. It is important to draw out the pastoral consequences of the Council's teaching, which reflects an ancient conviction of the Church. First, it needs to be said that in preaching the Gospel a fitting sense of proportion has to be maintained. This would be seen in the frequency with which certain themes are brought up and in the emphasis given to them in preaching. For example, if in the course of the liturgical year a parish priest speaks about temperance ten times but only mentions charity or justice two or three times, an imbalance results, and precisely those virtues which ought to be most present in preaching and catechesis are overlooked. The same thing happens when we speak more about law than about grace, more about the Church than about Christ, more about the Pope than about God's word.

39. Just as the organic unity existing among the virtues means that no one of them can be excluded from the Christian ideal, so no truth may be denied. The integrity of the Gospel message must not be deformed. What is more, each truth is better understood when related to the harmonious totality of the Christian message; in this context all of the truths are important and illumine one another. When preaching is faithful to the Gospel, the centrality of certain truths is evident and it becomes clear that Christian morality is not a form of stoicism, or self-denial, or merely a practical philosophy or a catalog of sins and faults. Before all else, the Gospel invites us to respond to the God of love who saves us, to see God in others and to go forth from ourselves to seek the good of others. Under no circumstance can this invitation be obscured! All of the virtues are at the service of this response of love. If this invitation does not radiate forcefully and attractively, the edifice of the Church's moral teaching risks becoming a house of cards, and this is our greatest risk. It would mean that it is not the Gospel which is being preached, but certain doctrinal or moral points based on specific ideological options. The message will run the risk of losing its freshness and will cease to have "the fragrance of the Gospel."

IV. A mission embodied within human limits

40. The Church is herself a missionary disciple; she needs to grow in her interpretation of the revealed word and in her understanding of truth. It is the task of exegetes and theologians to help "the judgment of the Church to mature."[42] The other sciences also help to accomplish this, each in its own way. With reference to the social sciences, for example, John Paul II said that the Church values their research, which helps her "to derive concrete indications helpful for her magisterial mission."[43] Within the Church countless issues are being studied and reflected upon with great freedom. Differing currents of thought in philosophy, theology, and pastoral practice, if open to being reconciled by the Spirit in respect and love, can enable the Church to grow, since all of them help to express more clearly the immense riches of God's word. For those who long for a monolithic body of doctrine guarded by all and leaving no room for nuance, this might appear as undesirable and leading to confusion. But in fact such variety serves to bring out and develop different facets of the inexhaustible riches of the Gospel.[44]

41. At the same time, today's vast and rapid cultural changes demand that we constantly seek ways of expressing unchanging truths in a language which brings out their abiding newness. "The deposit of the faith is one thing . . . the way it is expressed is another."[45] There are times when the faithful, in listening to completely orthodox language, take away something alien to the authentic Gospel of Jesus Christ, because that language is alien to their own way of speaking to and understanding one another. With the holy intent of communicating the truth about God and humanity, we sometimes give them a false god or a human ideal which is not really Christian. In this way, we hold fast to a formulation while failing to convey its substance. This is the greatest danger. Let us never forget that "the expression of truth can take different forms. The renewal of these forms of expression becomes necessary for the sake of transmitting to the people of today the Gospel message in its unchanging meaning."[46]

42. All of this has great relevance for the preaching of the Gospel, if we are really concerned to make its beauty more clearly recognized and

accepted by all. Of course, we will never be able to make the Church's teachings easily understood or readily appreciated by everyone. Faith always remains something of a cross; it retains a certain obscurity which does not detract from the firmness of its assent. Some things are understood and appreciated only from the standpoint of this assent, which is a sister to love, beyond the range of clear reasons and arguments. We need to remember that all religious teaching ultimately has to be reflected in the teacher's way of life, which awakens the assent of the heart by its nearness, love, and witness.

43. In her ongoing discernment, the Church can also come to see that certain customs not directly connected to the heart of the Gospel, even some which have deep historical roots, are no longer properly understood and appreciated. Some of these customs may be beautiful, but they no longer serve as means of communicating the Gospel. We should not be afraid to re-examine them. At the same time, the Church has rules or precepts which may have been quite effective in their time, but no longer have the same usefulness for directing and shaping people's lives. Saint Thomas Aquinas pointed out that the precepts which Christ and the apostles gave to the people of God "are very few."[47] Citing Saint Augustine, he noted that the precepts subsequently enjoined by the Church should be insisted upon with moderation "so as not to burden the lives of the faithful" and make our religion a form of servitude, whereas "God's mercy has willed that we should be free."[48] This warning, issued many centuries ago, is most timely today. It ought to be one of the criteria to be taken into account in considering a reform of the Church and her preaching which would enable it to reach everyone.

44. Moreover, pastors and the lay faithful who accompany their brothers and sisters in faith or on a journey of openness to God must always remember what the *Catechism of the Catholic Church* teaches quite clearly: "Imputability and responsibility for an action can be diminished or even nullified by ignorance, inadvertence, duress, fear, habit, inordinate attachments, and other psychological or social factors."[49] Consequently, without detracting from the evangelical ideal, they need to accompany with mercy and patience the eventual stages of personal growth as these

progressively occur.[50] I want to remind priests that the confessional must not be a torture chamber but rather an encounter with the Lord's mercy which spurs us on to do our best. A small step, in the midst of great human limitations, can be more pleasing to God than a life which appears outwardly in order but moves through the day without confronting great difficulties. Everyone needs to be touched by the comfort and attraction of God's saving love, which is mysteriously at work in each person, above and beyond their faults and failings.

45. We see then that the task of evangelization operates within the limits of language and of circumstances. It constantly seeks to communicate more effectively the truth of the Gospel in a specific context, without renouncing the truth, the goodness, and the light which it can bring whenever perfection is not possible. A missionary heart is aware of these limits and makes itself "weak with the weak . . . everything for everyone" (1 Cor 9:22). It never closes itself off, never retreats into its own security, never opts for rigidity and defensiveness. It realizes that it has to grow in its own understanding of the Gospel and in discerning the paths of the Spirit, and so it always does what good it can, even if in the process, its shoes get soiled by the mud of the street.

V. A mother with an open heart

46. A Church which "goes forth" is a Church whose doors are open. Going out to others in order to reach the fringes of humanity does not mean rushing out aimlessly into the world. Often it is better simply to slow down, to put aside our eagerness in order to see and listen to others, to stop rushing from one thing to another, and to remain with someone who has faltered along the way. At times we have to be like the father of the prodigal son, who always keeps his door open so that when the son returns, he can readily pass through it.

47. The Church is called to be the house of the Father, with doors always wide open. One concrete sign of such openness is that our church doors should always be open, so that if someone, moved by the Spirit, comes there looking for God, he or she will not find a closed door. There are

other doors that should not be closed either. Everyone can share in some way in the life of the Church; everyone can be part of the community, nor should the doors of the sacraments be closed for simply any reason. This is especially true of the sacrament which is itself "the door": baptism. The Eucharist, although it is the fullness of sacramental life, is not a prize for the perfect but a powerful medicine and nourishment for the weak.[51] These convictions have pastoral consequences that we are called to consider with prudence and boldness. Frequently, we act as arbiters of grace rather than its facilitators. But the Church is not a tollhouse; it is the house of the Father, where there is a place for everyone, with all their problems.

48. If the whole Church takes up this missionary impulse, she has to go forth to everyone without exception. But to whom should she go first? When we read the Gospel we find a clear indication: not so much our friends and wealthy neighbors, but above all the poor and the sick, those who are usually despised and overlooked, "those who cannot repay you" (Lk 14:14). There can be no room for doubt or for explanations which weaken so clear a message. Today and always, "the poor are the privileged recipients of the Gospel,"[52] and the fact that it is freely preached to them is a sign of the kingdom that Jesus came to establish. We have to state, without mincing words, that there is an inseparable bond between our faith and the poor. May we never abandon them.

49. Let us go forth, then, let us go forth to offer everyone the life of Jesus Christ. Here I repeat for the entire Church what I have often said to the priests and laity of Buenos Aires: I prefer a Church which is bruised, hurting, and dirty because it has been out on the streets, rather than a Church which is unhealthy from being confined and from clinging to its own security. I do not want a Church concerned with being at the center and which then ends by being caught up in a web of obsessions and procedures. If something should rightly disturb us and trouble our consciences, it is the fact that so many of our brothers and sisters are living without the strength, light, and consolation born of friendship with Jesus Christ, without a community of faith to support them, without meaning and a goal in life. More than by fear of going astray, my hope

is that we will be moved by the fear of remaining shut up within structures which give us a false sense of security, within rules which make us harsh judges, within habits which make us feel safe, while at our door people are starving and Jesus does not tire of saying to us: "Give them something to eat" (Mk 6:37).

CHAPTER TWO

AMID THE CRISIS OF COMMUNAL COMMITMENT

50. Before taking up some basic questions related to the work of evangelization, it may be helpful to mention briefly the context in which we all have to live and work. Today, we frequently hear of a "diagnostic overload" which is not always accompanied by improved and actually applicable methods of treatment. Nor would we be well served by a purely sociological analysis which would aim to embrace all of reality by employing an allegedly neutral and clinical method. What I would like to propose is something much more in the line of an evangelical discernment. It is the approach of a missionary disciple, an approach "nourished by the light and strength of the Holy Spirit."[53]

51. It is not the task of the Pope to offer a detailed and complete analysis of contemporary reality, but I do exhort all the communities to an "ever watchful scrutiny of the signs of the times."[54] This is in fact a grave responsibility, since certain present realities, unless effectively dealt with, are capable of setting off processes of dehumanization which would then be hard to reverse. We need to distinguish clearly what might be a fruit of the kingdom from what runs counter to God's plan. This involves not only recognizing and discerning spirits, but also—and this is decisive—choosing movements of the spirit of good and rejecting those of the spirit of evil. I take for granted the different analyses which other documents of the universal magisterium have offered, as well as those proposed by the regional and national conferences of bishops. In this Exhortation I claim only to consider briefly, and from a pastoral perspective, certain factors which can restrain or weaken the impulse of missionary renewal in the Church, either because they threaten the life and dignity of God's people or because they affect those who are directly involved in the Church's institutions and in her work of evangelization.

I. Some challenges of today's world

52. In our time humanity is experiencing a turning-point in its history, as we can see from the advances being made in so many fields. We can only praise the steps being taken to improve people's welfare in areas such as health care, education, and communications. At the same time we have to remember that the majority of our contemporaries are barely living from day to day, with dire consequences. A number of diseases are spreading. The hearts of many people are gripped by fear and desperation, even in the so-called rich countries. The joy of living frequently fades, lack of respect for others and violence are on the rise, and inequality is increasingly evident. It is a struggle to live and, often, to live with precious little dignity. This epochal change has been set in motion by the enormous qualitative, quantitative, rapid, and cumulative advances occurring in the sciences and in technology, and by their instant application in different areas of nature and of life. We are in an age of knowledge and information, which has led to new and often anonymous kinds of power.

No to an economy of exclusion

53. Just as the commandment "Thou shalt not kill" sets a clear limit in order to safeguard the value of human life, today we also have to say "thou shalt not" to an economy of exclusion and inequality. Such an economy kills. How can it be that it is not a news item when an elderly homeless person dies of exposure, but it is news when the stock market loses two points? This is a case of exclusion. Can we continue to stand by when food is thrown away while people are starving? This is a case of inequality. Today everything comes under the laws of competition and the survival of the fittest, where the powerful feed upon the powerless. As a consequence, masses of people find themselves excluded and marginalized: without work, without possibilities, without any means of escape.

Human beings are themselves considered consumer goods to be used and then discarded. We have created a "throw away" culture which is now spreading. It is no longer simply about exploitation and oppression, but something new. Exclusion ultimately has to do with what it means to be a part of the society in which we live; those excluded are no longer society's underside or its fringes or its disenfranchised—they are no longer even a part of it. The excluded are not the "exploited" but the outcast, the "leftovers."

54. In this context, some people continue to defend trickle-down theories which assume that economic growth, encouraged by a free market, will inevitably succeed in bringing about greater justice and inclusiveness in the world. This opinion, which has never been confirmed by the facts, expresses a crude and naïve trust in the goodness of those wielding economic power and in the sacralized workings of the prevailing economic system. Meanwhile, the excluded are still waiting. To sustain a lifestyle which excludes others, or to sustain enthusiasm for that selfish ideal, a globalization of indifference has developed. Almost without being aware of it, we end up being incapable of feeling compassion at the outcry of the poor, weeping for other people's pain, and feeling a need to help them, as though all this were someone else's responsibility and not our own. The culture of prosperity deadens us; we are thrilled if the market offers us something new to purchase. In the meantime all those lives stunted for lack of opportunity seem a mere spectacle; they fail to move us.

No to the new idolatry of money

55. One cause of this situation is found in our relationship with money, since we calmly accept its dominion over ourselves and our societies. The current financial crisis can make us overlook the fact that it originated in a profound human crisis: the denial of the primacy of the human person! We have created new idols. The worship of the ancient golden calf (cf. Ex 32:1–35) has returned in a new and ruthless guise in the idolatry of money and the dictatorship of an impersonal economy lacking a truly human purpose. The worldwide crisis affecting finance and the economy lays bare their imbalances and, above all, their lack of real concern for human beings; man is reduced to one of his needs alone: consumption.

56. While the earnings of a minority are growing exponentially, so too is the gap separating the majority from the prosperity enjoyed by those

happy few. This imbalance is the result of ideologies which defend the absolute autonomy of the marketplace and financial speculation. Consequently, they reject the right of states, charged with vigilance for the common good, to exercise any form of control. A new tyranny is thus born, invisible and often virtual, which unilaterally and relentlessly imposes its own laws and rules. Debt and the accumulation of interest also make it difficult for countries to realize the potential of their own economies and keep citizens from enjoying their real purchasing power. To all this we can add widespread corruption and self-serving tax evasion, which have taken on worldwide dimensions. The thirst for power and possessions knows no limits. In this system, which tends to devour everything which stands in the way of increased profits, whatever is fragile, like the environment, is defenseless before the interests of a deified market, which become the only rule.

No to a financial system which rules rather than serves

57. Behind this attitude lurks a rejection of ethics and a rejection of God. Ethics has come to be viewed with a certain scornful derision. It is seen as counterproductive, too human, because it makes money and power relative. It is felt to be a threat, since it condemns the manipulation and debasement of the person. In effect, ethics leads to a God who calls for a committed response which is outside the categories of the marketplace. When these latter are absolutized, God can only be seen as uncontrollable, unmanageable, even dangerous, since he calls human beings to their full realization and to freedom from all forms of enslavement. Ethics—a non-ideological ethics—would make it possible to bring about balance and a more humane social order. With this in mind, I encourage financial experts and political leaders to ponder the words of one of the sages of antiquity: "Not to share one's wealth with the poor is to steal from them and to take away their livelihood. It is not our own goods which we hold, but theirs."[55]

58. A financial reform open to such ethical considerations would require a vigorous change of approach on the part of political leaders. I urge them to face this challenge with determination and an eye to the future,

while not ignoring, of course, the specifics of each case. Money must serve, not rule! The Pope loves everyone, rich and poor alike, but he is obliged in the name of Christ to remind all that the rich must help, respect, and promote the poor. I exhort you to generous solidarity and to the return of economics and finance to an ethical approach which favors human beings.

No to the inequality which spawns violence

59. Today in many places we hear a call for greater security. But until exclusion and inequality in society and between peoples are reversed, it will be impossible to eliminate violence. The poor and the poorer peoples are accused of violence, yet without equal opportunities the different forms of aggression and conflict will find a fertile terrain for growth and eventually explode. When a society—whether local, national, or global—is willing to leave a part of itself on the fringes, no political programs or resources spent on law enforcement or surveillance systems can indefinitely guarantee tranquility. This is not the case simply because inequality provokes a violent reaction from those excluded from the system, but because the socioeconomic system is unjust at its root. Just as goodness tends to spread, the toleration of evil, which is injustice, tends to expand its baneful influence and quietly to undermine any political and social system, no matter how solid it may appear. If every action has its consequences, an evil embedded in the structures of a society has a constant potential for disintegration and death. It is evil crystallized in unjust social structures, which cannot be the basis of hope for a better future. We are far from the so-called "end of history," since the conditions for a sustainable and peaceful development have not yet been adequately articulated and realized.

60. Today's economic mechanisms promote inordinate consumption, yet it is evident that unbridled consumerism combined with inequality proves doubly damaging to the social fabric. Inequality eventually engenders a violence which recourse to arms cannot and never will be able to resolve. It serves only to offer false hopes to those clamoring for heightened security, even though nowadays we know that weapons and

violence, rather than providing solutions, create new and more serious conflicts. Some simply content themselves with blaming the poor and the poorer countries themselves for their troubles; indulging in unwarranted generalizations, they claim that the solution is an "education" that would tranquilize them, making them tame and harmless. All this becomes even more exasperating for the marginalized in the light of the widespread and deeply rooted corruption found in many countries—in their governments, businesses, and institutions—whatever the political ideology of their leaders.

Some cultural challenges

61. We also evangelize when we attempt to confront the various challenges which can arise.[56] On occasion these may take the form of veritable attacks on religious freedom or new persecutions directed against Christians; in some countries these have reached alarming levels of hatred and violence. In many places, the problem is more that of widespread indifference and relativism, linked to disillusionment and the crisis of ideologies which has come about as a reaction to anything which might appear totalitarian. This not only harms the Church but the fabric of society as a whole. We should recognize how in a culture where each person wants to be bearer of his or her own subjective truth, it becomes difficult for citizens to devise a common plan which transcends individual gain and personal ambitions.

62. In the prevailing culture, priority is given to the outward, the immediate, the visible, the quick, the superficial, and the provisional. What is real gives way to appearances. In many countries globalization has meant a hastened deterioration of their own cultural roots and the invasion of ways of thinking and acting proper to other cultures which are economically advanced but ethically debilitated. This fact has been brought up by bishops from various continents in different Synods. The African bishops, for example, taking up the Encyclical *Sollicitudo Rei Socialis*, pointed out years ago that there have been frequent attempts to make the African countries "parts of a machine, cogs on a gigantic wheel. This is often true also in the field of social communications which, being run by centers

mostly in the northern hemisphere, do not always give due consideration to the priorities and problems of such countries or respect their cultural makeup."[57] By the same token, the bishops of Asia "underlined the external influences being brought to bear on Asian cultures. New patterns of behavior are emerging as a result of over-exposure to the mass media. . . . As a result, the negative aspects of the media and entertainment industries are threatening traditional values, and in particular the sacredness of marriage and the stability of the family."[58]

63. The Catholic faith of many peoples is nowadays being challenged by the proliferation of new religious movements, some of which tend to fundamentalism while others seem to propose a spirituality without God. This is, on the one hand, a human reaction to a materialistic, consumerist, and individualistic society, but it is also a means of exploiting the weaknesses of people living in poverty and on the fringes of society, people who make ends meet amid great human suffering and are looking for immediate solutions to their needs. These religious movements, not without a certain shrewdness, come to fill, within a predominantly individualistic culture, a vacuum left by secularist rationalism. We must recognize that if part of our baptized people lack a sense of belonging to the Church, this is also due to certain structures and the occasionally unwelcoming atmosphere of some of our parishes and communities, or to a bureaucratic way of dealing with problems, be they simple or complex, in the lives of our people. In many places an administrative approach prevails over a pastoral approach, as does a concentration on administering the sacraments apart from other forms of evangelization.

64. The process of secularization tends to reduce the faith and the Church to the sphere of the private and personal. Furthermore, by completely rejecting the transcendent, it has produced a growing deterioration of ethics, a weakening of the sense of personal and collective sin, and a steady increase in relativism. These have led to a general sense of disorientation, especially in the periods of adolescence and young adulthood which are so vulnerable to change. As the bishops of the United States of America have rightly pointed out, while the Church insists on the existence of objective moral norms which are valid for everyone,

"there are those in our culture who portray this teaching as unjust, that is, as opposed to basic human rights. Such claims usually follow from a form of moral relativism that is joined, not without inconsistency, to a belief in the absolute rights of individuals. In this view, the Church is perceived as promoting a particular prejudice and as interfering with individual freedom."[59] We are living in an information-driven society which bombards us indiscriminately with data—all treated as being of equal importance—and which leads to remarkable superficiality in the area of moral discernment. In response, we need to provide an education which teaches critical thinking and encourages the development of mature moral values.

65. Despite the tide of secularism which has swept our societies, in many countries—even those where Christians are a minority—the Catholic Church is considered a credible institution by public opinion, and trusted for her solidarity and concern for those in greatest need. Again and again, the Church has acted as a mediator in finding solutions to problems affecting peace, social harmony, the land, the defense of life, human and civil rights, and so forth. And how much good has been done by Catholic schools and universities around the world! This is a good thing. Yet, we find it difficult to make people see that when we raise other questions less palatable to public opinion, we are doing so out of fidelity to precisely the same convictions about human dignity and the common good.

66. The family is experiencing a profound cultural crisis, as are all communities and social bonds. In the case of the family, the weakening of these bonds is particularly serious because the family is the fundamental cell of society, where we learn to live with others despite our differences and to belong to one another; it is also the place where parents pass on the faith to their children. Marriage now tends to be viewed as a form of mere emotional satisfaction that can be constructed in any way or modified at will. But the indispensable contribution of marriage to society transcends the feelings and momentary needs of the couple. As the French bishops have taught, it is not born "of loving sentiment, ephemeral by definition, but from the depth of the obligation assumed by the spouses who accept to enter a total communion of life."[60]

67. The individualism of our postmodern and globalized era favors a lifestyle which weakens the development and stability of personal relationships and distorts family bonds. Pastoral activity needs to bring out more clearly the fact that our relationship with the Father demands and encourages a communion which heals, promotes, and reinforces interpersonal bonds. In our world, especially in some countries, different forms of war and conflict are re-emerging, yet we Christians remain steadfast in our intention to respect others, to heal wounds, to build bridges, to strengthen relationships, and to "bear one another's burdens" (Gal 6:2). Today too, various associations for the defense of rights and the pursuit of noble goals are being founded. This is a sign of the desire of many people to contribute to social and cultural progress.

Challenges to inculturating the faith

68. The Christian substratum of certain peoples—most of all in the West—is a living reality. Here we find, especially among the most needy, a moral resource which preserves the values of an authentic Christian humanism. Seeing reality with the eyes of faith, we cannot fail to acknowledge what the Holy Spirit is sowing. It would show a lack of trust in his free and unstinting activity to think that authentic Christian values are absent where great numbers of people have received baptism and express their faith and solidarity with others in a variety of ways. This means more than acknowledging occasional "seeds of the word," since it has to do with an authentic Christian faith which has its own expressions and means of showing its relationship to the Church. The immense importance of a culture marked by faith cannot be overlooked; before the onslaught of contemporary secularism an evangelized culture, for all its limits, has many more resources than the mere sum total of believers. An evangelized popular culture contains values of faith and solidarity capable of encouraging the development of a more just and believing society, and possesses a particular wisdom which ought to be gratefully acknowledged.

69. It is imperative to evangelize cultures in order to inculturate the Gospel. In countries of Catholic tradition, this means encouraging, fostering,

and reinforcing a richness which already exists. In countries of other religious traditions, or profoundly secularized countries, it will mean sparking new processes for evangelizing culture, even though these will demand long-term planning. We must keep in mind, however, that we are constantly being called to grow. Each culture and social group needs purification and growth. In the case of the popular cultures of Catholic peoples, we can see deficiencies which need to be healed by the Gospel: machismo, alcoholism, domestic violence, low Mass attendance, fatalistic or superstitious notions which lead to sorcery, and the like. Popular piety itself can be the starting point for healing and liberation from these deficiencies.

70. It is also true that at times greater emphasis is placed on the outward expressions and traditions of some groups, or on alleged private revelations which would replace all else, than on the impulse of Christian piety. There is a kind of Christianity made up of devotions reflecting an individual and sentimental faith life which does not in fact correspond to authentic "popular piety." Some people promote these expressions while not being in the least concerned with the advancement of society or the formation of the laity, and in certain cases they do so in order to obtain economic benefits or some power over others. Nor can we overlook the fact that in recent decades there has been a breakdown in the way Catholics pass down the Christian faith to the young. It is undeniable that many people feel disillusioned and no longer identify with the Catholic tradition. Growing numbers of parents do not bring their children for baptism or teach them how to pray. There is also a certain exodus toward other faith communities. The causes of this breakdown include: a lack of opportunity for dialogue in families, the influence of the communications media, a relativistic subjectivism, unbridled consumerism which feeds the market, lack of pastoral care among the poor, the failure of our institutions to be welcoming, and our difficulty in restoring a mystical adherence to the faith in a pluralistic religious landscape.

Challenges from urban cultures

71. The new Jerusalem, the holy city (cf. Rv 21:2–4), is the goal toward which all of humanity is moving. It is curious that God's revelation tells us that the fullness of humanity and of history is realized in a city. We need to look at our cities with a contemplative gaze, a gaze of faith which sees God dwelling in their homes, in their streets and squares. God's presence accompanies the sincere efforts of individuals and groups to find encouragement and meaning in their lives. He dwells among them, fostering solidarity, fraternity, and the desire for goodness, truth, and justice. This presence must not be contrived but found, uncovered. God does not hide himself from those who seek him with a sincere heart, even though they do so tentatively, in a vague and haphazard manner.

72. In cities, as opposed to the countryside, the religious dimension of life is expressed by different lifestyles, daily rhythms linked to places and people. In their daily lives people must often struggle for survival, and this struggle contains within it a profound understanding of life which often includes a deep religious sense. We must examine this more closely in order to enter into a dialogue like that of our Lord and the Samaritan woman at the well where she sought to quench her thirst (cf. Jn 4:1–15).

73. New cultures are constantly being born in these vast new expanses where Christians are no longer the customary interpreters or generators of meaning. Instead, they themselves take from these cultures new languages, symbols, messages, and paradigms which propose new approaches to life, approaches often in contrast with the Gospel of Jesus. A completely new culture has come to life and continues to grow in the cities. The Synod noted that today the changes taking place in these great spaces and the culture which they create are a privileged locus of the new evangelization.[61] This challenges us to imagine innovative spaces and possibilities for prayer and communion which are more attractive and meaningful for city dwellers. Through the influence of the media, rural areas are being affected by the same cultural changes, which are significantly altering their way of life as well.

74. What is called for is an evangelization capable of shedding light on these new ways of relating to God, to others, and to the world around us, and inspiring essential values. It must reach the places where new narratives and paradigms are being formed, bringing the word of Jesus to the inmost soul of our cities. Cities are multicultural; in the larger cities, a connective network is found in which groups of people share a common imagination and dreams about life, and new human interactions arise, new cultures, invisible cities. Various subcultures exist side by side, and often practice segregation and violence. The Church is called to be at the service of a difficult dialogue. On the one hand, there are people who have the means needed to develop their personal and family lives, but there are also many "non-citizens," "half citizens," and "urban remnants." Cities create a sort of permanent ambivalence because, while they offer their residents countless possibilities, they also present many people with any number of obstacles to the full development of their lives. This contrast causes painful suffering. In many parts of the world, cities are the scene of mass protests where thousands of people call for freedom, a voice in public life, justice, and a variety of other demands which, if not properly understood, will not be silenced by force.

75. We cannot ignore the fact that in cities human trafficking, the narcotics trade, the abuse and exploitation of minors, the abandonment of the elderly and infirm, and various forms of corruption and criminal activity take place. At the same time, what could be significant places of encounter and solidarity often become places of isolation and mutual distrust. Houses and neighborhoods are more often built to isolate and protect than to connect and integrate. The proclamation of the Gospel will be a basis for restoring the dignity of human life in these contexts, for Jesus desires to pour out an abundance of life upon our cities (cf. Jn 10:10). The unified and complete sense of human life that the Gospel proposes is the best remedy for the ills of our cities, even though we have to realize that a uniform and rigid program of evangelization is not suited to this complex reality. But to live our human life to the fullest and to meet every challenge as a leaven of Gospel witness in every culture and in every city will make us better Christians and bear fruit in our cities.

II. Temptations faced by pastoral workers

76. I feel tremendous gratitude to all those who are committed to working in and for the Church. Here I do not wish to discuss at length the activities of the different pastoral workers, from bishops down to those who provide the most humble and hidden services. Rather, I would like to reflect on the challenges that all of them must face in the context of our current globalized culture. But in justice, I must say first that the contribution of the Church in today's world is enormous. The pain and the shame we feel at the sins of some members of the Church, and at our own, must never make us forget how many Christians are giving their lives in love. They help so many people to be healed or to die in peace in makeshift hospitals. They are present to those enslaved by different addictions in the poorest places on earth. They devote themselves to the education of children and young people. They take care of the elderly who have been forgotten by everyone else. They look for ways to communicate values in hostile environments. They are dedicated in many other ways to showing an immense love for humanity inspired by the God who became man. I am grateful for the beautiful example given to me by so many Christians who joyfully sacrifice their lives and their time. This witness comforts and sustains me in my own effort to overcome selfishness and to give more fully of myself.

77. As children of this age, though, all of us are in some way affected by the present globalized culture which, while offering us values and new possibilities, can also limit, condition, and ultimately harm us. I am aware that we need to create spaces where pastoral workers can be helped and healed, "places where faith itself in the crucified and risen Jesus is renewed, where the most profound questions and daily concerns are shared, where deeper discernment about our experiences and life itself is undertaken in the light of the Gospel, for the purpose of directing individual and social decisions toward the good and beautiful."[62] At the same time, I would like to call attention to certain particular temptations which affect pastoral workers.

Yes to the challenge of a missionary spirituality

78. Today we are seeing in many pastoral workers, including consecrated men and women, an inordinate concern for their personal freedom and relaxation, which leads them to see their work as a mere appendage to their life, as if it were not part of their very identity. At the same time, the spiritual life comes to be identified with a few religious exercises which can offer a certain comfort but which do not encourage encounter with others, engagement with the world, or a passion for evangelization. As a result, one can observe in many agents of evangelization, even though they pray, a heightened individualism, a crisis of identity, and a cooling of fervor. These are three evils which fuel one another.

79. At times our media culture and some intellectual circles convey a marked skepticism with regard to the Church's message, along with a certain cynicism. As a consequence, many pastoral workers, although they pray, develop a sort of inferiority complex which leads them to relativize or conceal their Christian identity and convictions. This produces a vicious circle. They end up being unhappy with who they are and what they do; they do not identify with their mission of evangelization and this weakens their commitment. They end up stifling the joy of mission with a kind of obsession about being like everyone else and possessing what everyone else possesses. Their work of evangelization thus becomes forced, and they devote little energy and very limited time to it.

80. Pastoral workers can thus fall into a relativism which, whatever their particular style of spirituality or way of thinking, proves even more dangerous than doctrinal relativism. It has to do with the deepest and inmost decisions that shape their way of life. This practical relativism consists in acting as if God did not exist, making decisions as if the poor did not exist, setting goals as if others did not exist, working as if people who have not received the Gospel did not exist. It is striking that even some who clearly have solid doctrinal and spiritual convictions frequently fall into a lifestyle which leads to an attachment to financial security, or to a desire for power or human glory at all cost, rather than giving

their lives to others in mission. Let us not allow ourselves to be robbed of missionary enthusiasm!

No to selfishness and spiritual sloth

81. At a time when we most need a missionary dynamism which will bring salt and light to the world, many lay people fear that they may be asked to undertake some apostolic work and they seek to avoid any responsibility that may take away from their free time. For example, it has become very difficult today to find trained parish catechists willing to persevere in this work for some years. Something similar is also happening with priests who are obsessed with protecting their free time. This is frequently due to the fact that people feel an overbearing need to guard their personal freedom, as though the task of evangelization was a dangerous poison rather than a joyful response to God's love which summons us to mission and makes us fulfilled and productive. Some resist giving themselves over completely to mission and thus end up in a state of paralysis and acedia.

82. The problem is not always an excess of activity, but rather activity undertaken badly, without adequate motivation, without a spirituality which would permeate it and make it pleasurable. As a result, work becomes more tiring than necessary, even leading at times to illness. Far from a content and happy tiredness, this is a tense, burdensome, dissatisfying, and, in the end, unbearable fatigue. This pastoral acedia can be caused by a number of things. Some fall into it because they throw themselves into unrealistic projects and are not satisfied simply to do what they reasonably can. Others, because they lack the patience to allow processes to mature; they want everything to fall from heaven. Others, because they are attached to a few projects or vain dreams of success. Others, because they have lost real contact with people and so depersonalize their work that they are more concerned with the road map than with the journey itself. Others fall into acedia because they are unable to wait; they want to dominate the rhythm of life. Today's obsession with immediate results makes it hard for pastoral workers to tolerate anything that smacks of disagreement, possible failure, criticism, the cross.

83. And so the biggest threat of all gradually takes shape: "the gray pragmatism of the daily life of the Church, in which all appears to proceed normally, while in reality faith is wearing down and degenerating into small-mindedness."[63] A tomb psychology thus develops and slowly transforms Christians into mummies in a museum. Disillusioned with reality, with the Church and with themselves, they experience a constant temptation to cling to a faint melancholy, lacking in hope, which seizes the heart like "the most precious of the devil's potions."[64] Called to radiate light and communicate life, in the end they are caught up in things that generate only darkness and inner weariness, and slowly consume all zeal for the apostolate. For all this, I repeat: Let us not allow ourselves to be robbed of the joy of evangelization!

No to a sterile pessimism

84. The joy of the Gospel is such that it cannot be taken away from us by anyone or anything (cf. Jn 16:22). The evils of our world—and those of the Church—must not be excuses for diminishing our commitment and our fervor. Let us look upon them as challenges which can help us to grow. With the eyes of faith, we can see the light which the Holy Spirit always radiates in the midst of darkness, never forgetting that "where sin increased, grace has abounded all the more" (Rom 5:20). Our faith is challenged to discern how wine can come from water and how wheat can grow in the midst of weeds. Fifty years after the Second Vatican Council, we are distressed by the troubles of our age and far from naive optimism; yet the fact that we are more realistic must not mean that we are any less trusting in the Spirit or less generous. In this sense, we can once again listen to the words of Blessed John XXIII on the memorable day of 11 October 1962: "At times we have to listen, much to our regret, to the voices of people who, though burning with zeal, lack a sense of discretion and measure. In this modern age they can see nothing but prevarication and ruin. . . . We feel that we must disagree with those prophets of doom who are always forecasting disaster, as though the end of the world were at hand. In our times, divine Providence is leading us to a new order of human relations which, by human effort and even

beyond all expectations, are directed to the fulfillment of God's superior and inscrutable designs, in which everything, even human setbacks, leads to the greater good of the Church."[65]

85. One of the more serious temptations which stifles boldness and zeal is a defeatism which turns us into querulous and disillusioned pessimists, "sourpusses." Nobody can go off to battle unless he is fully convinced of victory beforehand. If we start without confidence, we have already lost half the battle and we bury our talents. While painfully aware of our own frailties, we have to march on without giving in, keeping in mind what the Lord said to Saint Paul: "My grace is sufficient for you, for my power is made perfect in weakness" (2 Cor 12:9). Christian triumph is always a cross, yet a cross which is at the same time a victorious banner borne with aggressive tenderness against the assaults of evil. The evil spirit of defeatism is brother to the temptation to separate, before its time, the wheat from the weeds; it is the fruit of an anxious and self-centered lack of trust.

86. In some places a spiritual "desertification" has evidently come about, as the result of attempts by some societies to build without God or to eliminate their Christian roots. In those places "the Christian world is becoming sterile, and it is depleting itself like an overexploited ground, which transforms into a desert."[66] In other countries, violent opposition to Christianity forces Christians to hide their faith in their own beloved homeland. This is another painful kind of desert. But family and the workplace can also be a parched place where faith nonetheless has to be preserved and communicated. Yet "it is starting from the experience of this desert, from this void, that we can again discover the joy of believing, its vital importance for us men and women. In the desert we rediscover the value of what is essential for living; thus in today's world there are innumerable signs, often expressed implicitly or negatively, of the thirst for God, for the ultimate meaning of life. And in the desert people of faith are needed who, by the example of their own lives, point out the way to the Promised Land and keep hope alive."[67] In these situations we are called to be living sources of water from which others can drink. At times, this becomes a heavy cross, but it was from the cross, from his

pierced side, that our Lord gave himself to us as a source of living water. Let us not allow ourselves to be robbed of hope!

Yes to the new relationships brought by Christ

87. Today, when the networks and means of human communication have made unprecedented advances, we sense the challenge of finding and sharing a "mystique" of living together, of mingling and encounter, of embracing and supporting one another, of stepping into this flood tide which, while chaotic, can become a genuine experience of fraternity, a caravan of solidarity, a sacred pilgrimage. Greater possibilities for communication thus turn into greater possibilities for encounter and solidarity for everyone. If we were able to take this route, it would be so good, so soothing, so liberating and hope-filled! To go out of ourselves and to join others is healthy for us. To be self-enclosed is to taste the bitter poison of immanence, and humanity will be worse for every selfish choice we make.

88. The Christian ideal will always be a summons to overcome suspicion, habitual mistrust, fear of losing our privacy, all the defensive attitudes which today's world imposes on us. Many try to escape from others and take refuge in the comfort of their privacy or in a small circle of close friends, renouncing the realism of the social aspect of the Gospel. For just as some people want a purely spiritual Christ, without flesh and without the cross, they also want their interpersonal relationships provided by sophisticated equipment, by screens and systems which can be turned on and off on command. Meanwhile, the Gospel tells us constantly to run the risk of a face-to-face encounter with others, with their physical presence which challenges us, with their pain and their pleas, with their joy which infects us in our close and continuous interaction. True faith in the incarnate Son of God is inseparable from self-giving, from membership in the community, from service, from reconciliation with others. The Son of God, by becoming flesh, summoned us to the revolution of tenderness.

89. Isolation, which is a version of immanentism, can find expression in a false autonomy which has no place for God. But in the realm of religion it can also take the form of a spiritual consumerism tailored to one's

own unhealthy individualism. The return to the sacred and the quest for spirituality which mark our own time are ambiguous phenomena. Today, our challenge is not so much atheism as the need to respond adequately to many people's thirst for God, lest they try to satisfy it with alienating solutions or with a disembodied Jesus who demands nothing of us with regard to others. Unless these people find in the Church a spirituality which can offer healing and liberation, and fill them with life and peace, while at the same time summoning them to fraternal communion and missionary fruitfulness, they will end up by being taken in by solutions which neither make life truly human nor give glory to God.

90. Genuine forms of popular religiosity are incarnate, since they are born of the incarnation of Christian faith in popular culture. For this reason they entail a personal relationship, not with vague spiritual energies or powers, but with God, with Christ, with Mary, with the saints. These devotions are fleshy, they have a face. They are capable of fostering relationships and not just enabling escapism. In other parts of our society, we see the growing attraction to various forms of a "spirituality of well-being" divorced from any community life, or to a "theology of prosperity" detached from responsibility for our brothers and sisters, or to depersonalized experiences which are nothing more than a form of self-centeredness.

91. One important challenge is to show that the solution will never be found in fleeing from a personal and committed relationship with God which at the same time commits us to serving others. This happens frequently nowadays, as believers seek to hide or keep apart from others, or quietly flit from one place to another or from one task to another, without creating deep and stable bonds. "*Imaginatio locorum et mutatio multos fefellit.*"[68] This is a false remedy which cripples the heart and at times the body as well. We need to help others to realize that the only way is to learn how to encounter others with the right attitude, which is to accept and esteem them as companions along the way, without interior resistance. Better yet, it means learning to find Jesus in the faces of others, in their voices, in their pleas. And learning to suffer in the embrace

of the crucified Jesus whenever we are unjustly attacked or meet with ingratitude, never tiring of our decision to live in fraternity.[69]

92. There indeed we find true healing, since the way to relate to others which truly heals instead of debilitating us, is a *mystical* fraternity, a contemplative fraternity. It is a fraternal love capable of seeing the sacred grandeur of our neighbor, of finding God in every human being, of tolerating the nuisances of life in common by clinging to the love of God, of opening the heart to divine love and seeking the happiness of others just as their heavenly Father does. Here and now, especially where we are a "little flock" (Lk 12:32), the Lord's disciples are called to live as a community which is the salt of the earth and the light of the world (cf. Mt 5:13–16). We are called to bear witness to a constantly new way of living together in fidelity to the Gospel.[70] Let us not allow ourselves to be robbed of community!

No to spiritual worldliness

93. Spiritual worldliness, which hides behind the appearance of piety and even love for the Church, consists in seeking not the Lord's glory but human glory and personal well-being. It is what the Lord reprimanded the Pharisees for: "How can you believe, who receive glory from one another and do not seek the glory that comes from the only God?" (Jn 5:44). It is a subtle way of seeking one's "own interests, not those of Jesus Christ" (Phil 2:21). It takes on many forms, depending on the kinds of persons and groups into which it seeps. Since it is based on carefully cultivated appearances, it is not always linked to outward sin; from without, everything appears as it should be. But if it were to seep into the Church, "it would be infinitely more disastrous than any other worldliness which is simply moral."[71]

94. This worldliness can be fueled in two deeply interrelated ways. One is the attraction of gnosticism, a purely subjective faith whose only interest is a certain experience or a set of ideas and bits of information which are meant to console and enlighten, but which ultimately keep one imprisoned in his or her own thoughts and feelings. The other is the self-absorbed promethean neopelagianism of those who ultimately trust only in

their own powers and feel superior to others because they observe certain rules or remain intransigently faithful to a particular Catholic style from the past. A supposed soundness of doctrine or discipline leads instead to a narcissistic and authoritarian elitism, whereby instead of evangelizing, one analyzes and classifies others, and instead of opening the door to grace, one exhausts his or her energies in inspecting and verifying. In neither case is one really concerned about Jesus Christ or others. These are manifestations of an anthropocentric immanentism. It is impossible to think that a genuine evangelizing thrust could emerge from these adulterated forms of Christianity.

95. This insidious worldliness is evident in a number of attitudes which appear opposed, yet all have the same pretense of "taking over the space of the Church." In some people we see an ostentatious preoccupation for the liturgy, for doctrine, and for the Church's prestige, but without any concern that the Gospel have a real impact on God's faithful people and the concrete needs of the present time. In this way, the life of the Church turns into a museum piece or something which is the property of a select few. In others, this spiritual worldliness lurks behind a fascination with social and political gain, or pride in their ability to manage practical affairs, or an obsession with programs of self-help and self-realization. It can also translate into a concern to be seen, into a social life full of appearances, meetings, dinners, and receptions. It can also lead to a business mentality, caught up with management, statistics, plans, and evaluations whose principal beneficiary is not God's people but the Church as an institution. The mark of Christ, incarnate, crucified, and risen, is not present; closed and elite groups are formed, and no effort is made to go forth and seek out those who are distant or the immense multitudes who thirst for Christ. Evangelical fervor is replaced by the empty pleasure of complacency and self-indulgence.

96. This way of thinking also feeds the vainglory of those who are content to have a modicum of power and would rather be the general of a defeated army than a mere private in a unit which continues to fight. How often we dream up vast apostolic projects, meticulously planned, just like defeated generals! But this is to deny our history as a Church,

which is glorious precisely because it is a history of sacrifice, of hopes and daily struggles, of lives spent in service and fidelity to work, tiring as it may be, for all work is "the sweat of our brow." Instead, we waste time talking about "what needs to be done"—in Spanish we call this the sin of "habriaqueísmo"—like spiritual masters and pastoral experts who give instructions from on high. We indulge in endless fantasies and we lose contact with the real lives and difficulties of our people.

97. Those who have fallen into this worldliness look on from above and afar, they reject the prophecy of their brothers and sisters, they discredit those who raise questions, they constantly point out the mistakes of others, and they are obsessed by appearances. Their hearts are open only to the limited horizon of their own immanence and interests, and as a consequence they neither learn from their sins nor are they genuinely open to forgiveness. This is a tremendous corruption disguised as a good. We need to avoid it by making the Church constantly go out from herself, keeping her mission focused on Jesus Christ, and her commitment to the poor. God save us from a worldly Church with superficial spiritual and pastoral trappings! This stifling worldliness can only be healed by breathing in the pure air of the Holy Spirit who frees us from self-centeredness cloaked in an outward religiosity bereft of God. Let us not allow ourselves to be robbed of the Gospel!

No to warring among ourselves

98. How many wars take place within the people of God and in our different communities! In our neighborhoods and in the workplace, how many wars are caused by envy and jealousy, even among Christians! Spiritual worldliness leads some Christians to war with other Christians who stand in the way of their quest for power, prestige, pleasure, and economic security. Some are even no longer content to live as part of the greater Church community but stoke a spirit of exclusivity, creating an "inner circle." Instead of belonging to the whole Church in all its rich variety, they belong to this or that group which thinks itself different or special.

99. Our world is being torn apart by wars and violence, and wounded by a widespread individualism which divides human beings, setting them against one another as they pursue their own well-being. In various countries, conflicts and old divisions from the past are re-emerging. I especially ask Christians in communities throughout the world to offer a radiant and attractive witness of fraternal communion. Let everyone admire how you care for one another, and how you encourage and accompany one another: "By this everyone will know that you are my disciples, if you have love for one another" (Jn 13:35). This was Jesus' heartfelt prayer to the Father: "That they may all be one . . . in us . . . so that the world may believe" (Jn 17:21). Beware of the temptation of jealousy! We are all in the same boat and headed to the same port! Let us ask for the grace to rejoice in the gifts of each, which belong to all.

100. Those wounded by historical divisions find it difficult to accept our invitation to forgiveness and reconciliation, since they think that we are ignoring their pain or are asking them to give up their memory and ideals. But if they see the witness of authentically fraternal and reconciled communities, they will find that witness luminous and attractive. It always pains me greatly to discover how some Christian communities, and even consecrated persons, can tolerate different forms of enmity, division, calumny, defamation, vendetta, jealousy, and the desire to impose certain ideas at all costs, even to persecutions which appear as veritable witch hunts. Whom are we going to evangelize if this is the way we act?

101. Let us ask the Lord to help us understand the law of love. How good it is to have this law! How much good it does us to love one another, in spite of everything. Yes, in spite of everything! Saint Paul's exhortation is directed to each of us: "Do not be overcome by evil, but overcome evil with good" (Rom 12:21). And again: "Let us not grow weary in doing what is right" (Gal 6:9). We all have our likes and dislikes, and perhaps at this very moment we are angry with someone. At least let us say to the Lord: "Lord, I am angry with this person, with that person. I pray to you for him and for her." To pray for a person with whom I am irritated is a beautiful step forward in love, and an act of evangelization.

Let us do it today! Let us not allow ourselves to be robbed of the ideal of fraternal love!

Other ecclesial challenges

102. Lay people are, put simply, the vast majority of the people of God. The minority—ordained ministers—are at their service. There has been a growing awareness of the identity and mission of the laity in the Church. We can count on many lay persons, although still not nearly enough, who have a deeply-rooted sense of community and great fidelity to the tasks of charity, catechesis, and the celebration of the faith. At the same time, a clear awareness of this responsibility of the laity, grounded in their baptism and confirmation, does not appear in the same way in all places. In some cases, it is because lay persons have not been given the formation needed to take on important responsibilities. In others, it is because in their particular Churches room has not been made for them to speak and to act, due to an excessive clericalism which keeps them away from decision-making. Even if many are now involved in the lay ministries, this involvement is not reflected in a greater penetration of Christian values in the social, political, and economic sectors. It often remains tied to tasks within the Church, without a real commitment to applying the Gospel to the transformation of society. The formation of the laity and the evangelization of professional and intellectual life represent a significant pastoral challenge.

103. The Church acknowledges the indispensable contribution which women make to society through the sensitivity, intuition, and other distinctive skill sets which they, more than men, tend to possess. I think, for example, of the special concern which women show to others, which finds a particular, even if not exclusive, expression in motherhood. I readily acknowledge that many women share pastoral responsibilities with priests, helping to guide people, families, and groups and offering new contributions to theological reflection. But we need to create still broader opportunities for a more incisive female presence in the Church. Because "the feminine genius is needed in all expressions in the life of society, the presence of women must also be guaranteed in the workplace"[72] and in

the various other settings where important decisions are made, both in the Church and in social structures.

104. Demands that the legitimate rights of women be respected, based on the firm conviction that men and women are equal in dignity, present the Church with profound and challenging questions which cannot be lightly evaded. The reservation of the priesthood to males, as a sign of Christ the Spouse who gives himself in the Eucharist, is not a question open to discussion, but it can prove especially divisive if sacramental power is too closely identified with power in general. It must be remembered that when we speak of sacramental power "we are in the realm of function, not that of dignity or holiness."[73] The ministerial priesthood is one means employed by Jesus for the service of his people, yet our great dignity derives from baptism, which is accessible to all. The configuration of the priest to Christ the head—namely, as the principal source of grace—does not imply an exaltation which would set him above others. In the Church, functions "do not favor the superiority of some vis-à-vis the others."[74] Indeed, a woman, Mary, is more important than the bishops. Even when the function of ministerial priesthood is considered "hierarchical," it must be remembered that "it is totally ordered to the holiness of Christ's members."[75] Its key and axis is not power understood as domination, but the power to administer the sacrament of the Eucharist; this is the origin of its authority, which is always a service to God's people. This presents a great challenge for pastors and theologians, who are in a position to recognize more fully what this entails with regard to the possible role of women in decision-making in different areas of the Church's life.

105. Youth ministry, as traditionally organized, has also suffered the impact of social changes. Young people often fail to find responses to their concerns, needs, problems, and hurts in the usual structures. As adults, we find it hard to listen patiently to them, to appreciate their concerns and demands, and to speak to them in a language they can understand. For the same reason, our efforts in the field of education do not produce the results expected. The rise and growth of associations and movements mostly made up of young people can be seen as the work of the Holy Spirit, who blazes new trails to meet their expectations and

their search for a deep spirituality and a more real sense of belonging. There remains a need, however, to ensure that these associations actively participate in the Church's overall pastoral efforts.[76]

106. Even if it is not always easy to approach young people, progress has been made in two areas: the awareness that the entire community is called to evangelize and educate the young, and the urgent need for the young to exercise greater leadership. We should recognize that despite the present crisis of commitment and communal relationships, many young people are making common cause before the problems of our world and are taking up various forms of activism and volunteer work. Some take part in the life of the Church as members of service groups and various missionary initiatives in their own dioceses and in other places. How beautiful it is to see that young people are "street preachers" (*callejeros de la fe*), joyfully bringing Jesus to every street, every town square, and every corner of the earth!

107. Many places are experiencing a dearth of vocations to the priesthood and consecrated life. This is often due to a lack of contagious apostolic fervor in communities which results in a cooling of enthusiasm and attractiveness. Wherever there is life, fervor, and a desire to bring Christ to others, genuine vocations will arise. Even in parishes where priests are not particularly committed or joyful, the fraternal life and fervor of the community can awaken in the young a desire to consecrate themselves completely to God and to the preaching of the Gospel. This is particularly true if such a living community prays insistently for vocations and courageously proposes to its young people the path of special consecration. On the other hand, despite the scarcity of vocations, today we are increasingly aware of the need for a better process of selecting candidates to the priesthood. Seminaries cannot accept candidates on the basis of any motivation whatsoever, especially if those motivations have to do with affective insecurity or the pursuit of power, human glory, or economic well-being.

108. As I mentioned above, I have not sought to offer a complete diagnosis, but I invite communities to complete and enrich these perspectives

on the basis of their awareness of the challenges facing them and their neighbors. It is my hope that, in doing so, they will realize that whenever we attempt to read the signs of the times it is helpful to listen to young people and the elderly. Both represent a source of hope for every people. The elderly bring with them memory and the wisdom of experience, which warns us not to foolishly repeat our past mistakes. Young people call us to renewed and expansive hope, for they represent new directions for humanity and open us up to the future, lest we cling to a nostalgia for structures and customs which are no longer life-giving in today's world.

109. Challenges exist to be overcome! Let us be realists, but without losing our joy, our boldness, and our hope-filled commitment. Let us not allow ourselves to be robbed of missionary vigor!

CHAPTER THREE

THE PROCLAMATION OF THE GOSPEL

110. After having considered some of the challenges of the present, I would now like to speak of the task which bears upon us in every age and place, for "there can be no true evangelization without the explicit proclamation of Jesus as Lord," and without "the primacy of the proclamation of Jesus Christ in all evangelizing work."[77] Acknowledging the concerns of the Asian bishops, John Paul II told them that if the Church "is to fulfill its providential destiny, evangelization as the joyful, patient and progressive preaching of the saving death and resurrection of Jesus Christ must be your absolute priority."[78] These words hold true for all of us.

I. The entire people of God proclaims the Gospel

111. Evangelization is the task of the Church. The Church, as the agent of evangelization, is more than an organic and hierarchical institution; she is first and foremost a people advancing on its pilgrim way toward God. She is certainly a mystery rooted in the Trinity, yet she exists concretely in history as a people of pilgrims and evangelizers, transcending any institutional expression, however necessary. I would like to dwell briefly on this way of understanding the Church, whose ultimate foundation is in the free and gracious initiative of God.

A people for everyone

112. The salvation which God offers us is the work of his mercy. No human efforts, however good they may be, can enable us to merit so great a gift. God, by his sheer grace, draws us to himself and makes us one with him.[79] He sends his Spirit into our hearts to make us his children, transforming us and enabling us to respond to his love by our lives. The Church is sent by Jesus Christ as the sacrament of the salvation offered by God.[80] Through her evangelizing activity, she cooperates as an instrument of that divine grace which works unceasingly and inscrutably.

Benedict XVI put it nicely at the beginning of the Synod's reflections: "It is important always to know that the first word, the true initiative, the true activity comes from God and only by inserting ourselves into the divine initiative, only begging for this divine initiative, shall we too be able to become—with him and in him—evangelizers."[81] This principle of the primacy of grace must be a beacon which constantly illuminates our reflections on evangelization.

113. The salvation which God has wrought, and the Church joyfully proclaims, is for everyone.[82] God has found a way to unite himself to every human being in every age. He has chosen to call them together as a people and not as isolated individuals.[83] No one is saved by himself or herself, individually, or by his or her own efforts. God attracts us by taking into account the complex interweaving of personal relationships entailed in the life of a human community. This people which God has chosen and called is the Church. Jesus did not tell the apostles to form an exclusive and elite group. He said: "Go and make disciples of all nations" (Mt 28:19). Saint Paul tells us in the people of God, in the Church, "there is neither Jew or Greek . . . for you are all one in Christ Jesus" (Gal 3:28). To those who feel far from God and the Church, to all those who are fearful or indifferent, I would like to say this: the Lord, with great respect and love, is also calling you to be a part of his people!

114. Being Church means being God's people, in accordance with the great plan of his fatherly love. This means that we are to be God's leaven in the midst of humanity. It means proclaiming and bringing God's salvation into our world, which often goes astray and needs to be encouraged, given hope and strengthened on the way. The Church must be a place of mercy freely given, where everyone can feel welcomed, loved, forgiven, and encouraged to live the good life of the Gospel.

A people of many faces

115. The People of God is incarnate in the peoples of the earth, each of which has its own culture. The concept of culture is valuable for grasping the various expressions of the Christian life present in God's people. It has to do with the lifestyle of a given society, the specific way in which

its members relate to one another, to other creatures, and to God. Understood in this way, culture embraces the totality of a people's life.[84] Each people in the course of its history develops its culture with legitimate autonomy.[85] This is due to the fact that the human person, "by nature stands completely in need of life in society"[86] and always exists in reference to society, finding there a concrete way of relating to reality. The human person is always situated in a culture: "nature and culture are intimately linked."[87] Grace supposes culture, and God's gift becomes flesh in the culture of those who receive it.

116. In these first two Christian millennia, countless peoples have received the grace of faith, brought it to flower in their daily lives, and handed it on in the language of their own culture. Whenever a community receives the message of salvation, the Holy Spirit enriches its culture with the transforming power of the Gospel. The history of the Church shows that Christianity does not have simply one cultural expression, but rather, "remaining completely true to itself, with unswerving fidelity to the proclamation of the Gospel and the tradition of the Church, it will also reflect the different faces of the cultures and peoples in which it is received and takes root."[88] In the diversity of peoples who experience the gift of God, each in accordance with its own culture, the Church expresses her genuine catholicity and shows forth the "beauty of her varied face."[89] In the Christian customs of an evangelized people, the Holy Spirit adorns the Church, showing her new aspects of revelation and giving her a new face. Through inculturation, the Church "introduces peoples, together with their cultures, into her own community,"[90] for "every culture offers positive values and forms which can enrich the way the Gospel is preached, understood and lived."[91] In this way, the Church takes up the values of different cultures and becomes *sponsa ornata monilibus suis*, "the bride bedecked with her jewels" (cf. Is 61:10).[92]

117. When properly understood, cultural diversity is not a threat to Church unity. The Holy Spirit, sent by the Father and the Son, transforms our hearts and enables us to enter into the perfect communion of the blessed Trinity, where all things find their unity. He builds up the communion and harmony of the people of God. The same Spirit is

that harmony, just as he is the bond of love between the Father and the Son.[93] It is he who brings forth a rich variety of gifts, while at the same time creating a unity which is never uniformity but a multifaceted and inviting harmony. Evangelization joyfully acknowledges these varied treasures which the Holy Spirit pours out upon the Church. We would not do justice to the logic of the incarnation if we thought of Christianity as monocultural and monotonous. While it is true that some cultures have been closely associated with the preaching of the Gospel and the development of Christian thought, the revealed message is not identified with any of them; its content is transcultural. Hence in the evangelization of new cultures, or cultures which have not received the Christian message, it is not essential to impose a specific cultural form, no matter how beautiful or ancient it may be, together with the Gospel. The message that we proclaim always has a certain cultural dress, but we in the Church can sometimes fall into a needless hallowing of our own culture, and thus show more fanaticism than true evangelizing zeal.

118. The bishops of Oceania asked that the Church "develop an understanding and a presentation of the truth of Christ working from the traditions and cultures of the region" and invited "all missionaries to work in harmony with indigenous Christians so as to ensure that the faith and the life of the Church be expressed in legitimate forms appropriate for each culture."[94] We cannot demand that peoples of every continent, in expressing their Christian faith, imitate modes of expression which European nations developed at a particular moment of their history, because the faith cannot be constricted to the limits of understanding and expression of any one culture.[95] It is an indisputable fact that no single culture can exhaust the mystery of our redemption in Christ.

We are all missionary disciples

119. In all the baptized, from first to last, the sanctifying power of the Spirit is at work, impelling us to evangelization. The people of God is holy thanks to this anointing, which makes it infallible *in credendo*. This means that it does not err in faith, even though it may not find words to explain that faith. The Spirit guides it in truth and leads it to salvation.[96]

As part of his mysterious love for humanity, God furnishes the totality of the faithful with an instinct of faith—*sensus fidei*—which helps them to discern what is truly of God. The presence of the Spirit gives Christians a certain connaturality with divine realities, and a wisdom which enables them to grasp those realities intuitively, even when they lack the wherewithal to give them precise expression.

120. In virtue of their baptism, all the members of the People of God have become missionary disciples (cf. Mt 28:19). All the baptized, whatever their position in the Church or their level of instruction in the faith, are agents of evangelization, and it would be insufficient to envisage a plan of evangelization to be carried out by professionals while the rest of the faithful would simply be passive recipients. The new evangelization calls for personal involvement on the part of each of the baptized. Every Christian is challenged, here and now, to be actively engaged in evangelization; indeed, anyone who has truly experienced God's saving love does not need much time or lengthy training to go out and proclaim that love. Every Christian is a missionary to the extent that he or she has encountered the love of God in Christ Jesus: we no longer say that we are "disciples" and "missionaries," but rather that we are always "missionary disciples." If we are not convinced, let us look at those first disciples, who, immediately after encountering the gaze of Jesus, went forth to proclaim him joyfully: "We have found the Messiah!" (Jn 1:41). The Samaritan woman became a missionary immediately after speaking with Jesus and many Samaritans come to believe in him "because of the woman's testimony" (Jn 4:39). So too, Saint Paul, after his encounter with Jesus Christ, "immediately proclaimed Jesus" (Acts 9:20; cf. 22:6–21). So what are we waiting for?

121. Of course, all of us are called to mature in our work as evangelizers. We want to have better training, a deepening love, and a clearer witness to the Gospel. In this sense, we ought to let others be constantly evangelizing us. But this does not mean that we should postpone the evangelizing mission; rather, each of us should find ways to communicate Jesus wherever we are. All of us are called to offer others an explicit witness to the saving love of the Lord, who despite our imperfections

offers us his closeness, his word, and his strength, and gives meaning to our lives. In your heart you know that it is not the same to live without him; what you have come to realize, what has helped you to live and given you hope, is what you also need to communicate to others. Our falling short of perfection should be no excuse; on the contrary, mission is a constant stimulus not to remain mired in mediocrity but to continue growing. The witness of faith that each Christian is called to offer leads us to say with Saint Paul: "Not that I have already obtained this, or am already perfect; but I press on to make it my own, because Christ Jesus has made me his own" (Phil 3:12–13).

The evangelizing power of popular piety

122. In the same way, we can see that the different peoples among whom the Gospel has been inculturated are active collective subjects or agents of evangelization. This is because each people is the creator of their own culture and the protagonist of their own history. Culture is a dynamic reality which a people constantly recreates; each generation passes on a whole series of ways of approaching different existential situations to the next generation, which must in turn reformulate it as it confronts its own challenges. Being human means "being at the same time son and father of the culture to which one belongs."[97] Once the Gospel has been inculturated in a people, in their process of transmitting their culture they also transmit the faith in ever new forms; hence the importance of understanding evangelization as inculturation. Each portion of the people of God, by translating the gift of God into its own life and in accordance with its own genius, bears witness to the faith it has received and enriches it with new and eloquent expressions. One can say that "a people continuously evangelizes itself."[98] Herein lies the importance of popular piety, a true expression of the spontaneous missionary activity of the people of God. This is an ongoing and developing process, of which the Holy Spirit is the principal agent.[99]

123. Popular piety enables us to see how the faith, once received, becomes embodied in a culture and is constantly passed on. Once looked down upon, popular piety came to be appreciated once more in the decades

following the Council. In the Exhortation *Evangelii Nuntiandi*, Pope Paul VI gave a decisive impulse in this area. There he stated that popular piety "manifests a thirst for God which only the poor and the simple can know"[100] and that "it makes people capable of generosity and sacrifice even to the point of heroism, when it is a question of bearing witness to belief."[101] Closer to our own time, Benedict XVI, speaking about Latin America, pointed out that popular piety is "a precious treasure of the Catholic Church," in which "we see the soul of the Latin American peoples."[102]

124. The *Aparecida Document* describes the riches which the Holy Spirit pours forth in popular piety by his gratuitous initiative. On that beloved continent, where many Christians express their faith through popular piety, the bishops also refer to it as "popular spirituality" or "the people's mysticism."[103] It is truly "a spirituality incarnated in the culture of the lowly."[104] Nor is it devoid of content; rather it discovers and expresses that content more by way of symbols than by discursive reasoning, and in the act of faith greater accent is placed on *credere in Deum* than on *credere Deum*.[105] It is "a legitimate way of living the faith, a way of feeling part of the Church and a manner of being missionaries";[106] it brings with itself the grace of being a missionary, of coming out of oneself and setting out on pilgrimage: "Journeying together to shrines and taking part in other manifestations of popular piety, also by taking one's children or inviting others, is in itself an evangelizing gesture."[107] Let us not stifle or presume to control this missionary power!

125. To understand this reality we need to approach it with the gaze of the Good Shepherd, who seeks not to judge but to love. Only from the affective connaturality born of love can we appreciate the theological life present in the piety of Christian peoples, especially among their poor. I think of the steadfast faith of those mothers tending their sick children who, though perhaps barely familiar with the articles of the creed, cling to a rosary; or of all the hope poured into a candle lighted in a humble home with a prayer for help from Mary, or in the gaze of tender love directed to Christ crucified. No one who loves God's holy people will view these actions as the expression of a purely human search for the divine. They

are the manifestation of a theological life nourished by the working of the Holy Spirit who has been poured into our hearts (cf. Rom 5:5).

126. Underlying popular piety, as a fruit of the inculturated Gospel, is an active evangelizing power which we must not underestimate: to do so would be to fail to recognize the work of the Holy Spirit. Instead, we are called to promote and strengthen it, in order to deepen the never-ending process of inculturation. Expressions of popular piety have much to teach us; for those who are capable of reading them, they are a *locus theologicus* which demands our attention, especially at a time when we are looking to the new evangelization.

Person to person

127. Today, as the Church seeks to experience a profound missionary renewal, there is a kind of preaching which falls to each of us as a daily responsibility. It has to do with bringing the Gospel to the people we meet, whether they be our neighbors or complete strangers. This is the informal preaching which takes place in the middle of a conversation, something along the lines of what a missionary does when visiting a home. Being a disciple means being constantly ready to bring the love of Jesus to others, and this can happen unexpectedly and in any place: on the street, in a city square, during work, on a journey.

128. In this preaching, which is always respectful and gentle, the first step is personal dialogue, when the other person speaks and shares his or her joys, hopes, and concerns for loved ones, or so many other heartfelt needs. Only afterward is it possible to bring up God's word, perhaps by reading a Bible verse or relating a story, but always keeping in mind the fundamental message: the personal love of God who became man, who gave himself up for us, who is living, and who offers us his salvation and his friendship. This message has to be shared humbly as a testimony on the part of one who is always willing to learn, in the awareness that the message is so rich and so deep that it always exceeds our grasp. At times the message can be presented directly, at times by way of a personal witness or gesture, or in a way which the Holy Spirit may suggest in that particular situation. If it seems prudent and if the circumstances are right,

this fraternal and missionary encounter could end with a brief prayer related to the concerns which the person may have expressed. In this way they will have an experience of being listened to and understood; they will know that their particular situation has been placed before God, and that God's word really speaks to their lives.

129. We should not think, however, that the Gospel message must always be communicated by fixed formulations learned by heart or by specific words which express an absolutely invariable content. This communication takes place in so many different ways that it would be impossible to describe or catalog them all, and God's people, with all their many gestures and signs, are its collective subject. If the Gospel is embedded in a culture, the message is no longer transmitted solely from person to person. In countries where Christianity is a minority, then, along with encouraging each of the baptized to proclaim the Gospel, particular Churches should actively promote at least preliminary forms of inculturation. The ultimate aim should be that the Gospel, as preached in categories proper to each culture, will create a new synthesis with that particular culture. This is always a slow process and at times we can be overly fearful. But if we allow doubts and fears to dampen our courage, instead of being creative we will remain comfortable and make no progress whatsoever. In this case we will not take an active part in historical processes, but become mere onlookers as the Church gradually stagnates.

Charisms at the service of a communion which evangelizes

130. The Holy Spirit also enriches the entire evangelizing Church with different charisms. These gifts are meant to renew and build up the Church.[108] They are not an inheritance, safely secured and entrusted to a small group for safekeeping; rather they are gifts of the Spirit integrated into the body of the Church, drawn to the center which is Christ, and then channeled into an evangelizing impulse. A sure sign of the authenticity of a charism is its ecclesial character, its ability to be integrated harmoniously into the life of God's holy and faithful people for the good of all. Something truly new brought about by the Spirit need not overshadow other gifts and spiritualities in making itself felt. To

the extent that a charism is better directed to the heart of the Gospel, its exercise will be more ecclesial. It is in communion, even when this proves painful, that a charism is seen to be authentic and mysteriously fruitful. On the basis of her response to this challenge, the Church can be a model of peace in our world.

131. Differences between persons and communities can sometimes prove uncomfortable, but the Holy Spirit, who is the source of that diversity, can bring forth something good from all things and turn it into an attractive means of evangelization. Diversity must always be reconciled by the help of the Holy Spirit; he alone can raise up diversity, plurality, and multiplicity while at the same time bringing about unity. When we, for our part, aspire to diversity, we become self-enclosed, exclusive, and divisive; similarly, whenever we attempt to create unity on the basis of our human calculations, we end up imposing a monolithic uniformity. This is not helpful for the Church's mission.

Culture, thought, and education

132. Proclaiming the Gospel message to different cultures also involves proclaiming it to professional, scientific, and academic circles. This means an encounter between faith, reason, and the sciences with a view to developing new approaches and arguments on the issue of credibility, a creative apologetics[109] which would encourage greater openness to the Gospel on the part of all. When certain categories of reason and the sciences are taken up into the proclamation of the message, these categories then become tools of evangelization; water is changed into wine. Whatever is taken up is not just redeemed, but becomes an instrument of the Spirit for enlightening and renewing the world.

133. It is not enough that evangelizers be concerned to reach each person, or that the Gospel be proclaimed to the cultures as a whole. A theology—and not simply a pastoral theology—which is in dialogue with other sciences and human experiences is most important for our discernment on how best to bring the Gospel message to different cultural contexts and groups.[110] The Church, in her commitment to evangelization, appreciates and encourages the charism of theologians and their scholarly

efforts to advance dialogue with the world of cultures and sciences. I call on theologians to carry out this service as part of the Church's saving mission. In doing so, however, they must always remember that the Church and theology exist to evangelize, and not be content with a desk-bound theology.

134. Universities are outstanding environments for articulating and developing this evangelizing commitment in an interdisciplinary and integrated way. Catholic schools, which always strive to join their work of education with the explicit proclamation of the Gospel, are a most valuable resource for the evangelization of culture, even in those countries and cities where hostile situations challenge us to greater creativity in our search for suitable methods.[111]

II. The homily

135. Let us now look at preaching within the liturgy, which calls for serious consideration by pastors. I will dwell in particular, and even somewhat meticulously, on the homily and its preparation, since so many concerns have been expressed about this important ministry, and we cannot simply ignore them. The homily is the touchstone for judging a pastor's closeness and ability to communicate to his people. We know that the faithful attach great importance to it, and that both they and their ordained ministers suffer because of homilies: the laity from having to listen to them and the clergy from having to preach them! It is sad that this is the case. The homily can actually be an intense and happy experience of the Spirit, a consoling encounter with God's word, a constant source of renewal and growth.

136. Let us renew our confidence in preaching, based on the conviction that it is God who seeks to reach out to others through the preacher, and that he displays his power through human words. Saint Paul speaks forcefully about the need to preach, since the Lord desires to reach other people by means of our word (cf. Rom 10:14–17). By his words our Lord won over the hearts of the people; they came to hear him from all parts (cf. Mk 1:45); they were amazed at his teachings (cf. Mk 6:2); and they

sensed that he spoke to them as one with authority (cf. Mk 1:27). By their words the apostles, whom Christ established "to be with him and to be sent out to preach" (Mk 3:14), brought all nations to the bosom of the Church (cf. Mt 16:15–20).

The liturgical context

137. It is worth remembering that "the liturgical proclamation of the word of God, especially in the eucharistic assembly, is not so much a time for meditation and catechesis as a dialogue between God and his people, a dialogue in which the great deeds of salvation are proclaimed and the demands of the covenant are continually restated."[112] The homily has special importance due to its eucharistic context: it surpasses all forms of catechesis as the supreme moment in the dialogue between God and his people which lead up to sacramental communion. The homily takes up once more the dialogue which the Lord has already established with his people. The preacher must know the heart of his community, in order to realize where its desire for God is alive and ardent, as well as where that dialogue, once loving, has been thwarted and is now barren.

138. The homily cannot be a form of entertainment like those presented by the media, yet it does need to give life and meaning to the celebration. It is a distinctive genre, since it is preaching situated within the framework of a liturgical celebration; hence it should be brief and avoid taking on the semblance of a speech or a lecture. A preacher may be able to hold the attention of his listeners for a whole hour, but in this case his words become more important than the celebration of faith. If the homily goes on too long, it will affect two characteristic elements of the liturgical celebration: its balance and its rhythm. When preaching takes place within the context of the liturgy, it is part of the offering made to the Father and a mediation of the grace which Christ pours out during the celebration. This context demands that preaching should guide the assembly, and the preacher, to a life-changing communion with Christ in the Eucharist. This means that the words of the preacher must be measured, so that the Lord, more than his minister, will be the center of attention.

A mother's conversation

139. We said that the people of God, by the constant inner working of the Holy Spirit, is constantly evangelizing itself. What are the implications of this principle for preachers? It reminds us that the Church is a mother, and that she preaches in the same way that a mother speaks to her child, knowing that the child trusts that what she is teaching is for his or her benefit, for children know that they are loved. Moreover, a good mother can recognize everything that God is bringing about in her children, she listens to their concerns and learns from them. The spirit of love which reigns in a family guides both mother and child in their conversations; therein they teach and learn, experience correction, and grow in appreciation of what is good. Something similar happens in a homily. The same Spirit who inspired the Gospels and who acts in the Church also inspires the preacher to hear the faith of God's people and to find the right way to preach at each Eucharist. Christian preaching thus finds in the heart of people and their culture a source of living water, which helps the preacher to know what must be said and how to say it. Just as all of us like to be spoken to in our mother tongue, so too in the faith we like to be spoken to in our "mother culture," our native language (cf. 2 Mc 7:21, 27), and our heart is better disposed to listen. This language is a kind of music which inspires encouragement, strength, and enthusiasm.

140. This setting, both maternal and ecclesial, in which the dialogue between the Lord and his people takes place, should be encouraged by the closeness of the preacher, the warmth of his tone of voice, the unpretentiousness of his manner of speaking, the joy of his gestures. Even if the homily at times may be somewhat tedious, if this maternal and ecclesial spirit is present, it will always bear fruit, just as the tedious counsels of a mother bear fruit, in due time, in the hearts of her children.

141. One cannot but admire the resources that the Lord used to dialogue with his people, to reveal his mystery to all and to attract ordinary people by his lofty teachings and demands. I believe that the secret lies in the way Jesus looked at people, seeing beyond their weaknesses and failings: "Fear not little flock, for it is your Father's good pleasure to give you the

kingdom" (Lk 12:32); Jesus preaches with that spirit. Full of joy in the Spirit, he blesses the Father who draws the little ones to him: "I thank you Father, Lord of heaven and earth, that you have hidden these things from the wise and understanding and revealed them to babes" (Lk 10:21). The Lord truly enjoys talking with his people; the preacher should strive to communicate that same enjoyment to his listeners.

Words which set hearts on fire

142. Dialogue is much more than the communication of a truth. It arises from the enjoyment of speaking and it enriches those who express their love for one another through the medium of words. This is an enrichment which does not consist in objects but in persons who share themselves in dialogue. A preaching which would be purely moralistic or doctrinaire, or one which turns into a lecture on biblical exegesis, detracts from this heart-to-heart communication which takes place in the homily and possesses a quasi-sacramental character: "Faith comes from what is heard, and what is heard comes by the preaching of Christ" (Rom 10:17). In the homily, truth goes hand in hand with beauty and goodness. Far from dealing with abstract truths or cold syllogisms, it communicates the beauty of the images used by the Lord to encourage the practice of good. The memory of the faithful, like that of Mary, should overflow with the wondrous things done by God. Their hearts, growing in hope from the joyful and practical exercise of the love which they have received, will sense that each word of Scripture is a gift before it is a demand.

143. The challenge of an inculturated preaching consists in proclaiming a synthesis, not ideas or detached values. Where your synthesis is, there lies your heart. The difference between enlightening people with a synthesis and doing so with detached ideas is like the difference between boredom and heartfelt fervor. The preacher has the wonderful but difficult task of joining loving hearts, the hearts of the Lord and his people. The dialogue between God and his people further strengthens the covenant between them and consolidates the bond of charity. In the course of the homily, the hearts of believers keep silence and allow God to speak. The Lord and his people speak to one another in a thousand ways

directly, without intermediaries. But in the homily they want someone to serve as an instrument and to express their feelings in such a way that afterward, each one may choose how he or she will continue the conversation. The word is essentially a mediator and requires not just the two who dialogue but also an intermediary who presents it for what it is, out of the conviction that "what we preach is not ourselves, but Jesus Christ as Lord, with ourselves as your servants for Jesus' sake" (2 Cor 4:5).

144. To speak from the heart means that our hearts must not just be on fire, but also enlightened by the fullness of revelation and by the path traveled by God's word in the heart of the Church and our faithful people throughout history. This Christian identity, as the baptismal embrace which the Father gave us when we were little ones, makes us desire, as prodigal children—and favorite children in Mary—yet another embrace, that of the merciful Father who awaits us in glory. Helping our people to feel that they live in the midst of these two embraces is the difficult but beautiful task of one who preaches the Gospel.

III. Preparing to preach

145. Preparation for preaching is so important a task that a prolonged time of study, prayer, reflection, and pastoral creativity should be devoted to it. With great affection I wish to stop for a moment and offer a method of preparing homilies. Some may find these suggestions self-evident, but I consider it helpful to offer them as a way of emphasizing the need to devote quality time to this precious ministry. Some pastors argue that such preparation is not possible given the vast number of tasks which they must perform; nonetheless, I presume to ask that each week a sufficient portion of personal and community time be dedicated to this task, even if less time has to be given to other important activities. Trust that the Holy Spirit who is at work during the homily is not merely passive but active and creative. It demands that we offer ourselves and all our abilities as instruments (cf. Rom 12:1) which God can use. A preacher who does not prepare is not "spiritual"; he is dishonest and irresponsible with the gifts he has received.

Reverence for truth

146. The first step, after calling upon the Holy Spirit in prayer, is to give our entire attention to the biblical text, which needs to be the basis of our preaching. Whenever we stop and attempt to understand the message of a particular text, we are practicing "reverence for the truth."[113] This is the humility of heart which recognizes that the word is always beyond us, that "we are neither its masters or owners, but its guardians, heralds and servants."[114] This attitude of humble and awe-filled veneration of the word is expressed by taking the time to study it with the greatest care and a holy fear lest we distort it. To interpret a biblical text, we need to be patient, to put aside all other concerns, and to give it our time, interest, and undivided attention. We must leave aside any other pressing concerns and create an environment of serene concentration. It is useless to attempt to read a biblical text if all we are looking for are quick, easy, and immediate results. Preparation for preaching requires love. We only devote periods of quiet time to the things or the people whom we love; and here we are speaking of the God whom we love, a God who wishes to speak to us. Because of this love, we can take as much time as we need, like every true disciple: "Speak, Lord, for your servant is listening" (1 Sm 3:9).

147. First of all, we need to be sure that we understand the meaning of the words we read. I want to insist here on something which may seem obvious, but which is not always taken into account: the biblical text which we study is two or three thousand years old; its language is very different from that which we speak today. Even if we think we understand the words translated into our own language, this does not mean that we correctly understand what the sacred author wished to say. The different tools provided by literary analysis are well known: attention to words which are repeated or emphasized, recognition of the structure and specific movement of a text, consideration of the role played by the different characters, and so forth. But our own aim is not to understand every little detail of a text; our most important goal is to discover its principal message, the message which gives structure and unity to the text. If the preacher does not make this effort, his preaching will quite likely

have neither unity nor order; what he has to say will be a mere accumulation of various disjointed ideas incapable of inspiring others. The central message is what the author primarily wanted to communicate; this calls for recognizing not only the author's ideas but the effect which he wanted to produce. If a text was written to console, it should not be used to correct errors; if it was written as an exhortation, it should not be employed to teach doctrine; if it was written to teach something about God, it should not be used to expound various theological opinions; if it was written as a summons to praise or missionary outreach, let us not use it to talk about the latest news.

148. Certainly, to understand properly the meaning of the central message of a text we need to relate it to the teaching of the entire Bible as handed on by the Church. This is an important principle of biblical interpretation which recognizes that the Holy Spirit has inspired not just a part of the Bible, but the Bible as a whole, and that in some areas people have grown in their understanding of God's will on the basis of their personal experience. It also prevents erroneous or partial interpretations which would contradict other teachings of the same Scriptures. But it does not mean that we can weaken the distinct and specific emphasis of a text which we are called to preach. One of the defects of a tedious and ineffectual preaching is precisely its inability to transmit the intrinsic power of the text which has been proclaimed.

Personalizing the word

149. The preacher "ought first of all to develop a great personal familiarity with the word of God. Knowledge of its linguistic or exegetical aspects, though certainly necessary, is not enough. He needs to approach the word with a docile and prayerful heart so that it may deeply penetrate his thoughts and feelings and bring about a new outlook in him."[115] It is good for us to renew our fervor each day and every Sunday as we prepare the homily, examining ourselves to see if we have grown in love for the word which we preach. Nor should we forget that "the greater or lesser degree of the holiness of the minister has a real effect on the proclamation of the word."[116] As Saint Paul says, "we speak, not to please

men, but to please God who tests our hearts" (1 Thes 2:4). If we have a lively desire to be the first to hear the word which we must preach, this will surely be communicated to God's faithful people, for "out of the abundance of the heart, the mouth speaks" (Mt 12:34). The Sunday readings will resonate in all their brilliance in the hearts of the faithful if they have first done so in the heart of their pastor.

150. Jesus was angered by those supposed teachers who demanded much of others, teaching God's word but without being enlightened by it: "They bind heavy burdens, hard to bear, and lay them on the shoulders of others; but they themselves will not lift a finger to move them" (Mt 23:4). The apostle James exhorted: "Not many of you should become teachers, my brethren, for you know that we who teach shall be judged with greater strictness" (Jas 3:1). Whoever wants to preach must be the first to let the word of God move him deeply and become incarnate in his daily life. In this way preaching will consist in that activity, so intense and fruitful, which is "communicating to others what one has contemplated."[117] For all these reasons, before preparing what we will actually say when preaching, we need to let ourselves be penetrated by that word which will also penetrate others, for it is a living and active word, like a sword "which pierces to the division of soul and spirit, of joints and marrow, and discerns the thoughts and intentions of the heart" (Heb 4:12). This has great pastoral importance. Today too, people prefer to listen to witnesses: they "thirst for authenticity" and "call for evangelizers to speak of a God whom they themselves know and are familiar with, as if they were seeing him."[118]

151. We are not asked to be flawless, but to keep growing and wanting to grow as we advance along the path of the Gospel; our arms must never grow slack. What is essential is that the preacher be certain that God loves him, that Jesus Christ has saved him, and that his love always has the last word. Encountering such beauty, he will often feel that his life does not glorify God as it should, and he will sincerely desire to respond more fully to so great a love. Yet if he does not take time to hear God's word with an open heart, if he does not allow it to touch his life, to challenge him, to impel him, and if he does not devote time to pray with that word,

then he will indeed be a false prophet, a fraud, a shallow impostor. But by acknowledging his poverty and desiring to grow in his commitment, he will always be able to abandon himself to Christ, saying in the words of Peter: "I have no silver and gold, but what I have I give you" (Acts 3:6). The Lord wants to make use of us as living, free, and creative beings who let his word enter their own hearts before then passing it on to others. Christ's message must truly penetrate and possess the preacher, not just intellectually but in his entire being. The Holy Spirit, who inspired the word, "today, just as at the beginning of the Church, acts in every evangelizer who allows himself to be possessed and led by him. The Holy Spirit places on his lips the words which he could not find by himself."[119]

Spiritual reading

152. There is one particular way of listening to what the Lord wishes to tell us in his word and of letting ourselves be transformed by the Spirit. It is what we call lectio divina. It consists of reading God's word in a moment of prayer and allowing it to enlighten and renew us. This prayerful reading of the Bible is not something separate from the study undertaken by the preacher to ascertain the central message of the text; on the contrary, it should begin with that study and then go on to discern how that same message speaks to his own life. The spiritual reading of a text must start with its literal sense. Otherwise we can easily make the text say what we think is convenient, useful for confirming us in our previous decisions, suited to our own patterns of thought. Ultimately this would be tantamount to using something sacred for our own benefit and then passing on this confusion to God's people. We must never forget that sometimes "even Satan disguises himself as an angel of light" (2 Cor 11:14).

153. In the presence of God, during a recollected reading of the text, it is good to ask, for example: "Lord, what does this text say to me? What is it about my life that you want to change by this text? What troubles me about this text? Why am I not interested in this? Or perhaps: What do I find pleasant in this text? What is it about this word that moves me? What attracts me? Why does it attract me?" When we make an effort to

listen to the Lord, temptations usually arise. One of them is simply to feel troubled or burdened, and to turn away. Another common temptation is to think about what the text means for other people, and so avoid applying it to our own life. It can also happen that we look for excuses to water down the clear meaning of the text. Or we can wonder if God is demanding too much of us, asking for a decision which we are not yet prepared to make. This leads many people to stop taking pleasure in the encounter with God's word; but this would mean forgetting that no one is more patient than God our Father, that no one is more understanding and willing to wait. He always invites us to take a step forward, but does not demand a full response if we are not yet ready. He simply asks that we sincerely look at our life and present ourselves honestly before him, and that we be willing to continue to grow, asking from him what we ourselves cannot as yet achieve.

An ear to the people

154. The preacher also needs to keep his ear to the people and to discover what it is that the faithful need to hear. A preacher has to contemplate the word, but he also has to contemplate his people. In this way he learns "of the aspirations, of riches and limitations, of ways of praying, of loving, of looking at life and the world, which distinguish this or that human gathering," while paying attention "to actual people, to using their language, their signs and symbols, to answering the questions they ask."[120] He needs to be able to link the message of a biblical text to a human situation, to an experience which cries out for the light of God's word. This interest has nothing to do with shrewdness or calculation; it is profoundly religious and pastoral. Fundamentally it is a "spiritual sensitivity for reading God's message in events,"[121] and this is much more than simply finding something interesting to say. What we are looking for is "what the Lord has to say in this or that particular circumstance."[122] Preparation for preaching thus becomes an exercise in evangelical discernment, wherein we strive to recognize—in the light of the Spirit—"a call which God causes to resound in the historical situation itself. In this situation, and also through it, God calls the believer."[123]

155. In this effort we may need but think of some ordinary human experience such as a joyful reunion, a moment of disappointment, the fear of being alone, compassion at the sufferings of others, uncertainty about the future, concern for a loved one, and so forth. But we need to develop a broad and profound sensitivity to what really affects other people's lives. Let us also keep in mind that we should never respond to questions that nobody asks. Nor is it fitting to talk about the latest news in order to awaken people's interest; we have television programs for that. It is possible, however, to start with some fact or story so that God's word can forcefully resound in its call to conversion, worship, commitment to fraternity and service, and so forth. Yet there will always be some who readily listen to a preacher's commentaries on current affairs, while not letting themselves be challenged.

Homiletic resources

156. Some people think they can be good preachers because they know what ought to be said, but they pay no attention to how it should be said, that is, the concrete way of constructing a sermon. They complain when people do not listen to or appreciate them, but perhaps they have never taken the trouble to find the proper way of presenting their message. Let us remember that "the obvious importance of the content of evangelization must not overshadow the importance of its ways and means."[124] Concern for the way we preach is likewise a profoundly spiritual concern. It entails responding to the love of God by putting all our talents and creativity at the service of the mission which he has given us; at the same time, it shows a fine, active love of neighbor by refusing to offer others a product of poor quality. In the Bible, for example, we can find advice on how to prepare a homily so as best to reach people: "Speak concisely, say much in few words" (Sir 32:8).

157. Simply using a few examples, let us recall some practical resources which can enrich our preaching and make it more attractive. One of the most important things is to learn how to use images in preaching, how to appeal to imagery. Sometimes examples are used to clarify a certain point, but these examples usually appeal only to the mind; images, on

the other hand, help people better to appreciate and accept the message we wish to communicate. An attractive image makes the message seem familiar, close to home, practical, and related to everyday life. A successful image can make people savor the message, awaken a desire, and move the will toward the Gospel. A good homily, an old teacher once told me, should have "an idea, a sentiment, an image."

158. Paul VI said that "the faithful . . . expect much from preaching, and will greatly benefit from it, provided that it is simple, clear, direct, well-adapted."[125] Simplicity has to do with the language we use. It must be one that people understand, lest we risk speaking to a void. Preachers often use words learned during their studies and in specialized settings which are not part of the ordinary language of their hearers. These are words that are suitable in theology or catechesis, but whose meaning is incomprehensible to the majority of Christians. The greatest risk for a preacher is that he becomes so accustomed to his own language that he thinks that everyone else naturally understands and uses it. If we wish to adapt to people's language and to reach them with God's word, we need to share in their lives and pay loving attention to them. Simplicity and clarity are two different things. Our language may be simple but our preaching not very clear. It can end up being incomprehensible because it is disorganized, lacks logical progression, or tries to deal with too many things at one time. We need to ensure, then, that the homily has thematic unity, clear order, and correlation between sentences, so that people can follow the preacher easily and grasp his line of argument.

159. Another feature of a good homily is that it is positive. It is not so much concerned with pointing out what shouldn't be done, but with suggesting what we can do better. In any case, if it does draw attention to something negative, it will also attempt to point to a positive and attractive value, lest it remain mired in complaints, laments, criticisms, and reproaches. Positive preaching always offers hope, points to the future, does not leave us trapped in negativity. How good it is when priests, deacons, and the laity gather periodically to discover resources which can make preaching more attractive!

IV. Evangelization and the deeper understanding of the kerygma

160. The Lord's missionary mandate includes a call to growth in faith: "Teach them to observe all that I have commanded you" (Mt 28:20). Hence it is clear that that the first proclamation also calls for ongoing formation and maturation. Evangelization aims at a process of growth which entails taking seriously each person and God's plan for his or her life. All of us need to grow in Christ. Evangelization should stimulate a desire for this growth, so that each of us can say wholeheartedly: "It is no longer I who live, but Christ who lives in me" (Gal 2:20).

161. It would not be right to see this call to growth exclusively or primarily in terms of doctrinal formation. It has to do with "observing" all that the Lord has shown us as the way of responding to his love. Along with the virtues, this means above all the new commandment, the first and the greatest of the commandments, and the one that best identifies us as Christ's disciples: "This is my commandment, that you love one another as I have loved you" (Jn 15:12). Clearly, whenever the New Testament authors want to present the heart of the Christian moral message, they present the essential requirement of love for one's neighbor: "The one who loves *his neighbor* has fulfilled the whole law . . . therefore love of neighbor is the fulfilling of the law" (Rom 13:8, 10). These are the words of Saint Paul, for whom the commandment of love not only sums up the law but constitutes its very heart and purpose: "For the whole law is fulfilled in one word, 'you shall love your neighbor as yourself'" (Gal 5:14). To his communities Paul presents the Christian life as a journey of growth in love: "May the Lord make you increase and abound in love for one another and for all" (1 Thes 3:12). Saint James likewise exhorts Christians to fulfill "the royal law according to the Scripture: You shall love your neighbor as yourself" (2:8), in order not to fall short of any commandment.

162. On the other hand this process of response and growth is always preceded by God's gift, since the Lord first says: "Baptize them in the name . . ." (Mt 28:19). The Father's free gift which makes us his sons and

daughters, and the priority of the gift of his grace (cf. Eph 2:8–9; 1 Cor 4:7), enable that constant sanctification which pleases God and gives him glory. In this way, we allow ourselves to be transformed in Christ through a life lived "according to the Spirit" (Rom 8:5).

Kerygmatic and mystagogical catechesis

163. Education and catechesis are at the service of this growth. We already possess a number of magisterial documents and aids on catechesis issued by the Holy See and by various episcopates. I think in particular of the Apostolic Exhortation *Catechesi Tradendae* (1979), the *General Catechetical Directory* (1997), and other documents whose contents need not be repeated here. I would like to offer a few brief considerations which I believe to be of particular significance.

164. In catechesis too, we have rediscovered the fundamental role of the first announcement or kerygma, which needs to be the center of all evangelizing activity and all efforts at Church renewal. The kerygma is Trinitarian. The fire of the Spirit is given in the form of tongues and leads us to believe in Jesus Christ who, by his death and resurrection, reveals and communicates to us the Father's infinite mercy. On the lips of the catechist the first proclamation must ring out over and over: "Jesus Christ loves you; he gave his life to save you; and now he is living at your side every day to enlighten, strengthen, and free you." This first proclamation is called "first" not because it exists at the beginning and can then be forgotten or replaced by other more important things. It is first in a qualitative sense because it is the principal proclamation, the one which we must hear again and again in different ways, the one which we must announce one way or another throughout the process of catechesis, at every level and moment.[126] For this reason too, "the priest—like every other member of the Church—ought to grow in awareness that he himself is continually in need of being evangelized."[127]

165. We must not think that in catechesis the kerygma gives way to a supposedly more "solid" formation. Nothing is more solid, profound, secure, meaningful, and wisdom-filled than that initial proclamation. All Christian formation consists of entering more deeply into the kerygma,

which is reflected in and constantly illumines, the work of catechesis, thereby enabling us to understand more fully the significance of every subject which the latter treats. It is the message capable of responding to the desire for the infinite which abides in every human heart. The centrality of the kerygma calls for stressing those elements which are most needed today: it has to express God's saving love which precedes any moral and religious obligation on our part; it should not impose the truth but appeal to freedom; it should be marked by joy, encouragement, liveliness, and a harmonious balance which will not reduce preaching to a few doctrines which are at times more philosophical than evangelical. All this demands on the part of the evangelizer certain attitudes which foster openness to the message: approachability, readiness for dialogue, patience, a warmth and welcome which is non-judgmental.

166. Another aspect of catechesis which has developed in recent decades is *mystagogic* initiation.[128] This basically has to do with two things: a progressive experience of formation involving the entire community and a renewed appreciation of the liturgical signs of Christian initiation. Many manuals and programs have not yet taken sufficiently into account the need for a mystagogical renewal, one which would assume very different forms based on each educational community's discernment. Catechesis is a proclamation of the word and is always centered on that word, yet it also demands a suitable environment and an attractive presentation, the use of eloquent symbols, insertion into a broader growth process and the integration of every dimension of the person within a communal journey of hearing and response.

167. Every form of catechesis would do well to attend to the "way of beauty" (*via pulchritudinis*).[129] Proclaiming Christ means showing that to believe in and to follow him is not only something right and true, but also something beautiful, capable of filling life with new splendor and profound joy, even in the midst of difficulties. Every expression of true beauty can thus be acknowledged as a path leading to an encounter with the Lord Jesus. This has nothing to do with fostering an aesthetic relativism[130] which would downplay the inseparable bond between truth, goodness, and beauty, but rather a renewed esteem for beauty as a means

of touching the human heart and enabling the truth and goodness of the Risen Christ to radiate within it. If, as Saint Augustine says, we love only that which is beautiful,[131] the incarnate Son, as the revelation of infinite beauty, is supremely lovable and draws us to himself with bonds of love. So a formation in the *via pulchritudinis* ought to be part of our effort to pass on the faith. Each particular Church should encourage the use of the arts in evangelization, building on the treasures of the past but also drawing upon the wide variety of contemporary expressions so as to transmit the faith in a new "language of parables."[132] We must be bold enough to discover new signs and new symbols, new flesh to embody and communicate the word, and different forms of beauty which are valued in different cultural settings, including those unconventional modes of beauty which may mean little to the evangelizers, yet prove particularly attractive for others.

168. As for the moral component of catechesis, which promotes growth in fidelity to the Gospel way of life, it is helpful to stress again and again the attractiveness and the ideal of a life of wisdom, self-fulfillment, and enrichment. In the light of that positive message, our rejection of the evils which endanger that life can be better understood. Rather than experts in dire predictions, dour judges bent on rooting out every threat and deviation, we should appear as joyful messengers of challenging proposals, guardians of the goodness and beauty which shine forth in a life of fidelity to the Gospel.

Personal accompaniment in processes of growth

169. In a culture paradoxically suffering from anonymity and at the same time obsessed with the details of other people's lives, shamelessly given over to morbid curiosity, the Church must look more closely and sympathetically at others whenever necessary. In our world, ordained ministers and other pastoral workers can make present the fragrance of Christ's closeness and his personal gaze. The Church will have to initiate everyone—priests, religious, and laity—into this "art of accompaniment" which teaches us to remove our sandals before the sacred ground of the other (cf. Ex 3:5). The pace of this accompaniment must be steady and

reassuring, reflecting our closeness and our compassionate gaze which also heals, liberates, and encourages growth in the Christian life.

170. Although it sounds obvious, spiritual accompaniment must lead others ever closer to God, in whom we attain true freedom. Some people think they are free if they can avoid God; they fail to see that they remain existentially orphaned, helpless, homeless. They cease being pilgrims and become drifters, flitting around themselves and never getting anywhere. To accompany them would be counterproductive if it became a sort of therapy supporting their self-absorption and ceased to be a pilgrimage with Christ to the Father.

171. Today more than ever we need men and women who, on the basis of their experience of accompanying others, are familiar with processes which call for prudence, understanding, patience, and docility to the Spirit, so that they can protect the sheep from wolves who would scatter the flock. We need to practice the art of listening, which is more than simply hearing. Listening, in communication, is an openness of heart which makes possible that closeness without which genuine spiritual encounter cannot occur. Listening helps us to find the right gesture and word which shows that we are more than simply bystanders. Only through such respectful and compassionate listening can we enter on the paths of true growth and awaken a yearning for the Christian ideal: the desire to respond fully to God's love and to bring to fruition what he has sown in our lives. But this always demands the patience of one who knows full well what Saint Thomas Aquinas tells us: that anyone can have grace and charity, and yet falter in the exercise of the virtues because of persistent "contrary inclinations."[133] In other words, the organic unity of the virtues always and necessarily exists *in habitu*, even though forms of conditioning can hinder the operations of those virtuous habits. Hence the need for "a pedagogy which will introduce people step by step to the full appropriation of the mystery."[134] Reaching a level of maturity where individuals can make truly free and responsible decisions calls for much time and patience. As Blessed Peter Faber used to say: "Time is God's messenger."

172. One who accompanies others has to realize that each person's situation before God and their life in grace are mysteries which no one can fully know from without. The Gospel tells us to correct others and to help them to grow on the basis of a recognition of the objective evil of their actions (cf. Mt 18:15), but without making judgments about their responsibility and culpability (cf. Mt 7:1; Lk 6:37). Someone good at such accompaniment does not give in to frustrations or fears. He or she invites others to let themselves be healed, to take up their mat, embrace the cross, leave all behind, and go forth ever anew to proclaim the Gospel. Our personal experience of being accompanied and assisted, and of openness to those who accompany us, will teach us to be patient and compassionate with others, and to find the right way to gain their trust, their openness, and their readiness to grow.

173. Genuine spiritual accompaniment always begins and flourishes in the context of service to the mission of evangelization. Paul's relationship with Timothy and Titus provides an example of this accompaniment and formation which takes place in the midst of apostolic activity. Entrusting them with the mission of remaining in each city to "put in order what remains to be done" (Ti 1:5; cf. 1 Tm 1:3–5), Paul also gives them rules for their personal lives and their pastoral activity. This is clearly distinct from every kind of intrusive accompaniment or isolated self-realization. Missionary disciples accompany missionary disciples.

Centered on the word of God

174. Not only the homily has to be nourished by the word of God. All evangelization is based on that word, listened to, meditated upon, lived, celebrated, and witnessed to. The sacred Scriptures are the very source of evangelization. Consequently, we need to be constantly trained in hearing the word. The Church does not evangelize unless she constantly lets herself be evangelized. It is indispensable that the word of God "be ever more fully at the heart of every ecclesial activity."[135] God's word, listened to and celebrated, above all in the Eucharist, nourishes and inwardly strengthens Christians, enabling them to offer an authentic witness to the Gospel in daily life. We have long since moved beyond that old

contraposition between word and sacrament. The preaching of the word, living and effective, prepares for the reception of the sacrament, and in the sacrament that word attains its maximum efficacy.

175. The study of the sacred Scriptures must be a door opened to every believer.[136] It is essential that the revealed word radically enrich our catechesis and all our efforts to pass on the faith.[137] Evangelization demands familiarity with God's word, which calls for dioceses, parishes, and Catholic associations to provide for a serious, ongoing study of the Bible, while encouraging its prayerful individual and communal reading.[138] We do not blindly seek God, or wait for him to speak to us first, for "God has already spoken, and there is nothing further that we need to know, which has not been revealed to us."[139] Let us receive the sublime treasure of the revealed word.

CHAPTER FOUR

THE SOCIAL DIMENSION OF EVANGELIZATION

176. To evangelize is to make the kingdom of God present in our world. Yet "any partial or fragmentary definition which attempts to render the reality of evangelization in all its richness, complexity and dynamism does so only at the risk of impoverishing it and even of distorting it."[140] I would now like to share my concerns about the social dimension of evangelization, precisely because if this dimension is not properly brought out, there is a constant risk of distorting the authentic and integral meaning of the mission of evangelization.

I. Communal and societal repercussions of the kerygma

177. The kerygma has a clear social content: at the very heart of the Gospel is life in community and engagement with others. The content of the first proclamation has an immediate moral implication centered on charity.

Confession of faith and commitment to society

178. To believe in a Father who loves all men and women with an infinite love means realizing that "he thereby confers upon them an infinite dignity."[141] To believe that the Son of God assumed our human flesh means that each human person has been taken up into the very heart of God. To believe that Jesus shed his blood for us removes any doubt about the boundless love which ennobles each human being. Our redemption has a social dimension because "God, in Christ, redeems not only the individual person, but also the social relations existing between men."[142] To believe that the Holy Spirit is at work in everyone means realizing that he seeks to penetrate every human situation and all social bonds: "The Holy Spirit can be said to possess an infinite creativity, proper to the divine mind, which knows how to loosen the knots of human affairs, even the most complex and inscrutable."[143] Evangelization is meant to cooperate with this liberating work of the Spirit. The very mystery of the

Trinity reminds us that we have been created in the image of that divine communion, and so we cannot achieve fulfillment or salvation purely by our own efforts. From the heart of the Gospel we see the profound connection between evangelization and human advancement, which must necessarily find expression and develop in every work of evangelization. Accepting the first proclamation, which invites us to receive God's love and to love him in return with the very love which is his gift, brings forth in our lives and actions a primary and fundamental response: to desire, seek, and protect the good of others.

179. This inseparable bond between our acceptance of the message of salvation and genuine fraternal love appears in several scriptural texts which we would do well to meditate upon, in order to appreciate all their consequences. The message is one which we often take for granted, and can repeat almost mechanically, without necessarily ensuring that it has a real effect on our lives and in our communities. How dangerous and harmful this is, for it makes us lose our amazement, our excitement, and our zeal for living the Gospel of fraternity and justice! God's word teaches that our brothers and sisters are the prolongation of the incarnation for each of us: "As you did it to one of these, the least of my brethren, you did it to me" (Mt 25:40). The way we treat others has a transcendent dimension: "The measure you give will be the measure you get" (Mt 7:2). It corresponds to the mercy which God has shown us: "Be merciful, just as your Father is merciful. Do not judge, and you will not be judged; do not condemn, and you will not be condemned. Forgive, and you will be forgiven; give, and it will be given to you. . . . For the measure you give will be the measure you get back" (Lk 6:36–38). What these passages make clear is the absolute priority of "going forth from ourselves toward our brothers and sisters" as one of the two great commandments which ground every moral norm and as the clearest sign for discerning spiritual growth in response to God's completely free gift. For this reason, "the service of charity is also a constituent element of the Church's mission and an indispensable expression of her very being."[144] By her very nature the Church is missionary; she abounds in effective charity and a compassion which understands, assists, and promotes.

The kingdom and its challenge

180. Reading the Scriptures also makes it clear that the Gospel is not merely about our personal relationship with God. Nor should our loving response to God be seen simply as an accumulation of small personal gestures to individuals in need, a kind of "charity à la carte," or a series of acts aimed solely at easing our conscience. The Gospel is about the kingdom of God (cf. Lk 4:43); it is about loving God who reigns in our world. To the extent that he reigns within us, the life of society will be a setting for universal fraternity, justice, peace, and dignity. Both Christian preaching and life, then, are meant to have an impact on society. We are seeking God's kingdom: "Seek first God's kingdom and his righteousness, and all these things will be given to you as well" (Mt 6:33). Jesus' mission is to inaugurate the kingdom of his Father; he commands his disciples to proclaim the good news that "the kingdom of heaven is at hand" (Mt 10:7).

181. The kingdom, already present and growing in our midst, engages us at every level of our being and reminds us of the principle of discernment which Pope Paul VI applied to true development: it must be directed to "all men and the whole man."[145] We know that "evangelization would not be complete if it did not take account of the unceasing interplay of the Gospel and of man's concrete life, both personal and social."[146] This is the principle of universality intrinsic to the Gospel, for the Father desires the salvation of every man and woman, and his saving plan consists in "gathering up all things in Christ, things in heaven and things on earth" (Eph 1:10). Our mandate is to "go into all the world and proclaim the good news to the whole creation" (Mk 16:15), for "the creation waits with eager longing for the revealing of the children of God" (Rom 8:19). Here, "the creation" refers to every aspect of human life; consequently, "the mission of proclaiming the good news of Jesus Christ has a universal destination. Its mandate of charity encompasses all dimensions of existence, all individuals, all areas of community life, and all peoples. Nothing human can be alien to it."[147] True Christian hope, which seeks the eschatological kingdom, always generates history.

The Church's teaching on social questions

182. The Church's teachings concerning contingent situations are subject to new and further developments and can be open to discussion, yet we cannot help but be concrete—without presuming to enter into details—lest the great social principles remain mere generalities which challenge no one. There is a need to draw practical conclusions, so that they "will have greater impact on the complexities of current situations."[148] The Church's pastors, taking into account the contributions of the different sciences, have the right to offer opinions on all that affects people's lives, since the task of evangelization implies and demands the integral promotion of each human being. It is no longer possible to claim that religion should be restricted to the private sphere and that it exists only to prepare souls for heaven. We know that God wants his children to be happy in this world too, even though they are called to fulfillment in eternity, for he has created all things "for our enjoyment" (1 Tm 6:17), the enjoyment of everyone. It follows that Christian conversion demands reviewing especially those areas and aspects of life "related to the social order and the pursuit of the common good."[149]

183. Consequently, no one can demand that religion should be relegated to the inner sanctum of personal life, without influence on societal and national life, without concern for the soundness of civil institutions, without a right to offer an opinion on events affecting society. Who would claim to lock up in a church and silence the message of Saint Francis of Assisi or Blessed Teresa of Calcutta? They themselves would have found this unacceptable. An authentic faith—which is never comfortable or completely personal—always involves a deep desire to change the world, to transmit values, to leave this earth somehow better than we found it. We love this magnificent planet on which God has put us, and we love the human family which dwells here, with all its tragedies and struggles, its hopes and aspirations, its strengths and weaknesses. The earth is our common home and all of us are brothers and sisters. If indeed "the just ordering of society and of the state is a central responsibility of politics," the Church "cannot and must not remain on the sidelines in the fight for justice."[150] All Christians, their pastors included, are called

to show concern for the building of a better world. This is essential, for the Church's social thought is primarily positive: it offers proposals, it works for change, and in this sense it constantly points to the hope born of the loving heart of Jesus Christ. At the same time, it unites "its own commitment to that made in the social field by other Churches and Ecclesial Communities, whether at the level of doctrinal reflection or at the practical level."[151]

184. This is not the time or the place to examine in detail the many grave social questions affecting today's world, some of which I have dealt with in the second chapter. This Exhortation is not a social document, and for reflection on those different themes we have a most suitable tool in the *Compendium of the Social Doctrine of the Church,* whose use and study I heartily recommend. Furthermore, neither the Pope nor the Church has a monopoly on the interpretation of social realities or the proposal of solutions to contemporary problems. Here I can repeat the insightful observation of Pope Paul VI: "In the face of such widely varying situations, it is difficult for us to utter a unified message and to put forward a solution which has universal validity. This is not our ambition, nor is it our mission. It is up to the Christian communities to analyze with objectivity the situation which is proper to their own country."[152]

185. In what follows I intend to concentrate on two great issues which strike me as fundamental at this time in history. I will treat them more fully because I believe that they will shape the future of humanity. These issues are first, the inclusion of the poor in society, and second, peace and social dialogue.

II. The inclusion of the poor in society

186. Our faith in Christ, who became poor, and was always close to the poor and the outcast, is the basis of our concern for the integral development of society's most neglected members.

In union with God, we hear a plea

187. Each individual Christian and every community is called to be an instrument of God for the liberation and promotion of the poor, and

for enabling them to be fully a part of society. This demands that we be docile and attentive to the cry of the poor and to come to their aid. A mere glance at the Scriptures is enough to make us see how our gracious Father wants to hear the cry of the poor: "I have observed the misery of my people who are in Egypt; I have heard their cry on account of their taskmasters. Indeed, I know their sufferings, and I have come down to deliver them . . . so I will send you . . ." (Ex 3:7–8, 10). We also see how he is concerned for their needs: "When the Israelites cried out to the Lord, the Lord raised up for them a deliverer" (Jgs 3:15). If we, who are God's means of hearing the poor, turn deaf ears to this plea, we oppose the Father's will and his plan; that poor person "might cry to the Lord against you, and you would incur guilt" (Dt 15:9). A lack of solidarity toward his or her needs will directly affect our relationship with God: "For if in bitterness of soul he calls down a curse upon you, his Creator will hear his prayer" (Sir 4:6). The old question always returns: "How does God's love abide in anyone who has the world's goods, and sees a brother or sister in need and yet refuses help?" (1 Jn 3:17). Let us recall also how bluntly the apostle James speaks of the cry of the oppressed: "The wages of the laborers who mowed your fields, which you kept back by fraud, cry out, and the cries of the harvesters have reached the ears of the Lord of hosts" (5:4).

188. The Church has realized that the need to heed this plea is itself born of the liberating action of grace within each of us, and thus it is not a question of a mission reserved only to a few: "The Church, guided by the Gospel of mercy and by love for mankind, hears the cry for justice and intends to respond to it with all her might."[153] In this context we can understand Jesus' command to his disciples: "You yourselves give them something to eat!" (Mk 6:37): it means working to eliminate the structural causes of poverty and to promote the integral development of the poor, as well as small daily acts of solidarity in meeting the real needs which we encounter. The word "solidarity" is a little worn and at times poorly understood, but it refers to something more than a few sporadic acts of generosity. It presumes the creation of a new mindset which thinks in

terms of community and the priority of the life of all over the appropriation of goods by a few.

189. Solidarity is a spontaneous reaction by those who recognize that the social function of property and the universal destination of goods are realities which come before private property. The private ownership of goods is justified by the need to protect and increase them, so that they can better serve the common good; for this reason, solidarity must be lived as the decision to restore to the poor what belongs to them. These convictions and habits of solidarity, when they are put into practice, open the way to other structural transformations and make them possible. Changing structures without generating new convictions and attitudes will only ensure that those same structures will become, sooner or later, corrupt, oppressive, and ineffectual.

190. Sometimes it is a matter of hearing the cry of entire peoples, the poorest peoples of the earth, since "peace is founded not only on respect for human rights, but also on respect for the rights of peoples."[154] Sadly, even human rights can be used as a justification for an inordinate defense of individual rights or the rights of the richer peoples. With due respect for the autonomy and culture of every nation, we must never forget that the planet belongs to all mankind and is meant for all mankind; the mere fact that some people are born in places with fewer resources or less development does not justify the fact that they are living with less dignity. It must be reiterated that "the more fortunate should renounce some of their rights so as to place their goods more generously at the service of others."[155] To speak properly of our own rights, we need to broaden our perspective and to hear the plea of other peoples and other regions than those of our own country. We need to grow in a solidarity which "would allow all peoples to become the artisans of their destiny,"[156] since "every person is called to self-fulfillment."[157]

191. In all places and circumstances, Christians, with the help of their pastors, are called to hear the cry of the poor. This has been eloquently stated by the bishops of Brazil: "We wish to take up daily the joys and hopes, the difficulties and sorrows of the Brazilian people, especially

of those living in the barrios and the countryside—landless, homeless, lacking food and health care—to the detriment of their rights. Seeing their poverty, hearing their cries and knowing their sufferings, we are scandalized because we know that there is enough food for everyone and that hunger is the result of a poor distribution of goods and income. The problem is made worse by the generalized practice of wastefulness."[158]

192. Yet we desire even more than this; our dream soars higher. We are not simply talking about ensuring nourishment or a "dignified sustenance" for all people, but also their "general temporal welfare and prosperity."[159] This means education, access to health care, and above all employment, for it is through free, creative, participatory, and mutually supportive labor that human beings express and enhance the dignity of their lives. A just wage enables them to have adequate access to all the other goods which are destined for our common use.

Fidelity to the Gospel, lest we run in vain

193. We incarnate the duty of hearing the cry of the poor when we are deeply moved by the suffering of others. Let us listen to what God's word teaches us about mercy, and allow that word to resound in the life of the Church. The Gospel tells us: "Blessed are the merciful, because they shall obtain mercy" (Mt 5:7). The apostle James teaches that our mercy to others will vindicate us on the day of God's judgment: "So speak and so act as those who are to be judged under the law of liberty. For judgment is without mercy to one who has shown no mercy, yet mercy triumphs over judgment" (Jas 2:12–13). Here James is faithful to the finest tradition of post-exilic Jewish spirituality, which attributed a particular salutary value to mercy: "Break off your sins by practicing righteousness, and your iniquities by showing mercy to the oppressed, that there may perhaps be a lengthening of your tranquility" (Dn 4:27). The wisdom literature sees almsgiving as a concrete exercise of mercy toward those in need: "Almsgiving delivers from death, and it will purge away every sin" (Tb 12:9). The idea is expressed even more graphically by Sirach: "Water extinguishes blazing fire: so almsgiving atones for sin" (Sir 3:30). The same synthesis appears in the New Testament: "Maintain constant

love for one another, for love covers a multitude of sins" (1 Pt 4:8). This truth greatly influenced the thinking of the Fathers of the Church and helped create a prophetic, counter-cultural resistance to the self-centered hedonism of paganism. We can recall a single example: "If we were in peril from fire, we would certainly run to water in order to extinguish the fire . . . in the same way, if a spark of sin flares up from our straw, and we are troubled on that account, whenever we have an opportunity to perform a work of mercy, we should rejoice, as if a fountain opened before so that the fire might be extinguished."[160]

194. This message is so clear and direct, so simple and eloquent, that no ecclesial interpretation has the right to relativize it. The Church's reflection on these texts ought not to obscure or weaken their force, but urge us to accept their exhortations with courage and zeal. Why complicate something so simple? Conceptual tools exist to heighten contact with the realities they seek to explain, not to distance us from them. This is especially the case with those biblical exhortations which summon us so forcefully to brotherly love, to humble and generous service, to justice and mercy toward the poor. Jesus taught us this way of looking at others by his words and his actions. So why cloud something so clear? We should not be concerned simply about falling into doctrinal error, but about remaining faithful to this light-filled path of life and wisdom. For "defenders of orthodoxy are sometimes accused of passivity, indulgence, or culpable complicity regarding the intolerable situations of injustice and the political regimes which prolong them."[161]

195. When Saint Paul approached the apostles in Jerusalem to discern whether he was "running or had run in vain" (Gal 2:2), the key criterion of authenticity which they presented was that he should not forget the poor (cf. Gal 2:10). This important principle, namely that the Pauline communities should not succumb to the self-centered lifestyle of the pagans, remains timely today, when a new self-centered paganism is growing. We may not always be able to reflect adequately the beauty of the Gospel, but there is one sign which we should never lack: the option for those who are least, those whom society discards.

196. Sometimes we prove hard of heart and mind; we are forgetful, distracted and carried away by the limitless possibilities for consumption and distraction offered by contemporary society. This leads to a kind of alienation at every level, for "a society becomes alienated when its forms of social organization, production and consumption make it more difficult to offer the gift of self and to establish solidarity between people."[162]

The special place of the poor in God's people

197. God's heart has a special place for the poor, so much so that he himself "became poor" (2 Cor 8:9). The entire history of our redemption is marked by the presence of the poor. Salvation came to us from the "yes" uttered by a lowly maiden from a small town on the fringes of a great empire. The Savior was born in a manger, in the midst of animals, like children of poor families; he was presented at the Temple along with two turtledoves, the offering made by those who could not afford a lamb (cf. Lk 2:24; Lv 5:7); he was raised in a home of ordinary workers and worked with his own hands to earn his bread. When he began to preach the kingdom, crowds of the dispossessed followed him, illustrating his words: "The Spirit of the Lord is upon me, because he has anointed me to preach good news to the poor" (Lk 4:18). He assured those burdened by sorrow and crushed by poverty that God has a special place for them in his heart: "Blessed are you poor, yours is the kingdom of God" (Lk 6:20); he made himself one of them: "I was hungry and you gave me food to eat," and he taught them that mercy toward all of these is the key to heaven (cf. Mt 25:5ff.).

198. For the Church, the option for the poor is primarily a theological category rather than a cultural, sociological, political, or philosophical one. God shows the poor "his first mercy."[163] This divine preference has consequences for the faith life of all Christians, since we are called to have "this mind . . . which was in Jesus Christ" (Phil 2:5). Inspired by this, the Church has made an option for the poor which is understood as a "special form of primacy in the exercise of Christian charity, to which the whole tradition of the Church bears witness."[164] This option—as Benedict XVI has taught—"is implicit in our Christian faith in a God who

became poor for us, so as to enrich us with his poverty."[165] This is why I want a Church which is poor and for the poor. They have much to teach us. Not only do they share in the *sensus fidei*, but in their difficulties they know the suffering Christ. We need to let ourselves be evangelized by them. The new evangelization is an invitation to acknowledge the saving power at work in their lives and to put them at the center of the Church's pilgrim way. We are called to find Christ in them, to lend our voice to their causes, but also to be their friends, to listen to them, to speak for them, and to embrace the mysterious wisdom which God wishes to share with us through them.

199. Our commitment does not consist exclusively in activities or programs of promotion and assistance; what the Holy Spirit mobilizes is not an unruly activism, but above all an attentiveness which considers the other "in a certain sense as one with ourselves."[166] This loving attentiveness is the beginning of a true concern for their person which inspires me effectively to seek their good. This entails appreciating the poor in their goodness, in their experience of life, in their culture, and in their ways of living the faith. True love is always contemplative, and permits us to serve the other not out of necessity or vanity, but rather because he or she is beautiful above and beyond mere appearances: "The love by which we find the other pleasing leads us to offer him something freely."[167] The poor person, when loved, "is esteemed as of great value,"[168] and this is what makes the authentic option for the poor differ from any other ideology, from any attempt to exploit the poor for one's own personal or political interest. Only on the basis of this real and sincere closeness can we properly accompany the poor on their path of liberation. Only this will ensure that "in every Christian community the poor feel at home. Would not this approach be the greatest and most effective presentation of the good news of the kingdom?"[169] Without the preferential option for the poor, "the proclamation of the Gospel, which is itself the prime form of charity, risks being misunderstood or submerged by the ocean of words which daily engulfs us in today's society of mass communications."[170]

200. Since this Exhortation is addressed to members of the Catholic Church, I want to say, with regret, that the worst discrimination which

the poor suffer is the lack of spiritual care. The great majority of the poor have a special openness to the faith; they need God and we must not fail to offer them his friendship, his blessing, his word, the celebration of the sacraments, and a journey of growth and maturity in the faith. Our preferential option for the poor must mainly translate into a privileged and preferential religious care.

201. No one must say that they cannot be close to the poor because their own lifestyle demands more attention to other areas. This is an excuse commonly heard in academic, business or professional, and even ecclesial circles. While it is quite true that the essential vocation and mission of the lay faithful is to strive that earthly realities and all human activity may be transformed by the Gospel,[171] none of us can think we are exempt from concern for the poor and for social justice: "Spiritual conversion, the intensity of the love of God and neighbor, zeal for justice and peace, the Gospel meaning of the poor and of poverty, are required of everyone."[172] I fear that these words too may give rise to commentary or discussion with no real practical effect. That being said, I trust in the openness and readiness of all Christians, and I ask you to seek, as a community, creative ways of accepting this renewed call.

The economy and the distribution of income

202. The need to resolve the structural causes of poverty cannot be delayed, not only for the pragmatic reason of its urgency for the good order of society, but because society needs to be cured of a sickness which is weakening and frustrating it, and which can only lead to new crises. Welfare projects, which meet certain urgent needs, should be considered merely temporary responses. As long as the problems of the poor are not radically resolved by rejecting the absolute autonomy of markets and financial speculation and by attacking the structural causes of inequality,[173] no solution will be found for the world's problems or, for that matter, to any problems. Inequality is the root of social ills.

203. The dignity of each human person and the pursuit of the common good are concerns which ought to shape all economic policies. At times, however, they seem to be a mere addendum imported from without in

order to fill out a political discourse lacking in perspectives or plans for true and integral development. How many words prove irksome to this system! It is irksome when the question of ethics is raised, when global solidarity is invoked, when the distribution of goods is mentioned, when reference is made to protecting labor and defending the dignity of the powerless, when allusion is made to a God who demands a commitment to justice. At other times these issues are exploited by a rhetoric which cheapens them. Casual indifference in the face of such questions empties our lives and our words of all meaning. Business is a vocation, and a noble vocation, provided that those engaged in it see themselves challenged by a greater meaning in life; this will enable them truly to serve the common good by striving to increase the goods of this world and to make them more accessible to all.

204. We can no longer trust in the unseen forces and the invisible hand of the market. Growth in justice requires more than economic growth, while presupposing such growth: it requires decisions, programs, mechanisms, and processes specifically geared to a better distribution of income, the creation of sources of employment, and an integral promotion of the poor which goes beyond a simple welfare mentality. I am far from proposing an irresponsible populism, but the economy can no longer turn to remedies that are a new poison, such as attempting to increase profits by reducing the work force and thereby adding to the ranks of the excluded.

205. I ask God to give us more politicians capable of sincere and effective dialogue aimed at healing the deepest roots—and not simply the appearances—of the evils in our world! Politics, though often denigrated, remains a lofty vocation and one of the highest forms of charity, inasmuch as it seeks the common good.[174] We need to be convinced that charity "is the principle not only of micro-relationships (with friends, with family members or within small groups) but also of macro-relationships (social, economic and political ones)."[175] I beg the Lord to grant us more politicians who are genuinely disturbed by the state of society, the people, the lives of the poor! It is vital that government leaders and financial leaders take heed and broaden their horizons, working to ensure that all citizens have dignified work, education, and healthcare. Why not turn

to God and ask him to inspire their plans? I am firmly convinced that openness to the transcendent can bring about a new political and economic mindset which would help to break down the wall of separation between the economy and the common good of society.

206. Economy, as the very word indicates, should be the art of achieving a fitting management of our common home, which is the world as a whole. Each meaningful economic decision made in one part of the world has repercussions everywhere else; consequently, no government can act without regard for shared responsibility. Indeed, it is becoming increasingly difficult to find local solutions for enormous global problems which overwhelm local politics with difficulties to resolve. If we really want to achieve a healthy world economy, what is needed at this juncture of history is a more efficient way of interacting which, with due regard for the sovereignty of each nation, ensures the economic well-being of all countries, not just of a few.

207. Any Church community, if it thinks it can comfortably go its own way without creative concern and effective cooperation in helping the poor to live with dignity and reaching out to everyone, will also risk breaking down, however much it may talk about social issues or criticize governments. It will easily drift into a spiritual worldliness camouflaged by religious practices, unproductive meetings, and empty talk.

208. If anyone feels offended by my words, I would respond that I speak them with affection and with the best of intentions, quite apart from any personal interest or political ideology. My words are not those of a foe or an opponent. I am interested only in helping those who are in thrall to an individualistic, indifferent, and self-centered mentality to be freed from those unworthy chains and to attain a way of living and thinking which is more humane, noble, and fruitful, and which will bring dignity to their presence on this earth.

Concern for the vulnerable

209. Jesus, the evangelizer par excellence and the Gospel in person, identifies especially with the little ones (cf. Mt 25:40). This reminds us

Christians that we are called to care for the vulnerable of the earth. But the current model, with its emphasis on success and self-reliance, does not appear to favor an investment in efforts to help the slow, the weak, or the less talented to find opportunities in life.

210. It is essential to draw near to new forms of poverty and vulnerability, in which we are called to recognize the suffering Christ, even if this appears to bring us no tangible and immediate benefits. I think of the homeless, the addicted, refugees, indigenous peoples, the elderly who are increasingly isolated and abandoned, and many others. Migrants present a particular challenge for me, since I am the pastor of a Church without frontiers, a Church which considers herself mother to all. For this reason, I exhort all countries to a generous openness which, rather than fearing the loss of local identity, will prove capable of creating new forms of cultural synthesis. How beautiful are those cities which overcome paralyzing mistrust, integrate those who are different, and make this very integration a new factor of development! How attractive are those cities which, even in their architectural design, are full of spaces which connect, relate, and favor the recognition of others!

211. I have always been distressed at the lot of those who are victims of various kinds of human trafficking. How I wish that all of us would hear God's cry: "Where is your brother?" (Gn 4:9). Where is your brother or sister who is enslaved? Where is the brother and sister whom you are killing each day in clandestine warehouses, in rings of prostitution, in children used for begging, in exploiting undocumented labor? Let us not look the other way. There is greater complicity than we think. The issue involves everyone! This infamous network of crime is now well established in our cities, and many people have blood on their hands as a result of their comfortable and silent complicity.

212. Doubly poor are those women who endure situations of exclusion, mistreatment, and violence, since they are frequently less able to defend their rights. Even so, we constantly witness among them impressive examples of daily heroism in defending and protecting their vulnerable families.

213. Among the vulnerable for whom the Church wishes to care with particular love and concern are unborn children, the most defenseless and innocent among us. Nowadays efforts are made to deny them their human dignity and to do with them whatever one pleases, taking their lives and passing laws preventing anyone from standing in the way of this. Frequently, as a way of ridiculing the Church's effort to defend their lives, attempts are made to present her position as ideological, obscurantist, and conservative. Yet this defense of unborn life is closely linked to the defense of each and every other human right. It involves the conviction that a human being is always sacred and inviolable, in any situation and at every stage of development. Human beings are ends in themselves and never a means of resolving other problems. Once this conviction disappears, so do solid and lasting foundations for the defense of human rights, which would always be subject to the passing whims of the powers that be. Reason alone is sufficient to recognize the inviolable value of each single human life, but if we also look at the issue from the standpoint of faith, "every violation of the personal dignity of the human being cries out in vengeance to God and is an offense against the creator of the individual."[176]

214. Precisely because this involves the internal consistency of our message about the value of the human person, the Church cannot be expected to change her position on this question. I want to be completely honest in this regard. This is not something subject to alleged reforms or "modernizations." It is not "progressive" to try to resolve problems by eliminating a human life. On the other hand, it is also true that we have done little to adequately accompany women in very difficult situations, where abortion appears as a quick solution to their profound anguish, especially when the life developing within them is the result of rape or a situation of extreme poverty. Who can remain unmoved before such painful situations?

215. There are other weak and defenseless beings who are frequently at the mercy of economic interests or indiscriminate exploitation. I am speaking of creation as a whole. We human beings are not only the beneficiaries but also the stewards of other creatures. Thanks to our bodies,

God has joined us so closely to the world around us that we can feel the desertification of the soil almost as a physical ailment, and the extinction of a species as a painful disfigurement. Let us not leave in our wake a swath of destruction and death which will affect our own lives and those of future generations.[177] Here I would make my own the touching and prophetic lament voiced some years ago by the bishops of the Philippines: "An incredible variety of insects lived in the forest and were busy with all kinds of tasks. . . . Birds flew through the air, their bright plumes and varying calls adding color and song to the green of the forests. . . . God intended this land for us, his special creatures, but not so that we might destroy it and turn it into a wasteland. . . . After a single night's rain, look at the chocolate brown rivers in your locality and remember that they are carrying the life blood of the land into the sea. . . . How can fish swim in sewers like the Pasig and so many more rivers which we have polluted? Who has turned the wonderworld of the seas into underwater cemeteries bereft of color and life?"[178]

216. Small yet strong in the love of God, like Saint Francis of Assisi, all of us, as Christians, are called to watch over and protect the fragile world in which we live, and all its peoples.

III. The common good and peace in society

217. We have spoken at length about joy and love, but the word of God also speaks about the fruit of peace (cf. Gal 5:22).

218. Peace in society cannot be understood as pacification or the mere absence of violence resulting from the domination of one part of society over others. Nor does true peace act as a pretext for justifying a social structure which silences or appeases the poor, so that the more affluent can placidly support their lifestyle while others have to make do as they can. Demands involving the distribution of wealth, concern for the poor and human rights cannot be suppressed under the guise of creating a consensus on paper or a transient peace for a contented minority. The dignity of the human person and the common good rank higher than

the comfort of those who refuse to renounce their privileges. When these values are threatened, a prophetic voice must be raised.

219. Nor is peace "simply the absence of warfare, based on a precarious balance of power; it is fashioned by efforts directed day after day toward the establishment of the ordered universe willed by God, with a more perfect justice among men."[179] In the end, a peace which is not the result of integral development will be doomed; it will always spawn new conflicts and various forms of violence.

220. People in every nation enhance the social dimension of their lives by acting as committed and responsible citizens, not as a mob swayed by the powers that be. Let us not forget that "responsible citizenship is a virtue, and participation in political life is a moral obligation."[180] Yet becoming a people demands something more. It is an ongoing process in which every new generation must take part: a slow and arduous effort calling for a desire for integration and a willingness to achieve this through the growth of a peaceful and multifaceted culture of encounter.

221. Progress in building a people in peace, justice, and fraternity depends on four principles related to constant tensions present in every social reality. These derive from the pillars of the Church's social doctrine, which serve as "primary and fundamental parameters of reference for interpreting and evaluating social phenomena."[181] In their light I would now like to set forth these four specific principles which can guide the development of life in society and the building of a people where differences are harmonized within a shared pursuit. I do so out of the conviction that their application can be a genuine path to peace within each nation and in the entire world.

Time is greater than space

222. A constant tension exists between fullness and limitation. Fullness evokes the desire for complete possession, while limitation is a wall set before us. Broadly speaking, "time" has to do with fullness as an expression of the horizon which constantly opens before us, while each individual moment has to do with limitation as an expression of enclosure.

People live poised between each individual moment and the greater, brighter horizon of the utopian future as the final cause which draws us to itself. Here we see a first principle for progress in building a people: time is greater than space.

223. This principle enables us to work slowly but surely, without being obsessed with immediate results. It helps us patiently to endure difficult and adverse situations, or inevitable changes in our plans. It invites us to accept the tension between fullness and limitation, and to give a priority to time. One of the faults which we occasionally observe in sociopolitical activity is that spaces and power are preferred to time and processes. Giving priority to space means madly attempting to keep everything together in the present, trying to possess all the spaces of power and of self-assertion; it is to crystallize processes and presume to hold them back. Giving priority to time means being concerned about initiating processes rather than possessing spaces. Time governs spaces, illumines them and makes them links in a constantly expanding chain, with no possibility of return. What we need, then, is to give priority to actions which generate new processes in society and engage other persons and groups who can develop them to the point where they bear fruit in significant historical events. Without anxiety, but with clear convictions and tenacity.

224. Sometimes I wonder if there are people in today's world who are really concerned about generating processes of people-building, as opposed to obtaining immediate results which yield easy, quick short-term political gains, but do not enhance human fullness. History will perhaps judge the latter with the criterion set forth by Romano Guardini: "The only measure for properly evaluating an age is to ask to what extent it fosters the development and attainment of a full and authentically meaningful human existence, in accordance with the peculiar character and the capacities of that age."[182]

225. This criterion also applies to evangelization, which calls for attention to the bigger picture, openness to suitable processes, and concern for the long run. The Lord himself, during his earthly life, often warned his disciples that there were things they could not yet understand and that

they would have to await the Holy Spirit (cf. Jn 16:12–13). The parable of the weeds among the wheat (cf. Mt 13:24–30) graphically illustrates an important aspect of evangelization: the enemy can intrude upon the kingdom and sow harm, but ultimately he is defeated by the goodness of the wheat.

Unity prevails over conflict

226. Conflict cannot be ignored or concealed. It has to be faced. But if we remain trapped in conflict, we lose our perspective, our horizons shrink, and reality itself begins to fall apart. In the midst of conflict, we lose our sense of the profound unity of reality.

227. When conflict arises, some people simply look at it and go their way as if nothing happened; they wash their hands of it and get on with their lives. Others embrace it in such a way that they become its prisoners; they lose their bearings, project onto institutions their own confusion and dissatisfaction, and thus make unity impossible. But there is also a third way, and it is the best way to deal with conflict. It is the willingness to face conflict head on, to resolve it, and to make it a link in the chain of a new process. "Blessed are the peacemakers!" (Mt 5:9).

228. In this way it becomes possible to build communion amid disagreement, but this can only be achieved by those great persons who are willing to go beyond the surface of the conflict and to see others in their deepest dignity. This requires acknowledging a principle indispensable to the building of friendship in society: namely, that unity is greater than conflict. Solidarity, in its deepest and most challenging sense, thus becomes a way of making history in a life setting where conflicts, tensions, and oppositions can achieve a diversified and life-giving unity. This is not to opt for a kind of syncretism, or for the absorption of one into the other, but rather for a resolution which takes place on a higher plane and preserves what is valid and useful on both sides.

229. This principle, drawn from the Gospel, reminds us that Christ has made all things one in himself: heaven and earth, God and man, time and eternity, flesh and spirit, person and society. The sign of this unity

and reconciliation of all things in him is peace. Christ "is our peace" (Eph 2:14). The Gospel message always begins with a greeting of peace, and peace at all times crowns and confirms the relations between the disciples. Peace is possible because the Lord has overcome the world and its constant conflict "by making peace through the blood of his cross" (Col 1:20). But if we look more closely at these biblical texts, we find that the locus of this reconciliation of differences is within ourselves, in our own lives, ever threatened as they are by fragmentation and breakdown.[183] If hearts are shattered in thousands of pieces, it is not easy to create authentic peace in society.

230. The message of peace is not about a negotiated settlement but rather the conviction that the unity brought by the Spirit can harmonize every diversity. It overcomes every conflict by creating a new and promising synthesis. Diversity is a beautiful thing when it can constantly enter into a process of reconciliation and seal a sort of cultural covenant resulting in a "reconciled diversity." As the bishops of the Congo have put it: "Our ethnic diversity is our wealth. . . . It is only in unity, through conversion of hearts and reconciliation, that we will be able to help our country to develop on all levels."[184]

Realities are more important than ideas

231. There also exists a constant tension between ideas and realities. Realities simply are, whereas ideas are worked out. There has to be continuous dialogue between the two, lest ideas become detached from realities. It is dangerous to dwell in the realm of words alone, of images and rhetoric. So a third principle comes into play: realities are greater than ideas. This calls for rejecting the various means of masking reality: angelic forms of purity, dictatorships of relativism, empty rhetoric, objectives more ideal than real, brands of ahistorical fundamentalism, ethical systems bereft of kindness, intellectual discourse bereft of wisdom.

232. Ideas—conceptual elaborations—are at the service of communication, understanding, and praxis. Ideas disconnected from realities give rise to ineffectual forms of idealism and nominalism, capable at most of classifying and defining, but certainly not calling to action. What calls

us to action are realities illuminated by reason. Formal nominalism has to give way to harmonious objectivity. Otherwise, the truth is manipulated, cosmetics take the place of real care for our bodies.[185] We have politicians—and even religious leaders—who wonder why people do not understand and follow them, since their proposals are so clear and logical. Perhaps it is because they are stuck in the realm of pure ideas and end up reducing politics or faith to rhetoric. Others have left simplicity behind and have imported a rationality foreign to most people.

233. Realities are greater than ideas. This principle has to do with incarnation of the word and its being put into practice: "By this you know the Spirit of God: every spirit that confesses that Jesus Christ is come in the flesh is from God" (1 Jn 4:2). The principle of reality, of a word already made flesh and constantly striving to take flesh anew, is essential to evangelization. It helps us to see that the Church's history is a history of salvation, to be mindful of those saints who inculturated the Gospel in the life of our peoples and to reap the fruits of the Church's rich bimillennial tradition, without pretending to come up with a system of thought detached from this treasury, as if we wanted to reinvent the Gospel. At the same time, this principle impels us to put the word into practice, to perform works of justice and charity which make that word fruitful. Not to put the word into practice, not to make it reality, is to build on sand, to remain in the realm of pure ideas and to end up in a lifeless and unfruitful self-centeredness and gnosticism.

The whole is greater than the part

234. An innate tension also exists between globalization and localization. We need to pay attention to the global so as to avoid narrowness and banality. Yet we also need to look to the local, which keeps our feet on the ground. Together, the two prevent us from falling into one of two extremes. In the first, people get caught up in an abstract, globalized universe, falling into step behind everyone else, admiring the glitter of other people's world, gaping and applauding at all the right times. At the other extreme, they turn into a museum of local folklore, a world apart, doomed to doing the same things over and over, and incapable of being

challenged by novelty or appreciating the beauty which God bestows beyond their borders.

235. The whole is greater than the part, but it is also greater than the sum of its parts. There is no need, then, to be overly obsessed with limited and particular questions. We constantly have to broaden our horizons and see the greater good which will benefit us all. But this has to be done without evasion or uprooting. We need to sink our roots deeper into the fertile soil and history of our native place, which is a gift of God. We can work on a small scale, in our own neighborhood, but with a larger perspective. Nor do people who wholeheartedly enter into the life of a community need to lose their individualism or hide their identity; instead, they receive new impulses to personal growth. The global need not stifle, nor the particular prove barren.

236. Here our model is not the sphere, which is no greater than its parts, where every point is equidistant from the center, and there are no differences between them. Instead, it is the polyhedron, which reflects the convergence of all its parts, each of which preserves its distinctiveness. Pastoral and political activity alike seek to gather in this polyhedron the best of each. There is a place for the poor and their culture, their aspirations, and their potential. Even people who can be considered dubious on account of their errors have something to offer which must not be overlooked. It is the convergence of peoples who, within the universal order, maintain their own individuality; it is the sum total of persons within a society which pursues the common good, which truly has a place for everyone.

237. To Christians, this principle also evokes the totality or integrity of the Gospel which the Church passes down to us and sends us forth to proclaim. Its fullness and richness embrace scholars and workers, businessmen and artists, in a word, everyone. The genius of each people receives in its own way the entire Gospel and embodies it in expressions of prayer, fraternity, justice, struggle, and celebration. The good news is the joy of the Father who desires that none of his little ones be lost, the joy of the Good Shepherd who finds the lost sheep and brings it back to

the flock. The Gospel is the leaven which causes the dough to rise and the city on the hill whose light illumines all peoples. The Gospel has an intrinsic principle of totality: it will always remain good news until it has been proclaimed to all people, until it has healed and strengthened every aspect of humanity, until it has brought all men and women together at table in God's kingdom. The whole is greater than the part.

IV. Social dialogue as a contribution to peace

238. Evangelization also involves the path of dialogue. For the Church today, three areas of dialogue stand out where she needs to be present in order to promote full human development and to pursue the common good: dialogue with states, dialogue with society—including dialogue with cultures and the sciences—and dialogue with other believers who are not part of the Catholic Church. In each case, "the Church speaks from the light which faith offers,"[186] contributing her two thousand year experience and keeping ever in mind the life and sufferings of human beings. This light transcends human reason, yet it can also prove meaningful and enriching to those who are not believers, and it stimulates reason to broaden its perspectives.

239. The Church proclaims "the Gospel of peace" (Eph 6:15) and she wishes to cooperate with all national and international authorities in safeguarding this immense universal good. By preaching Jesus Christ, who is himself peace (cf. Eph 2:14), the new evangelization calls on every baptized person to be a peacemaker and a credible witness to a reconciled life.[187] In a culture which privileges dialogue as a form of encounter, it is time to devise a means for building consensus and agreement while seeking the goal of a just, responsive, and inclusive society. The principal author, the historic subject of this process, is the people as a whole and their culture, and not a single class, minority, group, or elite. We do not need plans drawn up by a few for the few, or an enlightened or outspoken minority which claims to speak for everyone. It is about agreeing to live together, a social and cultural pact.

240. It is the responsibility of the State to safeguard and promote the common good of society.[188] Based on the principles of subsidiarity and solidarity, and fully committed to political dialogue and consensus building, it plays a fundamental role, one which cannot be delegated, in working for the integral development of all. This role, at present, calls for profound social humility.

241. In her dialogue with the State and with society, the Church does not have solutions for every particular issue. Together with the various sectors of society, she supports those programs which best respond to the dignity of each person and the common good. In doing this, she proposes in a clear way the fundamental values of human life and convictions which can then find expression in political activity.

Dialogue between faith, reason, and science

242. Dialogue between science and faith also belongs to the work of evangelization at the service of peace.[189] Whereas positivism and scientism "refuse to admit the validity of forms of knowledge other than those of the positive sciences,"[190] the Church proposes another path, which calls for a synthesis between the responsible use of methods proper to the empirical sciences and other areas of knowledge such as philosophy, theology, as well as faith itself, which elevates us to the mystery transcending nature and human intelligence. Faith is not fearful of reason; on the contrary, it seeks and trusts reason, since "the light of reason and the light of faith both come from God"[191] and cannot contradict each other. Evangelization is attentive to scientific advances and wishes to shed on them the light of faith and the natural law so that they will remain respectful of the centrality and supreme value of the human person at every stage of life. All of society can be enriched thanks to this dialogue, which opens up new horizons for thought and expands the possibilities of reason. This too is a path of harmony and peace.

243. The Church has no wish to hold back the marvelous progress of science. On the contrary, she rejoices and even delights in acknowledging the enormous potential that God has given to the human mind. Whenever the sciences—rigorously focused on their specific field of

inquiry—arrive at a conclusion which reason cannot refute, faith does not contradict it. Neither can believers claim that a scientific opinion which is attractive but not sufficiently verified has the same weight as a dogma of faith. At times some scientists have exceeded the limits of their scientific competence by making certain statements or claims. But here the problem is not with reason itself, but with the promotion of a particular ideology which blocks the path to authentic, serene, and productive dialogue.

Ecumenical dialogue

244. Commitment to ecumenism responds to the prayer of the Lord Jesus that "they may all be one" (Jn 17:21). The credibility of the Christian message would be much greater if Christians could overcome their divisions and the Church could realize "the fullness of catholicity proper to her in those of her children who, though joined to her by baptism, are yet separated from full communion with her."[192] We must never forget that we are pilgrims journeying alongside one another. This means that we must have sincere trust in our fellow pilgrims, putting aside all suspicion or mistrust, and turn our gaze to what we are all seeking: the radiant peace of God's face. Trusting others is an art and peace is an art. Jesus told us: "Blessed are the peacemakers" (Mt 5:9). In taking up this task, also among ourselves, we fulfill the ancient prophecy: "They shall beat their swords into ploughshares" (Is 2:4).

245. In this perspective, ecumenism can be seen as a contribution to the unity of the human family. At the Synod, the presence of the Patriarch of Constantinople, His Holiness Bartholomaios I, and the Archbishop of Canterbury, His Grace Rowan Williams, was a true gift from God and a precious Christian witness.[193]

246. Given the seriousness of the counter-witness of division among Christians, particularly in Asia and Africa, the search for paths to unity becomes all the more urgent. Missionaries on those continents often mention the criticisms, complaints, and ridicule to which the scandal of divided Christians gives rise. If we concentrate on the convictions we share, and if we keep in mind the principle of the hierarchy of truths,

we will be able to progress decidedly toward common expressions of proclamation, service, and witness. The immense numbers of people who have not received the Gospel of Jesus Christ cannot leave us indifferent. Consequently, commitment to a unity which helps them to accept Jesus Christ can no longer be a matter of mere diplomacy or forced compliance, but rather an indispensable path to evangelization. Signs of division between Christians in countries ravaged by violence add further causes of conflict on the part of those who should instead be a leaven of peace. How many important things unite us! If we really believe in the abundantly free working of the Holy Spirit, we can learn so much from one another! It is not just about being better informed about others, but rather about reaping what the Spirit has sown in them, which is also meant to be a gift for us. To give but one example, in the dialogue with our Orthodox brothers and sisters, we Catholics have the opportunity to learn more about the meaning of episcopal collegiality and their experience of synodality. Through an exchange of gifts, the Spirit can lead us ever more fully into truth and goodness.

Relations with Judaism

247. We hold the Jewish people in special regard because their covenant with God has never been revoked, for "the gifts and the call of God are irrevocable" (Rom 11:29). The Church, which shares with Jews an important part of the sacred Scriptures, looks upon the people of the covenant and their faith as one of the sacred roots of her own Christian identity (cf. Rom 11:16–18). As Christians, we cannot consider Judaism as a foreign religion; nor do we include the Jews among those called to turn from idols and to serve the true God (cf. 1 Thes 1:9). With them, we believe in the one God who acts in history, and with them we accept his revealed word.

248. Dialogue and friendship with the children of Israel are part of the life of Jesus' disciples. The friendship which has grown between us makes us bitterly and sincerely regret the terrible persecutions which they have endured, and continue to endure, especially those that have involved Christians.

249. God continues to work among the people of the Old Covenant and to bring forth treasures of wisdom which flow from their encounter with his word. For this reason, the Church also is enriched when she receives the values of Judaism. While it is true that certain Christian beliefs are unacceptable to Judaism, and that the Church cannot refrain from proclaiming Jesus as Lord and Messiah, there exists as well a rich complementarity which allows us to read the texts of the Hebrew Scriptures together and to help one another to mine the riches of God's word. We can also share many ethical convictions and a common concern for justice and the development of peoples.

Interreligious dialogue

250. An attitude of openness in truth and in love must characterize the dialogue with the followers of non-Christian religions, in spite of various obstacles and difficulties, especially forms of fundamentalism on both sides. Interreligious dialogue is a necessary condition for peace in the world, and so it is a duty for Christians as well as other religious communities. This dialogue is in first place a conversation about human existence or simply, as the bishops of India have put it, a matter of "being open to them, sharing their joys and sorrows."[194] In this way we learn to accept others and their different ways of living, thinking, and speaking. We can then join one another in taking up the duty of serving justice and peace, which should become a basic principle of all our exchanges. A dialogue which seeks social peace and justice is in itself, beyond all merely practical considerations, an ethical commitment which brings about a new social situation. Efforts made in dealing with a specific theme can become a process in which, by mutual listening, both parts can be purified and enriched. These efforts, therefore, can also express love for truth.

251. In this dialogue, ever friendly and sincere, attention must always be paid to the essential bond between dialogue and proclamation, which leads the Church to maintain and intensify her relationship with non-Christians.[195] A facile syncretism would ultimately be a totalitarian gesture on the part of those who would ignore greater values of which

they are not the masters. True openness involves remaining steadfast in one's deepest convictions, clear and joyful in one's own identity, while at the same time being "open to understanding those of the other party" and "knowing that dialogue can enrich each side."[196] What is not helpful is a diplomatic openness which says "yes" to everything in order to avoid problems, for this would be a way of deceiving others and denying them the good which we have been given to share generously with others. Evangelization and interreligious dialogue, far from being opposed, mutually support and nourish one another.[197]

252. Our relationship with the followers of Islam has taken on great importance, since they are now significantly present in many traditionally Christian countries, where they can freely worship and become fully a part of society. We must never forget that they "profess to hold the faith of Abraham, and together with us they adore the one, merciful God, who will judge humanity on the last day."[198] The sacred writings of Islam have retained some Christian teachings; Jesus and Mary receive profound veneration and it is admirable to see how Muslims both young and old, men and women, make time for daily prayer and faithfully take part in religious services. Many of them also have a deep conviction that their life, in its entirety, is from God and for God. They also acknowledge the need to respond to God with an ethical commitment and with mercy toward those most in need.

253. In order to sustain dialogue with Islam, suitable training is essential for all involved, not only so that they can be solidly and joyfully grounded in their own identity, but so that they can also acknowledge the values of others, appreciate the concerns underlying their demands and shed light on shared beliefs. We Christians should embrace with affection and respect Muslim immigrants to our countries in the same way that we hope and ask to be received and respected in countries of Islamic tradition. I ask and I humbly entreat those countries to grant Christians freedom to worship and to practice their faith, in light of the freedom which followers of Islam enjoy in Western countries! Faced with disconcerting episodes of violent fundamentalism, our respect for true followers of Islam should lead us to avoid hateful generalizations,

for authentic Islam and the proper reading of the Koran are opposed to every form of violence.

254. Non-Christians, by God's gracious initiative, when they are faithful to their own consciences, can live "justified by the grace of God,"[199] and thus be "associated to the paschal mystery of Jesus Christ."[200] But due to the sacramental dimension of sanctifying grace, God's working in them tends to produce signs and rites, sacred expressions which in turn bring others to a communitarian experience of journeying toward God.[201] While these lack the meaning and efficacy of the sacraments instituted by Christ, they can be channels which the Holy Spirit raises up in order to liberate non-Christians from atheistic immanentism or from purely individual religious experiences. The same Spirit everywhere brings forth various forms of practical wisdom which help people to bear suffering and to live in greater peace and harmony. As Christians, we can also benefit from these treasures built up over many centuries, which can help us better to live our own beliefs.

Social dialogue in a context of religious freedom

255. The Synod Fathers spoke of the importance of respect for religious freedom, viewed as a fundamental human right.[202] This includes "the freedom to choose the religion which one judges to be true and to manifest one's beliefs in public."[203] A healthy pluralism, one which genuinely respects differences and values them as such, does not entail privatizing religions in an attempt to reduce them to the quiet obscurity of the individual's conscience or to relegate them to the enclosed precincts of churches, synagogues, or mosques. This would represent, in effect, a new form of discrimination and authoritarianism. The respect due to the agnostic or non-believing minority should not be arbitrarily imposed in a way that silences the convictions of the believing majority or ignores the wealth of religious traditions. In the long run, this would feed resentment rather than tolerance and peace.

256. When considering the effect of religion on public life, one must distinguish the different ways in which it is practiced. Intellectuals and serious journalists frequently descend to crude and superficial

generalizations in speaking of the shortcomings of religion, and often prove incapable of realizing that not all believers—or religious leaders—are the same. Some politicians take advantage of this confusion to justify acts of discrimination. At other times, contempt is shown for writings which reflect religious convictions, overlooking the fact that religious classics can prove meaningful in every age; they have an enduring power to open new horizons, to stimulate thought, to expand the mind and the heart. This contempt is due to the myopia of a certain rationalism. Is it reasonable and enlightened to dismiss certain writings simply because they arose in a context of religious belief? These writings include principles which are profoundly humanistic and, albeit tinged with religious symbols and teachings, they have a certain value for reason.

257. As believers, we also feel close to those who do not consider themselves part of any religious tradition, yet sincerely seek the truth, goodness, and beauty which we believe have their highest expression and source in God. We consider them as precious allies in the commitment to defending human dignity, in building peaceful coexistence between peoples, and in protecting creation. A special place of encounter is offered by new Areopagi such as the Court of the Gentiles, where "believers and non-believers are able to engage in dialogue about fundamental issues of ethics, art and science, and about the search for transcendence."[204] This too is a path to peace in our troubled world.

258. Starting from certain social issues of great importance for the future of humanity, I have tried to make explicit once again the inescapable social dimension of the Gospel message and to encourage all Christians to demonstrate it by their words, attitudes, and deeds.

CHAPTER FIVE

SPIRIT-FILLED EVANGELIZERS

259. Spirit-filled evangelizers means evangelizers fearlessly open to the working of the Holy Spirit. At Pentecost, the Spirit made the apostles go forth from themselves and turned them into heralds of God's wondrous deeds, capable of speaking to each person in his or her own language. The Holy Spirit also grants the courage to proclaim the newness of the Gospel with boldness (*parrhesía*) in every time and place, even when it meets with opposition. Let us call upon him today, firmly rooted in prayer, for without prayer all our activity risks being fruitless and our message empty. Jesus wants evangelizers who proclaim the good news not only with words, but above all by a life transfigured by God's presence.

260. In this final chapter, I do not intend to offer a synthesis of Christian spirituality, or to explore great themes like prayer, Eucharistic adoration, or the liturgical celebration of the faith. For all these we already have valuable texts of the magisterium and celebrated writings by great authors. I do not claim to replace or improve upon these treasures. I simply wish to offer some thoughts about the spirit of the new evangelization.

261. Whenever we say that something is "spirited," it usually refers to some interior impulse which encourages, motivates, nourishes, and gives meaning to our individual and communal activity. Spirit-filled evangelization is not the same as a set of tasks dutifully carried out despite one's own personal inclinations and wishes. How I long to find the right words to stir up enthusiasm for a new chapter of evangelization full of fervor, joy, generosity, courage, boundless love, and attraction! Yet I realize that no words of encouragement will be enough unless the fire of the Holy Spirit burns in our hearts. A spirit-filled evangelization is one guided by the Holy Spirit, for he is the soul of the Church called to proclaim the Gospel. Before offering some spiritual motivations and suggestions, I once more invoke the Holy Spirit. I implore him to come and renew the Church, to stir and impel her to go forth boldly to evangelize all peoples.

I. Reasons for a renewed missionary impulse

262. Spirit-filled evangelizers are evangelizers who pray and work. Mystical notions without a solid social and missionary outreach are of no help to evangelization, nor are dissertations or social or pastoral practices which lack a spirituality which can change hearts. These unilateral and incomplete proposals only reach a few groups and prove incapable of radiating beyond them because they curtail the Gospel. What is needed is the ability to cultivate an interior space which can give a Christian meaning to commitment and activity.[205] Without prolonged moments of adoration, of prayerful encounter with the word, of sincere conversation with the Lord, our work easily becomes meaningless; we lose energy as a result of weariness and difficulties, and our fervor dies out. The Church urgently needs the deep breath of prayer, and to my great joy groups devoted to prayer and intercession, the prayerful reading of God's word, and the perpetual adoration of the Eucharist are growing at every level of ecclesial life. Even so, "we must reject the temptation to offer a privatized and individualistic spirituality which ill accords with the demands of charity, to say nothing of the implications of the incarnation."[206] There is always the risk that some moments of prayer can become an excuse for not offering one's life in mission; a privatized lifestyle can lead Christians to take refuge in some false forms of spirituality.

263. We do well to keep in mind the early Christians and our many brothers and sisters throughout history who were filled with joy, unflagging courage, and zeal in proclaiming the Gospel. Some people nowadays console themselves by saying that things are not as easy as they used to be, yet we know that the Roman Empire was not conducive to the Gospel message, the struggle for justice, or the defense of human dignity. Every period of history is marked by the presence of human weakness, self-absorption, complacency, and selfishness, to say nothing of the concupiscence which preys upon us all. These things are ever present under one guise or another; they are due to our human limits rather than particular situations. Let us not say, then, that things are harder today; they are simply different. But let us learn also from the saints who have gone before us, who confronted the difficulties of their own day. So I propose

that we pause to rediscover some of the reasons which can help us to imitate them today.[207]

Personal encounter with the saving love of Jesus

264. The primary reason for evangelizing is the love of Jesus which we have received, the experience of salvation which urges us to ever greater love of him. What kind of love would not feel the need to speak of the beloved, to point him out, to make him known? If we do not feel an intense desire to share this love, we need to pray insistently that he will once more touch our hearts. We need to implore his grace daily, asking him to open our cold hearts and shake up our lukewarm and superficial existence. Standing before him with open hearts, letting him look at us, we see that gaze of love which Nathaniel glimpsed on the day when Jesus said to him: "I saw you under the fig tree" (Jn 1:48). How good it is to stand before a crucifix, or on our knees before the Blessed Sacrament, and simply to be in his presence! How much good it does us when he once more touches our lives and impels us to share his new life! What then happens is that "we speak of what we have seen and heard" (1 Jn 1:3). The best incentive for sharing the Gospel comes from contemplating it with love, lingering over its pages and reading it with the heart. If we approach it in this way, its beauty will amaze and constantly excite us. But if this is to come about, we need to recover a contemplative spirit which can help us to realize ever anew that we have been entrusted with a treasure which makes us more human and helps us to lead a new life. There is nothing more precious which we can give to others.

265. Jesus' whole life, his way of dealing with the poor, his actions, his integrity, his simple daily acts of generosity, and finally his complete self-giving, is precious and reveals the mystery of his divine life. Whenever we encounter this anew, we become convinced that it is exactly what others need, even though they may not recognize it: "What therefore you worship as unknown, this I proclaim to you" (Acts 17:23). Sometimes we lose our enthusiasm for mission because we forget that the Gospel responds to our deepest needs, since we were created for what the Gospel offers us: friendship with Jesus and love of our brothers and

sisters. If we succeed in expressing adequately and with beauty the essential content of the Gospel, surely this message will speak to the deepest yearnings of people's hearts: "The missionary is convinced that, through the working of the Spirit, there already exists in individuals and peoples an expectation, even if an unconscious one, of knowing the truth about God, about man, and about how we are to be set free from sin and death. The missionary's enthusiasm in proclaiming Christ comes from the conviction that he is responding to that expectation."[208] Enthusiasm for evangelization is based on this conviction. We have a treasure of life and love which cannot deceive, and a message which cannot mislead or disappoint. It penetrates to the depths of our hearts, sustaining and ennobling us. It is a truth which is never out of date because it reaches that part of us which nothing else can reach. Our infinite sadness can only be cured by an infinite love.

266. But this conviction has to be sustained by our own constantly renewed experience of savoring Christ's friendship and his message. It is impossible to persevere in a fervent evangelization unless we are convinced from personal experience that it is not the same thing to have known Jesus as not to have known him, not the same thing to walk with him as to walk blindly, not the same thing to hear his word as not to know it, and not the same thing to contemplate him, to worship him, to find our peace in him, as not to. It is not the same thing to try to build the world with his Gospel as to try to do so by our own lights. We know well that with Jesus life becomes richer and that with him it is easier to find meaning in everything. This is why we evangelize. A true missionary, who never ceases to be a disciple, knows that Jesus walks with him, speaks to him, breathes with him, works with him. He senses Jesus alive with him in the midst of the missionary enterprise. Unless we see him present at the heart of our missionary commitment, our enthusiasm soon wanes and we are no longer sure of what it is that we are handing on; we lack vigor and passion. A person who is not convinced, enthusiastic, certain, and in love, will convince nobody.

267. In union with Jesus, we seek what he seeks and we love what he loves. In the end, what we are seeking is the glory of the Father; we live

and act "for the praise of his glorious grace" (Eph 1:6). If we wish to commit ourselves fully and perseveringly, we need to leave behind every other motivation. This is our definitive, deepest, and greatest motivation, the ultimate reason and meaning behind all we do: the glory of the Father which Jesus sought at every moment of his life. As the Son, he rejoices eternally to be "close to the Father's heart" (Jn 1:18). If we are missionaries, it is primarily because Jesus told us that "by this my Father is glorified, that you bear much fruit" (Jn 15:8). Beyond all our own preferences and interests, our knowledge and motivations, we evangelize for the greater glory of the Father who loves us.

The spiritual savor of being a people

268. The word of God also invites us to recognize that we are a people: "Once you were no people but now you are God's people" (1 Pt 2:10). To be evangelizers of souls, we need to develop a spiritual taste for being close to people's lives and to discover that this is itself a source of greater joy. Mission is at once a passion for Jesus and a passion for his people. When we stand before Jesus crucified, we see the depth of his love which exalts and sustains us, but at the same time, unless we are blind, we begin to realize that Jesus' gaze, burning with love, expands to embrace all his people. We realize once more that he wants to make use of us to draw closer to his beloved people. He takes us from the midst of his people and he sends us to his people; without this sense of belonging we cannot understand our deepest identity.

269. Jesus himself is the model of this method of evangelization which brings us to the very heart of his people. How good it is for us to contemplate the closeness which he shows to everyone! If he speaks to someone, he looks into their eyes with deep love and concern: "Jesus, looking upon him, loved him" (Mk 10:21). We see how accessible he is, as he draws near the blind man (cf. Mk 10:46–52) and eats and drinks with sinners (cf. Mk 2:16) without worrying about being thought a glutton and a drunkard himself (cf. Mt 11:19). We see his sensitivity in allowing a sinful woman to anoint his feet (cf. Lk 7:36–50) and in receiving Nicodemus by night (cf. Jn 3:1–15). Jesus' sacrifice on the cross is nothing else than the

culmination of the way he lived his entire life. Moved by his example, we want to enter fully into the fabric of society, sharing the lives of all, listening to their concerns, helping them materially and spiritually in their needs, rejoicing with those who rejoice, weeping with those who weep; arm in arm with others, we are committed to building a new world. But we do so not from a sense of obligation, not as a burdensome duty, but as the result of a personal decision which brings us joy and gives meaning to our lives.

270. Sometimes we are tempted to be that kind of Christian who keeps the Lord's wounds at arm's length. Yet Jesus wants us to touch human misery, to touch the suffering flesh of others. He hopes that we will stop looking for those personal or communal niches which shelter us from the maelstrom of human misfortune and instead enter into the reality of other people's lives and know the power of tenderness. Whenever we do so, our lives become wonderfully complicated and we experience intensely what it is to be a people, to be part of a people.

271. It is true that in our dealings with the world, we are told to give reasons for our hope, but not as an enemy who critiques and condemns. We are told quite clearly: "do so with gentleness and reverence" (1 Pt 3:15) and "if possible, so far as it depends upon you, live peaceably with all" (Rom 12:18). We are also told to overcome "evil with good" (Rom 12:21) and to "work for the good of all" (Gal 6:10). Far from trying to appear better than others, we should "in humility count others better" than ourselves (Phil 2:3). The Lord's apostles themselves enjoyed "favor with all the people" (Acts 2:47; 4:21, 33; 5:13). Clearly Jesus does not want us to be grandees who look down upon others, but men and women of the people. This is not an idea of the Pope, or one pastoral option among others; they are injunctions contained in the word of God which are so clear, direct, and convincing that they need no interpretations which might diminish their power to challenge us. Let us live them *sine glossa*, without commentaries. By so doing we will know the missionary joy of sharing life with God's faithful people as we strive to light a fire in the heart of the world.

272. Loving others is a spiritual force drawing us to union with God; indeed, one who does not love others "walks in the darkness" (1 Jn 2:11), "remains in death" (1 Jn 3:14), and "does not know God" (1 Jn 4:8). Benedict XVI has said that "closing our eyes to our neighbor also blinds us to God,"[209] and that love is, in the end, the *only* light which "can always illuminate a world grown dim and give us the courage needed to keep living and working."[210] When we live out a spirituality of drawing nearer to others and seeking their welfare, our hearts are opened wide to the Lord's greatest and most beautiful gifts. Whenever we encounter another person in love, we learn something new about God. Whenever our eyes are opened to acknowledge the other, we grow in the light of faith and knowledge of God. If we want to advance in the spiritual life, then, we must constantly be missionaries. The work of evangelization enriches the mind and the heart, it opens up spiritual horizons, it makes us more and more sensitive to the workings of the Holy Spirit, and it takes us beyond our limited spiritual constructs. A committed missionary knows the joy of being a spring which spills over and refreshes others. Only the person who feels happiness in seeking the good of others, in desiring their happiness, can be a missionary. This openness of the heart is a source of joy, since "it is more blessed to give than to receive" (Acts 20:35). We do not live better when we flee, hide, refuse to share, stop giving, and lock ourselves up in our own comforts. Such a life is nothing less than slow suicide.

273. My mission of being in the heart of the people is not just a part of my life or a badge I can take off; it is not an "extra" or just another moment in life. Instead, it is something I cannot uproot from my being without destroying my very self. I am a mission on this earth; that is the reason why I am here in this world. We have to regard ourselves as sealed, even branded, by this mission of bringing light, blessing, enlivening, raising up, healing, and freeing. All around us we begin to see nurses with soul, teachers with soul, politicians with soul, people who have chosen deep down to be with others and for others. But once we separate our work from our private lives, everything turns gray and we will always be seeking recognition or asserting our needs. We stop being a people.

274. If we are to share our lives with others and generously give of ourselves, we also have to realize that every person is worthy of our giving. Not for their physical appearance, their abilities, their language, their way of thinking, or for any satisfaction that we might receive, but rather because they are God's handiwork, his creation. God created that person in his image, and he or she reflects something of God's glory. Every human being is the object of God's infinite tenderness, and he himself is present in their lives. Jesus offered his precious blood on the cross for that person. Appearances notwithstanding, every person is immensely holy and deserves our love. Consequently, if I can help at least one person to have a better life, that already justifies the offering of my life. It is a wonderful thing to be God's faithful people. We achieve fulfillment when we break down walls and our heart is filled with faces and names!

The mysterious working of the risen Christ and his Spirit

275. In the second chapter, we reflected on that lack of deep spirituality which turns into pessimism, fatalism, and mistrust. Some people do not commit themselves to mission because they think that nothing will change and that it is useless to make the effort. They think: "Why should I deny myself my comforts and pleasures if I won't see any significant result?" This attitude makes it impossible to be a missionary. It is only a malicious excuse for remaining caught up in comfort, laziness, vague dissatisfaction, and empty selfishness. It is a self-destructive attitude, for "man cannot live without hope: life would become meaningless and unbearable."[211] If we think that things are not going to change, we need to recall that Jesus Christ has triumphed over sin and death and is now almighty. Jesus Christ truly lives. Put another way, "if Christ has not been raised, then our preaching is in vain" (1 Cor 15:14). The Gospel tells us that when the first disciples went forth to preach, "the Lord worked with them and confirmed the message" (Mk 16:20). The same thing happens today. We are invited to discover this, to experience it. Christ, risen and glorified, is the wellspring of our hope, and he will not deprive us of the help we need to carry out the mission which he has entrusted to us.

276. Christ's resurrection is not an event of the past; it contains a vital power which has permeated this world. Where all seems to be dead, signs of the resurrection suddenly spring up. It is an irresistible force. Often it seems that God does not exist: all around us we see persistent injustice, evil, indifference, and cruelty. But it is also true that in the midst of darkness something new always springs to life and sooner or later produces fruit. On razed land life breaks through, stubbornly yet invincibly. However dark things are, goodness always re-emerges and spreads. Each day in our world beauty is born anew, it rises transformed through the storms of history. Values always tend to reappear under new guises, and human beings have arisen time after time from situations that seemed doomed. Such is the power of the resurrection, and all who evangelize are instruments of that power.

277. At the same time, new difficulties are constantly surfacing: experiences of failure and the human weaknesses which bring so much pain. We all know from experience that sometimes a task does not bring the satisfaction we seek, results are few and changes are slow, and we are tempted to grow weary. Yet lowering our arms momentarily out of weariness is not the same as lowering them for good, overcome by chronic discontent and by a listlessness that parches the soul. It also happens that our hearts can tire of the struggle because in the end we are caught up in ourselves, in a careerism which thirsts for recognition, applause, rewards, and status. In this case we do not lower our arms, but we no longer grasp what we seek; the resurrection is not there. In cases like these, the Gospel, the most beautiful message that this world can offer, is buried under a pile of excuses.

278. Faith also means believing in God, believing that he truly loves us, that he is alive, that he is mysteriously capable of intervening, that he does not abandon us and that he brings good out of evil by his power and his infinite creativity. It means believing that he marches triumphantly in history with those who "are called and chosen and faithful" (Rv 17:14). Let us believe the Gospel when it tells us that the kingdom of God is already present in this world and is growing, here and there, and in different ways: like the small seed which grows into a great tree

(cf. Mt 13:31–32), like the measure of leaven that makes the dough rise (cf. Mt 13:33), and like the good seed that grows amid the weeds (cf. Mt 13, 24–30) and can always pleasantly surprise us. The kingdom is here, it returns, it struggles to flourish anew. Christ's resurrection everywhere calls forth seeds of that new world; even if they are cut back, they grow again, for the resurrection is already secretly woven into the fabric of this history, for Jesus did not rise in vain. May we never remain on the sidelines of this march of living hope!

279. Because we do not always see these seeds growing, we need an interior certainty, a conviction that God is able to act in every situation, even amid apparent setbacks: "We have this treasure in earthen vessels" (2 Cor 4:7). This certainty is often called "a sense of mystery." It involves knowing with certitude that all those who entrust themselves to God in love will bear good fruit (cf. Jn 15:5). This fruitfulness is often invisible, elusive, and unquantifiable. We can know quite well that our lives will be fruitful, without claiming to know how, or where, or when. We may be sure that none of our acts of love will be lost, nor any of our acts of sincere concern for others. No single act of love for God will be lost, no generous effort is meaningless, no painful endurance is wasted. All of these encircle our world like a vital force. Sometimes it seems that our work is fruitless, but mission is not like a business transaction or investment, or even a humanitarian activity. It is not a show where we count how many people come as a result of our publicity; it is something much deeper, which escapes all measurement. It may be that the Lord uses our sacrifices to shower blessings in another part of the world which we will never visit. The Holy Spirit works as he wills, when he wills, and where he wills; we entrust ourselves without pretending to see striking results. We know only that our commitment is necessary. Let us learn to rest in the tenderness of the arms of the Father amid our creative and generous commitment. Let us keep marching forward; let us give him everything, allowing him to make our efforts bear fruit in his good time.

280. Keeping our missionary fervor alive calls for firm trust in the Holy Spirit, for it is he who "helps us in our weakness" (Rom 8:26). But this generous trust has to be nourished, and so we need to invoke the Spirit

constantly. He can heal whatever causes us to flag in the missionary endeavor. It is true that this trust in the unseen can cause us to feel disoriented: it is like being plunged into the deep and not knowing what we will find. I myself have frequently experienced this. Yet there is no greater freedom than that of allowing oneself to be guided by the Holy Spirit, renouncing the attempt to plan and control everything to the last detail, and instead letting him enlighten, guide, and direct us, leading us wherever he wills. The Holy Spirit knows well what is needed in every time and place. This is what it means to be mysteriously fruitful!

The missionary power of intercessory prayer

281. One form of prayer moves us particularly to take up the task of evangelization and to seek the good of others: it is the prayer of intercession. Let us peer for a moment into the heart of Saint Paul, to see what his prayer was like. It was full of people: ". . . I constantly pray with you in every one of my prayers for all of you . . . because I hold you in my heart" (Phil 1:4, 7). Here we see that intercessory prayer does not divert us from true contemplation, since authentic contemplation always has a place for others.

282. This attitude becomes a prayer of gratitude to God for others. "First, I thank my God through Jesus Christ for all of you" (Rom 1:8). It is constant thankfulness: "I give thanks to God always for you because of the grace of God which was given you in Christ Jesus" (1 Cor 1:4); "I thank my God in all my remembrance of you" (Phil 1:3). Far from being suspicious, negative, and despairing, it is a spiritual gaze born of deep faith which acknowledges what God is doing in the lives of others. At the same time, it is the gratitude which flows from a heart attentive to others. When evangelizers rise from prayer, their hearts are more open; freed of self-absorption, they are desirous of doing good and sharing their lives with others.

283. The great men and women of God were great intercessors. Intercession is like a "leaven" in the heart of the Trinity. It is a way of penetrating the Father's heart and discovering new dimensions which can shed light on concrete situations and change them. We can say that God's heart is

touched by our intercession, yet in reality he is always there first. What our intercession achieves is that his power, his love, and his faithfulness are shown ever more clearly in the midst of the people.

II. Mary, mother of evangelization

284. With the Holy Spirit, Mary is always present in the midst of the people. She joined the disciples in praying for the coming of the Holy Spirit (Acts 1:14) and thus made possible the missionary outburst which took place at Pentecost. She is the Mother of the Church which evangelizes, and without her we could never truly understand the spirit of the new evangelization.

Jesus' gift to his people

285. On the cross, when Jesus endured in his own flesh the dramatic encounter of the sin of the world and God's mercy, he could feel at his feet the consoling presence of his mother and his friend. At that crucial moment, before fully accomplishing the work which his Father had entrusted to him, Jesus said to Mary: "Woman, here is your son." Then he said to his beloved friend: "Here is your mother" (Jn 19:26–27). These words of the dying Jesus are not chiefly the expression of his devotion and concern for his mother; rather, they are a revelatory formula which manifests the mystery of a special saving mission. Jesus left us his mother to be our mother. Only after doing so did Jesus know that "all was now finished" (Jn 19:28). At the foot of the cross, at the supreme hour of the new creation, Christ led us to Mary. He brought us to her because he did not want us to journey without a mother, and our people read in this maternal image all the mysteries of the Gospel. The Lord did not want to leave the Church without this icon of womanhood. Mary, who brought him into the world with great faith, also accompanies "the rest of her offspring, those who keep the commandments of God and bear testimony to Jesus" (Rv 12:17). The close connection between Mary, the Church, and each member of the faithful, based on the fact that each in his or her own way brings forth Christ, has been beautifully expressed by Blessed Isaac of Stella: "In the inspired Scriptures, what is said in a

universal sense of the virgin mother, the Church, is understood in an individual sense of the Virgin Mary. . . . In a way, every Christian is also believed to be a bride of God's word, a mother of Christ, his daughter and sister, at once virginal and fruitful. . . . Christ dwelt for nine months in the tabernacle of Mary's womb. He dwells until the end of the ages in the tabernacle of the Church's faith. He will dwell forever in the knowledge and love of each faithful soul."[212]

286. Mary was able to turn a stable into a home for Jesus, with poor swaddling clothes and an abundance of love. She is the handmaid of the Father who sings his praises. She is the friend who is ever concerned that wine not be lacking in our lives. She is the woman whose heart was pierced by a sword and who understands all our pain. As mother of all, she is a sign of hope for peoples suffering the birth pangs of justice. She is the missionary who draws near to us and accompanies us throughout life, opening our hearts to faith by her maternal love. As a true mother, she walks at our side, she shares our struggles and she constantly surrounds us with God's love. Through her many titles, often linked to her shrines, Mary shares the history of each people which has received the Gospel and she becomes a part of their historic identity. Many Christian parents ask that their children be baptized in a Marian shrine, as a sign of their faith in her motherhood which brings forth new children for God. There, in these many shrines, we can see how Mary brings together her children who with great effort come as pilgrims to see her and to be seen by her. Here they find strength from God to bear the weariness and the suffering in their lives. As she did with Juan Diego, Mary offers them maternal comfort and love, and whispers in their ear: "Let your heart not be troubled. . . . Am I not here, who am your Mother?"[213]

Star of the new evangelization

287. We ask the Mother of the living Gospel to intercede that this invitation to a new phase of evangelization will be accepted by the entire ecclesial community. Mary is the woman of faith, who lives and advances in faith,[214] and "her exceptional pilgrimage of faith represents a constant point of reference for the Church."[215] Mary let herself be guided by the

Holy Spirit on a journey of faith toward a destiny of service and fruitfulness. Today we look to her and ask her to help us proclaim the message of salvation to all and to enable new disciples to become evangelizers in turn.[216] Along this journey of evangelization we will have our moments of aridity, darkness, and even fatigue. Mary herself experienced these things during the years of Jesus' childhood in Nazareth: "This is the beginning of the Gospel, the joyful good news. However, it is not difficult to see in that beginning a particular heaviness of heart, linked with a sort of night of faith—to use the words of Saint John of the Cross—a kind of 'veil' through which one has to draw near to the Invisible One and to live in intimacy with the mystery. And this is the way that Mary, for many years, lived in intimacy with the mystery of her Son, and went forward in her pilgrimage of faith."[217]

288. There is a Marian "style" to the Church's work of evangelization. Whenever we look to Mary, we come to believe once again in the revolutionary nature of love and tenderness. In her we see that humility and tenderness are not virtues of the weak but of the strong who need not treat others poorly in order to feel important themselves. Contemplating Mary, we realize that she who praised God for "bringing down the mighty from their thrones" and "sending the rich away empty" (Lk 1:52–53) is also the one who brings a homely warmth to our pursuit of justice. She is also the one who carefully keeps "all these things, pondering them in her heart" (Lk 2:19). Mary is able to recognize the traces of God's Spirit in events great and small. She constantly contemplates the mystery of God in our world, in human history, and in our daily lives. She is the woman of prayer and work in Nazareth, and she is also Our Lady of Help, who sets out from her town "with haste" (Lk 1:39) to be of service to others. This interplay of justice and tenderness, of contemplation and concern for others, is what makes the ecclesial community look to Mary as a model of evangelization. We implore her maternal intercession that the Church may become a home for many peoples, a mother for all peoples, and that the way may be opened to the birth of a new world. It is the Risen Christ who tells us, with a power that fills us with confidence and unshakeable hope: "Behold, I make all things new"

(Rv 21:5). With Mary we advance confidently toward the fulfillment of this promise, and to her we pray:

> Mary, Virgin and Mother,
> you who, moved by the Holy Spirit,
> welcomed the word of life
> in the depths of your humble faith:
> as you gave yourself completely to the Eternal One,
> help us to say our own "yes"
> to the urgent call, as pressing as ever,
> to proclaim the good news of Jesus.
>
> Filled with Christ's presence,
> you brought joy to John the Baptist,
> making him exult in the womb of his mother.
> Brimming over with joy,
> you sang of the great things done by God.
> Standing at the foot of the cross
> with unyielding faith,
> you received the joyful comfort of the resurrection,
> and joined the disciples in awaiting the Spirit
> so that the evangelizing Church might be born.
>
> Obtain for us now a new ardor born of the resurrection,
> that we may bring to all the Gospel of life
> which triumphs over death.
> Give us a holy courage to seek new paths,
> that the gift of unfading beauty
> may reach every man and woman.
>
> Virgin of listening and contemplation,
> Mother of love, Bride of the eternal wedding feast,
> pray for the Church, whose pure icon you are,
> that she may never be closed in on herself
> or lose her passion for establishing God's kingdom.

Star of the new evangelization,
help us to bear radiant witness to communion,
service, ardent and generous faith,
justice and love of the poor,
that the joy of the Gospel
may reach to the ends of the earth,
illuminating even the fringes of our world.

Mother of the living Gospel,
wellspring of happiness for God's little ones,
pray for us.
Amen. Alleluia!

Given in Rome, at Saint Peter's, on 24 November, the solemnity of Our Lord Jesus Christ, King of the Universe, and the conclusion of the Year of Faith, in the year 2013, the first of my Pontificate.

FRANCISCUS

Notes

1. Paul VI, Apostolic Exhortation *Gaudete in Domino* (9 May 1975), 22: AAS 67 (1975), 297.

2. Ibid., 8: AAS 67 (1975), 292.

3. Encyclical Letter *Deus Caritas Est* (25 December 2005), 1: AAS 98 (2006), 217.

4. Fifth General Conference of the Latin American and Caribbean Bishops, *Aparecida Document*, 29 June 2007, 360.

5. Ibid.

6. Paul VI, Apostolic Exhortation *Evangelii Nuntiandi* (8 December 1975), 80: AAS 68 (1976), 75.

7. *Spiritual Canticle*, 36, 10.

8. *Adversus Haereses*, IV, c. 34, n. 1: PG 7, pars prior, 1083: "*Omnem novitatem attulit, semetipsum afferens.*"

9. Paul VI, Apostolic Exhortation *Evangelii Nuntiandi* (8 December 1975), 7: AAS 68 (1976), 9.

10. Cf. *Propositio* 7.

11. Benedict XVI, Homily at Mass for the Conclusion of the Synod of Bishops (28 October 2012): AAS 104 (2012), 890.

12. Ibid.

13. Benedict XVI, Homily at Mass for the Opening of the Fifth General Conference of the Latin American and Caribbean Bishops (13 May 2007), Aparecida, Brazil: AAS 99 (2007), 437.

14. Encyclical Letter *Redemptoris Missio* (7 December 1990), 34: AAS 83 (1991), 280.

15. Ibid., 40: AAS 83 (1991), 287.

16. Ibid., 86: AAS 83 (1991), 333.

17. Fifth General Conference of the Latin American and Caribbean Bishops, *Aparecida Document*, 29 June 2007, 548.

18. Ibid., 370.

19. Cf. *Propositio* 1.

20. John Paul II, Post-Synodal Apostolic Exhortation *Christifideles Laici* (30 December 1988), 32: AAS 81 (1989), 451.

21. Fifth General Conference of the Latin American and Caribbean Bishops, *Aparecida Document*, 29 June 2007, 201.

22. Ibid., 551.

23. Paul VI, Encyclical Letter *Ecclesiam Suam* (6 August 1964), 9, 10, 11: AAS 56 (1964), 611–612.

24. Second Ecumenical Vatican Council, Decree on Ecumenism *Unitatis Redintegratio*, 6.

25. John Paul II, Post-Synodal Apostolic Exhortation *Ecclesia in Oceania* (22 November 2001), 19: AAS 94 (2002), 390.

26. John Paul II, Post-Synodal Apostolic Exhortation *Christifideles Laici* (30 September 1988), 26: AAS 81 (1989), 438.

27. Cf. *Propositio* 26.

28. Cf. *Propositio* 44.

29. Cf. *Propositio* 26.

30. Cf. *Propositio* 41.

31. Second Vatican Ecumenical Council, Decree on the Pastoral Office of Bishops *Christus Dominus*, 11.

32. Cf. Benedict XVI, Address for the Fortieth Anniversary of the Decree *Ad Gentes* (11 March 2006): AAS 98 (2006), 337.

33. Cf. *Propositio* 42.

34. Cf. Canons 460–468; 492–502; 511–514; 536–537.

35. Encyclical Letter *Ut Unum Sint* (25 May 1995), 95: AAS 87 (1995), 977–978.

36. Second Vatican Ecumenical Council, Dogmatic Constitution on the Church *Lumen Gentium*, 23.

37. John Paul II, Motu Proprio *Apostolos Suos* (21 May 1998): AAS 90 (1998), 641–658.

38. Second Vatican Ecumenical Council, Decree on Ecumenism *Unitatis Redintegratio*, 11.

39. Cf. *S. Th.*, I–II, q. 66, a. 4–6.

40. *S. Th.*, I–II, q. 108, a. 1.

41. *S. Th.*, II–II, q. 30, a. 4: "We do not worship God with sacrifices and exterior gifts for him, but rather for us and for our neighbor. He has no need of our sacrifices, but he does ask that these be offered by us as devotion and for the benefit of our neighbor. For him, mercy, which overcomes the defects of our devotion and sacrifice, is the sacrifice which is most pleasing, because it is mercy which above all seeks the good of one's neighbor" (*S. Th.*, II–II, q. 30, a. 4, ad 1).

42. Second Vatican Ecumenical Council, Dogmatic Constitution on Divine Revelation *Dei Verbum*, 12.

43. Motu Proprio *Socialium Scientiarum* (1 January 1994): AAS 86 (1994), 209.

44. Saint Thomas Aquinas noted that the multiplicity and variety "were the intention of the first agent," who wished that "what each individual thing lacked in order to reflect the divine goodness would be made up for by other things," since the Creator's goodness "could not be fittingly reflected by just one creature" (*S. Th.*, I, q. 47, a. 1). Consequently, we need to grasp the variety of things in their multiple relationships (cf. *S. Th.*, I, q. 47, a. 2, ad 1; q. 47, a. 3). By analogy, we need to listen to and complement one another in our partial reception of reality and the Gospel.

45. John XXIII, *Address for the Opening of the Second Vatican Council* (11 October 1962): AAS 54 (1962), 792: "*Est enim aliud ipsum depositum fidei, seu veritates, quae veneranda doctrina nostra continentur, aliud modus, quo eaedem enuntiantur.*"

46. John Paul II, Encyclical Letter *Ut Unum Sint* (25 May 1995), 19: AAS 87 (1995), 933.

47. *S. Th.*, I–II, q. 107, a. 4.

48. Ibid.

49. No. 1735.

50. Cf. John Paul II, Post-Synodal Apostolic Exhortation *Familiaris Consortio* (22 November 1981), 34: AAS 74 (1982), 123.

51. Cf. Saint Ambrose, *De Sacramentis*, IV, 6, 28: PL 16, 464: "I must receive it always, so that it may always forgive my sins. If I sin continually, I must always have a remedy"; ID., op. cit., IV, 5, 24: PL 16, 463: "Those who ate manna died; those who eat this body will obtain the forgiveness of their sins"; Saint Cyril of Alexandria, *In Joh. Evang.*, IV, 2: PG 73, 584–585: "I examined myself and I found myself unworthy. To those who speak thus I say: when will you be worthy? When at last you present yourself before Christ? And if your sins prevent you from drawing nigh, and you never cease to fall—for, as the Psalm says, 'what man knows his faults?'—will you remain without partaking of the sanctification that gives life for eternity?"

52. Benedict XVI, *Address to the Brazilian Bishops in the Cathedral of São Paulo*, Brazil (11 May 2007), 3: AAS 99 (2007), 428.

53. John Paul II, Post-Synodal Apostolic Exhortation *Pastores Dabo Vobis* (25 March 1992), 10: AAS 84 (1992), 673.

54. Paul VI, Encyclical Letter *Ecclesiam Suam* (6 August 1964), 19: AAS 56 (1964), 609.

55. Saint John Chrysostom, *De Lazaro Concio*, II, 6: PG 48, 992D.

56. Cf. *Propositio* 13.

57. John Paul II, Apostolic Exhortation *Ecclesia in Africa* (14 September 1995), 52: AAS 88 (1996), 32–33; ID., Encyclical Letter *Sollicitudo Rei Socialis* (30 December 1987), 22: AAS 80 (1988), 539.

58. John Paul II, Apostolic Exhortation *Ecclesia in Asia* (6 November 1999), 7: AAS 92 (2000), 458.

59. United States Conference of Catholic Bishops, *Ministry to Persons with a Homosexual Inclination: Guidelines for Pastoral Care* (2006), 17.

60. Conférence Des Évêques De France, Conseil Famille et Société, *Élargir le mariage aux personnes de même sexe? Ouvrons le débat!* (28 September 2012).

61. Cf. *Propositio* 25.

62. Azione Cattolica Italiana, *Messaggio della XIV Assemblea Nazionale alla Chiesa ed al Paese* (8 May 2011).

63. J. Ratzinger, *The Current Situation of Faith and Theology*. Conference given at the Meeting of Presidents of Latin American Episcopal Commissions for the Doctrine of the Faith, Guadalajara, Mexico, 1996. Translation in *L'Osservatore Romano*, English Language Edition, 6 November 1996. Cf. Fifth General Conference of the Latin American and Caribbean Bishops, *Aparecida Document*, 29 June 2007, 12.

64. G. Bernanos, *Journal d'un curé de campagne*, Paris, 1974, 135.

65. *Address for the Opening of the Second Vatican Council* (11 October 1962): 4, 2–4: AAS 54 (1962), 789.

66. J. H. Newman, Letter of 26 January 1833, in *The Letters and Diaries of John Henry Newman*, vol. III, Oxford, 1979, 204.

67. Benedict XVI, Homily at Mass for the Opening of the Year of Faith (11 October 2012): AAS 104 (2012), 881.

68. Thomas à Kempis, *De Imitatione Christi*, Lib. I, IX, 5: "Dreaming of different places, and moving from one to another, has misled many."

69. We can benefit from the testimony of Saint Thérèse of Lisieux, who speaks of one particular Sister whom she found especially disagreeable, where an interior experience had a decisive impact: "One winter afternoon I was engaged as usual in my little task. It was cold and growing dark. . . . Suddenly I heard in the distance the harmonious sounds of a musical instrument. I began to imagine a well-lit room, draped in gold, and in it, elegantly dressed young ladies exchanging worldly compliments and courtesies. Then I looked at the poor sick woman whom I was attending. In place of a melody, I heard her occasional groans and sighs. . . . I cannot express what took place in my soul. All that I do know is that the Lord illumined it with the rays of truth which so surpassed the flickering glow of earthly revels, that I could scarcely believe my happiness" (Ms. C, 29v–30r, in *Oeuvres Complètes*, Paris, 1992, 274–275).

70. Cf. *Propositio* 8.

71. H. de Lubac, *Méditation sur l'Église*, Paris, 1968, 321.

72. Pontifical Council for Justice and Peace, *Compendium of the Social Doctrine of the Church*, 295.

73. John Paul II, Post-Synodal Apostolic Exhortation *Christifideles Laici* (30 December 1988), 51: AAS 81 (1989), 413.

74. Congregation for the Doctrine of the Faith, Declaration *Inter Insigniores* on the Question of the Admission of Women to the Ministerial Priesthood (15 October 1976): AAS 68 (1977), 115, cited in John Paul II, Post-Synodal Apostolic Exhortation *Christifideles Laici* (30 December 1988), note 190: AAS 81 (1989), 493.

75. John Paul II, Apostolic Letter *Mulieris Dignitatem* (15 August 1988), 27: AAS 80 (1988), 1718.

76. Cf. *Propositio* 51.

77. John Paul II, Post-Synodal Apostolic Exhortation *Ecclesia in Asia* (6 November 1999), 19: AAS 92 (2000), 478.

78. Ibid., 2: AAS 92 (2000), 451.

79. Cf. *Propositio* 4.

80. Cf. Second Vatican Ecumenical Council, Dogmatic Constitution on the Church *Lumen Gentium*, 1.

81. Meditation during the First General Congregation of the XIII Ordinary General Assembly of the Synod of Bishops (8 October 2012): AAS 104 (2012), 897.

82. Cf. *Propositio* 6; Second Vatican Ecumenical Council, Pastoral Constitution on the Church in the Modern World *Gaudium et Spes*, 22.

83. Cf. Second Vatican Ecumenical Council, Dogmatic Constitution on the Church *Lumen Gentium*, 9.

84. Cf. Third General Conference of the Latin American and Caribbean Bishops, *Puebla Document*, 23 March 1979, Nos. 386–387.

85. Cf. Second Vatican Ecumenical Council, Pastoral Constitution on the Church in the Modern World *Gaudium et Spes*, 36.

86. Ibid., 25.

87. Ibid., 53.

88. John Paul II, Apostolic Letter *Novo Millennio Ineunte* (6 January 2001), 40: AAS 93 (2001), 295.

89. Ibid.

90. John Paul II, Encyclical Letter *Redemptoris Missio* (7 December 1990), 52: AAS 83 (1991), 300; cf. Apostolic Exhortation *Catechesi Tradendae* (16 October 1979), 53: AAS 71 (1979), 1321.

91. John Paul II, Post-Synodal Apostolic Exhortation *Ecclesia in Oceania* (22 November 2001), 16: AAS 94 (2002), 383.

92. John Paul II, Post-Synodal Apostolic Exhortation *Ecclesia in Africa* (14 September 1995), 61: AAS 88 (1996), 39.

93. Saint Thomas Aquinas, *S. Th.*, I, q. 39, a. 8, cons. 2: "Without the Holy Spirit who is the bond of both, one cannot understand the connecting unity between the Father and the Son"; cf. I, q. 37, a. 1, ad 3.

94. John Paul II, Post-Synodal Apostolic Exhortation *Ecclesia in Oceania* (22 November 2001), 17: AAS 94 (2002), 385.

95. John Paul II, Post-Synodal Apostolic Exhortation *Ecclesia in Asia* (6 November 1999), 20: AAS 92 (2000), 478–482.

96. Cf. Second Vatican Ecumenical Council, Dogmatic Constitution on the Church *Lumen Gentium*, 12.

97. John Paul II, Encyclical Letter *Fides et Ratio* (14 September 1998), 71: AAS 91 (1999), 60.

98. Third General Conference of the Latin American and Caribbean Bishops, *Puebla Document*, 23 March 1979, 450; cf. Fifth General Conference of the Latin American and Caribbean Bishops, *Aparecida Document*, 29 June 2007, 264.

99. John Paul II, Post-Synodal Apostolic Exhortation *Ecclesia in Asia* (6 November 1999), 21: AAS 92 (2000), 482–484.

100. No. 48: AAS 68 (1976), 38.

101. Ibid.

102. *Opening Address of the Fifth General Conference of the Latin American and Caribbean Bishops* (13 May 2007), 1: AAS 90 (2007), 446.

103. Fifth General Conference of the Latin American and Caribbean Bishops, *Aparecida Document*, 29 June 2007, 262.

104. Ibid., 263.

105. Cf. Saint Thomas Aquinas, *S. Th.*, II–II, q. 2, a. 2.

106. Fifth General Conference of the Latin American and Caribbean Bishops, *Aparecida Document*, 29 June 2007, 264.

107. Ibid.

108. Cf. Second Vatican Ecumenical Council, Dogmatic Constitution on the Church *Lumen Gentium*, 12.

109. Cf. *Propositio* 17.

110. Cf. *Propositio* 30.

111. Cf. *Propositio* 27.

112. John Paul II, Apostolic Letter *Dies Domini* (31 May 1998), 41: AAS 90 (1998), 738–739.

113. Paul VI, Apostolic Exhortation *Evangelii Nuntiandi* (8 December 1975), 78: AAS 68 (1976), 71.

114. Ibid.

115. John Paul II, Post-Synodal Apostolic Exhortation *Pastores Dabo Vobis* (25 March 1992), 26: AAS 84 (1992), 698.

116. Ibid., 25: AAS 84 (1992), 696.

117. Saint Thomas Aquinas, *S. Th.*, II–II, q. 188, a. 6.

118. Paul VI, Apostolic Exhortation *Evangelii Nuntiandi* (8 December 1975), 76: AAS 68 (1976), 68.

119. Ibid., 75: AAS 68 (1976), 65.

120. Ibid., 63: AAS 68 (1976), 53.

121. Ibid., 43: AAS 68 (1976), 33.

122. Ibid.

123. John Paul II, Post-Synodal Apostolic Exhortation *Pastores Dabo Vobis* (25 March 1992), 10: AAS 84 (1992), 672.

124. Paul VI, Apostolic Exhortation *Evangelii Nuntiandi* (8 December 1975), 40: AAS 68 (1976), 31.

125. Ibid., 43: AAS 68 (1976), 33.

126. Cf. *Propositio* 9.

127. John Paul II, Post-Synodal Apostolic Exhortation *Pastores Dabo Vobis* (25 March 1992), 26: AAS 84 (1992), 698.

128. Cf. *Propositio* 38.

129. Cf. *Propositio* 20.

130. Cf. Second Vatican Ecumenical Council, Decree on the Means of Social Communication *Inter Mirifica*, 6.

131. Cf. *De Musica*, VI, 13, 38: PL 32, 1183–1184; *Confessiones*, IV, 13.20: PL 32, 701.

132. Benedict XVI, *Address for the Screening of the Documentary "Art and Faith"—Via Pulchritudinis* (25 October 2012): *L'Osservatore Romano* (27 October 2012), 7.

133. *S. Th.*, I–II, q. 65, a. 3, ad 2: *"propter aliquas dispositiones contrarias."*

134. John Paul II, Post-Synodal Apostolic Exhortation *Ecclesia in Asia* (6 November 1999), 20: AAS 92 (2000), 481.

135. Benedict XVI, Post-Synodal Apostolic Exhortation *Verbum Domini* (30 September 2010), 1: AAS 102 (2010), 682.

136. Cf. *Propositio* 11.

137. Cf. Second Vatican Ecumenical Council, Dogmatic Constitution on Divine Revelation *Dei Verbum*, 21–22.

138. Cf. Benedict XVI, Post-Synodal Apostolic Exhortation *Verbum Domini* (30 September 2010), 86–87: AAS 102 (2010), 757–760.

139. *Benedict XVI, Address during the First General Congregation of the Synod of Bishops* (8 October 2012): AAS 104 (2012), 896.

140. Paul VI, Post-Synodal Apostolic Exhortation *Evangelii Nuntiandi* (8 December 1975), 17: AAS 68 (1976), 17.

141. John Paul II, Message to the Handicapped, *Angelus* (16 November 1980): *Insegnamenti*, 3/2 (1980), 1232.

142. Pontifical Council for Justice and Peace, *Compendium of the Social Doctrine of the Church*, 52.

143. John Paul, *Catechesis* (24 April 1991): *Insegnamenti*, 14/1 (1991), 853.

144. Benedict XVI, Motu Proprio *Intima Ecclesiae Natura* (11 November 2012): AAS 104 (2012), 996.

145. Encyclical Letter *Populorum Progressio* (16 March 1967), 14: AAS 59 (1967), 264.

146. Paul VI, Apostolic Exhortation *Evangelii Nuntiandi* (8 December 1975), 29: AAS 68 (1976), 25.

147. Fifth General Conference of the Latin American and Caribbean Bishops, *Aparecida Document*, 29 June 2007, 380.

148. Pontifical Council for Justice and Peace, *Compendium of the Social Doctrine of the Church*, 9.

149. John Paul II, Post-Synodal Apostolic Exhortation *Ecclesia in America* (22 January 1999), 27: AAS 91 (1999), 762.

150. Benedict XVI, Encyclical Letter *Deus Caritas Est* (25 December 2005), 28: AAS 98 (2006), 239–240.

151. Pontifical Council for Justice and Peace, *Compendium of the Social Doctrine of the Church*, 12.

152. Apostolic Letter *Octogesima Advenien* (14 May 1971), 4: AAS 63 (1971), 403.

153. Congregation for the Doctrine of the Faith, Instruction *Libertatis Nuntius* (6 August 1984), XI, 1: AAS 76 (1984), 903.

154. Pontifical Council for Justice and Peace, *Compendium of the Social Doctrine of the Church*, 157.

155. Paul VI, Apostolic Letter *Octogesima Adveniens* (14 May 1971), 23: AAS 63 (1971), 418.

156. Paul VI, Encyclical Letter *Populorum Progressio* (26 March 1967), 65: AAS 59 (1967), 289.

157. Ibid., 15: AAS 59 (1967), 265.

158. Conferência Nacional Dos Bispos Do Brazil, *"Exigências evangélicas e éticas de superação da miséria e da fome"* (April 2002), Introduction, 2.

159. John XIII, Encyclical Letter *Mater et Magistra* (15 May 1961), 3: AAS 53 (1961), 402.

160. Saint Augustine, *De Catechizandis Rudibus*, I, XIX, 22: PL 40, 327.

161. Congregation for the Doctrine of the Faith, Instruction *Libertatis Nuntius* (6 August 1984), XI, 18: AAS 76 (1984), 907–908.

162. John Paul II, Encyclical Letter *Centesimus Annus* (1 May 1991), 41: AAS 83 (1991), 844–845.

163. John Paul II, Homily at Mass for the Evangelization of Peoples in Santo Domingo (11 October 1984), 5: AAS 77 (1985), 358.

164. John Paul II, Encyclical Letter *Sollicitudo Rei Socialis* (30 December 1987), 42: AAS 80 (1988), 572.

165. *Address at the Inaugural Session of the Fifth General Conference of the Latin American and Caribbean Bishops* (13 May 2007), 3: AAS 99 (2007), 450.

166. Saint Thomas Aquinas, *S. Th.*, II–II, q. 27, a. 2.

167. Ibid., I–II, q. 110, a. 1.

168. Ibid., I–II, q. 26, a. 3.

169. John Paul II, Apostolic Letter *Novo Millennio Ineunte* (6 January 2001), 50: AAS 93 (2001), 303.

170. Ibid.

171. Cf. *Propositio* 45.

172. Congregation for the Doctrine of the Faith, Instruction *Libertatis Nuntius* (6 August 1984), XI, 18: AAS 76 (1984), 908.

173. This implies a commitment to "eliminate the structural causes of global economic dysfunction": Benedict XVI, *Address to the Diplomatic Corps* (8 January 2007): AAS 99 (2007), 73.

174. Cf. Commission Sociale de L'épiscopat Français, *Réhabiliter la politique* (17 February 1999); cf. Pius XI, Message of 18 December 1927.

175. Benedict XVI, Encyclical Letter *Caritas in Veritate* (29 June 2009), 2: AAS 101 (2009), 642.

176. John Paul II, Post-Synodal Apostolic Exhortation *Christifideles Laici* (30 December 1988), 37: AAS 81 (1989), 461.

177. Cf. *Propositio* 56.

178. Catholic Bishops Conference of the Philippines, Pastoral Letter *What Is Happening to Our Beautiful Land?* (29 January 1988).

179. Paul VI, Encyclical Letter *Populorum Progressio* (26 March 1967), 76: AAS 59 (1967), 294–295.

180. United States Conference of Catholic Bishops, Pastoral Letter *Forming Conscience for Faithful Citizenship* (November 2007), 13.

181. Pontifical Council for Justice and Peace, *Compendium of the Social Doctrine of the Church*, 161.

182. *Das Ende der Neuzeit*, Würzburg, 1965, 30–31.

183. Cf. I. Quiles, S.J., *Filosofía de la educación personalista*, Buenos Aires, 1981, 46–53.

184. Comité Permanent De La Conférence Épiscopale Nationale Du Congo, *Message sur la situation sécuritaire dans le pays* (5 December 2012), 11.

185. Cf. Plato, *Gorgias*, 465.

186. Benedict XVI, *Address to the Roman Curia* (21 December 2012): AAS 105 (2013), 51.

187. Cf. *Propositio* 14.

188. Cf. *Catechism of the Catholic Church*, 1910; Pontifical Council for Justice and Peace, *Compendium of the Social Doctrine of the Church*, 168.

189. Cf. *Propositio* 54.

190. John Paul II, Encyclical Letter *Fides et Ratio* (14 September 1998), 88: AAS 91 (1999), 74.

191. Saint Thomas Aquinas, *Summa contra Gentiles*, I, 7; cf. John Paul II, Encyclical Letter *Fides et Ratio* (14 September 1998), 43: AAS 91 (1999), 39.

192. Second Vatican Council, Decree on Ecumenism *Unitatis Redintegratio*, 4.

193. Cf. *Propositio* 52.

194. Indian Bishops' Conference, Final Declaration of the XXX Assembly: *The Role of the Church for a Better India* (8 March 2013), 8.9.

195. Cf. *Propositio* 53.

196. John Paul II, Encyclical Letter *Redemptoris Missio* (7 December 1990), 56: AAS 83 (1991), 304.

197. Cf. Benedict XVI, *Address to the Roman Curia* (21 December 2012): AAS 105 (2006), 51; Second Vatican Ecumenical Council, Decree on the Missionary Activity of the Church *Ad Gentes*, 9; *Catechism of the Catholic Church*, 856.

198. Second Vatican Ecumenical Council, Dogmatic Constitution on the Church *Lumen Gentium*, 16.

199. International Theological Commission, *Christianity and the World Religions* (1996), 72: *Enchiridion Vaticanum* 15, No. 1061.

200. Ibid.

201. Cf. ibid., 81–87: *Enchiridion Vaticanum* 15, Nos. 1070–1076.

202. Cf. *Propositio* 16.

203. Benedict XVI, Post-Synodal Apostolic Exhortation *Ecclesia in Medio Oriente* (14 September 2012), 26: AAS 104 (2012), 762.

204. Cf. *Propositio* 55.

205. Cf. *Propositio* 36.

206. John Paul II, Apostolic Letter *Novo Millennio Ineunte* (6 January 2001), 52: AAS 93 (2001), 304.

207. Cf. V. M. Fernández, "Espiritualidad para la esperanza activa. Discurso en la apertura del I Congreso Nacional de Doctrina Social de la Iglesia (Rosario 2011)," in *UCActualidad*, 142 (2011), 16.

208. John Paul II, Encyclical Letter *Redemptoris Missio* (7 December 1990), 45: AAS 83 (1991), 292.

209. Benedict XVI, Encyclical Letter, *Deus Caritas Est* (25 December 2005), 16: AAS 98 (2006), 230.

210. Ibid., 39: AAS 98 (2006), 250.

211. Second Special Assembly for Europe of the Synod of Bishops, Final Message, 1: *L'Osservatore Romano*, Weekly English-language edition, 27 October 1999, 5.

212. Isaac of Stella, *Sermo* 51: PL 194, 1863, 1865.

213. *Nican Mopohua*, 118–119.

214. Cf. Second Vatican Ecumenical Council, Dogmatic Constitution on the Church *Lumen Gentium*, 52–69.

215. John Paul II, Encyclical Letter *Redemptoris Mater* (25 March 1987), 6: AAS 79 (1987), 366–367.

216. Cf. *Propositio* 58.

217. John Paul II, Encyclical Letter *Redemptoris Mater* (25 March 1987), 17: AAS 79 (1987), 381.

Misericordiae Vultus
The Face of Mercy
April 11, 2015

MISERICORDIAE VULTUS

BULL OF INDICTION
OF THE EXTRAORDINARY
JUBILEE OF MERCY

FRANCIS

BISHOP OF ROME
SERVANT OF THE SERVANTS OF GOD
TO ALL WHO READ THIS LETTER
GRACE, MERCY, AND PEACE

1. Jesus Christ is the face of the Father's mercy. These words might well sum up the mystery of the Christian faith. Mercy has become living and visible in Jesus of Nazareth, reaching its culmination in him. The Father, "rich in mercy" (Eph 2:4), after having revealed his name to Moses as "a God merciful and gracious, slow to anger, and abounding in steadfast love and faithfulness" (Ex 34:6), has never ceased to show, in various ways throughout history, his divine nature. In the "fullness of time" (Gal 4:4), when everything had been arranged according to his plan of salvation, he sent his only Son into the world, born of the Virgin Mary, to reveal his love for us in a definitive way. Whoever sees Jesus sees the Father (cf. Jn 14:9). Jesus of Nazareth, by his words, his actions, and his entire person[1] reveals the mercy of God.

2. We need constantly to contemplate the mystery of mercy. It is a well-spring of joy, serenity, and peace. Our salvation depends on it. Mercy: the word reveals the very mystery of the Most Holy Trinity. Mercy: the ultimate and supreme act by which God comes to meet us. Mercy: the fundamental law that dwells in the heart of every person who looks sincerely into the eyes of his brothers and sisters on the path of life. Mercy: the bridge that connects God and man, opening our hearts to the hope of being loved forever despite our sinfulness.

3. At times we are called to gaze even more attentively on mercy so that we may become a more effective sign of the Father's action in our lives.

For this reason I have proclaimed an *Extraordinary Jubilee of Mercy* as a special time for the Church, a time when the witness of believers might grow stronger and more effective.

The Holy Year will open on 8 December 2015, the Solemnity of the Immaculate Conception. This liturgical feast day recalls God's action from the very beginning of the history of mankind. After the sin of Adam and Eve, God did not wish to leave humanity alone in the throes of evil. And so he turned his gaze to Mary, holy and immaculate in love (cf. Eph 1:4), choosing her to be the Mother of man's Redeemer. When faced with the gravity of sin, God responds with the fullness of mercy. Mercy will always be greater than any sin, and no one can place limits on the love of God who is ever ready to forgive. I will have the joy of opening the Holy Door on the Solemnity of the Immaculate Conception. On that day, the Holy Door will become a *Door of Mercy* through which anyone who enters will experience the love of God who consoles, pardons, and instills hope.

On the following Sunday, the Third Sunday of Advent, the Holy Door of the Cathedral of Rome—that is, the Basilica of Saint John Lateran—will be opened. In the following weeks, the Holy Doors of the other Papal Basilicas will be opened. On the same Sunday, I will announce that in every local church, at the cathedral—the mother church of the faithful in any particular area—or, alternatively, at the co-cathedral or another church of special significance, a Door of Mercy will be opened for the duration of the Holy Year. At the discretion of the local ordinary, a similar door may be opened at any shrine frequented by large groups of pilgrims, since visits to these holy sites are so often grace-filled moments, as people discover a path to conversion. Every Particular Church, therefore, will be directly involved in living out this Holy Year as an extraordinary moment of grace and spiritual renewal. Thus the Jubilee will be celebrated both in Rome and in the Particular Churches as a visible sign of the Church's universal communion.

4. I have chosen the date of 8 December because of its rich meaning in the recent history of the Church. In fact, I will open the Holy Door on the fiftieth anniversary of the closing of the Second Vatican Ecumenical

Council. The Church feels a great need to keep this event alive. With the Council, the Church entered a new phase of her history. The Council Fathers strongly perceived, as a true breath of the Holy Spirit, a need to talk about God to men and women of their time in a more accessible way. The walls which for too long had made the Church a kind of fortress were torn down and the time had come to proclaim the Gospel in a new way. It was a new phase of the same evangelization that had existed from the beginning. It was a fresh undertaking for all Christians to bear witness to their faith with greater enthusiasm and conviction. The Church sensed a responsibility to be a living sign of the Father's love in the world.

We recall the poignant words of Saint John XXIII when, opening the Council, he indicated the path to follow: "Now the Bride of Christ wishes to use the medicine of mercy rather than taking up arms of severity. . . . The Catholic Church, as she holds high the torch of Catholic truth at this Ecumenical Council, wants to show herself a loving mother to all; patient, kind, moved by compassion and goodness toward her separated children."[2] Blessed Paul VI spoke in a similar vein at the closing of the Council: "We prefer to point out how charity has been the principal religious feature of this Council . . . the old story of the Good Samaritan has been the model of the spirituality of the Council . . . a wave of affection and admiration flowed from the Council over the modern world of humanity. Errors were condemned, indeed, because charity demanded this no less than did truth, but for individuals themselves there was only admonition, respect and love. Instead of depressing diagnoses, encouraging remedies; instead of direful predictions, messages of trust issued from the Council to the present-day world. The modern world's values were not only respected but honored, its efforts approved, its aspirations purified and blessed. . . . Another point we must stress is this: all this rich teaching is channeled in one direction, the service of mankind, of every condition, in every weakness and need."[3]

With these sentiments of gratitude for everything the Church has received, and with a sense of responsibility for the task that lies ahead, we shall cross the threshold of the Holy Door fully confident that the strength of the Risen Lord, who constantly supports us on our pilgrim way, will sustain us. May the Holy Spirit, who guides the steps of believers in cooperating with the work of salvation wrought by Christ, lead the way and support the People of God so that they may contemplate the face of mercy.[4]

5. The Jubilee Year will close with the liturgical Solemnity of Christ the King on 20 November 2016. On that day, as we seal the Holy Door, we shall be filled, above all, with a sense of gratitude and thanksgiving to the Most Holy Trinity for having granted us an extraordinary time of grace. We will entrust the life of the Church, all humanity, and the entire cosmos to the Lordship of Christ, asking him to pour out his mercy upon us like the morning dew, so that everyone may work together to build a brighter future. How much I desire that the year to come will be steeped in mercy, so that we can go out to every man and woman, bringing the goodness and tenderness of God! May the balm of mercy reach everyone, both believers and those far away, as a sign that the kingdom of God is already present in our midst!

6. "It is proper to God to exercise mercy, and he manifests his omnipotence particularly in this way."[5] Saint Thomas Aquinas's words show that God's mercy, rather than a sign of weakness, is the mark of his omnipotence. For this reason the liturgy, in one of its most ancient collects, has us pray: "O God, who reveal your power above all in your mercy and forgiveness . . ."[6] Throughout the history of humanity, God will always be the One who is present, close, provident, holy, and merciful.

"Patient and merciful." These words often go together in the Old Testament to describe God's nature. His being merciful is concretely demonstrated in his many actions throughout the history of salvation where his goodness prevails over punishment and destruction. In a special way the Psalms bring to the fore the grandeur of his merciful action: "He forgives all your iniquity, he heals all your diseases, he redeems your life from the pit, he crowns you with steadfast love and mercy" (Ps 103:3–4). Another psalm, in an even more explicit way, attests to the concrete signs of his mercy: "He executes justice for the oppressed; he gives food to the hungry. The Lord sets the prisoners free; the Lord opens the eyes of the blind. The Lord lifts up those who are bowed down; the Lord loves the righteous. The Lord watches over the sojourners, he upholds the widow and the fatherless; but the way of the wicked he brings to ruin" (Ps 146:7–9). Here are some other expressions of the Psalmist: "He heals the brokenhearted, and binds up their wounds. . . . The Lord lifts up the downtrodden, he casts the wicked to the ground" (Ps 147:3, 6). In short, the mercy of God is not an abstract idea, but a concrete reality with which he reveals his love as of that of a father or a mother, moved to the very depths out of love for their child. It is hardly an exaggeration to say that this is a "visceral" love. It gushes forth from the depths naturally, full of tenderness and compassion, indulgence and mercy.

7. "For his mercy endures forever." This is the refrain that repeats after each verse in Psalm 136 as it narrates the history of God's revelation. By virtue of mercy, all the events of the Old Testament are replete with profound salvific import. Mercy renders God's history with Israel a history of salvation. To repeat continually "for his mercy endures forever," as the psalm does, seems to break through the dimensions of space and time, inserting everything into the eternal mystery of love. It is as if to say that not only in history, but for all eternity man will always be under the merciful gaze of the Father. It is no accident that the people of Israel wanted to include this psalm—the "Great *Hallel*," as it is called—in its most important liturgical feast days.

Before his Passion, Jesus prayed with this psalm of mercy. Matthew attests to this in his Gospel when he says that, "when they had sung a hymn" (26:30), Jesus and his disciples went out to the Mount of Olives. While he was instituting the Eucharist as an everlasting memorial of himself and his paschal sacrifice, he symbolically placed this supreme act of revelation in the light of his mercy. Within the very same context of mercy, Jesus entered upon his passion and death, conscious of the great mystery of love that he would consummate on the Cross. Knowing that Jesus himself prayed this psalm makes it even more important for us as Christians, challenging us to take up the refrain in our daily lives by praying these words of praise: "for his mercy endures forever."

8. With our eyes fixed on Jesus and his merciful gaze, we experience the love of the Most Holy Trinity. The mission Jesus received from the Father was that of revealing the mystery of divine love in its fullness. "God is love" (1 Jn 4:8, 16), John affirms for the first and only time in all of Holy Scripture. This love has now been made visible and tangible in Jesus' entire life. His person is nothing but love, a love given gratuitously. The relationships he forms with the people who approach him manifest something entirely unique and unrepeatable. The signs he works, especially in favor of sinners, the poor, the marginalized, the sick, and the suffering, are all meant to teach mercy. Everything in him speaks of mercy. Nothing in him is devoid of compassion.

Jesus, seeing the crowds of people who followed him, realized that they were tired and exhausted, lost and without a guide, and he felt deep compassion for them (cf. Mt 9:36). On the basis of this compassionate love he healed the sick who were presented to him (cf. Mt 14:14), and with just a few loaves of bread and fish he satisfied the enormous crowd (cf. Mt 15:37). What moved Jesus in all of these situations was nothing other than mercy, with which he read the hearts of those he encountered and responded to their deepest need. When he came upon the widow of Nain taking her son out for burial, he felt great compassion for the immense suffering of this grieving mother, and he gave back her son by raising him from the dead (cf. Lk 7:15). After freeing the demoniac in the country of the Gerasenes, Jesus entrusted him with this mission: "Go home to your friends, and tell them how much the Lord has done for you, and how he has had mercy on you" (Mk 5:19). The calling of Matthew is also presented within the context of mercy. Passing by the tax collector's booth, Jesus looked intently at Matthew. It was a look full of mercy that forgave the sins of that man, a sinner and a tax collector, whom Jesus chose—against the hesitation of the disciples—to become one of the Twelve. Saint Bede the Venerable, commenting on this Gospel passage, wrote that Jesus looked upon Matthew with merciful love and chose him: *miserando atque eligendo*.[7] This expression impressed me so much that I chose it for my episcopal motto.

9. In the parables devoted to mercy, Jesus reveals the nature of God as that of a Father who never gives up until he has forgiven the wrong and overcome rejection with compassion and mercy. We know these parables well, three in particular: the lost sheep, the lost coin, and the father with two sons (cf. Lk 15:1–32). In these parables, God is always presented as full of joy, especially when he pardons. In them we find the core of the Gospel and of our faith, because mercy is presented as a force that overcomes everything, filling the heart with love and bringing consolation through pardon.

From another parable, we cull an important teaching for our Christian lives. In reply to Peter's question about how many times it is necessary to forgive, Jesus says: "I do not say seven times, but seventy times seven times" (Mt 18:22). He then goes on to tell the parable of the "ruthless servant," who, called by his master to return a huge amount, begs him on his knees for mercy. His master cancels his debt. But he then meets a fellow servant who owes him a few cents and who in turn begs on his knees for mercy, but the first servant refuses his request and throws him into jail. When the master hears of the matter, he becomes infuriated and, summoning the first servant back to him, says, "Should not you have had mercy on your fellow servant, as I had mercy on you?" (Mt 18:33). Jesus concludes, "So also my heavenly Father will do to every one of you, if you do not forgive your brother from your heart" (Mt 18:35).

This parable contains a profound teaching for all of us. Jesus affirms that mercy is not only an action of the Father, it becomes a criterion for ascertaining who his true children are. In short, we are called to show mercy because mercy has first been shown to us. Pardoning offenses becomes the clearest expression of merciful love, and for us Christians it is an imperative from which we cannot excuse ourselves. At times how hard it seems to forgive! And yet pardon is the instrument placed into our fragile hands to attain serenity of heart. To let go of anger, wrath, violence, and revenge are necessary conditions to living joyfully. Let us therefore heed the Apostle's exhortation: "Do not let the sun go down on your anger" (Eph 4:26). Above all, let us listen to the words of Jesus who made mercy an ideal of life and a criterion for the credibility of our faith: "Blessed are the merciful, for they shall obtain mercy" (Mt 5:7): the beatitude to which we should particularly aspire in this Holy Year.

As we can see in sacred Scripture, mercy is a key word that indicates God's action toward us. He does not limit himself merely to affirming his love, but makes it visible and tangible. Love, after all, can never be just an abstraction. By its very nature, it indicates something concrete: intentions, attitudes, and behaviors that are shown in daily living. The mercy of God is his loving concern for each one of us. He feels responsible; that is, he desires our well-being and he wants to see us happy, full of joy, and peaceful. This is the path which the merciful love of Christians must also travel. As the Father loves, so do his children. Just as he is merciful, so we are called to be merciful to each other.

10. Mercy is the very foundation of the Church's life. All of her pastoral activity should be caught up in the tenderness she makes present to believers; nothing in her preaching and in her witness to the world can be lacking in mercy. The Church's very credibility is seen in how she shows merciful and compassionate love. The Church "has an endless desire to show mercy."[8] Perhaps we have long since forgotten how to show and live the way of mercy. The temptation, on the one hand, to focus exclusively on justice made us forget that this is only the first, albeit necessary and indispensable step. But the Church needs to go beyond and strive for a higher and more important goal. On the other hand, sad to say, we must admit that the practice of mercy is waning in the wider culture. In some cases the word seems to have dropped out of use. However, without a witness to mercy, life becomes fruitless and sterile, as if sequestered in a barren desert. The time has come for the Church to take up the joyful call to mercy once more. It is time to return to the basics and to bear the weaknesses and struggles of our brothers and sisters. Mercy is the force that reawakens us to new life and instills in us the courage to look to the future with hope.

11. Let us not forget the great teaching offered by Saint John Paul II in his second Encyclical, *Dives in Misericordia*, which at the time came unexpectedly, its theme catching many by surprise. There are two passages

in particular to which I would like to draw attention. First, Saint John Paul II highlighted the fact that we had forgotten the theme of mercy in today's cultural milieu: "The present-day mentality, more perhaps than that of people in the past, seems opposed to a God of mercy, and in fact tends to exclude from life and to remove from the human heart the very idea of mercy. The word and the concept of 'mercy' seem to cause uneasiness in man, who, thanks to the enormous development of science and technology, never before known in history, has become the master of the earth and has subdued and dominated it (cf. Gn 1:28). This dominion over the earth, sometimes understood in a one-sided and superficial way, seems to have no room for mercy. . . . And this is why, in the situation of the Church and the world today, many individuals and groups guided by a lively sense of faith are turning, I would say almost spontaneously, to the mercy of God."[9]

Furthermore, Saint John Paul II pushed for a more urgent proclamation and witness to mercy in the contemporary world: "It is dictated by love for man, for all that is human and which, according to the intuitions of many of our contemporaries, is threatened by an immense danger. The mystery of Christ . . . obliges me to proclaim mercy as God's merciful love, revealed in that same mystery of Christ. It likewise obliges me to have recourse to that mercy and to beg for it at this difficult, critical phase of the history of the Church and of the world."[10] This teaching is more pertinent than ever and deserves to be taken up once again in this Holy Year. Let us listen to his words once more: "The Church lives an authentic life when she professes and proclaims mercy—the most stupendous attribute of the Creator and of the Redeemer—and when she brings people close to the sources of the Savior's mercy, of which she is the trustee and dispenser."[11]

12. The Church is commissioned to announce the mercy of God, the beating heart of the Gospel, which in its own way must penetrate the heart and mind of every person. The Spouse of Christ must pattern her behavior after the Son of God who went out to everyone without exception. In the present day, as the Church is charged with the task of the new evangelization, the theme of mercy needs to be proposed again and

again with new enthusiasm and renewed pastoral action. It is absolutely essential for the Church and for the credibility of her message that she herself live and testify to mercy. Her language and her gestures must transmit mercy, so as to touch the hearts of all people and inspire them once more to find the road that leads to the Father.

The Church's first truth is the love of Christ. The Church makes herself a servant of this love and mediates it to all people: a love that forgives and expresses itself in the gift of oneself. Consequently, wherever the Church is present, the mercy of the Father must be evident. In our parishes, communities, associations, and movements, in a word, wherever there are Christians, everyone should find an oasis of mercy.

13. We want to live this Jubilee Year in light of the Lord's words: *Merciful like the Father.* The Evangelist reminds us of the teaching of Jesus who says, "Be merciful just as your Father is merciful" (Lk 6:36). It is a program of life as demanding as it is rich with joy and peace. Jesus' command is directed to anyone willing to listen to his voice (cf. Lk 6:27). In order to be capable of mercy, therefore, we must first of all dispose ourselves to listen to the Word of God. This means rediscovering the value of silence in order to meditate on the Word that comes to us. In this way, it will be possible to contemplate God's mercy and adopt it as our lifestyle.

14. The practice of *pilgrimage* has a special place in the Holy Year, because it represents the journey each of us makes in this life. Life itself is a pilgrimage, and the human being is a *viator*, a pilgrim traveling along the road, making his way to the desired destination. Similarly, to reach the Holy Door in Rome or in any other place in the world, everyone, each according to his or her ability, will have to make a pilgrimage. This will be a sign that mercy is also a goal to reach and requires dedication and sacrifice. May pilgrimage be an impetus to conversion: by crossing the threshold of the Holy Door, we will find the strength to embrace God's mercy and dedicate ourselves to being merciful with others as the Father has been with us.

The Lord Jesus shows us the steps of the pilgrimage to attain our goal: "Judge not, and you will not be judged; condemn not, and you will not be condemned; forgive, and you will be forgiven; give, and it will be given to you; good measure, pressed down, shaken together, running over, will be put into your lap. For the measure you give will be the measure you get back" (Lk 6:37–38). The Lord asks us above all *not to judge* and *not to condemn*. If anyone wishes to avoid God's judgment, he should not make himself the judge of his brother or sister. Human beings, whenever they judge, look no farther than the surface, whereas the Father looks into the very depths of the soul. How much harm words do when they are motivated by feelings of jealousy and envy! To speak ill of others puts them in a bad light, undermines their reputation, and leaves them prey to the whims of gossip. To refrain from judgment and condemnation means, in a positive sense, to know how to accept the good in every person and to spare him any suffering that might be caused by our partial judgment, our presumption to know everything about him. But this is still not sufficient to express mercy. Jesus asks us also to *forgive* and to *give*. To be instruments of mercy because it was we who first received mercy from God. To be generous with others, knowing that God showers his goodness upon us with immense generosity.

Merciful like the Father, therefore, is the "motto" of this Holy Year. In mercy, we find proof of how God loves us. He gives his entire self, always, freely, asking nothing in return. He comes to our aid whenever we call upon him. What a beautiful thing that the Church begins her daily prayer with the words, "O God, come to my assistance. O Lord, make haste to help me" (Ps 70:2)! The assistance we ask for is already the first step of God's mercy toward us. He comes to assist us in our weakness. And his help consists in helping us accept his presence and closeness to us. Day after day, touched by his compassion, we also can become compassionate toward others.

15. In this Holy Year, we look forward to the experience of opening our hearts to those living on the outermost fringes of society: fringes which modern society itself creates. How many uncertain and painful situations there are in the world today! How many are the wounds borne by the flesh of those who have no voice because their cry is muffled and drowned out by the indifference of the rich! During this Jubilee, the

Church will be called even more to heal these wounds, to assuage them with the oil of consolation, to bind them with mercy and cure them with solidarity and vigilant care. Let us not fall into humiliating indifference or a monotonous routine that prevents us from discovering what is new! Let us ward off destructive cynicism! Let us open our eyes and see the misery of the world, the wounds of our brothers and sisters who are denied their dignity, and let us recognize that we are compelled to heed their cry for help! May we reach out to them and support them so they can feel the warmth of our presence, our friendship, and our fraternity! May their cry become our own, and together may we break down the barriers of indifference that too often reign supreme and mask our hypocrisy and egoism!

It is my burning desire that, during this Jubilee, the Christian people may reflect on the *corporal and spiritual works of mercy*. It will be a way to reawaken our conscience, too often grown dull in the face of poverty. And let us enter more deeply into the heart of the Gospel where the poor have a special experience of God's mercy. Jesus introduces us to these works of mercy in his preaching so that we can know whether or not we are living as his disciples. Let us rediscover these *corporal works of mercy*: to feed the hungry, give drink to the thirsty, clothe the naked, welcome the stranger, heal the sick, visit the imprisoned, and bury the dead. And let us not forget the *spiritual works of mercy*: to counsel the doubtful, instruct the ignorant, admonish sinners, comfort the afflicted, forgive offenses, bear patiently those who do us ill, and pray for the living and the dead.

We cannot escape the Lord's words to us, and they will serve as the criteria upon which we will be judged: whether we have fed the hungry and given drink to the thirsty, welcomed the stranger and clothed the naked, or spent time with the sick and those in prison (cf. Mt 25:31–45). Moreover, we will be asked if we have helped others to escape the doubt that causes them to fall into despair and which is often a source of loneliness; if we have helped to overcome the ignorance in which millions of people live, especially children deprived of the necessary means to free them from the bonds of poverty; if we have been close to the lonely and afflicted; if we have forgiven those who have offended us and have rejected all forms of anger and hate that lead to violence; if we have had the kind of patience God shows, who is so patient with us; and if we have commended our brothers and sisters to the Lord in prayer. In each of these "little ones," Christ himself is present. His flesh becomes visible in the flesh of the tortured, the crushed, the scourged, the malnourished, and the exiled . . . to be acknowledged, touched, and cared for by us. Let us not forget the words of Saint John of the Cross: "as we prepare to leave this life, we will be judged on the basis of love."[12]

16. In the Gospel of Luke, we find another important element that will help us live the Jubilee with faith. Luke writes that Jesus, on the Sabbath, went back to Nazareth and, as was his custom, entered the synagogue. They called upon him to read the Scripture and to comment on it. The passage was from the Book of Isaiah where it is written: "The Spirit of the Lord God is upon me, because the Lord has anointed me to bring good tidings to the afflicted; he has sent me to bind up the brokenhearted, to proclaim liberty to the captives, and freedom to those in captivity; to proclaim the year of the Lord's favor" (Is 61:1–2). A "year of the Lord's favor" or "mercy": this is what the Lord proclaimed and this is what we wish to live now. This Holy Year will bring to the fore the richness of Jesus' mission echoed in the words of the prophet: to bring a word and gesture of consolation to the poor, to proclaim liberty to those bound by new forms of slavery in modern society, to restore sight to those who can see no more because they are caught up in themselves, to restore dignity to all those from whom it has been robbed. The preaching of Jesus is made visible once more in the response of faith which Christians are called to offer by their witness. May the words of the Apostle accompany us: he who does acts of mercy, let him do them with cheerfulness (cf. Rom 12:8).

17. The season of Lent during this Jubilee Year should also be lived more intensely as a privileged moment to celebrate and experience God's mercy. How many pages of sacred Scripture are appropriate for meditation during the weeks of Lent to help us rediscover the merciful face of the Father! We can repeat the words of the prophet Micah and make

them our own: You, O Lord, are a God who takes away iniquity and pardons sin, who does not hold your anger forever, but are pleased to show mercy. You, Lord, will return to us and have pity on your people. You will trample down our sins and toss them into the depths of the sea (cf. 7:18–19).

The pages of the prophet Isaiah can also be meditated upon concretely during this season of prayer, fasting, and works of charity: "Is not this the fast that I choose: to loosen the bonds of wickedness, to undo the thongs of the yoke, to let the oppressed go free, and to break every yoke? Is it not to share your bread with the hungry, and bring the homeless poor into your house; when you see the naked, to cover him, and not to hide yourself from your own flesh? Then shall your light break forth like the dawn, and your healing shall spring up speedily; your righteousness shall go before you, the glory of the Lord shall be your rear guard. Then you shall call, and the Lord will answer; you shall cry, and he will say, here I am. If you take away from the midst of you the yoke, the pointing of the finger, and speaking wickedness, if you pour yourself out for the hungry and satisfy the desire of the afflicted, then shall your light rise in the darkness and your gloom be as the noonday. And the Lord will guide you continually, and satisfy your desire with good things, and make your bones strong; and you shall be like a watered garden, like a spring of water, whose waters fail not" (58:6–11).

The initiative of "*24 Hours for the Lord,*" to be celebrated on the Friday and Saturday preceding the Fourth Week of Lent, should be implemented in every diocese. So many people, including young people, are returning to the sacrament of Reconciliation; through this experience they are rediscovering a path back to the Lord, living a moment of intense prayer and finding meaning in their lives. Let us place the sacrament of Reconciliation at the center once more in such a way that it will enable people to touch the grandeur of God's mercy with their own hands. For every penitent, it will be a source of true interior peace.

I will never tire of insisting that confessors be authentic signs of the Father's mercy. We do not become good confessors automatically. We become good confessors when, above all, we allow ourselves to be penitents in search of his mercy. Let us never forget that to be confessors means to participate in the very mission of Jesus to be a concrete sign of the constancy of divine love that pardons and saves. We priests have received the gift of the Holy Spirit for the forgiveness of sins, and we are responsible for this. None of us wields power over this Sacrament; rather, we are faithful servants of God's mercy through it. Every confessor must accept the faithful as the father in the parable of the prodigal son: a father who runs out to meet his son despite the fact that he has squandered away his inheritance. Confessors are called to embrace the repentant son who comes back home and to express the joy of having him back again. Let us never tire of also going out to the other son who stands outside, incapable of rejoicing, in order to explain to him that his judgment is severe and unjust and meaningless in light of the father's boundless mercy. May confessors not ask useless questions, but like the father in the parable, interrupt the speech prepared ahead of time by the prodigal son, so that confessors will learn to accept the plea for help and mercy pouring from the heart of every penitent. In short, confessors are called to be a sign of the primacy of mercy always, everywhere, and in every situation, no matter what.

18. During Lent of this Holy Year, I intend to send out *Missionaries of Mercy*. They will be a sign of the Church's maternal solicitude for the People of God, enabling them to enter the profound richness of this mystery so fundamental to the faith. There will be priests to whom I will grant the authority to pardon even those sins reserved to the Holy See, so that the breadth of their mandate as confessors will be even clearer. They will be, above all, living signs of the Father's readiness to welcome those in search of his pardon. They will be Missionaries of Mercy because they will be facilitators of a truly human encounter, a source of liberation, rich with responsibility for overcoming obstacles and taking up the new life of Baptism again. They will be led in their mission by the words of the Apostle: "For God has consigned all men to disobedience, that he may have mercy upon all" (Rom 11:32). Everyone, in fact, without exception, is called to embrace the call to mercy. May these Missionaries live this

call with the assurance that they can fix their eyes on Jesus, "the merciful and faithful high priest in the service of God" (Heb 2:17).

I ask my brother bishops to invite and welcome these Missionaries so that they can be, above all, persuasive preachers of mercy. May individual dioceses organize "missions to the people" in such a way that these Missionaries may be heralds of joy and forgiveness. Bishops are asked to celebrate the sacrament of Reconciliation with their people so that the time of grace made possible by the Jubilee Year makes it possible for many of God's sons and daughters to take up once again the journey to the Father's house. May pastors, especially during the liturgical season of Lent, be diligent in calling back the faithful "to the throne of grace, that we may receive mercy and find grace" (Heb 4:16).

19. May the message of mercy reach everyone, and may no one be indifferent to the call to experience mercy. I direct this invitation to conversion even more fervently to those whose behavior distances them from the grace of God. I particularly have in mind men and women belonging to criminal organizations of any kind. For their own good, I beg them to change their lives. I ask them this in the name of the Son of God who, though rejecting sin, never rejected the sinner. Do not fall into the terrible trap of thinking that life depends on money and that, in comparison with money, anything else is devoid of value or dignity. This is nothing but an illusion! We cannot take money with us into the life beyond. Money does not bring us happiness. Violence inflicted for the sake of amassing riches soaked in blood makes one neither powerful nor immortal. Everyone, sooner or later, will be subject to God's judgment, from which no one can escape.

The same invitation is extended to those who either perpetrate or participate in corruption. This festering wound is a grave sin that cries out to heaven for vengeance, because it threatens the very foundations of personal and social life. Corruption prevents us from looking to the future with hope, because its tyrannical greed shatters the plans of the weak and tramples upon the poorest of the poor. It is an evil that embeds itself into the actions of everyday life and spreads, causing great public scandal. Corruption is a sinful hardening of the heart that replaces

God with the illusion that money is a form of power. It is a work of darkness, fed by suspicion and intrigue. *Corruptio optimi pessima,* Saint Gregory the Great said with good reason, affirming that no one can think himself immune from this temptation. If we want to drive it out from personal and social life, we need prudence, vigilance, loyalty, transparency, together with the courage to denounce any wrongdoing. If it is not combated openly, sooner or later everyone will become an accomplice to it, and it will end up destroying our very existence.

This is the opportune moment to change our lives! This is the time to allow our hearts to be touched! When faced with evil deeds, even in the face of serious crimes, it is the time to listen to the cry of innocent people who are deprived of their property, their dignity, their feelings, and even their very lives. To stick to the way of evil will only leave one deluded and sad. True life is something entirely different. God never tires of reaching out to us. He is always ready to listen, as I am too, along with my brother bishops and priests. All one needs to do is to accept the invitation to conversion and submit oneself to justice during this special time of mercy offered by the Church.

20. It would not be out of place at this point to recall the relationship between *justice* and *mercy*. These are not two contradictory realities, but two dimensions of a single reality that unfolds progressively until it culminates in the fullness of love. Justice is a fundamental concept for civil society, which is meant to be governed by the rule of law. Justice is also understood as that which is rightly due to each individual. In the Bible, there are many references to divine justice and to God as "judge." In these passages, justice is understood as the full observance of the Law and the behavior of every good Israelite in conformity with God's commandments. Such a vision, however, has not infrequently led to legalism by distorting the original meaning of justice and obscuring its profound value. To overcome this legalistic perspective, we need to recall that in sacred Scripture, justice is conceived essentially as the faithful abandonment of oneself to God's will.

For his part, Jesus speaks several times of the importance of faith over and above the observance of the law. It is in this sense that we must understand his words when, reclining at table with Matthew and other tax collectors and sinners, he says to the Pharisees raising objections to him, "Go and learn the meaning of 'I desire mercy not sacrifice.' I have come not to call the righteous, but sinners" (Mt 9:13). Faced with a vision of justice as the mere observance of the law that judges people simply by dividing them into two groups—the just and sinners—Jesus is bent on revealing the great gift of mercy that searches out sinners and offers them pardon and salvation. One can see why, on the basis of such a liberating vision of mercy as a source of new life, Jesus was rejected by the Pharisees and the other teachers of the law. In an attempt to remain faithful to the law, they merely placed burdens on the shoulders of others and undermined the Father's mercy. The appeal to a faithful observance of the law must not prevent attention from being given to matters that touch upon the dignity of the person.

The appeal Jesus makes to the text from the book of the prophet Hosea—"I desire love and not sacrifice" (6:6)—is important in this regard. Jesus affirms that, from that time onward, the rule of life for his disciples must place mercy at the center, as Jesus himself demonstrated by sharing meals with sinners. Mercy, once again, is revealed as a fundamental aspect of Jesus' mission. This is truly challenging to his hearers, who would draw the line at a formal respect for the law. Jesus, on the other hand, goes beyond the law; the company he keeps with those the law considers sinners makes us realize the depth of his mercy.

The Apostle Paul makes a similar journey. Prior to meeting Jesus on the road to Damascus, he dedicated his life to pursuing the justice of the law with zeal (cf. Phil 3:6). His conversion to Christ led him to turn that vision upside down, to the point that he would write to the Galatians: "We have believed in Christ Jesus, in order to be justified by faith in Christ, and not by works of the law, because by works of the law shall no one be justified" (2:16).

Paul's understanding of justice changes radically. He now places faith first, not justice. Salvation comes not through the observance of the law, but through faith in Jesus Christ, who in his death and resurrection brings salvation together with a mercy that justifies. God's justice now becomes the liberating force for those oppressed by slavery to sin and its consequences. God's justice is his mercy (cf. Ps 51:11–16).

21. Mercy is not opposed to justice but rather expresses God's way of reaching out to the sinner, offering him a new chance to look at himself, convert, and believe. The experience of the prophet Hosea can help us see the way in which mercy surpasses justice. The era in which the prophet lived was one of the most dramatic in the history of the Jewish people. The kingdom was tottering on the edge of destruction; the people had not remained faithful to the covenant; they had wandered from God and lost the faith of their forefathers. According to human logic, it seems reasonable for God to think of rejecting an unfaithful people; they had not observed their pact with God and therefore deserved just punishment: in other words, exile. The prophet's words attest to this: "They shall not return to the land of Egypt, and Assyria shall be their king, because they have refused to return to me" (Hos 11:5). And yet, after this invocation of justice, the prophet radically changes his speech and reveals the true face of God: "How can I give you up, O Ephraim! How can I hand you over, O Israel! How can I make you like Admah! How can I treat you like Zeboiim! My heart recoils within me, my compassion grows warm and tender. I will not execute my fierce anger, I will not again destroy Ephraim; for I am God and not man, the Holy One in your midst, and I will not come to destroy" (11:8–9). Saint Augustine, almost as if he were commenting on these words of the prophet, says: "It is easier for God to hold back anger than mercy."[13] And so it is. God's anger lasts but a moment, his mercy forever.

If God limited himself to only justice, he would cease to be God, and would instead be like human beings who ask merely that the law be respected. But mere justice is not enough. Experience shows that an appeal to justice alone will result in its destruction. This is why God goes beyond justice with his mercy and forgiveness. Yet this does not mean that justice should be devalued or rendered superfluous. On the contrary: anyone who makes a mistake must pay the price. However, this is just the beginning of conversion, not its end, because one begins to feel the tenderness and mercy of God. God does not deny justice. He rather envelopes it and surpasses it with an even greater event in which we experience love as the foundation of true justice. We must pay close attention to what Saint Paul says if we want to avoid making the same mistake for which he reproaches the Jews of his time: "For, being ignorant of the righteousness that comes from God, and seeking to establish their own, they did not submit to God's righteousness. For Christ is the end of the law, that every one who has faith may be justified" (Rom 10:3–4). God's justice is his mercy given to everyone as a grace that flows from the death and resurrection of Jesus Christ. Thus the Cross of Christ is God's judgment on all of us and on the whole world, because through it he offers us the certitude of love and new life.

22. A Jubilee also entails the granting of *indulgences*. This practice will acquire an even more important meaning in the Holy Year of Mercy. God's forgiveness knows no bounds. In the death and resurrection of Jesus Christ, God makes even more evident his love and its power to destroy all human sin. Reconciliation with God is made possible through the paschal mystery and the mediation of the Church. Thus God is always ready to forgive, and he never tires of forgiving in ways that are continually new and surprising. Nevertheless, all of us know well the experience of sin. We know that we are called to perfection (cf. Mt 5:48), yet we feel the heavy burden of sin. Though we feel the transforming power of grace, we also feel the effects of sin typical of our fallen state. Despite being forgiven, the conflicting consequences of our sins remain. In the sacrament of Reconciliation, God forgives our sins, which he truly blots out; and yet sin leaves a negative effect on the way we think and act. But the mercy of God is stronger even than this. It becomes *indulgence* on the part of the Father who, through the Bride of Christ, his Church, reaches the pardoned sinner and frees him from every residue left by the consequences of sin, enabling him to act with charity, to grow in love rather than to fall back into sin.

The Church lives within the communion of the saints. In the Eucharist, this communion, which is a gift from God, becomes a spiritual union binding us to the saints and blessed ones whose number is beyond counting (cf. Rv 7:4). Their holiness comes to the aid of our weakness in a way that enables the Church, with her maternal prayers and her way of life, to fortify the weakness of some with the strength of others. Hence, to live the indulgence of the Holy Year means to approach the Father's mercy with the certainty that his forgiveness extends to the entire life of the believer. To gain an indulgence is to experience the holiness of the Church, who bestows upon all the fruits of Christ's redemption, so that God's love and forgiveness may extend everywhere. Let us live this Jubilee intensely, begging the Father to forgive our sins and to bathe us in his merciful "indulgence."

23. There is an aspect of mercy that goes beyond the confines of the Church. It relates us to Judaism and Islam, both of which consider mercy to be one of God's most important attributes. Israel was the first to receive this revelation which continues in history as the source of an inexhaustible richness meant to be shared with all mankind. As we have seen, the pages of the Old Testament are steeped in mercy, because they narrate the works that the Lord performed in favor of his people at the most trying moments of their history. Among the privileged names that Islam attributes to the Creator are "Merciful and Kind." This invocation is often on the lips of faithful Muslims who feel themselves accompanied and sustained by mercy in their daily weakness. They too believe that no one can place a limit on divine mercy because its doors are always open.

I trust that this Jubilee Year celebrating the mercy of God will foster an encounter with these religions and with other noble religious traditions; may it open us to even more fervent dialogue so that we might know and understand one another better; may it eliminate every form of closed-mindedness and disrespect, and drive out every form of violence and discrimination.

24. My thoughts now turn to the Mother of Mercy. May the sweetness of her countenance watch over us in this Holy Year, so that all of us may rediscover the joy of God's tenderness. No one has penetrated the profound mystery of the incarnation like Mary. Her entire life was patterned after the presence of mercy made flesh. The Mother of the Crucified and

Risen One has entered the sanctuary of divine mercy because she participated intimately in the mystery of His love.

Chosen to be the Mother of the Son of God, Mary, from the outset, was prepared by the love of God to be the *Ark of the Covenant* between God and man. She treasured divine mercy in her heart in perfect harmony with her Son Jesus. Her hymn of praise, sung at the threshold of the home of Elizabeth, was dedicated to the mercy of God which extends from "generation to generation" (Lk 1:50). We too were included in those prophetic words of the Virgin Mary. This will be a source of comfort and strength to us as we cross the threshold of the Holy Year to experience the fruits of divine mercy.

At the foot of the Cross, Mary, together with John, the disciple of love, witnessed the words of forgiveness spoken by Jesus. This supreme expression of mercy toward those who crucified him show us the point to which the mercy of God can reach. Mary attests that the mercy of the Son of God knows no bounds and extends to everyone, without exception. Let us address her in the words of the *Salve Regina*, a prayer ever ancient and ever new, so that she may never tire of turning her merciful eyes upon us, and make us worthy to contemplate the face of mercy, her Son Jesus.

Our prayer also extends to the saints and blessed ones who made divine mercy their mission in life. I think especially of the great apostle of mercy, Saint Faustina Kowalska. May she, who was called to enter the depths of divine mercy, intercede for us and obtain for us the grace of living and walking always according to the mercy of God and with an unwavering trust in his love.

25. I present, therefore, this Extraordinary Jubilee Year dedicated to living out in our daily lives the mercy which the Father constantly extends to all of us. In this Jubilee Year, let us allow God to surprise us. He never tires of casting open the doors of his heart and of repeating that he loves us and wants to share his love with us. The Church feels the urgent need to proclaim God's mercy. Her life is authentic and credible only when she becomes a convincing herald of mercy. She knows that her primary task, especially at a moment full of great hopes and signs of contradiction, is

to introduce everyone to the great mystery of God's mercy by contemplating the face of Christ. The Church is called above all to be a credible witness to mercy, professing it and living it as the core of the revelation of Jesus Christ. From the heart of the Trinity, from the depths of the mystery of God, the great river of mercy wells up and overflows unceasingly. It is a spring that will never run dry, no matter how many people draw from it. Every time someone is in need, he or she can approach it, because the mercy of God never ends. The profundity of the mystery surrounding it is as inexhaustible as the richness which springs up from it.

In this Jubilee Year, may the Church echo the word of God that resounds strong and clear as a message and a sign of pardon, strength, aid, and love. May she never tire of extending mercy, and be ever patient in offering compassion and comfort. May the Church become the voice of every man and woman, and repeat confidently without end: "Be mindful of your mercy, O Lord, and your steadfast love, for they have been from of old" (Ps 25:6).

Given in Rome, at Saint Peter's, on 11 April, the Vigil of the Second Sunday of Easter, or the Sunday of Divine Mercy, in the year of our Lord 2015, the third of my Pontificate.

FRANCISCUS

Notes

1. Cf. Second Vatican Ecumenical Council, Dogmatic Constitution on Divine Revelation *Dei Verbum*, 4.

2. Opening Address of the Second Vatican Ecumenical Council *Gaudet Mater Ecclesia*, 11 October 1962, 2–3.

3. Speech at the Final Public Session of the Second Vatican Ecumenical Council, 7 December 1965.

4. Cf. Second Vatican Ecumenical Council, Dogmatic Constitution on the Church *Lumen Gentium*, 16: Pastoral Constitution on the Church in the Modern World *Gaudium et Spes*, 15.

5. Saint Thomas Aquinas, *Summa Theologiae*, II–II, q. 30. a. 4.

6. XXVI Sunday in Ordinary Time. This Collect already appears in the eighth century among the euchological texts of the Gelasian Sacramentary (1198).

7. Cf. *Homily 22*: *CCL*, 122, 149–151.

8. Apostolic Exhortation *Evangelii Gaudium*, 24.

9. No. 2.

10. Saint John Paul II, Encyclical Letter *Dives in Misericordia*, 15.

11. Ibid., 13.

12. *Words of Light and Love*, 57.

13. *Homilies on the Psalms*, 76, 11.

Laudato Si'

Praise Be to You: On Care for Our Common Home

May 24, 2015

ENCYCLICAL LETTER
LAUDATO SI'
OF THE HOLY FATHER
FRANCIS
ON CARE FOR OUR COMMON HOME

1. *"Laudato Si', mi' Signore"—"Praise be to you, my Lord."* In the words of this beautiful canticle, Saint Francis of Assisi reminds us that our common home is like a sister with whom we share our life and a beautiful mother who opens her arms to embrace us. "Praise be to you, my Lord, through our Sister, Mother Earth, who sustains and governs us, and who produces various fruit with colored flowers and herbs."[1]

2. This sister now cries out to us because of the harm we have inflicted on her by our irresponsible use and abuse of the goods with which God has endowed her. We have come to see ourselves as her lords and masters, entitled to plunder her at will. The violence present in our hearts, wounded by sin, is also reflected in the symptoms of sickness evident in the soil, in the water, in the air, and in all forms of life. This is why the earth herself, burdened and laid waste, is among the most abandoned and maltreated of our poor; she "groans in travail" (Rom 8:22). We have forgotten that we ourselves are dust of the earth (cf. Gn 2:7); our very bodies are made up of her elements, we breathe her air, and we receive life and refreshment from her waters.

Nothing in this world is indifferent to us

3. More than fifty years ago, with the world teetering on the brink of nuclear crisis, Pope Saint John XXIII wrote an Encyclical which not only rejected war but offered a proposal for peace. He addressed his message *Pacem in Terris* to the entire "Catholic world" and indeed "to all men and women of good will." Now, faced as we are with global environmental deterioration, I wish to address every person living on this planet. In my Apostolic Exhortation *Evangelii Gaudium,* I wrote to all the members of the Church with the aim of encouraging ongoing missionary renewal. In

this Encyclical, I would like to enter into dialogue with all people about our common home.

4. In 1971, eight years after *Pacem in Terris*, Blessed Pope Paul VI referred to the ecological concern as "a tragic consequence" of unchecked human activity: "Due to an ill-considered exploitation of nature, humanity runs the risk of destroying it and becoming in turn a victim of this degradation."[2] He spoke in similar terms to the Food and Agriculture Organization of the United Nations about the potential for an "ecological catastrophe under the effective explosion of industrial civilization," and stressed "the urgent need for a radical change in the conduct of humanity," inasmuch as "the most extraordinary scientific advances, the most amazing technical abilities, the most astonishing economic growth, unless they are accompanied by authentic social and moral progress, will definitively turn against man."[3]

5. Saint John Paul II became increasingly concerned about this issue. In his first Encyclical he warned that human beings frequently seem "to see no other meaning in their natural environment than what serves for immediate use and consumption."[4] Subsequently, he would call for a global ecological *conversion*.[5] At the same time, he noted that little effort had been made to "safeguard the moral conditions for an authentic *human ecology*."[6] The destruction of the human environment is extremely serious, not only because God has entrusted the world to us men and women, but because human life is itself a gift which must be defended from various forms of debasement. Every effort to protect and improve our world entails profound changes in "lifestyles, models of production and consumption, and the established structures of power which today govern societies."[7] Authentic human development has a moral character. It presumes full respect for the human person, but it must also be concerned for the world around us and "take into account the nature of each being and of its mutual connection in an ordered system."[8] Accordingly, our human ability to transform reality must proceed in line with God's original gift of all that is.[9]

6. My predecessor Benedict XVI likewise proposed "eliminating the structural causes of the dysfunctions of the world economy and correcting models of growth which have proved incapable of ensuring respect for the environment."[10] He observed that the world cannot be analyzed by isolating only one of its aspects, since "the book of nature is one and indivisible," and includes the environment, life, sexuality, the family, social relations, and so forth. It follows that "the deterioration of nature is closely connected to the culture which shapes human coexistence."[11] Pope Benedict asked us to recognize that the natural environment has been gravely damaged by our irresponsible behavior. The social environment has also suffered damage. Both are ultimately due to the same evil: the notion that there are no indisputable truths to guide our lives, and hence human freedom is limitless. We have forgotten that "man is not only a freedom which he creates for himself. Man does not create himself. He is spirit and will, but also nature."[12] With paternal concern, Benedict urged us to realize that creation is harmed "where we ourselves have the final word, where everything is simply our property and we use it for ourselves alone. The misuse of creation begins when we no longer recognize any higher instance than ourselves, when we see nothing else but ourselves."[13]

United by the same concern

7. These statements of the Popes echo the reflections of numerous scientists, philosophers, theologians, and civic groups, all of which have enriched the Church's thinking on these questions. Outside the Catholic Church, other Churches and Christian communities—and other religions as well—have expressed deep concern and offered valuable reflections on issues which all of us find disturbing. To give just one striking example, I would mention the statements made by the beloved Ecumenical Patriarch Bartholomew, with whom we share the hope of full ecclesial communion.

8. Patriarch Bartholomew has spoken in particular of the need for each of us to repent of the ways we have harmed the planet, for "inasmuch as we all generate small ecological damage," we are called to acknowledge "our

contribution, smaller or greater, to the disfigurement and destruction of creation."[14] He has repeatedly stated this firmly and persuasively, challenging us to acknowledge our sins against creation: "For human beings . . . to destroy the biological diversity of God's creation; for human beings to degrade the integrity of the earth by causing changes in its climate, by stripping the earth of its natural forests or destroying its wetlands; for human beings to contaminate the earth's waters, its land, its air, and its life—these are sins."[15] For "to commit a crime against the natural world is a sin against ourselves and a sin against God."[16]

9. At the same time, Bartholomew has drawn attention to the ethical and spiritual roots of environmental problems, which require that we look for solutions not only in technology but in a change of humanity; otherwise we would be dealing merely with symptoms. He asks us to replace consumption with sacrifice, greed with generosity, wastefulness with a spirit of sharing, an asceticism which "entails learning to give, and not simply to give up. It is a way of loving, of moving gradually away from what I want to what God's world needs. It is liberation from fear, greed and compulsion."[17] As Christians, we are also called "to accept the world as a sacrament of communion, as a way of sharing with God and our neighbors on a global scale. It is our humble conviction that the divine and the human meet in the slightest detail in the seamless garment of God's creation, in the last speck of dust of our planet."[18]

Saint Francis of Assisi

10. I do not want to write this Encyclical without turning to that attractive and compelling figure, whose name I took as my guide and inspiration when I was elected Bishop of Rome. I believe that Saint Francis is the example par excellence of care for the vulnerable and of an integral ecology lived out joyfully and authentically. He is the patron saint of all who study and work in the area of ecology, and he is also much loved by non-Christians. He was particularly concerned for God's creation and for the poor and outcast. He loved, and was deeply loved for his joy, his generous self-giving, his openheartedness. He was a mystic and a pilgrim who lived in simplicity and in wonderful harmony with God, with

others, with nature, and with himself. He shows us just how inseparable the bond is between concern for nature, justice for the poor, commitment to society, and interior peace.

11. Francis helps us to see that an integral ecology calls for openness to categories which transcend the language of mathematics and biology, and take us to the heart of what it is to be human. Just as happens when we fall in love with someone, whenever he would gaze at the sun, the moon, or the smallest of animals, he burst into song, drawing all other creatures into his praise. He communed with all creation, even preaching to the flowers, inviting them "to praise the Lord, just as if they were endowed with reason."[19] His response to the world around him was so much more than intellectual appreciation or economic calculus, for to him each and every creature was a sister united to him by bonds of affection. That is why he felt called to care for all that exists. His disciple Saint Bonaventure tells us that, "from a reflection on the primary source of all things, filled with even more abundant piety, he would call creatures, no matter how small, by the name of 'brother' or 'sister.'"[20] Such a conviction cannot be written off as naive romanticism, for it affects the choices which determine our behavior. If we approach nature and the environment without this openness to awe and wonder, if we no longer speak the language of fraternity and beauty in our relationship with the world, our attitude will be that of masters, consumers, ruthless exploiters, unable to set limits on their immediate needs. By contrast, if we feel intimately united with all that exists, then sobriety and care will well up spontaneously. The poverty and austerity of Saint Francis were no mere veneer of asceticism, but something much more radical: a refusal to turn reality into an object simply to be used and controlled.

12. What is more, Saint Francis, faithful to Scripture, invites us to see nature as a magnificent book in which God speaks to us and grants us a glimpse of his infinite beauty and goodness. "Through the greatness and the beauty of creatures one comes to know by analogy their maker" (Ws 13:5); indeed, "his eternal power and divinity have been made known through his works since the creation of the world" (Rom 1:20). For this reason, Francis asked that part of the friary garden always

be left untouched, so that wild flowers and herbs could grow there, and those who saw them could raise their minds to God, the Creator of such beauty.[21] Rather than a problem to be solved, the world is a joyful mystery to be contemplated with gladness and praise.

My appeal

13. The urgent challenge to protect our common home includes a concern to bring the whole human family together to seek a sustainable and integral development, for we know that things can change. The Creator does not abandon us; he never forsakes his loving plan or repents of having created us. Humanity still has the ability to work together in building our common home. Here I want to recognize, encourage, and thank all those striving in countless ways to guarantee the protection of the home which we share. Particular appreciation is owed to those who tirelessly seek to resolve the tragic effects of environmental degradation on the lives of the world's poorest. Young people demand change. They wonder how anyone can claim to be building a better future without thinking of the environmental crisis and the sufferings of the excluded.

14. I urgently appeal, then, for a new dialogue about how we are shaping the future of our planet. We need a conversation which includes everyone, since the environmental challenge we are undergoing, and its human roots, concern and affect us all. The worldwide ecological movement has already made considerable progress and led to the establishment of numerous organizations committed to raising awareness of these challenges. Regrettably, many efforts to seek concrete solutions to the environmental crisis have proved ineffective, not only because of powerful opposition but also because of a more general lack of interest. Obstructionist attitudes, even on the part of believers, can range from denial of the problem to indifference, nonchalant resignation or blind confidence in technical solutions. We require a new and universal solidarity. As the bishops of Southern Africa have stated: "Everyone's talents and involvement are needed to redress the damage caused by human abuse of God's creation."[22] All of us can cooperate as instruments of

God for the care of creation, each according to his or her own culture, experience, involvements, and talents.

15. It is my hope that this Encyclical Letter, which is now added to the body of the Church's social teaching, can help us to acknowledge the appeal, immensity, and urgency of the challenge we face. I will begin by briefly reviewing several aspects of the present ecological crisis, with the aim of drawing on the results of the best scientific research available today, letting them touch us deeply and provide a concrete foundation for the ethical and spiritual itinerary that follows. I will then consider some principles drawn from the Judeo-Christian tradition which can render our commitment to the environment more coherent. I will then attempt to get to the roots of the present situation, so as to consider not only its symptoms but also its deepest causes. This will help to provide an approach to ecology which respects our unique place as human beings in this world and our relationship to our surroundings. In light of this reflection, I will advance some broader proposals for dialogue and action which would involve each of us as individuals, and also affect international policy. Finally, convinced as I am that change is impossible without motivation and a process of education, I will offer some inspired guidelines for human development to be found in the treasure of Christian spiritual experience.

16. Although each chapter will have its own subject and specific approach, it will also take up and re-examine important questions previously dealt with. This is particularly the case with a number of themes which will reappear as the Encyclical unfolds. As examples, I will point to the intimate relationship between the poor and the fragility of the planet, the conviction that everything in the world is connected, the critique of new paradigms and forms of power derived from technology, the call to seek other ways of understanding the economy and progress, the value proper to each creature, the human meaning of ecology, the need for forthright and honest debate, the serious responsibility of international and local policy, the throwaway culture and the proposal of a new lifestyle. These questions will not be dealt with once and for all, but reframed and enriched again and again.

CHAPTER ONE

WHAT IS HAPPENING TO OUR COMMON HOME

17. Theological and philosophical reflections on the situation of humanity and the world can sound tiresome and abstract, unless they are grounded in a fresh analysis of our present situation, which is in many ways unprecedented in the history of humanity. So, before considering how faith brings new incentives and requirements with regard to the world of which we are a part, I will briefly turn to what is happening to our common home.

18. The continued acceleration of changes affecting humanity and the planet is coupled today with a more intensified pace of life and work which might be called "rapidification." Although change is part of the working of complex systems, the speed with which human activity has developed contrasts with the naturally slow pace of biological evolution. Moreover, the goals of this rapid and constant change are not necessarily geared to the common good or to integral and sustainable human development. Change is something desirable, yet it becomes a source of anxiety when it causes harm to the world and to the quality of life of much of humanity.

19. Following a period of irrational confidence in progress and human abilities, some sectors of society are now adopting a more critical approach. We see increasing sensitivity to the environment and the need to protect nature, along with a growing concern, both genuine and distressing, for what is happening to our planet. Let us review, however cursorily, those questions which are troubling us today and which we can no longer sweep under the carpet. Our goal is not to amass information or to satisfy curiosity, but rather to become painfully aware, to dare to turn what is happening to the world into our own personal suffering and thus to discover what each of us can do about it.

I. Pollution and climate change

Pollution, waste, and the throwaway culture

20. Some forms of pollution are part of people's daily experience. Exposure to atmospheric pollutants produces a broad spectrum of health hazards, especially for the poor, and causes millions of premature deaths. People take sick, for example, from breathing high levels of smoke from fuels used in cooking or heating. There is also pollution that affects everyone, caused by transport, industrial fumes, substances which contribute to the acidification of soil and water, fertilizers, insecticides, fungicides, herbicides, and agrotoxins in general. Technology, which, linked to business interests, is presented as the only way of solving these problems, in fact proves incapable of seeing the mysterious network of relations between things and so sometimes solves one problem only to create others.

21. Account must also be taken of the pollution produced by residue, including dangerous waste present in different areas. Each year hundreds of millions of tons of waste are generated, much of it non-biodegradable, highly toxic, and radioactive, from homes and businesses, from construction and demolition sites, from clinical, electronic, and industrial sources. The earth, our home, is beginning to look more and more like an immense pile of filth. In many parts of the planet, the elderly lament that once beautiful landscapes are now covered with rubbish. Industrial waste and chemical products utilized in cities and agricultural areas can lead to bioaccumulation in the organisms of the local population, even when levels of toxins in those places are low. Frequently no measures are taken until after people's health has been irreversibly affected.

22. These problems are closely linked to a throwaway culture which affects the excluded just as it quickly reduces things to rubbish. To cite one example, most of the paper we produce is thrown away and not recycled. It is hard for us to accept that the way natural ecosystems work is exemplary: plants synthesize nutrients which feed herbivores; these in turn become food for carnivores, which produce significant quantities of organic waste which give rise to new generations of plants. But our

industrial system, at the end of its cycle of production and consumption, has not developed the capacity to absorb and reuse waste and by-products. We have not yet managed to adopt a circular model of production capable of preserving resources for present and future generations, while limiting as much as possible the use of non-renewable resources, moderating their consumption, maximizing their efficient use, reusing and recycling them. A serious consideration of this issue would be one way of counteracting the throwaway culture which affects the entire planet, but it must be said that only limited progress has been made in this regard.

Climate as a common good

23. The climate is a common good, belonging to all and meant for all. At the global level, it is a complex system linked to many of the essential conditions for human life. A very solid scientific consensus indicates that we are presently witnessing a disturbing warming of the climatic system. In recent decades this warming has been accompanied by a constant rise in the sea level and, it would appear, by an increase of extreme weather events, even if a scientifically determinable cause cannot be assigned to each particular phenomenon. Humanity is called to recognize the need for changes of lifestyle, production, and consumption, in order to combat this warming or at least the human causes which produce or aggravate it. It is true that there are other factors (such as volcanic activity, variations in the earth's orbit and axis, the solar cycle), yet a number of scientific studies indicate that most global warming in recent decades is due to the great concentration of greenhouse gases (carbon dioxide, methane, nitrogen oxides, and others) released mainly as a result of human activity. As these gases build up in the atmosphere, they hamper the escape of heat produced by sunlight at the earth's surface. The problem is aggravated by a model of development based on the intensive use of fossil fuels, which is at the heart of the worldwide energy system. Another determining factor has been an increase in changed uses of the soil, principally deforestation for agricultural purposes.

24. Warming has effects on the carbon cycle. It creates a vicious circle which aggravates the situation even more, affecting the availability of

essential resources like drinking water, energy, and agricultural production in warmer regions, and leading to the extinction of part of the planet's biodiversity. The melting in the polar ice caps and in high altitude plains can lead to the dangerous release of methane gas, while the decomposition of frozen organic material can further increase the emission of carbon dioxide. Things are made worse by the loss of tropical forests which would otherwise help to mitigate climate change. Carbon dioxide pollution increases the acidification of the oceans and compromises the marine food chain. If present trends continue, this century may well witness extraordinary climate change and an unprecedented destruction of ecosystems, with serious consequences for all of us. A rise in the sea level, for example, can create extremely serious situations, if we consider that a quarter of the world's population lives on the coast or nearby, and that the majority of our megacities are situated in coastal areas.

25. Climate change is a global problem with grave implications: environmental, social, economic, political, and for the distribution of goods. It represents one of the principal challenges facing humanity in our day. Its worst impact will probably be felt by developing countries in coming decades. Many of the poor live in areas particularly affected by phenomena related to warming, and their means of subsistence are largely dependent on natural reserves and ecosystemic services such as agriculture, fishing, and forestry. They have no other financial activities or resources which can enable them to adapt to climate change or to face natural disasters, and their access to social services and protection is very limited. For example, changes in climate, to which animals and plants cannot adapt, lead them to migrate; this in turn affects the livelihood of the poor, who are then forced to leave their homes, with great uncertainty for their future and that of their children. There has been a tragic rise in the number of migrants seeking to flee from the growing poverty caused by environmental degradation. They are not recognized by international conventions as refugees; they bear the loss of the lives they have left behind, without enjoying any legal protection whatsoever. Sadly, there is widespread indifference to such suffering, which is even

now taking place throughout our world. Our lack of response to these tragedies involving our brothers and sisters points to the loss of that sense of responsibility for our fellow men and women upon which all civil society is founded.

26. Many of those who possess more resources and economic or political power seem mostly to be concerned with masking the problems or concealing their symptoms, simply making efforts to reduce some of the negative impacts of climate change. However, many of these symptoms indicate that such effects will continue to worsen if we continue with current models of production and consumption. There is an urgent need to develop policies so that, in the next few years, the emission of carbon dioxide and other highly polluting gases can be drastically reduced, for example, substituting for fossil fuels and developing sources of renewable energy. Worldwide there is minimal access to clean and renewable energy. There is still a need to develop adequate storage technologies. Some countries have made considerable progress, although it is far from constituting a significant proportion. Investments have also been made in means of production and transportation which consume less energy and require fewer raw materials, as well as in methods of construction and renovating buildings which improve their energy efficiency. But these good practices are still far from widespread.

II. The issue of water

27. Other indicators of the present situation have to do with the depletion of natural resources. We all know that it is not possible to sustain the present level of consumption in developed countries and wealthier sectors of society, where the habit of wasting and discarding has reached unprecedented levels. The exploitation of the planet has already exceeded acceptable limits and we still have not solved the problem of poverty.

28. Fresh drinking water is an issue of primary importance, since it is indispensable for human life and for supporting terrestrial and aquatic ecosystems. Sources of fresh water are necessary for health care, agriculture, and industry. Water supplies used to be relatively constant, but now

in many places demand exceeds the sustainable supply, with dramatic consequences in the short and long term. Large cities dependent on significant supplies of water have experienced periods of shortage, and at critical moments these have not always been administered with sufficient oversight and impartiality. Water poverty especially affects Africa where large sectors of the population have no access to safe drinking water or experience droughts which impede agricultural production. Some countries have areas rich in water while others endure drastic scarcity.

29. One particularly serious problem is the quality of water available to the poor. Every day, unsafe water results in many deaths and the spread of water-related diseases, including those caused by microorganisms and chemical substances. Dysentery and cholera, linked to inadequate hygiene and water supplies, are a significant cause of suffering and of infant mortality. Underground water sources in many places are threatened by the pollution produced in certain mining, farming, and industrial activities, especially in countries lacking adequate regulation or controls. It is not only a question of industrial waste. Detergents and chemical products, commonly used in many places of the world, continue to pour into our rivers, lakes, and seas.

30. Even as the quality of available water is constantly diminishing, in some places there is a growing tendency, despite its scarcity, to privatize this resource, turning it into a commodity subject to the laws of the market. Yet *access to safe drinkable water is a basic and universal human right, since it is essential to human survival and, as such, is a condition for the exercise of other human rights.* Our world has a grave social debt toward the poor who lack access to drinking water, because *they are denied the right to a life consistent with their inalienable dignity.* This debt can be paid partly by an increase in funding to provide clean water and sanitary services among the poor. But water continues to be wasted, not only in the developed world but also in developing countries which possess it in abundance. This shows that the problem of water is partly an educational and cultural issue, since there is little awareness of the seriousness of such behavior within a context of great inequality.

31. Greater scarcity of water will lead to an increase in the cost of food and the various products which depend on its use. Some studies warn that an acute water shortage may occur within a few decades unless urgent action is taken. The environmental repercussions could affect billions of people; it is also conceivable that the control of water by large multinational businesses may become a major source of conflict in this century.[23]

III. Loss of biodiversity

32. The earth's resources are also being plundered because of short-sighted approaches to the economy, commerce, and production. The loss of forests and woodlands entails the loss of species which may constitute extremely important resources in the future, not only for food but also for curing disease and other uses. Different species contain genes which could be key resources in years ahead for meeting human needs and regulating environmental problems.

33. It is not enough, however, to think of different species merely as potential "resources" to be exploited, while overlooking the fact that they have value in themselves. Each year sees the disappearance of thousands of plant and animal species which we will never know, which our children will never see, because they have been lost forever. The great majority become extinct for reasons related to human activity. Because of us, thousands of species will no longer give glory to God by their very existence, nor convey their message to us. We have no such right.

34. It may well disturb us to learn of the extinction of mammals or birds, since they are more visible. But the good functioning of ecosystems also requires fungi, algae, worms, insects, reptiles, and an innumerable variety of microorganisms. Some less numerous species, although generally unseen, nonetheless play a critical role in maintaining the equilibrium of a particular place. Human beings must intervene when a geosystem reaches a critical state. But nowadays, such intervention in nature has become more and more frequent. As a consequence, serious problems arise, leading to further interventions; human activity becomes

ubiquitous, with all the risks which this entails. Often a vicious circle results, as human intervention to resolve a problem further aggravates the situation. For example, many birds and insects which disappear due to synthetic agrotoxins are helpful for agriculture: their disappearance will have to be compensated for by yet other techniques which may well prove harmful. We must be grateful for the praiseworthy efforts being made by scientists and engineers dedicated to finding solutions to man-made problems. But a sober look at our world shows that the degree of human intervention, often in the service of business interests and consumerism, is actually making our earth less rich and beautiful, ever more limited and gray, even as technological advances and consumer goods continue to abound limitlessly. We seem to think that we can substitute an irreplaceable and irretrievable beauty with something which we have created ourselves.

35. In assessing the environmental impact of any project, concern is usually shown for its effects on soil, water, and air, yet few careful studies are made of its impact on biodiversity, as if the loss of species or animals and plant groups were of little importance. Highways, new plantations, the fencing-off of certain areas, the damming of water sources, and similar developments, crowd out natural habitats and, at times, break them up in such a way that animal populations can no longer migrate or roam freely. As a result, some species face extinction. Alternatives exist which at least lessen the impact of these projects, like the creation of biological corridors, but few countries demonstrate such concern and foresight. Frequently, when certain species are exploited commercially, little attention is paid to studying their reproductive patterns in order to prevent their depletion and the consequent imbalance of the ecosystem.

36. Caring for ecosystems demands far-sightedness, since no one looking for quick and easy profit is truly interested in their preservation. But the cost of the damage caused by such selfish lack of concern is much greater than the economic benefits to be obtained. Where certain species are destroyed or seriously harmed, the values involved are incalculable. We can be silent witnesses to terrible injustices if we think that we can

obtain significant benefits by making the rest of humanity, present and future, pay the extremely high costs of environmental deterioration.

37. Some countries have made significant progress in establishing sanctuaries on land and in the oceans where any human intervention is prohibited which might modify their features or alter their original structures. In the protection of biodiversity, specialists insist on the need for particular attention to be shown to areas richer both in the number of species and in endemic, rare, or less protected species. Certain places need greater protection because of their immense importance for the global ecosystem, or because they represent important water reserves and thus safeguard other forms of life.

38. Let us mention, for example, those richly biodiverse lungs of our planet which are the Amazon and the Congo basins, or the great aquifers and glaciers. We know how important these are for the entire earth and for the future of humanity. The ecosystems of tropical forests possess an enormously complex biodiversity which is almost impossible to appreciate fully, yet when these forests are burned down or leveled for purposes of cultivation, within the space of a few years countless species are lost and the areas frequently become arid wastelands. A delicate balance has to be maintained when speaking about these places, for we cannot overlook the huge global economic interests which, under the guise of protecting them, can undermine the sovereignty of individual nations. In fact, there are "proposals to internationalize the Amazon, which only serve the economic interests of transnational corporations."[24] We cannot fail to praise the commitment of international agencies and civil society organizations which draw public attention to these issues and offer critical cooperation, employing legitimate means of pressure, to ensure that each government carries out its proper and inalienable responsibility to preserve its country's environment and natural resources, without capitulating to spurious local or international interests.

39. The replacement of virgin forest with plantations of trees, usually monocultures, is rarely adequately analyzed. Yet this can seriously compromise a biodiversity which the new species being introduced does not

accommodate. Similarly, wetlands converted into cultivated land lose the enormous biodiversity which they formerly hosted. In some coastal areas the disappearance of ecosystems sustained by mangrove swamps is a source of serious concern.

40. Oceans not only contain the bulk of our planet's water supply, but also most of the immense variety of living creatures, many of them still unknown to us and threatened for various reasons. What is more, marine life in rivers, lakes, seas, and oceans, which feeds a great part of the world's population, is affected by uncontrolled fishing, leading to a drastic depletion of certain species. Selective forms of fishing which discard much of what they collect continue unabated. Particularly threatened are marine organisms which we tend to overlook, like some forms of plankton; they represent a significant element in the ocean food chain, and species used for our food ultimately depend on them.

41. In tropical and subtropical seas, we find coral reefs comparable to the great forests on dry land, for they shelter approximately a million species, including fish, crabs, molluscs, sponges, and algae. Many of the world's coral reefs are already barren or in a state of constant decline. "Who turned the wonderworld of the seas into underwater cemeteries bereft of color and life?"[25] This phenomenon is due largely to pollution which reaches the sea as the result of deforestation, agricultural monocultures, industrial waste, and destructive fishing methods, especially those using cyanide and dynamite. It is aggravated by the rise in temperature of the oceans. All of this helps us to see that every intervention in nature can have consequences which are not immediately evident, and that certain ways of exploiting resources prove costly in terms of degradation which ultimately reaches the ocean bed itself.

42. Greater investment needs to be made in research aimed at understanding more fully the functioning of ecosystems and adequately analyzing the different variables associated with any significant modification of the environment. Because all creatures are connected, each must be cherished with love and respect, for all of us as living creatures are dependent on one another. Each area is responsible for the care of this family.

This will require undertaking a careful inventory of the species which it hosts, with a view to developing programs and strategies of protection with particular care for safeguarding species heading toward extinction.

IV. Decline in the quality of human life and the breakdown of society

43. Human beings too are creatures of this world, enjoying a right to life and happiness, and endowed with unique dignity. So we cannot fail to consider the effects on people's lives of environmental deterioration, current models of development, and the throwaway culture.

44. Nowadays, for example, we are conscious of the disproportionate and unruly growth of many cities, which have become unhealthy to live in, not only because of pollution caused by toxic emissions but also as a result of urban chaos, poor transportation, and visual pollution and noise. Many cities are huge, inefficient structures, excessively wasteful of energy and water. Neighborhoods, even those recently built, are congested, chaotic, and lacking in sufficient green space. We were not meant to be inundated by cement, asphalt, glass, and metal, and deprived of physical contact with nature.

45. In some places, rural and urban alike, the privatization of certain spaces has restricted people's access to places of particular beauty. In others, "ecological" neighborhoods have been created which are closed to outsiders in order to ensure an artificial tranquility. Frequently, we find beautiful and carefully manicured green spaces in so-called "safer" areas of cities, but not in the more hidden areas where the disposable of society live.

46. The social dimensions of global change include the effects of technological innovations on employment, social exclusion, an inequitable distribution and consumption of energy and other services, social breakdown, increased violence and a rise in new forms of social aggression, drug trafficking, growing drug use by young people, and the loss of identity. These are signs that the growth of the past two centuries has not always led to an integral development and an improvement in the

quality of life. Some of these signs are also symptomatic of real social decline, the silent rupture of the bonds of integration and social cohesion.

47. Furthermore, when media and the digital world become omnipresent, their influence can stop people from learning how to live wisely, to think deeply, and to love generously. In this context, the great sages of the past run the risk of going unheard amid the noise and distractions of an information overload. Efforts need to be made to help these media become sources of new cultural progress for humanity and not a threat to our deepest riches. True wisdom, as the fruit of self-examination, dialogue, and generous encounter between persons, is not acquired by a mere accumulation of data which eventually leads to overload and confusion, a sort of mental pollution. Real relationships with others, with all the challenges they entail, now tend to be replaced by a type of internet communication which enables us to choose or eliminate relationships at whim, thus giving rise to a new type of contrived emotion which has more to do with devices and displays than with other people and with nature. Today's media do enable us to communicate and to share our knowledge and affections. Yet at times they also shield us from direct contact with the pain, the fears, and the joys of others and the complexity of their personal experiences. For this reason, we should be concerned that, alongside the exciting possibilities offered by these media, a deep and melancholic dissatisfaction with interpersonal relations, or a harmful sense of isolation, can also arise.

V. Global inequality

48. The human environment and the natural environment deteriorate together; we cannot adequately combat environmental degradation unless we attend to causes related to human and social degradation. In fact, the deterioration of the environment and of society affects the most vulnerable people on the planet: "Both everyday experience and scientific research show that the gravest effects of all attacks on the environment are suffered by the poorest."[26] For example, the depletion of fishing reserves especially hurts small fishing communities without the means to replace those resources; water pollution particularly affects

the poor who cannot buy bottled water; and rises in the sea level mainly affect impoverished coastal populations who have nowhere else to go. The impact of present imbalances is also seen in the premature death of many of the poor, in conflicts sparked by the shortage of resources, and in any number of other problems which are insufficiently represented on global agendas.[27]

49. It needs to be said that, generally speaking, there is little in the way of clear awareness of problems which especially affect the excluded. Yet they are the majority of the planet's population, billions of people. These days, they are mentioned in international political and economic discussions, but one often has the impression that their problems are brought up as an afterthought, a question which gets added almost out of duty or in a tangential way, if not treated merely as collateral damage. Indeed, when all is said and done, they frequently remain at the bottom of the pile. This is due partly to the fact that many professionals, opinion makers, communications media, and centers of power, being located in affluent urban areas, are far removed from the poor, with little direct contact with their problems. They live and reason from the comfortable position of a high level of development and a quality of life well beyond the reach of the majority of the world's population. This lack of physical contact and encounter, encouraged at times by the disintegration of our cities, can lead to a numbing of conscience and to tendentious analyses which neglect parts of reality. At times this attitude exists side by side with a "green" rhetoric. Today, however, we have to realize that a true ecological approach *always* becomes a social approach; it must integrate questions of justice in debates on the environment, so as to hear *both the cry of the earth and the cry of the poor*.

50. Instead of resolving the problems of the poor and thinking of how the world can be different, some can only propose a reduction in the birth rate. At times, developing countries face forms of international pressure which make economic assistance contingent on certain policies of "reproductive health." Yet "while it is true that an unequal distribution of the population and of available resources creates obstacles to development and a sustainable use of the environment, it must nonetheless be

recognized that demographic growth is fully compatible with an integral and shared development."[28] To blame population growth instead of extreme and selective consumerism on the part of some, is one way of refusing to face the issues. It is an attempt to legitimize the present model of distribution, where a minority believes that it has the right to consume in a way which can never be universalized, since the planet could not even contain the waste products of such consumption. Besides, we know that approximately a third of all food produced is discarded, and "whenever food is thrown out it is as if it were stolen from the table of the poor."[29] Still, attention needs to be paid to imbalances in population density, on both national and global levels, since a rise in consumption would lead to complex regional situations, as a result of the interplay between problems linked to environmental pollution, transport, waste treatment, loss of resources, and quality of life.

51. Inequity affects not only individuals but entire countries; it compels us to consider an ethics of international relations. A true "ecological debt" exists, particularly between the global north and south, connected to commercial imbalances with effects on the environment, and the disproportionate use of natural resources by certain countries over long periods of time. The export of raw materials to satisfy markets in the industrialized north has caused harm locally, as for example in mercury pollution in gold mining or sulphur dioxide pollution in copper mining. There is a pressing need to calculate the use of environmental space throughout the world for depositing gas residues which have been accumulating for two centuries and have created a situation which currently affects all the countries of the world. The warming caused by huge consumption on the part of some rich countries has repercussions on the poorest areas of the world, especially Africa, where a rise in temperature, together with drought, has proved devastating for farming. There is also the damage caused by the export of solid waste and toxic liquids to developing countries, and by the pollution produced by companies which operate in less developed countries in ways they could never do at home, in the countries in which they raise their capital: "We note that often the businesses which operate this way are multinationals. They do here

what they would never do in developed countries or the so-called first world. Generally, after ceasing their activity and withdrawing, they leave behind great human and environmental liabilities such as unemployment, abandoned towns, the depletion of natural reserves, deforestation, the impoverishment of agriculture and local stock breeding, open pits, riven hills, polluted rivers and a handful of social works which are no longer sustainable."[30]

52. The foreign debt of poor countries has become a way of controlling them, yet this is not the case where ecological debt is concerned. In different ways, developing countries, where the most important reserves of the biosphere are found, continue to fuel the development of richer countries at the cost of their own present and future. The land of the southern poor is rich and mostly unpolluted, yet access to ownership of goods and resources for meeting vital needs is inhibited by a system of commercial relations and ownership which is structurally perverse. The developed countries ought to help pay this debt by significantly limiting their consumption of non-renewable energy and by assisting poorer countries to support policies and programs of sustainable development. The poorest areas and countries are less capable of adopting new models for reducing environmental impact because they lack the wherewithal to develop the necessary processes and to cover their costs. We must continue to be aware that, regarding climate change, there are *differentiated responsibilities*. As the United States bishops have said, greater attention must be given to "the needs of the poor, the weak and the vulnerable, in a debate often dominated by more powerful interests."[31] We need to strengthen the conviction that we are one single human family. There are no frontiers or barriers, political or social, behind which we can hide, still less is there room for the globalization of indifference.

VI. Weak responses

53. These situations have caused sister earth, along with all the abandoned of our world, to cry out, pleading that we take another course. Never have we so hurt and mistreated our common home as we have in the last two hundred years. Yet we are called to be instruments of God our

Father, so that our planet might be what he desired when he created it and correspond with his plan for peace, beauty, and fullness. The problem is that we still lack the culture needed to confront this crisis. We lack leadership capable of striking out on new paths and meeting the needs of the present with concern for all and without prejudice toward coming generations. The establishment of a legal framework which can set clear boundaries and ensure the protection of ecosystems has become indispensable; otherwise, the new power structures based on the techno-economic paradigm may overwhelm not only our politics but also freedom and justice.

54. It is remarkable how weak international political responses have been. The failure of global summits on the environment make it plain that our politics are subject to technology and finance. There are too many special interests, and economic interests easily end up trumping the common good and manipulating information so that their own plans will not be affected. The *Aparecida Document* urges that "the interests of economic groups which irrationally demolish sources of life should not prevail in dealing with natural resources."[32] The alliance between the economy and technology ends up sidelining anything unrelated to its immediate interests. Consequently the most one can expect is superficial rhetoric, sporadic acts of philanthropy, and perfunctory expressions of concern for the environment, whereas any genuine attempt by groups within society to introduce change is viewed as a nuisance based on romantic illusions or an obstacle to be circumvented.

55. Some countries are gradually making significant progress, developing more effective controls and working to combat corruption. People may well have a growing ecological sensitivity but it has not succeeded in changing their harmful habits of consumption which, rather than decreasing, appear to be growing all the more. A simple example is the increasing use and power of air-conditioning. The markets, which immediately benefit from sales, stimulate ever greater demand. An outsider looking at our world would be amazed at such behavior, which at times appears self-destructive.

56. In the meantime, economic powers continue to justify the current global system where priority tends to be given to speculation and the pursuit of financial gain, which fail to take the context into account, let alone the effects on human dignity and the natural environment. Here we see how environmental deterioration and human and ethical degradation are closely linked. Many people will deny doing anything wrong because distractions constantly dull our consciousness of just how limited and finite our world really is. As a result, "whatever is fragile, like the environment, is defenseless before the interests of a deified market, which become the only rule."[33]

57. It is foreseeable that, once certain resources have been depleted, the scene will be set for new wars, albeit under the guise of noble claims. War always does grave harm to the environment and to the cultural riches of peoples, risks which are magnified when one considers nuclear arms and biological weapons. "Despite the international agreements which prohibit chemical, bacteriological and biological warfare, the fact is that laboratory research continues to develop new offensive weapons capable of altering the balance of nature."[34] Politics must pay greater attention to foreseeing new conflicts and addressing the causes which can lead to them. But powerful financial interests prove most resistant to this effort, and political planning tends to lack breadth of vision. What would induce anyone, at this stage, to hold on to power only to be remembered for their inability to take action when it was urgent and necessary to do so?

58. In some countries, there are positive examples of environmental improvement: rivers, polluted for decades, have been cleaned up; native woodlands have been restored; landscapes have been beautified thanks to environmental renewal projects; beautiful buildings have been erected; advances have been made in the production of non-polluting energy and in the improvement of public transportation. These achievements do not solve global problems, but they do show that men and women are still capable of intervening positively. For all our limitations, gestures of generosity, solidarity, and care cannot but well up within us, since we were made for love.

59. At the same time we can note the rise of a false or superficial ecology which bolsters complacency and a cheerful recklessness. As often occurs in periods of deep crisis which require bold decisions, we are tempted to think that what is happening is not entirely clear. Superficially, apart from a few obvious signs of pollution and deterioration, things do not look that serious, and the planet could continue as it is for some time. Such evasiveness serves as a license to carrying on with our present lifestyles and models of production and consumption. This is the way human beings contrive to feed their self-destructive vices: trying not to see them, trying not to acknowledge them, delaying the important decisions, and pretending that nothing will happen.

VII. A variety of opinions

60. Finally, we need to acknowledge that different approaches and lines of thought have emerged regarding this situation and its possible solutions. At one extreme, we find those who doggedly uphold the myth of progress and tell us that ecological problems will solve themselves simply with the application of new technology and without any need for ethical considerations or deep change. At the other extreme are those who view men and women and all their interventions as no more than a threat, jeopardizing the global ecosystem, and consequently the presence of human beings on the planet should be reduced and all forms of intervention prohibited. Viable future scenarios will have to be generated between these extremes, since there is no one path to a solution. This makes a variety of proposals possible, all capable of entering into dialogue with a view to developing comprehensive solutions.

61. On many concrete questions, the Church has no reason to offer a definitive opinion; she knows that honest debate must be encouraged among experts, while respecting divergent views. But we need only take a frank look at the facts to see that our common home is falling into serious disrepair. Hope would have us recognize that there is always a way out, that we can always redirect our steps, that we can always do something to solve our problems. Still, we can see signs that things are now reaching a breaking point, due to the rapid pace of change and

degradation; these are evident in large-scale natural disasters as well as social and even financial crises, for the world's problems cannot be analyzed or explained in isolation. There are regions now at high risk and, aside from all doomsday predictions, the present world system is certainly unsustainable from a number of points of view, for we have stopped thinking about the goals of human activity. "If we scan the regions of our planet, we immediately see that humanity has disappointed God's expectations."[35]

CHAPTER TWO

THE GOSPEL OF CREATION

62. Why should this document, addressed to all people of good will, include a chapter dealing with the convictions of believers? I am well aware that in the areas of politics and philosophy there are those who firmly reject the idea of a Creator, or consider it irrelevant, and consequently dismiss as irrational the rich contribution which religions can make toward an integral ecology and the full development of humanity. Others view religions simply as a subculture to be tolerated. Nonetheless, science and religion, with their distinctive approaches to understanding reality, can enter into an intense dialogue fruitful for both.

I. The light offered by faith

63. Given the complexity of the ecological crisis and its multiple causes, we need to realize that the solutions will not emerge from just one way of interpreting and transforming reality. Respect must also be shown for the various cultural riches of different peoples, their art and poetry, their interior life and spirituality. If we are truly concerned to develop an ecology capable of remedying the damage we have done, no branch of the sciences and no form of wisdom can be left out, and that includes religion and the language particular to it. The Catholic Church is open to dialogue with philosophical thought; this has enabled her to produce various syntheses between faith and reason. The development of the Church's social teaching represents such a synthesis with regard to social issues; this teaching is called to be enriched by taking up new challenges.

64. Furthermore, although this Encyclical welcomes dialogue with everyone so that together we can seek paths of liberation, I would like from the outset to show how faith convictions can offer Christians, and some other believers as well, ample motivation to care for nature and for the most vulnerable of their brothers and sisters. If the simple fact of being human moves people to care for the environment of which they are a part, Christians in their turn "realize that their responsibility within

creation, and their duty toward nature and the Creator, are an essential part of their faith."[36] It is good for humanity and the world at large when we believers better recognize the ecological commitments which stem from our convictions.

II. The wisdom of the biblical accounts

65. Without repeating the entire theology of creation, we can ask what the great biblical narratives say about the relationship of human beings with the world. In the first creation account in the Book of Genesis, God's plan includes creating humanity. After the creation of man and woman, "God saw everything that he had made, and behold it was *very good*" (Gn 1:31). The Bible teaches that every man and woman is created out of love and made in God's image and likeness (cf. Gn 1:26). This shows us the immense dignity of each person, "who is not just something, but someone. He is capable of self-knowledge, of self-possession and of freely giving himself and entering into communion with other persons."[37] Saint John Paul II stated that the special love of the Creator for each human being "confers upon him or her an infinite dignity."[38] Those who are committed to defending human dignity can find in the Christian faith the deepest reasons for this commitment. How wonderful is the certainty that each human life is not adrift in the midst of hopeless chaos, in a world ruled by pure chance or endlessly recurring cycles! The Creator can say to each one of us: "Before I formed you in the womb, I knew you" (Jer 1:5). We were conceived in the heart of God, and for this reason "each of us is the result of a thought of God. Each of us is willed, each of us is loved, each of us is necessary."[39]

66. The creation accounts in the book of Genesis contain, in their own symbolic and narrative language, profound teachings about human existence and its historical reality. They suggest that human life is grounded in three fundamental and closely intertwined relationships: with God, with our neighbor, and with the earth itself. According to the Bible, these three vital relationships have been broken, both outwardly and within us. This rupture is sin. The harmony between the Creator, humanity, and creation as a whole was disrupted by our presuming to take the place of

God and refusing to acknowledge our creaturely limitations. This in turn distorted our mandate to "have dominion" over the earth (cf. Gn 1:28), to "till it and keep it" (Gn 2:15). As a result, the originally harmonious relationship between human beings and nature became conflictual (cf. Gn 3:17–19). It is significant that the harmony which Saint Francis of Assisi experienced with all creatures was seen as a healing of that rupture. Saint Bonaventure held that, through universal reconciliation with every creature, Saint Francis in some way returned to the state of original innocence.[40] This is a far cry from our situation today, where sin is manifest in all its destructive power in wars, the various forms of violence and abuse, the abandonment of the most vulnerable, and attacks on nature.

67. We are not God. The earth was here before us and it has been given to us. This allows us to respond to the charge that Judeo-Christian thinking, on the basis of the Genesis account which grants man "dominion" over the earth (cf. Gn 1:28), has encouraged the unbridled exploitation of nature by painting him as domineering and destructive by nature. This is not a correct interpretation of the Bible as understood by the Church. Although it is true that we Christians have at times incorrectly interpreted the Scriptures, nowadays we must forcefully reject the notion that our being created in God's image and given dominion over the earth justifies absolute domination over other creatures. The biblical texts are to be read in their context, with an appropriate hermeneutic, recognizing that they tell us to "till and keep" the garden of the world (cf. Gn 2:15). "Tilling" refers to cultivating, ploughing, or working, while "keeping" means caring, protecting, overseeing, and preserving. This implies a relationship of mutual responsibility between human beings and nature. Each community can take from the bounty of the earth whatever it needs for subsistence, but it also has the duty to protect the earth and to ensure its fruitfulness for coming generations. "The earth is the Lord's" (Ps 24:1); to him belongs "the earth with all that is within it" (Dt 10:14). Thus God rejects every claim to absolute ownership: "The land shall not be sold in perpetuity, for the land is mine; for you are strangers and sojourners with me" (Lv 25:23).

68. This responsibility for God's earth means that human beings, endowed with intelligence, must respect the laws of nature and the delicate equilibria existing between the creatures of this world, for "he commanded and they were created; and he established them for ever and ever; he fixed their bounds and he set a law which cannot pass away" (Ps 148:5b–6). The laws found in the Bible dwell on relationships, not only among individuals but also with other living beings. "You shall not see your brother's donkey or his ox fallen down by the way and withhold your help. . . . If you chance to come upon a bird's nest in any tree or on the ground, with young ones or eggs and the mother sitting upon the young or upon the eggs; you shall not take the mother with the young" (Dt 22:4, 6). Along these same lines, rest on the seventh day is meant not only for human beings, but also so "that your ox and your donkey may have rest" (Ex 23:12). Clearly, the Bible has no place for a tyrannical anthropocentrism unconcerned for other creatures.

69. Together with our obligation to use the earth's goods responsibly, we are called to recognize that other living beings have a value of their own in God's eyes: "by their mere existence they bless him and give him glory,"[41] and indeed, "the Lord rejoices in all his works" (Ps 104:31). By virtue of our unique dignity and our gift of intelligence, we are called to respect creation and its inherent laws, for "the Lord by wisdom founded the earth" (Prv 3:19). In our time, the Church does not simply state that other creatures are completely subordinated to the good of human beings, as if they have no worth in themselves and can be treated as we wish. The German bishops have taught that, where other creatures are concerned, "we can speak of the priority of *being* over that of *being useful*."[42] The *Catechism* clearly and forcefully criticizes a distorted anthropocentrism: "Each creature possesses its own particular goodness and perfection. . . . Each of the various creatures, willed in its own being, reflects in its own way a ray of God's infinite wisdom and goodness. Man must therefore respect the particular goodness of every creature, to avoid any disordered use of things."[43]

70. In the story of Cain and Abel, we see how envy led Cain to commit the ultimate injustice against his brother, which in turn ruptured the

relationship between Cain and God, and between Cain and the earth from which he was banished. This is seen clearly in the dramatic exchange between God and Cain. God asks: "Where is Abel your brother?" Cain answers that he does not know, and God persists: "What have you done? The voice of your brother's blood is crying to me from the ground. And now you are cursed from the ground" (Gn 4:9–11). Disregard for the duty to cultivate and maintain a proper relationship with my neighbor, for whose care and custody I am responsible, ruins my relationship with my own self, with others, with God, and with the earth. When all these relationships are neglected, when justice no longer dwells in the land, the Bible tells us that life itself is endangered. We see this in the story of Noah, where God threatens to do away with humanity because of its constant failure to fulfill the requirements of justice and peace: "I have determined to make an end of all flesh; for the earth is filled with violence through them" (Gn 6:13). These ancient stories, full of symbolism, bear witness to a conviction which we today share, that everything is interconnected, and that genuine care for our own lives and our relationships with nature is inseparable from fraternity, justice, and faithfulness to others.

71. Although "the wickedness of man was great in the earth" (Gn 6:5) and the Lord "was sorry that he had made man on the earth" (Gn 6:6), nonetheless, through Noah, who remained innocent and just, God decided to open a path of salvation. In this way he gave humanity the chance of a new beginning. All it takes is one good person to restore hope! The biblical tradition clearly shows that this renewal entails recovering and respecting the rhythms inscribed in nature by the hand of the Creator. We see this, for example, in the law of the Sabbath. On the seventh day, God rested from all his work. He commanded Israel to set aside each seventh day as a day of rest, a *Sabbath* (cf. Gn 2:2–3; Ex 16:23; 20:10). Similarly, every seven years, a sabbatical year was set aside for Israel, a complete rest for the land (cf. Lv 25:1–4), when sowing was forbidden and one reaped only what was necessary to live on and to feed one's household (cf. Lv 25:4–6). Finally, after seven weeks of years, which is to say forty-nine years, the Jubilee was celebrated as a year of general

forgiveness and "liberty throughout the land for all its inhabitants" (cf. Lv 25:10). This law came about as an attempt to ensure balance and fairness in their relationships with others and with the land on which they lived and worked. At the same time, it was an acknowledgment that the gift of the earth with its fruits belongs to everyone. Those who tilled and kept the land were obliged to share its fruits, especially with the poor, with widows, orphans, and foreigners in their midst: "When you reap the harvest of your land, you shall not reap your field to its very border, neither shall you gather the gleanings after the harvest. And you shall not strip your vineyard bare, neither shall you gather the fallen grapes of your vineyard; you shall leave them for the poor and for the sojourner" (Lv 19:9–10).

72. The Psalms frequently exhort us to praise God the Creator, "who spread out the earth on the waters, for his steadfast love endures for ever" (Ps 136:6). They also invite other creatures to join us in this praise: "Praise him, sun and moon, praise him, all you shining stars! Praise him, you highest heavens, and you waters above the heavens! Let them praise the name of the Lord, for he commanded and they were created" (Ps 148:3–5). We do not only exist by God's mighty power; we also live with him and beside him. This is why we adore him.

73. The writings of the prophets invite us to find renewed strength in times of trial by contemplating the all-powerful God who created the universe. Yet God's infinite power does not lead us to flee his fatherly tenderness, because in him affection and strength are joined. Indeed, all sound spirituality entails both welcoming divine love and adoration, confident in the Lord because of his infinite power. In the Bible, the God who liberates and saves is the same God who created the universe, and these two divine ways of acting are intimately and inseparably connected: "Ah Lord God! It is you who made the heavens and the earth by your great power and by your outstretched arm! Nothing is too hard for you. . . . You brought your people Israel out of the land of Egypt with signs and wonders" (Jer 32:17, 21). "The Lord is the everlasting God, the Creator of the ends of the earth. He does not faint or grow weary; his understanding

is unsearchable. He gives power to the faint, and strengthens the powerless" (Is 40:28b–29).

74. The experience of the Babylonian captivity provoked a spiritual crisis which led to deeper faith in God. Now his creative omnipotence was given pride of place in order to exhort the people to regain their hope in the midst of their wretched predicament. Centuries later, in another age of trial and persecution, when the Roman Empire was seeking to impose absolute dominion, the faithful would once again find consolation and hope in a growing trust in the all-powerful God: "Great and wonderful are your deeds, O Lord God the Almighty! Just and true are your ways!" (Rv 15:3). The God who created the universe out of nothing can also intervene in this world and overcome every form of evil. Injustice is not invincible.

75. A spirituality which forgets God as all-powerful and Creator is not acceptable. That is how we end up worshiping earthly powers, or ourselves usurping the place of God, even to the point of claiming an unlimited right to trample his creation underfoot. The best way to restore men and women to their rightful place, putting an end to their claim to absolute dominion over the earth, is to speak once more of the figure of a Father who creates and who alone owns the world. Otherwise, human beings will always try to impose their own laws and interests on reality.

III. The mystery of the universe

76. In the Judeo-Christian tradition, the word "creation" has a broader meaning than "nature," for it has to do with God's loving plan in which every creature has its own value and significance. Nature is usually seen as a system which can be studied, understood, and controlled, whereas creation can only be understood as a gift from the outstretched hand of the Father of all, and as a reality illuminated by the love which calls us together into universal communion.

77. "By the word of the Lord the heavens were made" (Ps 33:6). This tells us that the world came about as the result of a decision, not from chaos or chance, and this exalts it all the more. The creating word expresses a

free choice. The universe did not emerge as the result of arbitrary omnipotence, a show of force, or a desire for self-assertion. Creation is of the order of love. God's love is the fundamental moving force in all created things: "For you love all things that exist, and detest none of the things that you have made; for you would not have made anything if you had hated it" (Ws 11:24). Every creature is thus the object of the Father's tenderness, who gives it its place in the world. Even the fleeting life of the least of beings is the object of his love, and in its few seconds of existence, God enfolds it with his affection. Saint Basil the Great described the Creator as "goodness without measure,"[44] while Dante Alighieri spoke of "the love which moves the sun and the stars."[45] Consequently, we can ascend from created things "to the greatness of God and to his loving mercy."[46]

78. At the same time, Judeo-Christian thought demythologized nature. While continuing to admire its grandeur and immensity, it no longer saw nature as divine. In doing so, it emphasizes all the more our human responsibility for nature. This rediscovery of nature can never be at the cost of the freedom and responsibility of human beings who, as part of the world, have the duty to cultivate their abilities in order to protect it and develop its potential. If we acknowledge the value and the fragility of nature and, at the same time, our God-given abilities, we can finally leave behind the modern myth of unlimited material progress. A fragile world, entrusted by God to human care, challenges us to devise intelligent ways of directing, developing, and limiting our power.

79. In this universe, shaped by open and intercommunicating systems, we can discern countless forms of relationship and participation. This leads us to think of the whole as open to God's transcendence, within which it develops. Faith allows us to interpret the meaning and the mysterious beauty of what is unfolding. We are free to apply our intelligence toward things evolving positively, or toward adding new ills, new causes of suffering and real setbacks. This is what makes for the excitement and drama of human history, in which freedom, growth, salvation, and love can blossom, or lead toward decadence and mutual destruction. The work of the Church seeks not only to remind everyone of the duty to

care for nature, but at the same time "she must above all protect mankind from self-destruction."[47]

80. Yet God, who wishes to work with us and who counts on our cooperation, can also bring good out of the evil we have done. "The Holy Spirit can be said to possess an infinite creativity, proper to the divine mind, which knows how to loosen the knots of human affairs, including the most complex and inscrutable."[48] Creating a world in need of development, God in some way sought to limit himself in such a way that many of the things we think of as evils, dangers, or sources of suffering, are in reality part of the pains of childbirth which he uses to draw us into the act of cooperation with the Creator.[49] God is intimately present to each being, without impinging on the autonomy of his creature, and this gives rise to the rightful autonomy of earthly affairs.[50] His divine presence, which ensures the subsistence and growth of each being, "continues the work of creation."[51] The Spirit of God has filled the universe with possibilities and therefore, from the very heart of things, something new can always emerge: "Nature is nothing other than a certain kind of art, namely God's art, impressed upon things, whereby those things are moved to a determinate end. It is as if a shipbuilder were able to give timbers the wherewithal to move themselves to take the form of a ship."[52]

81. Human beings, even if we postulate a process of evolution, also possess a uniqueness which cannot be fully explained by the evolution of other open systems. Each of us has his or her own personal identity and is capable of entering into dialogue with others and with God himself. Our capacity to reason, to develop arguments, to be inventive, to interpret reality, and to create art, along with other not yet discovered capacities, are signs of a uniqueness which transcends the spheres of physics and biology. The sheer novelty involved in the emergence of a personal being within a material universe presupposes a direct action of God and a particular call to life and to relationship on the part of a "Thou" who addresses himself to another "thou." The biblical accounts of creation invite us to see each human being as a subject who can never be reduced to the status of an object.

82. Yet it would also be mistaken to view other living beings as mere objects subjected to arbitrary human domination. When nature is viewed solely as a source of profit and gain, this has serious consequences for society. This vision of "might is right" has engendered immense inequality, injustice, and acts of violence against the majority of humanity, since resources end up in the hands of the first comer or the most powerful: the winner takes all. Completely at odds with this model are the ideals of harmony, justice, fraternity, and peace as proposed by Jesus. As he said of the powers of his own age: "You know that the rulers of the Gentiles lord it over them, and their great men exercise authority over them. It shall not be so among you; but whoever would be great among you must be your servant" (Mt 20:25–26).

83. The ultimate destiny of the universe is in the fullness of God, which has already been attained by the risen Christ, the measure of the maturity of all things.[53] Here we can add yet another argument for rejecting every tyrannical and irresponsible domination of human beings over other creatures. The ultimate purpose of other creatures is not to be found in us. Rather, all creatures are moving forward with us and through us toward a common point of arrival, which is God, in that transcendent fullness where the risen Christ embraces and illumines all things. Human beings, endowed with intelligence and love, and drawn by the fullness of Christ, are called to lead all creatures back to their Creator.

IV. The message of each creature in the harmony of creation

84. Our insistence that each human being is an image of God should not make us overlook the fact that each creature has its own purpose. None is superfluous. The entire material universe speaks of God's love, his boundless affection for us. Soil, water, mountains: everything is, as it were, a caress of God. The history of our friendship with God is always linked to particular places which take on an intensely personal meaning; we all remember places, and revisiting those memories does us much good. Anyone who has grown up in the hills or used to sit by the spring to drink, or played outdoors in the neighborhood square; going back to these places is a chance to recover something of their true selves.

85. God has written a precious book, "whose letters are the multitude of created things present in the universe."[54] The Canadian bishops rightly pointed out that no creature is excluded from this manifestation of God: "From panoramic vistas to the tiniest living form, nature is a constant source of wonder and awe. It is also a continuing revelation of the divine."[55] The bishops of Japan, for their part, made a thought-provoking observation: "To sense each creature singing the hymn of its existence is to live joyfully in God's love and hope."[56] This contemplation of creation allows us to discover in each thing a teaching which God wishes to hand on to us, since "for the believer, to contemplate creation is to hear a message, to listen to a paradoxical and silent voice."[57] We can say that "alongside revelation properly so-called, contained in sacred Scripture, there is a divine manifestation in the blaze of the sun and the fall of night."[58] Paying attention to this manifestation, we learn to see ourselves in relation to all other creatures: "I express myself in expressing the world; in my effort to decipher the sacredness of the world, I explore my own."[59]

86. The universe as a whole, in all its manifold relationships, shows forth the inexhaustible riches of God. Saint Thomas Aquinas wisely noted that multiplicity and variety "come from the intention of the first agent" who willed that "what was wanting to one in the representation of the divine goodness might be supplied by another,"[60] inasmuch as God's goodness "could not be represented fittingly by any one creature."[61] Hence we need to grasp the variety of things in their multiple relationships.[62] We understand better the importance and meaning of each creature if we contemplate it within the entirety of God's plan. As the *Catechism* teaches: "God wills the interdependence of creatures. The sun and the moon, the cedar and the little flower, the eagle and the sparrow: the spectacle of their countless diversities and inequalities tells us that no creature is self-sufficient. Creatures exist only in dependence on each other, to complete each other, in the service of each other."[63]

87. When we can see God reflected in all that exists, our hearts are moved to praise the Lord for all his creatures and to worship him in union with them. This sentiment finds magnificent expression in the hymn of Saint Francis of Assisi:

Praised be you, my Lord, with all your creatures,
especially Sir Brother Sun,
who is the day and through whom you give us light.
And he is beautiful and radiant with great splendor;
and bears a likeness of you, Most High.
Praised be you, my Lord, through Sister Moon and the stars,
in heaven you formed them clear and precious and beautiful.
Praised be you, my Lord, through Brother Wind,
and through the air, cloudy and serene, and every kind of weather
through whom you give sustenance to your creatures.
Praised be you, my Lord, through Sister Water,
who is very useful and humble and precious and chaste.
Praised be you, my Lord, through Brother Fire,
through whom you light the night,
and he is beautiful and playful and robust and strong.[64]

88. The bishops of Brazil have pointed out that nature as a whole not only manifests God but is also a locus of his presence. The Spirit of life dwells in every living creature and calls us to enter into relationship with him.[65] Discovering this presence leads us to cultivate the "ecological virtues."[66] This is not to forget that there is an infinite distance between God and the things of this world, which do not possess his fullness. Otherwise, we would not be doing the creatures themselves any good either, for we would be failing to acknowledge their right and proper place. We would end up unduly demanding of them something which they, in their smallness, cannot give us.

V. A universal communion

89. The created things of this world are not free of ownership: "For they are yours, O Lord, who love the living" (Ws 11:26). This is the basis of our conviction that, as part of the universe, called into being by one Father, all of us are linked by unseen bonds and together form a kind of universal family, a sublime communion which fills us with a sacred, affectionate, and humble respect. Here I would reiterate that "God has joined us so

closely to the world around us that we can feel the desertification of the soil almost as a physical ailment, and the extinction of a species as a painful disfigurement."[67]

90. This is not to put all living beings on the same level nor to deprive human beings of their unique worth and the tremendous responsibility it entails. Nor does it imply a divinization of the earth which would prevent us from working on it and protecting it in its fragility. Such notions would end up creating new imbalances which would deflect us from the reality which challenges us.[68] At times we see an obsession with denying any pre-eminence to the human person; more zeal is shown in protecting other species than in defending the dignity which all human beings share in equal measure. Certainly, we should be concerned lest other living beings be treated irresponsibly. But we should be particularly indignant at the enormous inequalities in our midst, whereby we continue to tolerate some considering themselves more worthy than others. We fail to see that some are mired in desperate and degrading poverty, with no way out, while others have not the faintest idea of what to do with their possessions, vainly showing off their supposed superiority and leaving behind them so much waste which, if it were the case everywhere, would destroy the planet. In practice, we continue to tolerate that some consider themselves more human than others, as if they had been born with greater rights.

91. A sense of deep communion with the rest of nature cannot be real if our hearts lack tenderness, compassion, and concern for our fellow human beings. It is clearly inconsistent to combat trafficking in endangered species while remaining completely indifferent to human trafficking, unconcerned about the poor, or undertaking to destroy another human being deemed unwanted. This compromises the very meaning of our struggle for the sake of the environment. It is no coincidence that, in the canticle in which Saint Francis praises God for his creatures, he goes on to say: "Praised be you my Lord, through those who give pardon for your love." Everything is connected. Concern for the environment thus needs to be joined to a sincere love for our fellow human beings and an unwavering commitment to resolving the problems of society.

92. Moreover, when our hearts are authentically open to universal communion, this sense of fraternity excludes nothing and no one. It follows that our indifference or cruelty toward fellow creatures of this world sooner or later affects the treatment we mete out to other human beings. We have only one heart, and the same wretchedness which leads us to mistreat an animal will not be long in showing itself in our relationships with other people. Every act of cruelty toward any creature is "contrary to human dignity."[69] We can hardly consider ourselves to be fully loving if we disregard any aspect of reality: "Peace, justice and the preservation of creation are three absolutely interconnected themes, which cannot be separated and treated individually without once again falling into reductionism."[70] Everything is related, and we human beings are united as brothers and sisters on a wonderful pilgrimage, woven together by the love God has for each of his creatures and which also unites us in fond affection with brother sun, sister moon, brother river, and mother earth.

VI. The common destination of goods

93. Whether believers or not, we are agreed today that the earth is essentially a shared inheritance, whose fruits are meant to benefit everyone. For believers, this becomes a question of fidelity to the Creator, since God created the world for everyone. Hence every ecological approach needs to incorporate a social perspective which takes into account the fundamental rights of the poor and the underprivileged. The principle of the subordination of private property to the universal destination of goods, and thus the right of everyone to their use, is a golden rule of social conduct and "the first principle of the whole ethical and social order."[71] The Christian tradition has never recognized the right to private property as absolute or inviolable, and has stressed the social purpose of all forms of private property. Saint John Paul II forcefully reaffirmed this teaching, stating that "God gave the earth to the whole human race for the sustenance of all its members, *without excluding or favoring anyone*."[72] These are strong words. He noted that "a type of development which did not respect and promote human rights—personal and social, economic and political, including the rights of nations and of peoples—would

not be really worthy of man."[73] He clearly explained that "the Church does indeed defend the legitimate right to private property, but she also teaches no less clearly that there is always a social mortgage on all private property, in order that goods may serve the general purpose that God gave them."[74] Consequently, he maintained, "it is not in accord with God's plan that this gift be used in such a way that its benefits favor only a few."[75] This calls into serious question the unjust habits of a part of humanity.[76]

94. The rich and the poor have equal dignity, for "the Lord is the maker of them all" (Prv 22:2). "He himself made both small and great" (Ws 6:7), and "he makes his sun rise on the evil and on the good" (Mt 5:45). This has practical consequences, such as those pointed out by the bishops of Paraguay: "Every *campesino* has a natural right to possess a reasonable allotment of land where he can establish his home, work for subsistence of his family and a secure life. This right must be guaranteed so that its exercise is not illusory but real. That means that apart from the ownership of property, rural people must have access to means of technical education, credit, insurance, and markets."[77]

95. The natural environment is a collective good, the patrimony of all humanity and the responsibility of everyone. If we make something our own, it is only to administer it for the good of all. If we do not, we burden our consciences with the weight of having denied the existence of others. That is why the New Zealand bishops asked what the commandment "Thou shall not kill" means when "twenty percent of the world's population consumes resources at a rate that robs the poor nations and future generations of what they need to survive."[78]

VII. The gaze of Jesus

96. Jesus took up the biblical faith in God the Creator, emphasizing a fundamental truth: God is Father (cf. Mt 11:25). In talking with his disciples, Jesus would invite them to recognize the paternal relationship God has with all his creatures. With moving tenderness he would remind them that each one of them is important in God's eyes: "Are not five sparrows

sold for two pennies? And not one of them is forgotten before God" (Lk 12:6). "Look at the birds of the air: they neither sow nor reap nor gather into barns, and yet your heavenly Father feeds them" (Mt 6:26).

97. The Lord was able to invite others to be attentive to the beauty that there is in the world because he himself was in constant touch with nature, lending it an attention full of fondness and wonder. As he made his way throughout the land, he often stopped to contemplate the beauty sown by his Father, and invited his disciples to perceive a divine message in things: "Lift up your eyes, and see how the fields are already white for harvest" (Jn 4:35). "The kingdom of God is like a grain of mustard seed which a man took and sowed in his field; it is the smallest of all seeds, but once it has grown, it is the greatest of plants" (Mt 13:31–32).

98. Jesus lived in full harmony with creation, and others were amazed: "What sort of man is this, that even the winds and the sea obey him?" (Mt 8:27). His appearance was not that of an ascetic set apart from the world, nor of an enemy to the pleasant things of life. Of himself he said: "The Son of Man came eating and drinking and they say, 'Look, a glutton and a drunkard!'" (Mt 11:19). He was far removed from philosophies which despised the body, matter, and the things of the world. Such unhealthy dualisms, nonetheless, left a mark on certain Christian thinkers in the course of history and disfigured the Gospel. Jesus worked with his hands, in daily contact with the matter created by God, to which he gave form by his craftsmanship. It is striking that most of his life was dedicated to this task in a simple life which awakened no admiration at all: "Is not this the carpenter, the son of Mary?" (Mk 6:3). In this way he sanctified human labor and endowed it with a special significance for our development. As Saint John Paul II taught, "by enduring the toil of work in union with Christ crucified for us, man in a way collaborates with the Son of God for the redemption of humanity."[79]

99. In the Christian understanding of the world, the destiny of all creation is bound up with the mystery of Christ, present from the beginning: "All things have been created though him and for him" (Col 1:16).[80] The prologue of the Gospel of John (1:1–18) reveals Christ's creative work as the

Divine Word (*Logos*). But then, unexpectedly, the prologue goes on to say that this same Word "became flesh" (Jn 1:14). One Person of the Trinity entered into the created cosmos, throwing in his lot with it, even to the cross. From the beginning of the world, but particularly through the incarnation, the mystery of Christ is at work in a hidden manner in the natural world as a whole, without thereby impinging on its autonomy.

100. The New Testament does not only tell us of the earthly Jesus and his tangible and loving relationship with the world. It also shows him risen and glorious, present throughout creation by his universal Lordship: "For in him all the fullness of God was pleased to dwell, and through him to reconcile to himself all things, whether on earth or in heaven, making peace by the blood of his cross" (Col 1:19–20). This leads us to direct our gaze to the end of time, when the Son will deliver all things to the Father, so that "God may be everything to every one" (1 Cor 15:28). Thus, the creatures of this world no longer appear to us under merely natural guise because the risen One is mysteriously holding them to himself and directing them toward fullness as their end. The very flowers of the field and the birds which his human eyes contemplated and admired are now imbued with his radiant presence.

CHAPTER THREE

THE HUMAN ROOTS OF THE ECOLOGICAL CRISIS

101. It would hardly be helpful to describe symptoms without acknowledging the human origins of the ecological crisis. A certain way of understanding human life and activity has gone awry, to the serious detriment of the world around us. Should we not pause and consider this? At this stage, I propose that we focus on the dominant technocratic paradigm and the place of human beings and of human action in the world.

I. Technology: creativity and power

102. Humanity has entered a new era in which our technical prowess has brought us to a crossroads. We are the beneficiaries of two centuries of enormous waves of change: steam engines, railways, the telegraph, electricity, automobiles, airplanes, chemical industries, modern medicine, information technology, and, more recently, the digital revolution, robotics, biotechnologies, and nanotechnologies. It is right to rejoice in these advances and to be excited by the immense possibilities which they continue to open up before us, for "science and technology are wonderful products of a God-given human creativity."[81] The modification of nature for useful purposes has distinguished the human family from the beginning; technology itself "expresses the inner tension that impels man gradually to overcome material limitations."[82] Technology has remedied countless evils which used to harm and limit human beings. How can we not feel gratitude and appreciation for this progress, especially in the fields of medicine, engineering, and communications? How could we not acknowledge the work of many scientists and engineers who have provided alternatives to make development sustainable?

103. Technoscience, when well directed, can produce important means of improving the quality of human life, from useful domestic appliances to great transportation systems, bridges, buildings, and public spaces. It can also produce art and enable men and women immersed in the material world to "leap" into the world of beauty. Who can deny the beauty of

an aircraft or a skyscraper? Valuable works of art and music now make use of new technologies. So, in the beauty intended by the one who uses new technical instruments and in the contemplation of such beauty, a quantum leap occurs, resulting in a fulfillment which is uniquely human.

104. Yet it must also be recognized that nuclear energy, biotechnology, information technology, knowledge of our DNA, and many other abilities which we have acquired, have given us tremendous power. More precisely, they have given those with the knowledge, and especially the economic resources to use them, an impressive dominance over the whole of humanity and the entire world. Never has humanity had such power over itself, yet nothing ensures that it will be used wisely, particularly when we consider how it is currently being used. We need but think of the nuclear bombs dropped in the middle of the twentieth century, or the array of technology which Nazism, Communism, and other totalitarian regimes have employed to kill millions of people, to say nothing of the increasingly deadly arsenal of weapons available for modern warfare. In whose hands does all this power lie, or will it eventually end up? It is extremely risky for a small part of humanity to have it.

105. There is a tendency to believe that every increase in power means "an increase of 'progress' itself," an advance in "security, usefulness, welfare and vigor; . . . an assimilation of new values into the stream of culture,"[83] as if reality, goodness, and truth automatically flow from technological and economic power as such. The fact is that "contemporary man has not been trained to use power well,"[84] because our immense technological development has not been accompanied by a development in human responsibility, values, and conscience. Each age tends to have only a meager awareness of its own limitations. It is possible that we do not grasp the gravity of the challenges now before us. "The risk is growing day by day that man will not use his power as he should"; in effect, "power is never considered in terms of the responsibility of choice which is inherent in freedom" since its "only norms are taken from alleged necessity, from either utility or security."[85] But human beings are not completely autonomous. Our freedom fades when it is handed over to the blind forces of the unconscious, of immediate needs, of self-interest,

and of violence. In this sense, we stand naked and exposed in the face of our ever-increasing power, lacking the wherewithal to control it. We have certain superficial mechanisms, but we cannot claim to have a sound ethics, a culture and spirituality genuinely capable of setting limits and teaching clear-minded self-restraint.

II. The globalization of the technocratic paradigm

106. The basic problem goes even deeper: it is the way that humanity has taken up technology and its development *according to an undifferentiated and one-dimensional paradigm*. This paradigm exalts the concept of a subject who, using logical and rational procedures, progressively approaches and gains control over an external object. This subject makes every effort to establish the scientific and experimental method, which in itself is already a technique of possession, mastery, and transformation. It is as if the subject were to find itself in the presence of something formless, completely open to manipulation. Men and women have constantly intervened in nature, but for a long time this meant being in tune with and respecting the possibilities offered by the things themselves. It was a matter of receiving what nature itself allowed, as if from its own hand. Now, by contrast, we are the ones to lay our hands on things, attempting to extract everything possible from them while frequently ignoring or forgetting the reality in front of us. Human beings and material objects no longer extend a friendly hand to one another; the relationship has become confrontational. This has made it easy to accept the idea of infinite or unlimited growth, which proves so attractive to economists, financiers, and experts in technology. It is based on the lie that there is an infinite supply of the earth's goods, and this leads to the planet being squeezed dry beyond every limit. It is the false notion that "an infinite quantity of energy and resources are available, that it is possible to renew them quickly, and that the negative effects of the exploitation of the natural order can be easily absorbed."[86]

107. It can be said that many problems of today's world stem from the tendency, at times unconscious, to make the method and aims of science and technology an epistemological paradigm which shapes the lives of

individuals and the workings of society. The effects of imposing this model on reality as a whole, human and social, are seen in the deterioration of the environment, but this is just one sign of a reductionism which affects every aspect of human and social life. We have to accept that technological products are not neutral, for they create a framework which ends up conditioning lifestyles and shaping social possibilities along the lines dictated by the interests of certain powerful groups. Decisions which may seem purely instrumental are in reality decisions about the kind of society we want to build.

108. The idea of promoting a different cultural paradigm and employing technology as a mere instrument is nowadays inconceivable. The technological paradigm has become so dominant that it would be difficult to do without its resources and even more difficult to utilize them without being dominated by their internal logic. It has become countercultural to choose a lifestyle whose goals are even partly independent of technology, of its costs and its power to globalize and make us all the same. Technology tends to absorb everything into its ironclad logic, and those who are surrounded with technology "know full well that it moves forward in the final analysis neither for profit nor for the well-being of the human race," that "in the most radical sense of the term power is its motive—a lordship over all."[87] As a result, "man seizes hold of the naked elements of both nature and human nature."[88] Our capacity to make decisions, a more genuine freedom, and the space for each one's alternative creativity are diminished.

109. The technocratic paradigm also tends to dominate economic and political life. The economy accepts every advance in technology with a view to profit, without concern for its potentially negative impact on human beings. Finance overwhelms the real economy. The lessons of the global financial crisis have not been assimilated, and we are learning all too slowly the lessons of environmental deterioration. Some circles maintain that current economics and technology will solve all environmental problems, and argue, in popular and non-technical terms, that the problems of global hunger and poverty will be resolved simply by market growth. They are less concerned with certain economic theories which

today scarcely anybody dares defend, than with their actual operation in the functioning of the economy. They may not affirm such theories with words, but nonetheless support them with their deeds by showing no interest in more balanced levels of production, a better distribution of wealth, concern for the environment and the rights of future generations. Their behavior shows that for them maximizing profits is enough. Yet by itself the market cannot guarantee integral human development and social inclusion.[89] At the same time, we have "a sort of 'superdevelopment' of a wasteful and consumerist kind which forms an unacceptable contrast with the ongoing situations of dehumanizing deprivation,"[90] while we are all too slow in developing economic institutions and social initiatives which can give the poor regular access to basic resources. We fail to see the deepest roots of our present failures, which have to do with the direction, goals, meaning, and social implications of technological and economic growth.

110. The specialization which belongs to technology makes it difficult to see the larger picture. The fragmentation of knowledge proves helpful for concrete applications, and yet it often leads to a loss of appreciation for the whole, for the relationships between things, and for the broader horizon, which then becomes irrelevant. This very fact makes it hard to find adequate ways of solving the more complex problems of today's world, particularly those regarding the environment and the poor; these problems cannot be dealt with from a single perspective or from a single set of interests. A science which would offer solutions to the great issues would necessarily have to take into account the data generated by other fields of knowledge, including philosophy and social ethics; but this is a difficult habit to acquire today. Nor are there genuine ethical horizons to which one can appeal. Life gradually becomes a surrender to situations conditioned by technology, itself viewed as the principal key to the meaning of existence. In the concrete situation confronting us, there are a number of symptoms which point to what is wrong, such as environmental degradation, anxiety, a loss of the purpose of life and of community living. Once more we see that "realities are more important than ideas."[91]

111. Ecological culture cannot be reduced to a series of urgent and partial responses to the immediate problems of pollution, environmental decay, and the depletion of natural resources. There needs to be a distinctive way of looking at things, a way of thinking, policies, an educational program, a lifestyle, and a spirituality which together generate resistance to the assault of the technocratic paradigm. Otherwise, even the best ecological initiatives can find themselves caught up in the same globalized logic. To seek only a technical remedy to each environmental problem which comes up is to separate what is in reality interconnected and to mask the true and deepest problems of the global system.

112. Yet we can once more broaden our vision. We have the freedom needed to limit and direct technology; we can put it at the service of another type of progress, one which is healthier, more human, more social, more integral. Liberation from the dominant technocratic paradigm does in fact happen sometimes, for example, when cooperatives of small producers adopt less polluting means of production, and opt for a non-consumerist model of life, recreation, and community. Or when technology is directed primarily to resolving people's concrete problems, truly helping them live with more dignity and less suffering. Or indeed when the desire to create and contemplate beauty manages to overcome reductionism through a kind of salvation which occurs in beauty and in those who behold it. An authentic humanity, calling for a new synthesis, seems to dwell in the midst of our technological culture, almost unnoticed, like a mist seeping gently beneath a closed door. Will the promise last, in spite of everything, with all that is authentic rising up in stubborn resistance?

113. There is also the fact that people no longer seem to believe in a happy future; they no longer have blind trust in a better tomorrow based on the present state of the world and our technical abilities. There is a growing awareness that scientific and technological progress cannot be equated with the progress of humanity and history, a growing sense that the way to a better future lies elsewhere. This is not to reject the possibilities which technology continues to offer us. But humanity has changed profoundly, and the accumulation of constant novelties exalts

a superficiality which pulls us in one direction. It becomes difficult to pause and recover depth in life. If architecture reflects the spirit of an age, our megastructures and drab apartment blocks express the spirit of globalized technology, where a constant flood of new products coexists with a tedious monotony. Let us refuse to resign ourselves to this, and continue to wonder about the purpose and meaning of everything. Otherwise we would simply legitimate the present situation and need new forms of escapism to help us endure the emptiness.

114. All of this shows the urgent need for us to move forward in a bold cultural revolution. Science and technology are not neutral; from the beginning to the end of a process, various intentions and possibilities are in play and can take on distinct shapes. Nobody is suggesting a return to the Stone Age, but we do need to slow down and look at reality in a different way, to appropriate the positive and sustainable progress which has been made, but also to recover the values and the great goals swept away by our unrestrained delusions of grandeur.

III. The crisis and effects of modern anthropocentrism

115. Modern anthropocentrism has paradoxically ended up prizing technical thought over reality, since "the technological mind sees nature as an insensate order, as a cold body of facts, as a mere 'given,' as an object of utility, as raw material to be hammered into useful shape; it views the cosmos similarly as a mere 'space' into which objects can be thrown with complete indifference."[92] The intrinsic dignity of the world is thus compromised. When human beings fail to find their true place in this world, they misunderstand themselves and end up acting against themselves: "Not only has God given the earth to man, who must use it with respect for the original good purpose for which it was given, but, man too is God's gift to man. He must therefore respect the natural and moral structure with which he has been endowed."[93]

116. Modernity has been marked by an excessive anthropocentrism which today, under another guise, continues to stand in the way of shared understanding and of any effort to strengthen social bonds. The time has

come to pay renewed attention to reality and the limits it imposes; this in turn is the condition for a more sound and fruitful development of individuals and society. An inadequate presentation of Christian anthropology gave rise to a wrong understanding of the relationship between human beings and the world. Often, what was handed on was a Promethean vision of mastery over the world, which gave the impression that the protection of nature was something that only the faint-hearted cared about. Instead, our "dominion" over the universe should be understood more properly in the sense of responsible stewardship.[94]

117. Neglecting to monitor the harm done to nature and the environmental impact of our decisions is only the most striking sign of a disregard for the message contained in the structures of nature itself. When we fail to acknowledge as part of reality the worth of a poor person, a human embryo, a person with disabilities—to offer just a few examples—it becomes difficult to hear the cry of nature itself; everything is connected. Once the human being declares independence from reality and behaves with absolute dominion, the very foundations of our life begin to crumble, for "instead of carrying out his role as a cooperator with God in the work of creation, man sets himself up in place of God and thus ends up provoking a rebellion on the part of nature."[95]

118. This situation has led to a constant schizophrenia, wherein a technocracy which sees no intrinsic value in lesser beings coexists with the other extreme, which sees no special value in human beings. But one cannot prescind from humanity. There can be no renewal of our relationship with nature without a renewal of humanity itself. There can be no ecology without an adequate anthropology. When the human person is considered as simply one being among others, the product of chance or physical determinism, then "our overall sense of responsibility wanes."[96] A misguided anthropocentrism need not necessarily yield to "biocentrism," for that would entail adding yet another imbalance, failing to solve present problems and adding new ones. Human beings cannot be expected to feel responsibility for the world unless, at the same time, their unique capacities of knowledge, will, freedom, and responsibility are recognized and valued.

119. Nor must the critique of a misguided anthropocentrism underestimate the importance of interpersonal relations. If the present ecological crisis is one small sign of the ethical, cultural, and spiritual crisis of modernity, we cannot presume to heal our relationship with nature and the environment without healing all fundamental human relationships. Christian thought sees human beings as possessing a particular dignity above other creatures; it thus inculcates esteem for each person and respect for others. Our openness to others, each of whom is a "thou" capable of knowing, loving, and entering into dialogue, remains the source of our nobility as human persons. A correct relationship with the created world demands that we not weaken this social dimension of openness to others, much less the transcendent dimension of our openness to the "Thou" of God. Our relationship with the environment can never be isolated from our relationship with others and with God. Otherwise, it would be nothing more than romantic individualism dressed up in ecological garb, locking us into a stifling immanence.

120. Since everything is interrelated, concern for the protection of nature is also incompatible with the justification of abortion. How can we genuinely teach the importance of concern for other vulnerable beings, however troublesome or inconvenient they may be, if we fail to protect a human embryo, even when its presence is uncomfortable and creates difficulties? "If personal and social sensitivity toward the acceptance of the new life is lost, then other forms of acceptance that are valuable for society also wither away."[97]

121. We need to develop a new synthesis capable of overcoming the false arguments of recent centuries. Christianity, in fidelity to its own identity and the rich deposit of truth which it has received from Jesus Christ, continues to reflect on these issues in fruitful dialogue with changing historical situations. In doing so, it reveals its eternal newness.[98]

Practical relativism

122. A misguided anthropocentrism leads to a misguided lifestyle. In the Apostolic Exhortation *Evangelii Gaudium*, I noted that the practical relativism typical of our age is "even more dangerous than doctrinal

relativism."[99] When human beings place themselves at the center, they give absolute priority to immediate convenience and all else becomes relative. Hence we should not be surprised to find, in conjunction with the omnipresent technocratic paradigm and the cult of unlimited human power, the rise of a relativism which sees everything as irrelevant unless it serves one's own immediate interests. There is a logic in all this whereby different attitudes can feed on one another, leading to environmental degradation and social decay.

123. The culture of relativism is the same disorder which drives one person to take advantage of another, to treat others as mere objects, imposing forced labor on them or enslaving them to pay their debts. The same kind of thinking leads to the sexual exploitation of children and abandonment of the elderly who no longer serve our interests. It is also the mindset of those who say: Let us allow the invisible forces of the market to regulate the economy, and consider their impact on society and nature as collateral damage. In the absence of objective truths or sound principles other than the satisfaction of our own desires and immediate needs, what limits can be placed on human trafficking, organized crime, the drug trade, commerce in blood diamonds, and the fur of endangered species? Is it not the same relativistic logic which justifies buying the organs of the poor for resale or use in experimentation, or eliminating children because they are not what their parents wanted? This same "use and throw away" logic generates so much waste, because of the disordered desire to consume more than what is really necessary. We should not think that political efforts or the force of law will be sufficient to prevent actions which affect the environment because, when the culture itself is corrupt and objective truth and universally valid principles are no longer upheld, then laws can only be seen as arbitrary impositions or obstacles to be avoided.

The need to protect employment

124. Any approach to an integral ecology, which by definition does not exclude human beings, needs to take account of the value of labor, as Saint John Paul II wisely noted in his Encyclical *Laborem Exercens*. According

to the biblical account of creation, God placed man and woman in the garden he had created (cf. Gn 2:15) not only to preserve it ("keep") but also to make it fruitful ("till"). Laborers and craftsmen thus "maintain the fabric of the world" (Sir 38:34). Developing the created world in a prudent way is the best way of caring for it, as this means that we ourselves become the instrument used by God to bring out the potential which he himself inscribed in things: "The Lord created medicines out of the earth, and a sensible man will not despise them" (Sir 38:4).

125. If we reflect on the proper relationship between human beings and the world around us, we see the need for a correct understanding of work; if we talk about the relationship between human beings and things, the question arises as to the meaning and purpose of all human activity. This has to do not only with manual or agricultural labor but with any activity involving a modification of existing reality, from producing a social report to the design of a technological development. Underlying every form of work is a concept of the relationship which we can and must have with what is other than ourselves. Together with the awe-filled contemplation of creation which we find in Saint Francis of Assisi, the Christian spiritual tradition has also developed a rich and balanced understanding of the meaning of work, as, for example, in the life of Blessed Charles de Foucauld and his followers.

126. We can also look to the great tradition of monasticism. Originally, it was a kind of flight from the world, an escape from the decadence of the cities. The monks sought the desert, convinced that it was the best place for encountering the presence of God. Later, Saint Benedict of Norcia proposed that his monks live in community, combining prayer and spiritual reading with manual labor (*ora et labora*). Seeing manual labor as spiritually meaningful proved revolutionary. Personal growth and sanctification came to be sought in the interplay of recollection and work. This way of experiencing work makes us more protective and respectful of the environment; it imbues our relationship to the world with a healthy sobriety.

127. We are convinced that "man is the source, the focus and the aim of all economic and social life."[100] Nonetheless, once our human capacity for contemplation and reverence is impaired, it becomes easy for the meaning of work to be misunderstood.[101] We need to remember that men and women have "the capacity to improve their lot, to further their moral growth and to develop their spiritual endowments."[102] Work should be the setting for this rich personal growth, where many aspects of life enter into play: creativity, planning for the future, developing our talents, living out our values, relating to others, giving glory to God. It follows that, in the reality of today's global society, it is essential that "we continue to prioritize the goal of access to steady employment for everyone,"[103] no matter the limited interests of business and dubious economic reasoning.

128. We were created with a vocation to work. The goal should not be that technological progress increasingly replace human work, for this would be detrimental to humanity. Work is a necessity, part of the meaning of life on this earth, a path to growth, human development, and personal fulfillment. Helping the poor financially must always be a provisional solution in the face of pressing needs. The broader objective should always be to allow them a dignified life through work. Yet the orientation of the economy has favored a kind of technological progress in which the costs of production are reduced by laying off workers and replacing them with machines. This is yet another way in which we can end up working against ourselves. The loss of jobs also has a negative impact on the economy "through the progressive erosion of social capital: the network of relationships of trust, dependability, and respect for rules, all of which are indispensable for any form of civil coexistence."[104] In other words, "human costs always include economic costs, and economic dysfunctions always involve human costs."[105] To stop investing in people, in order to gain greater short-term financial gain, is bad business for society.

129. In order to continue providing employment, it is imperative to promote an economy which favors productive diversity and business creativity. For example, there is a great variety of small-scale food production systems which feed the greater part of the world's peoples, using a modest amount of land and producing less waste, be it in small

agricultural parcels, in orchards and gardens, hunting and wild harvesting, or local fishing. Economies of scale, especially in the agricultural sector, end up forcing smallholders to sell their land or to abandon their traditional crops. Their attempts to move to other, more diversified, means of production prove fruitless because of the difficulty of linkage with regional and global markets, or because the infrastructure for sales and transport is geared to larger businesses. Civil authorities have the right and duty to adopt clear and firm measures in support of small producers and differentiated production. To ensure economic freedom from which all can effectively benefit, restraints occasionally have to be imposed on those possessing greater resources and financial power. To claim economic freedom while real conditions bar many people from actual access to it, and while possibilities for employment continue to shrink, is to practice a doublespeak which brings politics into disrepute. Business is a noble vocation, directed to producing wealth and improving our world. It can be a fruitful source of prosperity for the areas in which it operates, especially if it sees the creation of jobs as an essential part of its service to the common good.

New biological technologies

130. In the philosophical and theological vision of the human being and of creation which I have presented, it is clear that the human person, endowed with reason and knowledge, is not an external factor to be excluded. While human intervention on plants and animals is permissible when it pertains to the necessities of human life, the *Catechism of the Catholic Church* teaches that experimentation on animals is morally acceptable only "if it remains within reasonable limits [and] contributes to caring for or saving human lives."[106] The *Catechism* firmly states that human power has limits and that "it is contrary to human dignity to cause animals to suffer or die needlessly."[107] All such use and experimentation "requires a religious respect for the integrity of creation."[108]

131. Here I would recall the balanced position of Saint John Paul II, who stressed the benefits of scientific and technological progress as evidence of "the nobility of the human vocation to participate responsibly in God's

creative action," while also noting that "we cannot interfere in one area of the ecosystem without paying due attention to the consequences of such interference in other areas."[109] He made it clear that the Church values the benefits which result "from the study and applications of molecular biology, supplemented by other disciplines such as genetics, and its technological application in agriculture and industry."[110] But he also pointed out that this should not lead to "indiscriminate genetic manipulation"[111] which ignores the negative effects of such interventions. Human creativity cannot be suppressed. If an artist cannot be stopped from using his or her creativity, neither should those who possess particular gifts for the advancement of science and technology be prevented from using their God-given talents for the service of others. We need constantly to rethink the goals, effects, overall context, and ethical limits of this human activity, which is a form of power involving considerable risks.

132. This, then, is the correct framework for any reflection concerning human intervention on plants and animals, which at present includes genetic manipulation by biotechnology for the sake of exploiting the potential present in material reality. The respect owed by faith to reason calls for close attention to what the biological sciences, through research uninfluenced by economic interests, can teach us about biological structures, their possibilities and their mutations. Any legitimate intervention will act on nature only in order "to favor its development in its own line, that of creation, as intended by God."[112]

133. It is difficult to make a general judgment about genetic modification (GM), whether vegetable or animal, medical or agricultural, since these vary greatly among themselves and call for specific considerations. The risks involved are not always due to the techniques used, but rather to their improper or excessive application. Genetic mutations, in fact, have often been, and continue to be, caused by nature itself. Nor are mutations caused by human intervention a modern phenomenon. The domestication of animals, the crossbreeding of species, and other older and universally accepted practices can be mentioned as examples. We need but recall that scientific developments in GM cereals began with the observation of natural bacteria which spontaneously modified plant

genomes. In nature, however, this process is slow and cannot be compared to the fast pace induced by contemporary technological advances, even when the latter build upon several centuries of scientific progress.

134. Although no conclusive proof exists that GM cereals may be harmful to human beings, and in some regions their use has brought about economic growth which has helped to resolve problems, there remain a number of significant difficulties which should not be underestimated. In many places, following the introduction of these crops, productive land is concentrated in the hands of a few owners due to "the progressive disappearance of small producers, who, as a consequence of the loss of the exploited lands, are obliged to withdraw from direct production."[113] The most vulnerable of these become temporary laborers, and many rural workers end up moving to poverty-stricken urban areas. The expansion of these crops has the effect of destroying the complex network of ecosystems, diminishing the diversity of production, and affecting regional economies, now and in the future. In various countries, we see an expansion of oligopolies for the production of cereals and other products needed for their cultivation. This dependency would be aggravated were the production of infertile seeds to be considered; the effect would be to force farmers to purchase them from larger producers.

135. Certainly, these issues require constant attention and a concern for their ethical implications. A broad, responsible scientific and social debate needs to take place, one capable of considering all the available information and of calling things by their name. It sometimes happens that complete information is not put on the table; a selection is made on the basis of particular interests, be they politico-economic or ideological. This makes it difficult to reach a balanced and prudent judgment on different questions, one which takes into account all the pertinent variables. Discussions are needed in which all those directly or indirectly affected (farmers, consumers, civil authorities, scientists, seed producers, people living near fumigated fields, and others) can make known their problems and concerns, and have access to adequate and reliable information in order to make decisions for the common good, present and future. This is a complex environmental issue; it calls for a comprehensive approach

which would require, at the very least, greater efforts to finance various lines of independent, interdisciplinary research capable of shedding new light on the problem.

136. On the other hand, it is troubling that, when some ecological movements defend the integrity of the environment, rightly demanding that certain limits be imposed on scientific research, they sometimes fail to apply those same principles to human life. There is a tendency to justify transgressing all boundaries when experimentation is carried out on living human embryos. We forget that the inalienable worth of a human being transcends his or her degree of development. In the same way, when technology disregards the great ethical principles, it ends up considering any practice whatsoever as licit. As we have seen in this chapter, a technology severed from ethics will not easily be able to limit its own power.

CHAPTER FOUR

INTEGRAL ECOLOGY

137. Since everything is closely interrelated, and today's problems call for a vision capable of taking into account every aspect of the global crisis, I suggest that we now consider some elements of an *integral ecology*, one which clearly respects its human and social dimensions.

I. Environmental, economic, and social ecology

138. Ecology studies the relationship between living organisms and the environment in which they develop. This necessarily entails reflection and debate about the conditions required for the life and survival of society, and the honesty needed to question certain models of development, production, and consumption. It cannot be emphasized enough how everything is interconnected. Time and space are not independent of one another, and not even atoms or subatomic particles can be considered in isolation. Just as the different aspects of the planet—physical, chemical, and biological—are interrelated, so too living species are part of a network which we will never fully explore and understand. A good part of our genetic code is shared by many living beings. It follows that the fragmentation of knowledge and the isolation of bits of information can actually become a form of ignorance, unless they are integrated into a broader vision of reality.

139. When we speak of the "environment," what we really mean is a relationship existing between nature and the society which lives in it. Nature cannot be regarded as something separate from ourselves or as a mere setting in which we live. We are part of nature, included in it and thus in constant interaction with it. Recognizing the reasons why a given area is polluted requires a study of the workings of society, its economy, its behavior patterns, and the ways it grasps reality. Given the scale of change, it is no longer possible to find a specific, discrete answer for each part of the problem. It is essential to seek comprehensive solutions which consider the interactions within natural systems themselves

and with social systems. We are faced not with two separate crises, one environmental and the other social, but rather with one complex crisis which is both social and environmental. Strategies for a solution demand an integrated approach to combating poverty, restoring dignity to the excluded, and at the same time protecting nature.

140. Due to the number and variety of factors to be taken into account when determining the environmental impact of a concrete undertaking, it is essential to give researchers their due role, to facilitate their interaction, and to ensure broad academic freedom. Ongoing research should also give us a better understanding of how different creatures relate to one another in making up the larger units which today we term "ecosystems." We take these systems into account not only to determine how best to use them, but also because they have an intrinsic value independent of their usefulness. Each organism, as a creature of God, is good and admirable in itself; the same is true of the harmonious ensemble of organisms existing in a defined space and functioning as a system. Although we are often not aware of it, we depend on these larger systems for our own existence. We need only recall how ecosystems interact in dispersing carbon dioxide, purifying water, controlling illnesses and epidemics, forming soil, breaking down waste, and in many other ways which we overlook or simply do not know about. Once they become conscious of this, many people realize that we live and act on the basis of a reality which has previously been given to us, which precedes our existence and our abilities. So, when we speak of "sustainable use," consideration must always be given to each ecosystem's regenerative ability in its different areas and aspects.

141. Economic growth, for its part, tends to produce predictable reactions and a certain standardization with the aim of simplifying procedures and reducing costs. This suggests the need for an "economic ecology" capable of appealing to a broader vision of reality. The protection of the environment is in fact "an integral part of the development process and cannot be considered in isolation from it."[114] We urgently need a humanism capable of bringing together the different fields of knowledge, including economics, in the service of a more integral and integrating vision. Today,

the analysis of environmental problems cannot be separated from the analysis of human, family, work-related, and urban contexts, nor from how individuals relate to themselves, which leads in turn to how they relate to others and to the environment. There is an interrelation between ecosystems and between the various spheres of social interaction, demonstrating yet again that "the whole is greater than the part."[115]

142. If everything is related, then the health of a society's institutions has consequences for the environment and the quality of human life. "Every violation of solidarity and civic friendship harms the environment."[116] In this sense, social ecology is necessarily institutional, and gradually extends to the whole of society, from the primary social group, the family, to the wider local, national, and international communities. Within each social stratum, and between them, institutions develop to regulate human relationships. Anything which weakens those institutions has negative consequences, such as injustice, violence, and loss of freedom. A number of countries have a relatively low level of institutional effectiveness, which results in greater problems for their people while benefiting those who profit from this situation. Whether in the administration of the state, the various levels of civil society, or relationships between individuals themselves, lack of respect for the law is becoming more common. Laws may be well framed yet remain a dead letter. Can we hope, then, that in such cases, legislation and regulations dealing with the environment will really prove effective? We know, for example, that countries which have clear legislation about the protection of forests continue to keep silent as they watch laws repeatedly being broken. Moreover, what takes place in any one area can have a direct or indirect influence on other areas. Thus, for example, drug use in affluent societies creates a continual and growing demand for products imported from poorer regions, where behavior is corrupted, lives are destroyed, and the environment continues to deteriorate.

II. Cultural ecology

143. Together with the patrimony of nature, there is also an historic, artistic, and cultural patrimony which is likewise under threat. This

patrimony is a part of the shared identity of each place and a foundation upon which to build a habitable city. It is not a matter of tearing down and building new cities, supposedly more respectful of the environment yet not always more attractive to live in. Rather, there is a need to incorporate the history, culture, and architecture of each place, thus preserving its original identity. Ecology, then, also involves protecting the cultural treasures of humanity in the broadest sense. More specifically, it calls for greater attention to local cultures when studying environmental problems, favoring a dialogue between scientific-technical language and the language of the people. Culture is more than what we have inherited from the past; it is also, and above all, a living, dynamic, and participatory present reality, which cannot be excluded as we rethink the relationship between human beings and the environment.

144. A consumerist vision of human beings, encouraged by the mechanisms of today's globalized economy, has a leveling effect on cultures, diminishing the immense variety which is the heritage of all humanity. Attempts to resolve all problems through uniform regulations or technical interventions can lead to overlooking the complexities of local problems which demand the active participation of all members of the community. New processes taking shape cannot always fit into frameworks imported from outside; they need to be based in the local culture itself. As life and the world are dynamic realities, so our care for the world must also be flexible and dynamic. Merely technical solutions run the risk of addressing symptoms and not the more serious underlying problems. There is a need to respect the rights of peoples and cultures, and to appreciate that the development of a social group presupposes an historical process which takes place within a cultural context and demands the constant and active involvement of local people *from within their proper culture*. Nor can the notion of the quality of life be imposed from without, for quality of life must be understood within the world of symbols and customs proper to each human group.

145. Many intensive forms of environmental exploitation and degradation not only exhaust the resources which provide local communities with their livelihood, but also undo the social structures which, for a long

time, shaped cultural identity and their sense of the meaning of life and community. The disappearance of a culture can be just as serious, or even more serious, than the disappearance of a species of plant or animal. The imposition of a dominant lifestyle linked to a single form of production can be just as harmful as the altering of ecosystems.

146. In this sense, it is essential to show special care for indigenous communities and their cultural traditions. They are not merely one minority among others, but should be the principal dialogue partners, especially when large projects affecting their land are proposed. For them, land is not a commodity but rather a gift from God and from their ancestors who rest there, a sacred space with which they need to interact if they are to maintain their identity and values. When they remain on their land, they themselves care for it best. Nevertheless, in various parts of the world, pressure is being put on them to abandon their homelands to make room for agricultural or mining projects which are undertaken without regard for the degradation of nature and culture.

III. Ecology of daily life

147. Authentic development includes efforts to bring about an integral improvement in the quality of human life, and this entails considering the setting in which people live their lives. These settings influence the way we think, feel, and act. In our rooms, our homes, our workplaces and neighborhoods, we use our environment as a way of expressing our identity. We make every effort to adapt to our environment, but when it is disorderly, chaotic, or saturated with noise and ugliness, such overstimulation makes it difficult to find ourselves integrated and happy.

148. An admirable creativity and generosity is shown by persons and groups who respond to environmental limitations by alleviating the adverse effects of their surroundings and learning to orient their lives amid disorder and uncertainty. For example, in some places, where the façades of buildings are derelict, people show great care for the interior of their homes, or find contentment in the kindness and friendliness of others. A wholesome social life can light up a seemingly undesirable

environment. At times a commendable human ecology is practiced by the poor despite numerous hardships. The feeling of asphyxiation brought on by densely populated residential areas is countered if close and warm relationships develop, if communities are created, if the limitations of the environment are compensated for in the interior of each person who feels held within a network of solidarity and belonging. In this way, any place can turn from being a hell on earth into the setting for a dignified life.

149. The extreme poverty experienced in areas lacking harmony, open spaces, or potential for integration, can lead to incidents of brutality and to exploitation by criminal organizations. In the unstable neighborhoods of mega-cities, the daily experience of overcrowding and social anonymity can create a sense of uprootedness which spawns antisocial behavior and violence. Nonetheless, I wish to insist that love always proves more powerful. Many people in these conditions are able to weave bonds of belonging and togetherness which convert overcrowding into an experience of community in which the walls of the ego are torn down and the barriers of selfishness overcome. This experience of a communitarian salvation often generates creative ideas for the improvement of a building or a neighborhood.[117]

150. Given the interrelationship between living space and human behavior, those who design buildings, neighborhoods, public spaces, and cities, ought to draw on the various disciplines which help us to understand people's thought processes, symbolic language, and ways of acting. It is not enough to seek the beauty of design. More precious still is the service we offer to another kind of beauty: people's quality of life, their adaptation to the environment, encounter and mutual assistance. Here too, we see how important it is that urban planning always take into consideration the views of those who will live in these areas.

151. There is also a need to protect those common areas, visual landmarks, and urban landscapes which increase our sense of belonging, of rootedness, of "feeling at home" within a city which includes us and brings us together. It is important that the different parts of a city be well integrated and that those who live there have a sense of the whole,

rather than being confined to one neighborhood and failing to see the larger city as space which they share with others. Interventions which affect the urban or rural landscape should take into account how various elements combine to form a whole which is perceived by its inhabitants as a coherent and meaningful framework for their lives. Others will then no longer be seen as strangers, but as part of a "we" which all of us are working to create. For this same reason, in both urban and rural settings, it is helpful to set aside some places which can be preserved and protected from constant changes brought by human intervention.

152. Lack of housing is a grave problem in many parts of the world, both in rural areas and in large cities, since state budgets usually cover only a small portion of the demand. Not only the poor, but many other members of society as well, find it difficult to own a home. Having a home has much to do with a sense of personal dignity and the growth of families. This is a major issue for human ecology. In some places, where makeshift shanty towns have sprung up, this will mean developing those neighborhoods rather than razing or displacing them. When the poor live in unsanitary slums or in dangerous tenements, "in cases where it is necessary to relocate them, in order not to heap suffering upon suffering, adequate information needs to be given beforehand, with choices of decent housing offered, and the people directly involved must be part of the process."[118] At the same time, creativity should be shown in integrating rundown neighborhoods into a welcoming city: "How beautiful those cities which overcome paralyzing mistrust, integrate those who are different and make this very integration a new factor of development! How attractive are those cities which, even in their architectural design, are full of spaces which connect, relate and favor the recognition of others!"[119]

153. The quality of life in cities has much to do with systems of transport, which are often a source of much suffering for those who use them. Many cars, used by one or more people, circulate in cities, causing traffic congestion, raising the level of pollution, and consuming enormous quantities of non-renewable energy. This makes it necessary to build more roads and parking areas which spoil the urban landscape. Many specialists agree on the need to give priority to public transportation.

Yet some measures needed will not prove easily acceptable to society unless substantial improvements are made in the systems themselves, which in many cities force people to put up with undignified conditions due to crowding, inconvenience, infrequent service, and lack of safety.

154. Respect for our dignity as human beings often jars with the chaotic realities that people have to endure in city life. Yet this should not make us overlook the abandonment and neglect also experienced by some rural populations which lack access to essential services and where some workers are reduced to conditions of servitude, without rights or even the hope of a more dignified life.

155. Human ecology also implies another profound reality: the relationship between human life and the moral law, which is inscribed in our nature and is necessary for the creation of a more dignified environment. Pope Benedict XVI spoke of an "ecology of man," based on the fact that "man too has a nature that he must respect and that he cannot manipulate at will."[120] It is enough to recognize that our body itself establishes us in a direct relationship with the environment and with other living beings. The acceptance of our bodies as God's gift is vital for welcoming and accepting the entire world as a gift from the Father and our common home, whereas thinking that we enjoy absolute power over our own bodies turns, often subtly, into thinking that we enjoy absolute power over creation. Learning to accept our body, to care for it, and to respect its fullest meaning, is an essential element of any genuine human ecology. Also, valuing one's own body in its femininity or masculinity is necessary if I am going to be able to recognize myself in an encounter with someone who is different. In this way we can joyfully accept the specific gifts of another man or woman, the work of God the Creator, and find mutual enrichment. It is not a healthy attitude which would seek "to cancel out sexual difference because it no longer knows how to confront it."[121]

IV. The principle of the common good

156. An integral ecology is inseparable from the notion of the common good, a central and unifying principle of social ethics. The common good

is "the sum of those conditions of social life which allow social groups and their individual members relatively thorough and ready access to their own fulfillment."[122]

157. Underlying the principle of the common good is respect for the human person as such, endowed with basic and inalienable rights ordered to his or her integral development. It has also to do with the overall welfare of society and the development of a variety of intermediate groups, applying the principle of subsidiarity. Outstanding among those groups is the family, as the basic cell of society. Finally, the common good calls for social peace, the stability and security provided by a certain order which cannot be achieved without particular concern for distributive justice; whenever this is violated, violence always ensues. Society as a whole, and the state in particular, are obliged to defend and promote the common good.

158. In the present condition of global society, where injustices abound and growing numbers of people are deprived of basic human rights and considered expendable, the principle of the common good immediately becomes, logically and inevitably, a summons to solidarity and a preferential option for the poorest of our brothers and sisters. This option entails recognizing the implications of the universal destination of the world's goods, but, as I mentioned in the Apostolic Exhortation *Evangelii Gaudium*,[123] it demands before all else an appreciation of the immense dignity of the poor in the light of our deepest convictions as believers. We need only look around us to see that, today, this option is in fact an ethical imperative essential for effectively attaining the common good.

V. Justice between the generations

159. The notion of the common good also extends to future generations. The global economic crises have made painfully obvious the detrimental effects of disregarding our common destiny, which cannot exclude those who come after us. We can no longer speak of sustainable development apart from intergenerational solidarity. Once we start to think about the kind of world we are leaving to future generations, we look at

things differently; we realize that the world is a gift which we have freely received and must share with others. Since the world has been given to us, we can no longer view reality in a purely utilitarian way, in which efficiency and productivity are entirely geared to our individual benefit. Intergenerational solidarity is not optional, but rather a basic question of justice, since the world we have received also belongs to those who will follow us. The Portuguese bishops have called upon us to acknowledge this obligation of justice: "The environment is part of a logic of receptivity. It is on loan to each generation, which must then hand it on to the next."[124] An integral ecology is marked by this broader vision.

160. What kind of world do we want to leave to those who come after us, to children who are now growing up? This question not only concerns the environment in isolation; the issue cannot be approached piecemeal. When we ask ourselves what kind of world we want to leave behind, we think in the first place of its general direction, its meaning, and its values. Unless we struggle with these deeper issues, I do not believe that our concern for ecology will produce significant results. But if these issues are courageously faced, we are led inexorably to ask other pointed questions: What is the purpose of our life in this world? Why are we here? What is the goal of our work and all our efforts? What need does the earth have of us? It is no longer enough, then, simply to state that we should be concerned for future generations. We need to see that what is at stake is our own dignity. Leaving an inhabitable planet to future generations is, first and foremost, up to us. The issue is one which dramatically affects us, for it has to do with the ultimate meaning of our earthly sojourn.

161. Doomsday predictions can no longer be met with irony or disdain. We may well be leaving to coming generations debris, desolation, and filth. The pace of consumption, waste, and environmental change has so stretched the planet's capacity that our contemporary lifestyle, unsustainable as it is, can only precipitate catastrophes, such as those which even now periodically occur in different areas of the world. The effects of the present imbalance can only be reduced by our decisive action, here and now. We need to reflect on our accountability before those who will have to endure the dire consequences.

162. Our difficulty in taking up this challenge seriously has much to do with an ethical and cultural decline which has accompanied the deterioration of the environment. Men and women of our postmodern world run the risk of rampant individualism, and many problems of society are connected with today's self-centered culture of instant gratification. We see this in the crisis of family and social ties and the difficulties of recognizing the other. Parents can be prone to impulsive and wasteful consumption, which then affects their children who find it increasingly difficult to acquire a home of their own and build a family. Furthermore, our inability to think seriously about future generations is linked to our inability to broaden the scope of our present interests and to give consideration to those who remain excluded from development. Let us not only keep the poor of the future in mind, but also today's poor, whose life on this earth is brief and who cannot keep on waiting. Hence, "in addition to a fairer sense of intergenerational solidarity there is also an urgent moral need for a renewed sense of intragenerational solidarity."[125]

CHAPTER FIVE

LINES OF APPROACH AND ACTION

163. So far I have attempted to take stock of our present situation, pointing to the cracks in the planet that we inhabit as well as to the profoundly human causes of environmental degradation. Although the contemplation of this reality in itself has already shown the need for a change of direction and other courses of action, now we shall try to outline the major paths of dialogue which can help us escape the spiral of self-destruction which currently engulfs us.

I. Dialogue on the environment in the international community

164. Beginning in the middle of the last century and overcoming many difficulties, there has been a growing conviction that our planet is a homeland and that humanity is one people living in a common home. An interdependent world not only makes us more conscious of the negative effects of certain lifestyles and models of production and consumption which affect us all; more importantly, it motivates us to ensure that solutions are proposed from a global perspective, and not simply to defend the interests of a few countries. Interdependence obliges us to think of *one world with a common plan*. Yet the same ingenuity which has brought about enormous technological progress has so far proved incapable of finding effective ways of dealing with grave environmental and social problems worldwide. A global consensus is essential for confronting the deeper problems, which cannot be resolved by unilateral actions on the part of individual countries. Such a consensus could lead, for example, to planning a sustainable and diversified agriculture, developing renewable and less polluting forms of energy, encouraging a more efficient use of energy, promoting a better management of marine and forest resources, and ensuring universal access to drinking water.

165. We know that technology based on the use of highly polluting fossil fuels—especially coal, but also oil and, to a lesser degree, gas—needs to

be progressively replaced without delay. Until greater progress is made in developing widely accessible sources of renewable energy, it is legitimate to choose the less harmful alternative or to find short-term solutions. But the international community has still not reached adequate agreements about the responsibility for paying the costs of this energy transition. In recent decades, environmental issues have given rise to considerable public debate and have elicited a variety of committed and generous civic responses. Politics and business have been slow to react in a way commensurate with the urgency of the challenges facing our world. Although the post-industrial period may well be remembered as one of the most irresponsible in history, nonetheless there is reason to hope that humanity at the dawn of the twenty-first century will be remembered for having generously shouldered its grave responsibilities.

166. Worldwide, the ecological movement has made significant advances, thanks also to the efforts of many organizations of civil society. It is impossible here to mention them all, or to review the history of their contributions. But thanks to their efforts, environmental questions have increasingly found a place on public agendas and encouraged more far-sighted approaches. This notwithstanding, recent World Summits on the environment have not lived up to expectations because, due to lack of political will, they were unable to reach truly meaningful and effective global agreements on the environment.

167. The 1992 Earth Summit in Rio de Janeiro is worth mentioning. It proclaimed that "human beings are at the center of concerns for sustainable development."[126] Echoing the 1972 Stockholm Declaration, it enshrined international cooperation to care for the ecosystem of the entire earth, the obligation of those who cause pollution to assume its costs, and the duty to assess the environmental impact of given projects and works. It set the goal of limiting greenhouse gas concentration in the atmosphere, in an effort to reverse the trend of global warming. It also drew up an agenda with an action plan and a convention on biodiversity, and stated principles regarding forests. Although the summit was a real step forward, and prophetic for its time, its accords have been poorly implemented, due to the lack of suitable mechanisms for oversight, periodic review, and

penalties in cases of non-compliance. The principles which it proclaimed still await an efficient and flexible means of practical implementation.

168. Among positive experiences in this regard, we might mention, for example, the Basel Convention on hazardous wastes, with its system of reporting, standards, and controls. There is also the binding Convention on International Trade in Endangered Species of Wild Fauna and Flora, which includes on-site visits for verifying effective compliance. Thanks to the Vienna Convention for the Protection of the Ozone Layer and its implementation through the Montreal Protocol and amendments, the problem of the layer's thinning seems to have entered a phase of resolution.

169. As far as the protection of biodiversity and issues related to desertification are concerned, progress has been far less significant. With regard to climate change, the advances have been regrettably few. Reducing greenhouse gases requires honesty, courage, and responsibility, above all on the part of those countries which are more powerful and pollute the most. The Conference of the United Nations on Sustainable Development, "Rio+20" (Rio de Janeiro 2012), issued a wide-ranging but ineffectual outcome document. International negotiations cannot make significant progress due to positions taken by countries which place their national interests above the global common good. Those who will have to suffer the consequences of what we are trying to hide will not forget this failure of conscience and responsibility. Even as this Encyclical was being prepared, the debate was intensifying. We believers cannot fail to ask God for a positive outcome to the present discussions, so that future generations will not have to suffer the effects of our ill-advised delays.

170. Some strategies for lowering pollutant gas emissions call for the internationalization of environmental costs, which would risk imposing on countries with fewer resources burdensome commitments to reducing emissions comparable to those of the more industrialized countries. Imposing such measures penalizes those countries most in need of development. A further injustice is perpetrated under the guise of protecting the environment. Here also, the poor end up paying the price.

Furthermore, since the effects of climate change will be felt for a long time to come, even if stringent measures are taken now, some countries with scarce resources will require assistance in adapting to the effects already being produced, which affect their economies. In this context, there is a need for common and differentiated responsibilities. As the bishops of Bolivia have stated, "the countries which have benefited from a high degree of industrialization, at the cost of enormous emissions of greenhouse gases, have a greater responsibility for providing a solution to the problems they have caused."[127]

171. The strategy of buying and selling "carbon credits" can lead to a new form of speculation which would not help reduce the emission of polluting gases worldwide. This system seems to provide a quick and easy solution under the guise of a certain commitment to the environment, but in no way does it allow for the radical change which present circumstances require. Rather, it may simply become a ploy which permits maintaining the excessive consumption of some countries and sectors.

172. For poor countries, the priorities must be to eliminate extreme poverty and to promote the social development of their people. At the same time, they need to acknowledge the scandalous level of consumption in some privileged sectors of their population and to combat corruption more effectively. They are likewise bound to develop less polluting forms of energy production, but to do so they require the help of countries which have experienced great growth at the cost of the ongoing pollution of the planet. Taking advantage of abundant solar energy will require the establishment of mechanisms and subsidies which allow developing countries access to technology transfer, technical assistance, and financial resources, but in a way which respects their concrete situations, since "the compatibility of [infrastructures] with the context for which they have been designed is not always adequately assessed."[128] The costs of this would be low, compared to the risks of climate change. In any event, these are primarily ethical decisions, rooted in solidarity between all peoples.

173. Enforceable international agreements are urgently needed, since local authorities are not always capable of effective intervention. Relations between states must be respectful of each other's sovereignty, but must also lay down mutually agreed means of averting regional disasters which would eventually affect everyone. Global regulatory norms are needed to impose obligations and prevent unacceptable actions, for example, when powerful companies or countries dump contaminated waste or offshore polluting industries in other countries.

174. Let us also mention the system of governance of the oceans. International and regional conventions do exist, but fragmentation and the lack of strict mechanisms of regulation, control, and penalization end up undermining these efforts. The growing problem of marine waste and the protection of the open seas represent particular challenges. What is needed, in effect, is an agreement on systems of governance for the whole range of so-called "global commons."

175. The same mindset which stands in the way of making radical decisions to reverse the trend of global warming also stands in the way of achieving the goal of eliminating poverty. A more responsible overall approach is needed to deal with both problems: the reduction of pollution and the development of poorer countries and regions. The twenty-first century, while maintaining systems of governance inherited from the past, is witnessing a weakening of the power of nation-states, chiefly because the economic and financial sectors, being transnational, tend to prevail over the political. Given this situation, it is essential to devise stronger and more efficiently organized international institutions, with functionaries who are appointed fairly by agreement among national governments, and empowered to impose sanctions. As Benedict XVI has affirmed in continuity with the social teaching of the Church: "To manage the global economy; to revive economies hit by the crisis; to avoid any deterioration of the present crisis and the greater imbalances that would result; to bring about integral and timely disarmament, food security and peace; to guarantee the protection of the environment and to regulate migration: for all this, there is urgent need of a true world political authority, as my predecessor Blessed John XXIII indicated some

years ago."[129] Diplomacy also takes on new importance in the work of developing international strategies which can anticipate serious problems affecting us all.

II. Dialogue for new national and local policies

176. There are not just winners and losers among countries, but within poorer countries themselves. Hence different responsibilities need to be identified. Questions related to the environment and economic development can no longer be approached only from the standpoint of differences between countries; they also call for greater attention to policies on the national and local levels.

177. Given the real potential for a misuse of human abilities, individual states can no longer ignore their responsibility for planning, coordination, oversight, and enforcement within their respective borders. How can a society plan and protect its future amid constantly developing technological innovations? One authoritative source of oversight and coordination is the law, which lays down rules for admissible conduct in the light of the common good. The limits which a healthy, mature, and sovereign society must impose are those related to foresight and security, regulatory norms, timely enforcement, the elimination of corruption, effective responses to undesired side-effects of production processes, and appropriate intervention where potential or uncertain risks are involved. There is a growing jurisprudence dealing with the reduction of pollution by business activities. But political and institutional frameworks do not exist simply to avoid bad practice, but also to promote best practice, to stimulate creativity in seeking new solutions and to encourage individual or group initiatives.

178. A politics concerned with immediate results, supported by consumerist sectors of the population, is driven to produce short-term growth. In response to electoral interests, governments are reluctant to upset the public with measures which could affect the level of consumption or create risks for foreign investment. The myopia of power politics delays the inclusion of a far-sighted environmental agenda within the

overall agenda of governments. Thus we forget that "time is greater than space,"[130] that we are always more effective when we generate processes rather than holding on to positions of power. True statecraft is manifest when, in difficult times, we uphold high principles and think of the long-term common good. Political powers do not find it easy to assume this duty in the work of nation-building.

179. In some places, cooperatives are being developed to exploit renewable sources of energy which ensure local self-sufficiency and even the sale of surplus energy. This simple example shows that, while the existing world order proves powerless to assume its responsibilities, local individuals and groups can make a real difference. They are able to instill a greater sense of responsibility, a strong sense of community, a readiness to protect others, a spirit of creativity, and a deep love for the land. They are also concerned about what they will eventually leave to their children and grandchildren. These values are deeply rooted in indigenous peoples. Because the enforcement of laws is at times inadequate due to corruption, public pressure has to be exerted in order to bring about decisive political action. Society, through non-governmental organizations and intermediate groups, must put pressure on governments to develop more rigorous regulations, procedures, and controls. Unless citizens control political power—national, regional, and municipal—it will not be possible to control damage to the environment. Local legislation can be more effective, too, if agreements exist between neighboring communities to support the same environmental policies.

180. There are no uniform recipes, because each country or region has its own problems and limitations. It is also true that political realism may call for transitional measures and technologies, so long as these are accompanied by the gradual framing and acceptance of binding commitments. At the same time, on the national and local levels, much still needs to be done, such as promoting ways of conserving energy. These would include favoring forms of industrial production with maximum energy efficiency and diminished use of raw materials, removing from the market products which are less energy efficient or more polluting, improving transport systems, and encouraging the construction and

repair of buildings aimed at reducing their energy consumption and levels of pollution. Political activity on the local level could also be directed to modifying consumption, developing an economy of waste disposal and recycling, protecting certain species, and planning a diversified agriculture and the rotation of crops. Agriculture in poorer regions can be improved through investment in rural infrastructures, a better organization of local or national markets, systems of irrigation, and the development of techniques of sustainable agriculture. New forms of cooperation and community organization can be encouraged in order to defend the interests of small producers and preserve local ecosystems from destruction. Truly, much can be done!

181. Here, continuity is essential, because policies related to climate change and environmental protection cannot be altered with every change of government. Results take time and demand immediate outlays which may not produce tangible effects within any one government's term. That is why, in the absence of pressure from the public and from civic institutions, political authorities will always be reluctant to intervene, all the more when urgent needs must be met. To take up these responsibilities and the costs they entail, politicians will inevitably clash with the mindset of short-term gain and results which dominates present-day economics and politics. But if they are courageous, they will attest to their God-given dignity and leave behind a testimony of selfless responsibility. A healthy politics is sorely needed, capable of reforming and coordinating institutions, promoting best practices and overcoming undue pressure and bureaucratic inertia. It should be added, though, that even the best mechanisms can break down when there are no worthy goals and values, or a genuine and profound humanism to serve as the basis of a noble and generous society.

III. Dialogue and transparency in decision-making

182. An assessment of the environmental impact of business ventures and projects demands transparent political processes involving a free exchange of views. On the other hand, the forms of corruption which conceal the actual environmental impact of a given project, in exchange

for favors, usually produce specious agreements which fail to inform adequately and to allow for full debate.

183. Environmental impact assessment should not come after the drawing up of a business proposition or the proposal of a particular policy, plan, or program. It should be part of the process from the beginning, and be carried out in a way which is interdisciplinary, transparent, and free of all economic or political pressure. It should be linked to a study of working conditions and possible effects on people's physical and mental health, on the local economy and on public safety. Economic returns can thus be forecast more realistically, taking into account potential scenarios and the eventual need for further investment to correct possible undesired effects. A consensus should always be reached between the different stakeholders, who can offer a variety of approaches, solutions, and alternatives. The local population should have a special place at the table; they are concerned about their own future and that of their children, and can consider goals transcending immediate economic interest. We need to stop thinking in terms of "interventions" to save the environment in favor of policies developed and debated by all interested parties. The participation of the latter also entails being fully informed about such projects and their different risks and possibilities; this includes not just preliminary decisions but also various follow-up activities and continued monitoring. Honesty and truth are needed in scientific and political discussions; these should not be limited to the issue of whether or not a particular project is permitted by law.

184. In the face of possible risks to the environment which may affect the common good now and in the future, decisions must be made "based on a comparison of the risks and benefits foreseen for the various possible alternatives."[131] This is especially the case when a project may lead to a greater use of natural resources, higher levels of emission or discharge, an increase of refuse, or significant changes to the landscape, the habitats of protected species, or public spaces. Some projects, if insufficiently studied, can profoundly affect the quality of life of an area due to very different factors such as unforeseen noise pollution, the shrinking of visual horizons, the loss of cultural values, or the effects of nuclear energy

use. The culture of consumerism, which prioritizes short-term gain and private interest, can make it easy to rubber-stamp authorizations or to conceal information.

185. In any discussion about a proposed venture, a number of questions need to be asked in order to discern whether or not it will contribute to genuine integral development. What will it accomplish? Why? Where? When? How? For whom? What are the risks? What are the costs? Who will pay those costs and how? In this discernment, some questions must have higher priority. For example, we know that water is a scarce and indispensable resource and a fundamental right which conditions the exercise of other human rights. This indisputable fact overrides any other assessment of environmental impact on a region.

186. The Rio Declaration of 1992 states that "where there are threats of serious or irreversible damage, lack of full scientific certainty shall not be used as a pretext for postponing cost-effective measures"[132] which prevent environmental degradation. This precautionary principle makes it possible to protect those who are most vulnerable and whose ability to defend their interests and to assemble incontrovertible evidence is limited. If objective information suggests that serious and irreversible damage may result, a project should be halted or modified, even in the absence of indisputable proof. Here the burden of proof is effectively reversed, since in such cases objective and conclusive demonstrations will have to be brought forward to demonstrate that the proposed activity will not cause serious harm to the environment or to those who inhabit it.

187. This does not mean being opposed to any technological innovations which can bring about an improvement in the quality of life. But it does mean that profit cannot be the sole criterion to be taken into account, and that, when significant new information comes to light, a reassessment should be made, with the involvement of all interested parties. The outcome may be a decision not to proceed with a given project, to modify it, or to consider alternative proposals.

188. There are certain environmental issues where it is not easy to achieve a broad consensus. Here I would state once more that the Church does

not presume to settle scientific questions or to replace politics. But I am concerned to encourage an honest and open debate so that particular interests or ideologies will not prejudice the common good.

IV. Politics and economy in dialogue for human fulfillment

189. Politics must not be subject to the economy, nor should the economy be subject to the dictates of an efficiency-driven paradigm of technocracy. Today, in view of the common good, there is urgent need for politics and economics to enter into a frank dialogue in the service of life, especially human life. Saving banks at any cost, making the public pay the price, foregoing a firm commitment to reviewing and reforming the entire system, only reaffirms the absolute power of a financial system, a power which has no future and will only give rise to new crises after a slow, costly, and only apparent recovery. The financial crisis of 2007–08 provided an opportunity to develop a new economy, more attentive to ethical principles, and new ways of regulating speculative financial practices and virtual wealth. But the response to the crisis did not include rethinking the outdated criteria which continue to rule the world. Production is not always rational, and is usually tied to economic variables which assign to products a value that does not necessarily correspond to their real worth. This frequently leads to an overproduction of some commodities, with unnecessary impact on the environment and with negative results on regional economies.[133] The financial bubble also tends to be a productive bubble. The problem of the real economy is not confronted with vigor, yet it is the real economy which makes diversification and improvement in production possible, helps companies to function well, and enables small and medium businesses to develop and create employment.

190. Here too, it should always be kept in mind that "environmental protection cannot be assured solely on the basis of financial calculations of costs and benefits. The environment is one of those goods that cannot be adequately safeguarded or promoted by market forces."[134] Once more, we need to reject a magical conception of the market, which would suggest that problems can be solved simply by an increase in the profits

of companies or individuals. Is it realistic to hope that those who are obsessed with maximizing profits will stop to reflect on the environmental damage which they will leave behind for future generations? Where profits alone count, there can be no thinking about the rhythms of nature, its phases of decay and regeneration, or the complexity of ecosystems which may be gravely upset by human intervention. Moreover, biodiversity is considered at most a deposit of economic resources available for exploitation, with no serious thought for the real value of things, their significance for persons and cultures, or the concerns and needs of the poor.

191. Whenever these questions are raised, some react by accusing others of irrationally attempting to stand in the way of progress and human development. But we need to grow in the conviction that a decrease in the pace of production and consumption can at times give rise to another form of progress and development. Efforts to promote a sustainable use of natural resources are not a waste of money, but rather an investment capable of providing other economic benefits in the medium term. If we look at the larger picture, we can see that more diversified and innovative forms of production which impact less on the environment can prove very profitable. It is a matter of openness to different possibilities which do not involve stifling human creativity and its ideals of progress, but rather directing that energy along new channels.

192. For example, a path of productive development, which is more creative and better directed, could correct the present disparity between excessive technological investment in consumption and insufficient investment in resolving urgent problems facing the human family. It could generate intelligent and profitable ways of reusing, revamping, and recycling, and it could also improve the energy efficiency of cities. Productive diversification offers the fullest possibilities to human ingenuity to create and innovate, while at the same time protecting the environment and creating more sources of employment. Such creativity would be a worthy expression of our most noble human qualities, for we would be striving intelligently, boldly, and responsibly to promote a sustainable and equitable development within the context of a broader

concept of quality of life. On the other hand, to find ever new ways of despoiling nature, purely for the sake of new consumer items and quick profit, would be, in human terms, less worthy and creative, and more superficial.

193. In any event, if in some cases sustainable development were to involve new forms of growth, then in other cases, given the insatiable and irresponsible growth produced over many decades, we need also to think of containing growth by setting some reasonable limits and even retracing our steps before it is too late. We know how unsustainable is the behavior of those who constantly consume and destroy, while others are not yet able to live in a way worthy of their human dignity. That is why the time has come to accept decreased growth in some parts of the world, in order to provide resources for other places to experience healthy growth. Benedict XVI has said that "technologically advanced societies must be prepared to encourage more sober lifestyles, while reducing their energy consumption and improving its efficiency."[135]

194. For new models of progress to arise, there is a need to change "models of global development";[136] this will entail a responsible reflection on "the meaning of the economy and its goals with an eye to correcting its malfunctions and misapplications."[137] It is not enough to balance, in the medium term, the protection of nature with financial gain, or the preservation of the environment with progress. Halfway measures simply delay the inevitable disaster. Put simply, it is a matter of redefining our notion of progress. A technological and economic development which does not leave in its wake a better world and an integrally higher quality of life cannot be considered progress. Frequently, in fact, people's quality of life actually diminishes—by the deterioration of the environment, the low quality of food, or the depletion of resources—in the midst of economic growth. In this context, talk of sustainable growth usually becomes a way of distracting attention and offering excuses. It absorbs the language and values of ecology into the categories of finance and technocracy, and the social and environmental responsibility of businesses often gets reduced to a series of marketing and image-enhancing measures.

195. The principle of the maximization of profits, frequently isolated from other considerations, reflects a misunderstanding of the very concept of the economy. As long as production is increased, little concern is given to whether it is at the cost of future resources or the health of the environment; as long as the clearing of a forest increases production, no one calculates the losses entailed in the desertification of the land, the harm done to biodiversity, or the increased pollution. In a word, businesses profit by calculating and paying only a fraction of the costs involved. Yet only when "the economic and social costs of using up shared environmental resources are recognized with transparency and fully borne by those who incur them, not by other peoples or future generations,"[138] can those actions be considered ethical. An instrumental way of reasoning, which provides a purely static analysis of realities in the service of present needs, is at work whether resources are allocated by the market or by state central planning.

196. What happens with politics? Let us keep in mind the principle of subsidiarity, which grants freedom to develop the capabilities present at every level of society, while also demanding a greater sense of responsibility for the common good from those who wield greater power. Today, it is the case that some economic sectors exercise more power than states themselves. But economics without politics cannot be justified, since this would make it impossible to favor other ways of handling the various aspects of the present crisis. The mindset which leaves no room for sincere concern for the environment is the same mindset which lacks concern for the inclusion of the most vulnerable members of society. For "the current model, with its emphasis on success and self-reliance, does not appear to favor an investment in efforts to help the slow, the weak or the less talented to find opportunities in life."[139]

197. What is needed is a politics which is far-sighted and capable of a new, integral, and interdisciplinary approach to handling the different aspects of the crisis. Often, politics itself is responsible for the disrepute in which it is held, on account of corruption and the failure to enact sound public policies. If in a given region the state does not carry out its responsibilities, some business groups can come forward in the guise

of benefactors, wield real power, and consider themselves exempt from certain rules, to the point of tolerating different forms of organized crime, human trafficking, the drug trade and violence, all of which become very difficult to eradicate. If politics shows itself incapable of breaking such a perverse logic, and remains caught up in inconsequential discussions, we will continue to avoid facing the major problems of humanity. A strategy for real change calls for rethinking processes in their entirety, for it is not enough to include a few superficial ecological considerations while failing to question the logic which underlies present-day culture. A healthy politics needs to be able to take up this challenge.

198. Politics and the economy tend to blame each other when it comes to poverty and environmental degradation. It is to be hoped that they can acknowledge their own mistakes and find forms of interaction directed to the common good. While some are concerned only with financial gain, and others with holding on to or increasing their power, what we are left with are conflicts or spurious agreements where the last thing either party is concerned about is caring for the environment and protecting those who are most vulnerable. Here too, we see how true it is that "unity is greater than conflict."[140]

V. Religions in dialogue with science

199. It cannot be maintained that empirical science provides a complete explanation of life, the interplay of all creatures, and the whole of reality. This would be to breach the limits imposed by its own methodology. If we reason only within the confines of the latter, little room would be left for aesthetic sensibility, poetry, or even reason's ability to grasp the ultimate meaning and purpose of things.[141] I would add that "religious classics can prove meaningful in every age; they have an enduring power to open new horizons. . . . Is it reasonable and enlightened to dismiss certain writings simply because they arose in the context of religious belief?"[142] It would be quite simplistic to think that ethical principles present themselves purely in the abstract, detached from any context. Nor does the fact that they may be couched in religious language detract from their value in public debate. The ethical principles capable of being

apprehended by reason can always reappear in different guise and find expression in a variety of languages, including religious language.

200. Any technical solution which science claims to offer will be powerless to solve the serious problems of our world if humanity loses its compass, if we lose sight of the great motivations which make it possible for us to live in harmony, to make sacrifices, and to treat others well. Believers themselves must constantly feel challenged to live in a way consonant with their faith and not to contradict it by their actions. They need to be encouraged to be ever open to God's grace and to draw constantly from their deepest convictions about love, justice, and peace. If a mistaken understanding of our own principles has at times led us to justify mistreating nature, to exercise tyranny over creation, to engage in war, injustice, and acts of violence, we believers should acknowledge that by so doing we were not faithful to the treasures of wisdom which we have been called to protect and preserve. Cultural limitations in different eras often affected the perception of these ethical and spiritual treasures, yet by constantly returning to their sources, religions will be better equipped to respond to today's needs.

201. The majority of people living on our planet profess to be believers. This should spur religions to dialogue among themselves for the sake of protecting nature, defending the poor, and building networks of respect and fraternity. Dialogue among the various sciences is likewise needed, since each can tend to become enclosed in its own language, while specialization leads to a certain isolation and the absolutization of its own field of knowledge. This prevents us from confronting environmental problems effectively. An open and respectful dialogue is also needed between the various ecological movements, among which ideological conflicts are not infrequently encountered. The gravity of the ecological crisis demands that we all look to the common good, embarking on a path of dialogue which demands patience, self-discipline, and generosity, always keeping in mind that "realities are greater than ideas."[143]

CHAPTER SIX

ECOLOGICAL EDUCATION AND SPIRITUALITY

202. Many things have to change course, but it is we human beings above all who need to change. We lack an awareness of our common origin, of our mutual belonging, and of a future to be shared with everyone. This basic awareness would enable the development of new convictions, attitudes and forms of life. A great cultural, spiritual, and educational challenge stands before us, and it will demand that we set out on the long path of renewal.

I. Toward a new lifestyle

203. Since the market tends to promote extreme consumerism in an effort to sell its products, people can easily get caught up in a whirlwind of needless buying and spending. Compulsive consumerism is one example of how the techno-economic paradigm affects individuals. Romano Guardini had already foreseen this: "The gadgets and technics forced upon him by the patterns of machine production and of abstract planning mass man accepts quite simply; they are the forms of life itself. To either a greater or lesser degree mass man is convinced that his conformity is both reasonable and just."[144] This paradigm leads people to believe that they are free as long as they have the supposed freedom to consume. But those really free are the minority who wield economic and financial power. Amid this confusion, postmodern humanity has not yet achieved a new self-awareness capable of offering guidance and direction, and this lack of identity is a source of anxiety. We have too many means and only a few insubstantial ends.

204. The current global situation engenders a feeling of instability and uncertainty, which in turn becomes "a seedbed for collective selfishness."[145] When people become self-centered and self-enclosed, their greed increases. The emptier a person's heart is, the more he or she needs things to buy, own, and consume. It becomes almost impossible to accept the limits imposed by reality. In this horizon, a genuine sense of the common

good also disappears. As these attitudes become more widespread, social norms are respected only to the extent that they do not clash with personal needs. So our concern cannot be limited merely to the threat of extreme weather events, but must also extend to the catastrophic consequences of social unrest. Obsession with a consumerist lifestyle, above all when few people are capable of maintaining it, can only lead to violence and mutual destruction.

205. Yet all is not lost. Human beings, while capable of the worst, are also capable of rising above themselves, choosing again what is good, and making a new start, despite their mental and social conditioning. We are able to take an honest look at ourselves, to acknowledge our deep dissatisfaction, and to embark on new paths to authentic freedom. No system can completely suppress our openness to what is good, true, and beautiful, or our God-given ability to respond to his grace at work deep in our hearts. I appeal to everyone throughout the world not to forget this dignity which is ours. No one has the right to take it from us.

206. A change in lifestyle could bring healthy pressure to bear on those who wield political, economic, and social power. This is what consumer movements accomplish by boycotting certain products. They prove successful in changing the way businesses operate, forcing them to consider their environmental footprint and their patterns of production. When social pressure affects their earnings, businesses clearly have to find ways to produce differently. This shows us the great need for a sense of social responsibility on the part of consumers. "Purchasing is always a moral—and not simply economic—act."[146] Today, in a word, "the issue of environmental degradation challenges us to examine our lifestyle."[147]

207. The Earth Charter asked us to leave behind a period of self-destruction and make a new start, but we have not as yet developed a universal awareness needed to achieve this. Here, I would echo that courageous challenge: "As never before in history, common destiny beckons us to seek a new beginning. . . . Let ours be a time remembered for the awakening of a new reverence for life, the firm resolve to achieve sustainability,

the quickening of the struggle for justice and peace, and the joyful celebration of life."[148]

208. We are always capable of going out of ourselves toward the other. Unless we do this, other creatures will not be recognized for their true worth; we are unconcerned about caring for things for the sake of others; we fail to set limits on ourselves in order to avoid the suffering of others or the deterioration of our surroundings. Disinterested concern for others, and the rejection of every form of self-centeredness and self-absorption, are essential if we truly wish to care for our brothers and sisters and for the natural environment. These attitudes also attune us to the moral imperative of assessing the impact of our every action and personal decision on the world around us. If we can overcome individualism, we will truly be able to develop a different lifestyle and bring about significant changes in society.

II. Educating for the covenant between humanity and the environment

209. An awareness of the gravity of today's cultural and ecological crisis must be translated into new habits. Many people know that our current progress and the mere amassing of things and pleasures are not enough to give meaning and joy to the human heart, yet they feel unable to give up what the market sets before them. In those countries which should be making the greatest changes in consumer habits, young people have a new ecological sensitivity and a generous spirit, and some of them are making admirable efforts to protect the environment. At the same time, they have grown up in a milieu of extreme consumerism and affluence which makes it difficult to develop other habits. We are faced with an educational challenge.

210. Environmental education has broadened its goals. Whereas in the beginning it was mainly centered on scientific information, consciousness-raising, and the prevention of environmental risks, it tends now to include a critique of the "myths" of a modernity grounded in a utilitarian mindset (individualism, unlimited progress, competition, consumerism,

the unregulated market). It seeks also to restore the various levels of ecological equilibrium, establishing harmony within ourselves, with others, with nature and other living creatures, and with God. Environmental education should facilitate making the leap toward the transcendent which gives ecological ethics its deepest meaning. It needs educators capable of developing an ethics of ecology, and helping people, through effective pedagogy, to grow in solidarity, responsibility, and compassionate care.

211. Yet this education, aimed at creating an "ecological citizenship," is at times limited to providing information, and fails to instill good habits. The existence of laws and regulations is insufficient in the long run to curb bad conduct, even when effective means of enforcement are present. If the laws are to bring about significant, long-lasting effects, the majority of the members of society must be adequately motivated to accept them, and personally transformed to respond. Only by cultivating sound virtues will people be able to make a selfless ecological commitment. A person who could afford to spend and consume more but regularly uses less heating and wears warmer clothes, shows the kind of convictions and attitudes which help to protect the environment. There is a nobility in the duty to care for creation through little daily actions, and it is wonderful how education can bring about real changes in lifestyle. Education in environmental responsibility can encourage ways of acting which directly and significantly affect the world around us, such as avoiding the use of plastic and paper, reducing water consumption, separating refuse, cooking only what can reasonably be consumed, showing care for other living beings, using public transport or car-pooling, planting trees, turning off unnecessary lights, or any number of other practices. All of these reflect a generous and worthy creativity which brings out the best in human beings. Reusing something instead of immediately discarding it, when done for the right reasons, can be an act of love which expresses our own dignity.

212. We must not think that these efforts are not going to change the world. They benefit society, often unbeknown to us, for they call forth a goodness which, albeit unseen, inevitably tends to spread. Furthermore,

such actions can restore our sense of self-esteem; they can enable us to live more fully and to feel that life on earth is worthwhile.

213. Ecological education can take place in a variety of settings: at school, in families, in the media, in catechesis, and elsewhere. Good education plants seeds when we are young, and these continue to bear fruit throughout life. Here, though, I would stress the great importance of the family, which is "the place in which life—the gift of God—can be properly welcomed and protected against the many attacks to which it is exposed, and can develop in accordance with what constitutes authentic human growth. In the face of the so-called culture of death, the family is the heart of the culture of life."[149] In the family we first learn how to show love and respect for life; we are taught the proper use of things, order and cleanliness, respect for the local ecosystem, and care for all creatures. In the family we receive an integral education, which enables us to grow harmoniously in personal maturity. In the family we learn to ask without demanding, to say "thank you" as an expression of genuine gratitude for what we have been given, to control our aggressivity and greed, and to ask forgiveness when we have caused harm. These simple gestures of heartfelt courtesy help to create a culture of shared life and respect for our surroundings.

214. Political institutions and various other social groups are also entrusted with helping to raise people's awareness. So too is the Church. All Christian communities have an important role to play in ecological education. It is my hope that our seminaries and houses of formation will provide an education in responsible simplicity of life, in grateful contemplation of God's world, and in concern for the needs of the poor and the protection of the environment. Because the stakes are so high, we need institutions empowered to impose penalties for damage inflicted on the environment. But we also need the personal qualities of self-control and willingness to learn from one another.

215. In this regard, "the relationship between a good aesthetic education and the maintenance of a healthy environment cannot be overlooked."[150] By learning to see and appreciate beauty, we learn to reject self-interested

pragmatism. If someone has not learned to stop and admire something beautiful, we should not be surprised if he or she treats everything as an object to be used and abused without scruple. If we want to bring about deep change, we need to realize that certain mindsets really do influence our behavior. Our efforts at education will be inadequate and ineffectual unless we strive to promote a new way of thinking about human beings, life, society, and our relationship with nature. Otherwise, the paradigm of consumerism will continue to advance, with the help of the media and the highly effective workings of the market.

III. Ecological conversion

216. The rich heritage of Christian spirituality, the fruit of twenty centuries of personal and communal experience, has a precious contribution to make to the renewal of humanity. Here, I would like to offer Christians a few suggestions for an ecological spirituality grounded in the convictions of our faith, since the teachings of the Gospel have direct consequences for our way of thinking, feeling, and living. More than in ideas or concepts as such, I am interested in how such a spirituality can motivate us to a more passionate concern for the protection of our world. A commitment this lofty cannot be sustained by doctrine alone, without a spirituality capable of inspiring us, without an "interior impulse which encourages, motivates, nourishes and gives meaning to our individual and communal activity."[151] Admittedly, Christians have not always appropriated and developed the spiritual treasures bestowed by God upon the Church, where the life of the spirit is not dissociated from the body or from nature or from worldly realities, but lived in and with them, in communion with all that surrounds us.

217. "The external deserts in the world are growing, because the internal deserts have become so vast."[152] For this reason, the ecological crisis is also a summons to profound interior conversion. It must be said that some committed and prayerful Christians, with the excuse of realism and pragmatism, tend to ridicule expressions of concern for the environment. Others are passive; they choose not to change their habits and thus become inconsistent. So what they all need is an "ecological conversion,"

whereby the effects of their encounter with Jesus Christ become evident in their relationship with the world around them. Living our vocation to be protectors of God's handiwork is essential to a life of virtue; it is not an optional or a secondary aspect of our Christian experience.

218. In calling to mind the figure of Saint Francis of Assisi, we come to realize that a healthy relationship with creation is one dimension of overall personal conversion, which entails the recognition of our errors, sins, faults, and failures, and leads to heartfelt repentance and desire to change. The Australian bishops spoke of the importance of such conversion for achieving reconciliation with creation: "To achieve such reconciliation, we must examine our lives and acknowledge the ways in which we have harmed God's creation through our actions and our failure to act. We need to experience a conversion, or change of heart."[153]

219. Nevertheless, self-improvement on the part of individuals will not by itself remedy the extremely complex situation facing our world today. Isolated individuals can lose their ability and freedom to escape the utilitarian mindset, and end up prey to an unethical consumerism bereft of social or ecological awareness. Social problems must be addressed by community networks and not simply by the sum of individual good deeds. This task "will make such tremendous demands of man that he could never achieve it by individual initiative or even by the united effort of men bred in an individualistic way. The work of dominating the world calls for a union of skills and a unity of achievement that can only grow from quite a different attitude."[154] The ecological conversion needed to bring about lasting change is also a community conversion.

220. This conversion calls for a number of attitudes which together foster a spirit of generous care, full of tenderness. First, it entails gratitude and gratuitousness, a recognition that the world is God's loving gift, and that we are called quietly to imitate his generosity in self-sacrifice and good works: "Do not let your left hand know what your right hand is doing . . . and your Father who sees in secret will reward you" (Mt 6:3-4). It also entails a loving awareness that we are not disconnected from the rest of creatures, but joined in a splendid universal communion. As believers,

we do not look at the world from without but from within, conscious of the bonds with which the Father has linked us to all beings. By developing our individual, God-given capacities, an ecological conversion can inspire us to greater creativity and enthusiasm in resolving the world's problems and in offering ourselves to God "as a living sacrifice, holy and acceptable" (Rom 12:1). We do not understand our superiority as a reason for personal glory or irresponsible dominion, but rather as a different capacity which, in its turn, entails a serious responsibility stemming from our faith.

221. Various convictions of our faith, developed at the beginning of this Encyclical can help us to enrich the meaning of this conversion. These include the awareness that each creature reflects something of God and has a message to convey to us, and the security that Christ has taken unto himself this material world and now, risen, is intimately present to each being, surrounding it with his affection and penetrating it with his light. Then too, there is the recognition that God created the world, writing into it an order and a dynamism that human beings have no right to ignore. We read in the Gospel that Jesus says of the birds of the air that "not one of them is forgotten before God" (Lk 12:6). How then can we possibly mistreat them or cause them harm? I ask all Christians to recognize and to live fully this dimension of their conversion. May the power and the light of the grace we have received also be evident in our relationship to other creatures and to the world around us. In this way, we will help nurture that sublime fraternity with all creation which Saint Francis of Assisi so radiantly embodied.

IV. Joy and peace

222. Christian spirituality proposes an alternative understanding of the quality of life, and encourages a prophetic and contemplative lifestyle, one capable of deep enjoyment free of the obsession with consumption. We need to take up an ancient lesson, found in different religious traditions and also in the Bible. It is the conviction that "less is more." A constant flood of new consumer goods can baffle the heart and prevent us from cherishing each thing and each moment. To be serenely present

to each reality, however small it may be, opens us to much greater horizons of understanding and personal fulfillment. Christian spirituality proposes a growth marked by moderation and the capacity to be happy with little. It is a return to that simplicity which allows us to stop and appreciate the small things, to be grateful for the opportunities which life affords us, to be spiritually detached from what we possess, and not to succumb to sadness for what we lack. This implies avoiding the dynamic of dominion and the mere accumulation of pleasures.

223. Such sobriety, when lived freely and consciously, is liberating. It is not a lesser life or one lived with less intensity. On the contrary, it is a way of living life to the full. In reality, those who enjoy more and live better each moment are those who have given up dipping here and there, always on the look-out for what they do not have. They experience what it means to appreciate each person and each thing, learning familiarity with the simplest things and how to enjoy them. So they are able to shed unsatisfied needs, reducing their obsessiveness and weariness. Even living on little, they can live a lot, above all when they cultivate other pleasures and find satisfaction in fraternal encounters, in service, in developing their gifts, in music and art, in contact with nature, in prayer. Happiness means knowing how to limit some needs which only diminish us, and being open to the many different possibilities which life can offer.

224. Sobriety and humility were not favorably regarded in the last century. And yet, when there is a general breakdown in the exercise of a certain virtue in personal and social life, it ends up causing a number of imbalances, including environmental ones. That is why it is no longer enough to speak only of the integrity of ecosystems. We have to dare to speak of the integrity of human life, of the need to promote and unify all the great values. Once we lose our humility, and become enthralled with the possibility of limitless mastery over everything, we inevitably end up harming society and the environment. It is not easy to promote this kind of healthy humility or happy sobriety when we consider ourselves autonomous, when we exclude God from our lives or replace him with our own ego, and think that our subjective feelings can define what is right and what is wrong.

225. On the other hand, no one can cultivate a sober and satisfying life without being at peace with him or herself. An adequate understanding of spirituality consists in filling out what we mean by peace, which is much more than the absence of war. Inner peace is closely related to care for ecology and for the common good because, lived out authentically, it is reflected in a balanced lifestyle together with a capacity for wonder which takes us to a deeper understanding of life. Nature is filled with words of love, but how can we listen to them amid constant noise, interminable and nerve-wracking distractions, or the cult of appearances? Many people today sense a profound imbalance which drives them to frenetic activity and makes them feel busy, in a constant hurry which in turn leads them to ride rough-shod over everything around them. This too affects how they treat the environment. An integral ecology includes taking time to recover a serene harmony with creation, reflecting on our lifestyle and our ideals, and contemplating the Creator who lives among us and surrounds us, whose presence "must not be contrived but found, uncovered."[155]

226. We are speaking of an attitude of the heart, one which approaches life with serene attentiveness, which is capable of being fully present to someone without thinking of what comes next, which accepts each moment as a gift from God to be lived to the full. Jesus taught us this attitude when he invited us to contemplate the lilies of the field and the birds of the air, or when seeing the rich young man and knowing his restlessness, "he looked at him with love" (Mk 10:21). He was completely present to everyone and to everything, and in this way he showed us the way to overcome that unhealthy anxiety which makes us superficial, aggressive, and compulsive consumers.

227. One expression of this attitude is when we stop and give thanks to God before and after meals. I ask all believers to return to this beautiful and meaningful custom. That moment of blessing, however brief, reminds us of our dependence on God for life; it strengthens our feeling of gratitude for the gifts of creation; it acknowledges those who by their labors provide us with these goods; and it reaffirms our solidarity with those in greatest need.

V. Civic and political love

228. Care for nature is part of a lifestyle which includes the capacity for living together and communion. Jesus reminded us that we have God as our common Father and that this makes us brothers and sisters. Fraternal love can only be gratuitous; it can never be a means of repaying others for what they have done or will do for us. That is why it is possible to love our enemies. This same gratuitousness inspires us to love and accept the wind, the sun, and the clouds, even though we cannot control them. In this sense, we can speak of a "universal fraternity."

229. We must regain the conviction that we need one another, that we have a shared responsibility for others and the world, and that being good and decent are worth it. We have had enough of immorality and the mockery of ethics, goodness, faith, and honesty. It is time to acknowledge that light-hearted superficiality has done us no good. When the foundations of social life are corroded, what ensues are battles over conflicting interests, new forms of violence and brutality, and obstacles to the growth of a genuine culture of care for the environment.

230. Saint Thérèse of Lisieux invites us to practice the little way of love, not to miss out on a kind word, a smile, or any small gesture which sows peace and friendship. An integral ecology is also made up of simple daily gestures which break with the logic of violence, exploitation, and selfishness. In the end, a world of exacerbated consumption is at the same time a world which mistreats life in all its forms.

231. Love, overflowing with small gestures of mutual care, is also civic and political, and it makes itself felt in every action that seeks to build a better world. Love for society and commitment to the common good are outstanding expressions of a charity which affects not only relationships between individuals but also "macro-relationships, social, economic and political ones."[156] That is why the Church set before the world the ideal of a "civilization of love."[157] Social love is the key to authentic development: "In order to make society more human, more worthy of the human person, love in social life—political, economic, and cultural—must be given renewed value, becoming the constant and highest norm

for all activity."[158] In this framework, along with the importance of little everyday gestures, social love moves us to devise larger strategies to halt environmental degradation and to encourage a "culture of care" which permeates all of society. When we feel that God is calling us to intervene with others in these social dynamics, we should realize that this too is part of our spirituality, which is an exercise of charity and, as such, matures and sanctifies us.

232. Not everyone is called to engage directly in political life. Society is also enriched by a countless array of organizations which work to promote the common good and to defend the environment, whether natural or urban. Some, for example, show concern for a public place (a building, a fountain, an abandoned monument, a landscape, a square), and strive to protect, restore, improve, or beautify it as something belonging to everyone. Around these community actions, relationships develop or are recovered and a new social fabric emerges. Thus, a community can break out of the indifference induced by consumerism. These actions cultivate a shared identity, with a story which can be remembered and handed on. In this way, the world, and the quality of life of the poorest, are cared for, with a sense of solidarity which is at the same time aware that we live in a common home which God has entrusted to us. These community actions, when they express self-giving love, can also become intense spiritual experiences.

VI. Sacramental signs and the celebration of rest

233. The universe unfolds in God, who fills it completely. Hence, there is a mystical meaning to be found in a leaf, in a mountain trail, in a dewdrop, in a poor person's face.[159] The ideal is not only to pass from the exterior to the interior to discover the action of God in the soul, but also to discover God in all things. Saint Bonaventure teaches us that "contemplation deepens the more we feel the working of God's grace within our hearts, and the better we learn to encounter God in creatures outside ourselves."[160]

234. Saint John of the Cross taught that all the goodness present in the realities and experiences of this world "is present in God eminently and infinitely, or more properly, in each of these sublime realities is God."[161] This is not because the finite things of this world are really divine, but because the mystic experiences the intimate connection between God and all beings, and thus feels that "all things are God."[162] Standing awestruck before a mountain, he or she cannot separate this experience from God, and perceives that the interior awe being lived has to be entrusted to the Lord: "Mountains have heights and they are plentiful, vast, beautiful, graceful, bright, and fragrant. These mountains are what my Beloved is to me. Lonely valleys are quiet, pleasant, cool, shady, and flowing with fresh water; in the variety of their groves and in the sweet song of the birds, they afford abundant recreation and delight to the senses, and in their solitude and silence, they refresh us and give rest. These valleys are what my Beloved is to me."[163]

235. The sacraments are a privileged way in which nature is taken up by God to become a means of mediating supernatural life. Through our worship of God, we are invited to embrace the world on a different plane. Water, oil, fire, and colors are taken up in all their symbolic power and incorporated in our act of praise. The hand that blesses is an instrument of God's love and a reflection of the closeness of Jesus Christ, who came to accompany us on the journey of life. Water poured over the body of a child in Baptism is a sign of new life. Encountering God does not mean fleeing from this world or turning our back on nature. This is especially clear in the spirituality of the Christian East. "Beauty, which in the East is one of the best loved names expressing the divine harmony and the model of humanity transfigured, appears everywhere: in the shape of a church, in the sounds, in the colors, in the lights, in the scents."[164] For Christians, all the creatures of the material universe find their true meaning in the incarnate Word, for the Son of God has incorporated in his person part of the material world, planting in it a seed of definitive transformation. "Christianity does not reject matter. Rather, bodiliness is considered in all its value in the liturgical act, whereby the human body is disclosed in its inner nature as a temple of the Holy

Spirit and is united with the Lord Jesus, who himself took a body for the world's salvation."[165]

236. It is in the Eucharist that all that has been created finds its greatest exaltation. Grace, which tends to manifest itself tangibly, found unsurpassable expression when God himself became man and gave himself as food for his creatures. The Lord, in the culmination of the mystery of the Incarnation, chose to reach our intimate depths through a fragment of matter. He comes not from above, but from within; he comes that we might find him in this world of ours. In the Eucharist, fullness is already achieved; it is the living center of the universe, the overflowing core of love and of inexhaustible life. Joined to the incarnate Son, present in the Eucharist, the whole cosmos gives thanks to God. Indeed the Eucharist is itself an act of cosmic love: "Yes, cosmic! Because even when it is celebrated on the humble altar of a country church, the Eucharist is always in some way celebrated on the altar of the world."[166] The Eucharist joins heaven and earth; it embraces and penetrates all creation. The world which came forth from God's hands returns to him in blessed and undivided adoration: in the bread of the Eucharist, "creation is projected toward divinization, toward the holy wedding feast, toward unification with the Creator himself."[167] Thus, the Eucharist is also a source of light and motivation for our concerns for the environment, directing us to be stewards of all creation.

237. On Sunday, our participation in the Eucharist has special importance. Sunday, like the Jewish Sabbath, is meant to be a day which heals our relationships with God, with ourselves, with others, and with the world. Sunday is the day of the Resurrection, the "first day" of the new creation, whose first fruits are the Lord's risen humanity, the pledge of the final transfiguration of all created reality. It also proclaims "man's eternal rest in God."[168] In this way, Christian spirituality incorporates the value of relaxation and festivity. We tend to demean contemplative rest as something unproductive and unnecessary, but this is to do away with the very thing which is most important about work: its meaning. We are called to include in our work a dimension of receptivity and gratuity, which is quite different from mere inactivity. Rather, it is another way

of working, which forms part of our very essence. It protects human action from becoming empty activism; it also prevents that unfettered greed and sense of isolation which make us seek personal gain to the detriment of all else. The law of weekly rest forbade work on the seventh day, "so that your ox and your donkey may have rest, and the son of your maidservant, and the stranger, may be refreshed" (Ex 23:12). Rest opens our eyes to the larger picture and gives us renewed sensitivity to the rights of others. And so the day of rest, centered on the Eucharist, sheds it light on the whole week, and motivates us to greater concern for nature and the poor.

VII. The Trinity and the relationship between creatures

238. The Father is the ultimate source of everything, the loving and self-communicating foundation of all that exists. The Son, his reflection, through whom all things were created, united himself to this earth when he was formed in the womb of Mary. The Spirit, infinite bond of love, is intimately present at the very heart of the universe, inspiring and bringing new pathways. The world was created by the three Persons acting as a single divine principle, but each one of them performed this common work in accordance with his own personal property. Consequently, "when we contemplate with wonder the universe in all its grandeur and beauty, we must praise the whole Trinity."[169]

239. For Christians, believing in one God who is Trinitarian communion suggests that the Trinity has left its mark on all creation. Saint Bonaventure went so far as to say that human beings, before sin, were able to see how each creature "testifies that God is three." The reflection of the Trinity was there to be recognized in nature "when that book was open to man and our eyes had not yet become darkened."[170] The Franciscan saint teaches us that *each creature bears in itself a specifically Trinitarian structure,* so real that it could be readily contemplated if only the human gaze were not so partial, dark, and fragile. In this way, he points out to us the challenge of trying to read reality in a Trinitarian key.

240. The divine Persons are subsistent relations, and the world, created according to the divine model, is a web of relationships. Creatures tend toward God, and in turn it is proper to every living being to tend toward other things, so that throughout the universe we can find any number of constant and secretly interwoven relationships.[171] This leads us not only to marvel at the manifold connections existing among creatures, but also to discover a key to our own fulfillment. The human person grows more, matures more, and is sanctified more to the extent that he or she enters into relationships, going out from themselves to live in communion with God, with others, and with all creatures. In this way, they make their own that Trinitarian dynamism which God imprinted in them when they were created. Everything is interconnected, and this invites us to develop a spirituality of that global solidarity which flows from the mystery of the Trinity.

VIII. Queen of all creation

241. Mary, the Mother who cared for Jesus, now cares with maternal affection and pain for this wounded world. Just as her pierced heart mourned the death of Jesus, so now she grieves for the sufferings of the crucified poor and for the creatures of this world laid waste by human power. Completely transfigured, she now lives with Jesus, and all creatures sing of her fairness. She is the Woman, "clothed in the sun, with the moon under her feet, and on her head a crown of twelve stars" (Rv 12:1). Carried up into heaven, she is the Mother and Queen of all creation. In her glorified body, together with the Risen Christ, part of creation has reached the fullness of its beauty. She treasures the entire life of Jesus in her heart (cf. Lk 2:19, 51), and now understands the meaning of all things. Hence, we can ask her to enable us to look at this world with eyes of wisdom.

242. At her side in the Holy Family of Nazareth, stands the figure of Saint Joseph. Through his work and generous presence, he cared for and defended Mary and Jesus, delivering them from the violence of the unjust by bringing them to Egypt. The Gospel presents Joseph as a just man, hard-working and strong. But he also shows great tenderness,

which is not a mark of the weak but of those who are genuinely strong, fully aware of reality and ready to love and serve in humility. That is why he was proclaimed custodian of the universal Church. He too can teach us how to show care; he can inspire us to work with generosity and tenderness in protecting this world which God has entrusted to us.

IX. Beyond the sun

243. At the end, we will find ourselves face to face with the infinite beauty of God (cf. 1 Cor 13:12), and be able to read with admiration and happiness the mystery of the universe, which with us will share in unending plenitude. Even now we are journeying toward the sabbath of eternity, the new Jerusalem, toward our common home in heaven. Jesus says: "I make all things new" (Rv 21:5). Eternal life will be a shared experience of awe, in which each creature, resplendently transfigured, will take its rightful place and have something to give those poor men and women who will have been liberated once and for all.

244. In the meantime, we come together to take charge of this home which has been entrusted to us, knowing that all the good which exists here will be taken up into the heavenly feast. In union with all creatures, we journey through this land seeking God, for "if the world has a beginning and if it has been created, we must enquire who gave it this beginning, and who was its Creator."[172] Let us sing as we go. May our struggles and our concern for this planet never take away the joy of our hope.

245. God, who calls us to generous commitment and to give him our all, offers us the light and the strength needed to continue on our way. In the heart of this world, the Lord of life, who loves us so much, is always present. He does not abandon us, he does not leave us alone, for he has united himself definitively to our earth, and his love constantly impels us to find new ways forward. *Praise be to him*!

• • •

246. At the conclusion of this lengthy reflection which has been both joyful and troubling, I propose that we offer two prayers. The first we can share with all who believe in a God who is the all-powerful Creator,

while in the other we Christians ask for inspiration to take up the commitment to creation set before us by the Gospel of Jesus.

A prayer for our earth

All-powerful God, you are present in the whole universe
and in the smallest of your creatures.
You embrace with your tenderness all that exists.
Pour out upon us the power of your love,
that we may protect life and beauty.
Fill us with peace, that we may live
as brothers and sisters, harming no one.
O God of the poor,
help us to rescue the abandoned and forgotten of this earth,
so precious in your eyes.
Bring healing to our lives,
that we may protect the world and not prey on it,
that we may sow beauty, not pollution and destruction.
Touch the hearts
of those who look only for gain
at the expense of the poor and the earth.
Teach us to discover the worth of each thing,
to be filled with awe and contemplation,
to recognize that we are profoundly united
with every creature
as we journey toward your infinite light.
We thank you for being with us each day.
Encourage us, we pray, in our struggle
for justice, love, and peace.

A Christian prayer in union with creation

Father, we praise you with all your creatures.
They came forth from your all-powerful hand;
they are yours, filled with your presence and your tender love.
Praise be to you!

Son of God, Jesus,
through you all things were made.
You were formed in the womb of Mary our Mother,
you became part of this earth,
and you gazed upon this world with human eyes.
Today you are alive in every creature
in your risen glory.
Praise be to you!

Holy Spirit, by your light
you guide this world toward the Father's love
and accompany creation as it groans in travail.
You also dwell in our hearts
and you inspire us to do what is good.
Praise be to you!

Triune Lord, wondrous community of infinite love,
teach us to contemplate you
in the beauty of the universe,
for all things speak of you.
Awaken our praise and thankfulness
for every being that you have made.
Give us the grace to feel profoundly joined
to everything that is.

God of love, show us our place in this world
as channels of your love
for all the creatures of this earth,
for not one of them is forgotten in your sight.
Enlighten those who possess power and money
that they may avoid the sin of indifference,
that they may love the common good, advance the weak,
and care for this world in which we live.
The poor and the earth are crying out.
O Lord, seize us with your power and light,
help us to protect all life,

to prepare for a better future,
for the coming of your kingdom
of justice, peace, love, and beauty.
Praise be to you!
Amen.

Given in Rome at Saint Peter's on 24 May, the Solemnity of Pentecost, in the year 2015, the third of my Pontificate.

FRANCISCUS

Notes

1. *Canticle of the Creatures*, in *Francis of Assisi: Early Documents*, vol. 1, New York-London-Manila, 1999, 113–114.

2. Apostolic Letter *Octogesima Adveniens* (14 May 1971), 21: AAS 63 (1971), 416–417.

3. *Address to FAO on the 25th Anniversary of Its Institution* (16 November 1970), 4: AAS 62 (1970), 833.

4. Encyclical Letter *Redemptor Hominis* (4 March 1979), 15: AAS 71 (1979), 287.

5. Cf. *Catechesis* (17 January 2001), 4: *Insegnamenti* 41 / 1 (2001), 179.

6. Encyclical Letter *Centesimus Annus* (1 May 1991), 38: AAS 83 (1991), 841.

7. Ibid., 58: AAS 83 (1991), 863.

8. John Paul II, Encyclical Letter *Sollicitudo Rei Socialis* (30 December 1987), 34: AAS 80 (1988), 559.

9. Cf. id., Encyclical Letter *Centesimus Annus* (1 May 1991), 37: AAS 83 (1991), 840.

10. *Address to the Diplomatic Corps Accredited to the Holy See* (8 January 2007): AAS 99 (2007), 73.

11. Encyclical Letter *Caritas in Veritate* (29 June 2009), 51: AAS 101 (2009), 687.

12. *Address to the Bundestag*, Berlin (22 September 2011): AAS 103 (2011), 664.

13. *Address to the Clergy of the Diocese of Bolzano-Bressanone* (6 August 2008): AAS 100 (2008), 634.

14. *Message for the Day of Prayer for the Protection of Creation* (1 September 2012).

15. *Address in Santa Barbara, California* (8 November 1997); cf. John Chryssavgis, *On Earth As in Heaven: Ecological Vision and Initiatives of Ecumenical Patriarch Bartholomew*, Bronx, New York, 2012.

16. Ibid.

17. *Lecture at the Monastery of Utstein, Norway* (23 June 2003).

18. "Global Responsibility and Ecological Sustainability," Closing Remarks, Halki Summit I, Istanbul (20 June 2012).

19. Thomas of Celano, *The Life of Saint Francis*, I, 29, 81: in *Francis of Assisi: Early Documents*, vol. 1, New York-London-Manila, 1999, 251.

20. *The Major Legend of Saint Francis*, VIII, 6, in *Francis of Assisi: Early Documents*, vol. 2, New York-London-Manila, 2000, 590.

21. Cf. Thomas of Celano, *The Remembrance of the Desire of a Soul*, II, 124, 165, in *Francis of Assisi: Early Documents*, vol. 2, New York-London-Manila, 2000, 354.

22. Southern African Catholic Bishops' Conference, *Pastoral Statement on the Environmental Crisis* (5 September 1999).

23. Cf. *Greeting to the Staff of FAO* (20 November 2014): AAS 106 (2014), 985.

24. Fifth General Conference of the Latin American and Caribbean Bishops, *Aparecida Document* (29 June 2007), 86.

25. Catholic Bishops' Conference of the Philippines, Pastoral Letter *What Is Happening to Our Beautiful Land?* (29 January 1988).

26. Bolivian Bishops' Conference, Pastoral Letter on the Environment and Human Development in Bolivia *El universo, don de Dios para la vida* (23 March 2012), 17.

27. Cf. German Bishops' Conference, Commission for Social Issues, *Der Klimawandel: Brennpunkt globaler, intergenerationeller und ökologischer Gerechtigkeit* (September 2006), 28–30.

28. Pontifical Council for Justice and Peace, *Compendium of the Social Doctrine of the Church*, 483.

29. *Catechesis* (5 June 2013): *Insegnamenti* 1 / 1 (2013), 280.

30. Bishops of the Patagonia-Comahue Region (Argentina), *Christmas Message* (December 2009), 2.

31. United States Conference of Catholic Bishops, *Global Climate Change: A Plea for Dialogue, Prudence, and the Common Good* (15 June 2001).

32. Fifth General Conference of the Latin American and Caribbean Bishops, *Aparecida Document* (29 June 2007), 471.

33. Apostolic Exhortation *Evangelii Gaudium* (24 November 2013), 56: AAS 105 (2013), 1043.

34. John Paul II, *Message for the 1990 World Day of Peace*, 12: AAS 82 (1990), 154.

35. Id., *Catechesis* (17 January 2001), 3: *Insegnamenti* 24 / 1 (2001), 178.

36. John Paul II, *Message for the 1990 World Day of Peace*, 15: AAS 82 (1990), 156.

37. *Catechism of the Catholic Church*, 357.

38. Angelus in Osnabrück (Germany) with the disabled, 16 November 1980: *Insegnamenti* 3 / 2 (1980), 1232.

39. Benedict XVI, Homily for the Solemn Inauguration of the Petrine Ministry (24 April 2005): AAS 97 (2005), 711.

40. Cf. Bonaventure, *The Major Legend of Saint Francis*, VIII, 1, in *Francis of Assisi: Early Documents*, vol. 2, New York-London-Manila, 2000, 586.

41. *Catechism of the Catholic Church*, 2416.

42. German Bishops' Conference, *Zukunft der Schöpfung—Zukunft der Menschheit. Einklärung der Deutschen Bischofskonferenz zu Fragen der Umwelt und der Energieversorgung*, (1980), II, 2.

43. *Catechism of the Catholic Church*, 339.

44. *Hom. in Hexaemeron*, I, 2, 10: PG 29, 9.

45. *Divine Comedy, Paradiso*, Canto XXXIII, 145.

46. Benedict XVI, *Catechesis* (9 November 2005), 3: *Insegnamenti* 1 (2005), 768.

47. Id., Encyclical Letter *Caritas in Veritate* (29 June 2009), 51: AAS 101 (2009), 687.

48. John Paul II, *Catechesis* (24 April 1991), 6: *Insegnamenti* 14 (1991), 856.

49. The *Catechism* explains that God wished to create a world which is "journeying toward its ultimate perfection," and that this implies the presence of imperfection and physical evil; cf. *Catechism of the Catholic Church*, 310.

50. Cf. Second Vatican Ecumenical Council, Pastoral Constitution on the Church in the Modern World *Gaudium et Spes*, 36.

51. Thomas Aquinas, *Summa Theologiae*, I, q. 104, art. 1, ad 4.

52. Id., *In octo libros Physicorum Aristotelis expositio*, Lib. II, lectio 14.

53. Against this horizon we can set the contribution of Fr. Teilhard de Chardin; cf. Paul VI, *Address in a Chemical and Pharmaceutical Plant* (24 February 1966): *Insegnamenti* 4 (1966), 992–993; John Paul II, *Letter to the Reverend George Coyne* (1 June 1988): *Insegnamenti* 11 / 2 (1988), 1715; Benedict XVI, Homily for the Celebration of Vespers in Aosta (24 July 2009): *Insegnamenti* 5 / 2 (2009), 60.

54. John Paul II, *Catechesis* (30 January 2002), 6: *Insegnamenti* 25 / 1 (2002), 140.

55. Canadian Conference of Catholic Bishops, Social Affairs Commission, Pastoral Letter *You Love All That Exists . . . All Things Are Yours, God, Lover of Life* (4 October 2003), 1.

56. Catholic Bishops' Conference of Japan, *Reverence for Life: A Message for the Twenty-First Century* (1 January 2000), 89.

57. John Paul II, *Catechesis* (26 January 2000), 5: *Insegnamenti* 23 / 1 (2000), 123.

58. Id., *Catechesis* (2 August 2000), 3: *Insegnamenti* 23 / 2 (2000), 112.

59. Paul Ricoeur, *Philosophie de la Volonté*, t. II: *Finitude et Culpabilité*, Paris, 2009, 216.

60. *Summa Theologiae*, I, q. 47, art. 1.

61. Ibid.

62. Cf. ibid., art. 2, ad 1; art. 3.

63. *Catechism of the Catholic Church*, 340.

64. *Canticle of the Creatures*, in *Francis of Assisi: Early Documents*, New York-London-Manila, 1999, 113–114.

65. Cf. National Conference of the Bishops of Brazil, *A Igreja e a Questão Ecológica*, 1992, 53–54.

66. Ibid., 61.

67. Apostolic Exhortation *Evangelii Gaudium* (24 November 2013), 215: AAS 105 (2013), 1109.

68. Cf. Benedict XVI, Encyclical Letter *Caritas in Veritate* (29 June 2009), 14: AAS 101 (2009), 650.

69. *Catechism of the Catholic Church*, 2418.

70. Conference of Dominican Bishops, Pastoral Letter *Sobre la relación del hombre con la naturaleza* (21 January 1987).

71. John Paul II, Encyclical Letter *Laborem Exercens* (14 September 1981), 19: AAS 73 (1981), 626.

72. Encyclical Letter *Centesimus Annus* (1 May 1991), 31: AAS 83 (1991), 831.

73. Encyclical Letter *Sollicitudo Rei Socialis* (30 December 1987), 33: AAS 80 (1988), 557.

74. *Address to Indigenous and Rural People*, Cuilapán, Mexico (29 January 1979), 6: AAS 71 (1979), 209.

75. Homily at Mass for Farmers, Recife, Brazil (7 July 1980): AAS 72 (1980), 926.

76. Cf. *Message for the 1990 World Day of Peace*, 8: AAS 82 (1990), 152.

77. Paraguayan Bishops' Conference, Pastoral Letter *El campesino paraguayo y la tierra* (12 June 1983), 2, 4, d.

78. New Zealand Catholic Bishops Conference, *Statement on Environmental Issues* (1 September 2006).

79. Encyclical Letter *Laborem Exercens* (14 September 1981), 27: AAS 73 (1981), 645.

80. Hence Saint Justin could speak of "seeds of the Word" in the world; cf. *II Apologia* 8, 1–2; 13, 3–6: PG 6, 457–458, 467.

81. John Paul II, *Address to Scientists and Representatives of the United Nations University,* Hiroshima (25 February 1981), 3: AAS 73 (1981), 422.

82. Benedict XVI, Encyclical Letter *Caritas in Veritate* (29 June 2009), 69: AAS 101 (2009), 702.

83. Romano Guardini, *Das Ende der Neuzeit*, 9th ed., Würzburg, 1965, 87 (English: *The End of the Modern World*, Wilmington, 1998, 82).

84. Ibid.

85. Ibid., 87–88 (*The End of the Modern World*, 83).

86. Pontifical Council for Justice and Peace, *Compendium of the Social Doctrine of the Church*, 462.

87. Romano Guardini, *Das Ende der Neuzeit*, 63–64 (*The End of the Modern World*, 56).

88. Ibid., 64 (*The End of the Modern World*, 56).

89. Cf. Benedict XVI, Encyclical Letter *Caritas in Veritate* (29 June 2009), 35: AAS 101 (2009), 671.

90. Ibid., 22: 657.

91. Apostolic Exhortation *Evangelii Gaudium* (24 November 2013), 231: AAS 105 (2013), 1114.

92. Romano Guardini, *Das Ende der Neuzeit*, 63 (*The End of the Modern World*, 55).

93. John Paul II, Encyclical Letter *Centesimus Annus* (1 May 1991), 38: AAS 83 (1991), 841.

94. Cf. *Love for Creation: An Asian Response to the Ecological Crisis,* Declaration of the Colloquium sponsored by the Federation of Asian Bishops' Conferences (Tagatay, 31 January–5 February 1993), 3.3.2.

95. John Paul II, Encyclical Letter *Centesimus Annus* (1 May 1991), 37: AAS 83 (1991), 840.

96. Benedict XVI, *Message for the 2010 World Day of Peace,* 2: AAS 102 (2010), 41.

97. Id., Encyclical Letter *Caritas in Veritate* (29 June 2009), 28: AAS 101 (2009), 663.

98. Cf. Vincent of Lerins, *Commonitorium Primum*, ch. 23: PL 50, 688: "*Ut annis scilicet consolidetur, dilatetur tempore, sublimetur aetate.*"

99. No. 80: AAS 105 (2013), 1053.

100. Second Vatican Ecumenical Council, Pastoral Constitution on the Church in the Modern World *Gaudium et Spes*, 63.

101. Cf. John Paul II, Encyclical Letter *Centesimus Annus* (1 May 1991), 37: AAS 83 (1991), 840.

102. Paul VI, Encyclical Letter *Populorum Progressio* (26 March 1967), 34: AAS 59 (1967), 274.

103. Benedict XVI, Encyclical Letter *Caritas in Veritate* (29 June 2009), 32: AAS 101 (2009), 666.

104. Ibid.

105. Ibid.

106. *Catechism of the Catholic Church*, 2417.

107. Ibid., 2418.

108. Ibid., 2415.

109. *Message for the 1990 World Day of Peace*, 6: AAS 82 (1990), 150.

110. *Address to the Pontifical Academy of Sciences* (3 October 1981), 3: *Insegnamenti* 4/2 (1981), 333.

111. *Message for the 1990 World Day of Peace*, 7: AAS 82 (1990), 151.

112. John Paul II, *Address to the 35th General Assembly of the World Medical Association* (29 October 1983), 6: AAS 76 (1984), 394.

113. Episcopal Commission for Pastoral Concerns in Argentina, *Una tierra para todos* (June 2005), 19.

114. *Rio Declaration on Environment and Development* (14 June 1992), Principle 4.

115. Apostolic Exhortation *Evangelii Gaudium* (24 November 2013), 237: AAS 105 (2013), 1116.

116. Benedict XVI, Encyclical Letter *Caritas in Veritate* (29 June 2009), 51: AAS 101 (2009), 687.

117. Some authors have emphasized the values frequently found, for example, in the *villas, chabolas*, or *favelas* of Latin America: cf. Juan Carlos Scannone, S.J., "La irrupción del pobre y la lógica de la gratuidad," in Juan Carlos Scannone and Marcelo Perine (eds.), *Irrupción del pobre y quehacer filosófico. Hacia una nueva racionalidad*, Buenos Aires, 1993, 225–230.

118. Pontifical Council for Justice and Peace, *Compendium of the Social Doctrine of the Church*, 482.

119. Apostolic Exhortation *Evangelii Gaudium* (24 November 2013), 210: AAS 105 (2013), 1107.

120. *Address to the Bundestag*, Berlin (22 September 2011): AAS 103 (2011), 668.

121. *Catechesis* (15 April 2015): *L'Osservatore Romano*, 16 April 2015, 8.

122. Second Vatican Ecumenical Council, Pastoral Constitution on the Church in the Modern World *Gaudium et Spes*, 26.

123. Cf. Nos. 186–201: AAS 105 (2013), 1098–1105.

124. Portuguese Bishops' Conference, Pastoral Letter *Responsabilidade Solidária pelo Bem Comum* (15 September 2003), 20.

125. Benedict XVI, *Message for the 2010 World Day of Peace*, 8: AAS 102 (2010), 45.

126. *Rio Declaration on Environment and Development* (14 June 1992), Principle 1.

127. Bolivian Bishops' Conference, Pastoral Letter on the Environment and Human Development in Bolivia *El universo, don de Dios para la vida* (March 2012), 86.

128. Pontifical Council for Justice and Peace, *Energy, Justice, and Peace*, IV, 1, Vatican City (2014), 53.

129. Benedict XVI, Encyclical Letter *Caritas in Veritate* (29 June 2009), 67: AAS 101 (2009).

130. Apostolic Exhortation *Evangelii Gaudium* (24 November 2013), 222: AAS 105 (2013), 1111.

131. Pontifical Council for Justice and Peace, *Compendium of the Social Doctrine of the Church*, 469.

132. *Rio Declaration on the Environment and Development* (14 June 1992), Principle 15.

133. Cf. Mexican Bishops' Conference, Episcopal Commission for Pastoral and Social Concerns, *Jesucristo, vida y esperanza de los indígenas e campesinos* (14 January 2008).

134. Pontifical Council for Justice and Peace, *Compendium of the Social Doctrine of the Church*, 470.

135. *Message for the 2010 World Day of Peace*, 9: AAS 102 (2010), 46.

136. Ibid.

137. Ibid., 5: 43.

138. Benedict XVI, Encyclical Letter *Caritas in Veritate* (29 June 2009), 50: AAS 101 (2009), 686.

139. Apostolic Exhortation *Evangelii Gaudium* (24 November 2013), 209: AAS 105 (2013), 1107.

140. Ibid., 228: AAS 105 (2013), 1113.

141. Cf. Encyclical Letter *Lumen Fidei* (29 June 2013), 34: AAS 105 (2013), 577: "Nor is the light of faith, joined to the truth of love, extraneous to the material world, for love is always lived out in body and spirit; the light of faith is an incarnate light radiating from the luminous life of Jesus. It also illumines the material world, trusts its inherent order, and knows that it calls us to an ever widening path of harmony and understanding. The gaze of science thus benefits from faith: faith encourages the scientist to remain constantly open to reality in all its inexhaustible richness. Faith awakens the critical sense by preventing research from being satisfied with its own formulae and helps it to realize that nature is always greater. By stimulating wonder before the profound mystery of creation, faith broadens the horizons of reason to shed greater light on the world which discloses itself to scientific investigation."

142. Apostolic Exhortation *Evangelii Gaudium* (24 November 2013), 256: AAS 105 (2013), 1123.

143. Ibid., 231: 1114.

144. Romano Guardini, *Das Ende der Neuzeit*, 66–67 (*The End of the Modern World*, 60).

145. John Paul II, *Message for the 1990 World Day of Peace*, 1: AAS 82 (1990), 147.

146. Benedict XVI, Encyclical Letter *Caritas in Veritate* (29 June 2009), 66: AAS 101 (2009), 699.

147. Id., *Message for the 2010 World Day of Peace*, 11: AAS 102 (2010), 48.

148. *Earth Charter*, The Hague (29 June 2000).

149. John Paul II, Encyclical Letter *Centesimus Annus* (1 May 1991), 39: AAS 83 (1991), 842.

150. Id., *Message for the 1990 World Day of Peace*, 14: AAS 82 (1990), 155.

151. Apostolic Exhortation *Evangelii Gaudium* (24 Nov 2013), 261: AAS 105 (2013), 1124.

152. Benedict XVI, Homily for the Solemn Inauguration of the Petrine Ministry (24 April 2005): AAS 97 (2005), 710.

153. Australian Catholic Bishops' Conference, *A New Earth—The Environmental Challenge* (2002).

154. Romano Guardini, *Das Ende der Neuzeit*, 72 (*The End of the Modern World*, 65–66).

155. Apostolic Exhortation *Evangelii Gaudium* (24 November 2013), 71: AAS 105 (2013), 1050.

156. Benedict XVI, Encyclical Letter *Caritas in Veritate* (29 June 2009) 2: AAS 101 (2009), 642.

157. Paul VI, *Message for the 1977 World Day of Peace*: AAS 68 (1976), 709.

158. Pontifical Council for Justice and Peace, *Compendium of the Social Doctrine of the Church*, 582.

159. The spiritual writer Ali al-Khawas stresses from his own experience the need not to put too much distance between the creatures of the world and the interior experience of God. As he puts it: "Prejudice should not have us criticize those who seek ecstasy in music or poetry. There is a subtle mystery in each of the movements and sounds of this world. The initiate will capture what is being said when the wind blows, the trees sway, water flows, flies buzz, doors creak, birds sing, or in the sound of strings or flutes, the sighs of the sick, the groans of the afflicted . . ." (Eva De Vitray-Meyerovitch [ed.], *Anthologie du soufisme*, Paris 1978, 200).

160. *In II Sent.*, 23, 2, 3.

161. *Cántico Espiritual*, XIV, 5.

162. Ibid.

163. Ibid., XIV, 6–7.

164. John Paul II, Apostolic Letter *Orientale Lumen* (2 May 1995), 11: AAS 87 (1995), 757.

165. Ibid.

166. Id., Encyclical Letter *Ecclesia de Eucharistia* (17 April 2003), 8: AAS 95 (2003), 438.

167. Benedict XVI, Homily for the Mass of Corpus Domini (15 June 2006): AAS 98 (2006), 513.

168. *Catechism of the Catholic Church*, 2175.

169. John Paul II, *Catechesis* (2 August 2000), 4: *Insegnamenti* 23/2 (2000), 112.

170. *Quaest. Disp. de Myst. Trinitatis*, 1, 2 concl.

171. Cf. Thomas Aquinas, *Summa Theologiae*, I, q. 11, art. 3; q. 21, art. 1, ad 3; q. 47, art. 3.

172. Basil the Great, *Hom. in Hexaemeron*, I, 2, 6: PG 29, 8.

Amoris Laetitia

The Joy of Love: On Love in the Family

March 19, 2016

POST-SYNODAL APOSTOLIC EXHORTATION
AMORIS LAETITIA
OF THE HOLY FATHER
FRANCIS
TO BISHOPS, PRIESTS, AND DEACONS, CONSECRATED PERSONS, CHRISTIAN MARRIED COUPLES, AND ALL THE LAY FAITHFUL ON LOVE IN THE FAMILY

1. The Joy of Love experienced by families is also the joy of the Church. As the Synod Fathers noted, for all the many signs of crisis in the institution of marriage, "the desire to marry and form a family remains vibrant, especially among young people, and this is an inspiration to the Church."[1] As a response to that desire, "the Christian proclamation on the family is good news indeed."[2]

2. The Synod process allowed for an examination of the situation of families in today's world, and thus for a broader vision and a renewed awareness of the importance of marriage and the family. The complexity of the issues that arose revealed the need for continued open discussion of a number of doctrinal, moral, spiritual, and pastoral questions. The thinking of pastors and theologians, if faithful to the Church, honest, realistic, and creative, will help us to achieve greater clarity. The debates carried on in the media, in certain publications, and even among the Church's ministers, range from an immoderate desire for total change without sufficient reflection or grounding, to an attitude that would solve everything by applying general rules or deriving undue conclusions from particular theological considerations.

3. Since "time is greater than space," I would make it clear that not all discussions of doctrinal, moral, or pastoral issues need to be settled by interventions of the magisterium. Unity of teaching and practice is certainly necessary in the Church, but this does not preclude various ways

of interpreting some aspects of that teaching or drawing certain consequences from it. This will always be the case as the Spirit guides us toward the entire truth (cf. Jn 16:13), until he leads us fully into the mystery of Christ and enables us to see all things as he does. Each country or region, moreover, can seek solutions better suited to its culture and sensitive to its traditions and local needs. For "cultures are in fact quite diverse and every general principle . . . needs to be inculturated, if it is to be respected and applied."[3]

4. I must also say that the Synod process proved both impressive and illuminating. I am grateful for the many contributions that helped me to appreciate more fully the problems faced by families throughout the world. The various interventions of the Synod Fathers, to which I paid close heed, made up, as it were, a multifaceted gem reflecting many legitimate concerns and honest questions. For this reason, I thought it appropriate to prepare a post-synodal Apostolic Exhortation to gather the contributions of the two recent Synods on the family, while adding other considerations as an aid to reflection, dialogue, and pastoral practice, and as a help and encouragement to families in their daily commitments and challenges.

5. This Exhortation is especially timely in this Jubilee Year of Mercy. First, because it represents an invitation to Christian families to value the gifts of marriage and the family, and to persevere in a love strengthened by the virtues of generosity, commitment, fidelity, and patience. Second, because it seeks to encourage everyone to be a sign of mercy and closeness wherever family life remains imperfect or lacks peace and joy.

6. I will begin with an opening chapter inspired by the Scriptures, to set a proper tone. I will then examine the actual situation of families, in order to keep firmly grounded in reality. I will go on to recall some essential aspects of the Church's teaching on marriage and the family, thus paving the way for two central chapters dedicated to love. I will then highlight some pastoral approaches that can guide us in building sound and fruitful homes in accordance with God's plan, with a full chapter devoted to the raising of children. Finally, I will offer an invitation to

mercy and the pastoral discernment of those situations that fall short of what the Lord demands of us, and conclude with a brief discussion of family spirituality.

7. Given the rich fruits of the two-year Synod process, this Exhortation will treat, in different ways, a wide variety of questions. This explains its inevitable length. Consequently, I do not recommend a rushed reading of the text. The greatest benefit, for families themselves and for those engaged in the family apostolate, will come if each part is read patiently and carefully, or if attention is paid to the parts dealing with their specific needs. It is likely, for example, that married couples will be more concerned with Chapters Four and Five, and pastoral ministers with Chapter Six, while everyone should feel challenged by Chapter Eight. It is my hope that, in reading this text, all will feel called to love and cherish family life, for "families are not a problem; they are first and foremost an opportunity."[4]

CHAPTER ONE

IN THE LIGHT OF THE WORD

8. The Bible is full of families, births, love stories, and family crises. This is true from its very first page, with the appearance of Adam and Eve's family with all its burden of violence but also its enduring strength (cf. Gn 4) to its very last page, where we behold the wedding feast of the Bride and the Lamb (Rv 21:2, 9). Jesus' description of the two houses, one built on rock and the other on sand (cf. Mt 7:24–27), symbolizes any number of family situations shaped by the exercise of their members' freedom, for, as the poet says, "every home is a lampstand."[5] Let us now enter one of those houses, led by the Psalmist with a song that even today resounds in both Jewish and Christian wedding liturgies:

> Blessed is every one who fears the Lord,
> who walks in his ways!
> You shall eat the fruit of the labor of your hands;
> you shall be happy, and it shall go well with you.
> Your wife will be like a fruitful vine
> within your house;
> your children will be like olive shoots
> round your table.
> Thus shall the man be blessed
> who fears the Lord.
> The Lord bless you from Zion!
> May you see the prosperity of Jerusalem
> all the days of your life!
> May you see your children's children!
> Peace be upon Israel! (Ps 128:1–6)

You and your wife

9. Let us cross the threshold of this tranquil home, with its family sitting around the festive table. At the center we see the father and mother, a couple with their personal story of love. They embody the primordial

divine plan clearly spoken of by Christ himself: "Have you not read that he who made them from the beginning made them male and female?" (Mt 19:4). We hear an echo of the command found in the Book of Genesis: "Therefore a man shall leave his father and mother and cleave to his wife, and they shall become one flesh" (Gn 2:24).

10. The majestic early chapters of Genesis present the human couple in its deepest reality. Those first pages of the Bible make a number of very clear statements. The first, which Jesus paraphrases, says that "God created man in his own image, in the image of God he created them; male and female he created them" (1:27). It is striking that the "image of God" here refers to the couple, "male and female." Does this mean that sex is a property of God himself, or that God has a divine female companion, as some ancient religions held? Naturally, the answer is no. We know how clearly the Bible rejects as idolatrous such beliefs, found among the Canaanites of the Holy Land. God's transcendence is preserved, yet inasmuch as he is also the Creator, the fruitfulness of the human couple is a living and effective "image," a visible sign of his creative act.

11. The couple that loves and begets life is a true, living icon—not an idol like those of stone or gold prohibited by the Decalogue—capable of revealing God the Creator and Savior. For this reason, fruitful love becomes a symbol of God's inner life (cf. Gn 1:28; 9:7; 17:2–5, 16; 28:3; 35:11; 48:3–4). This is why the Genesis account, following the "priestly tradition," is interwoven with various genealogical accounts (cf. 4:17–22, 25–26; 5; 10; 11:10–32; 25:1–4, 12–17, 19–26; 36). The ability of human couples to beget life is the path along which the history of salvation progresses. Seen this way, the couple's fruitful relationship becomes an image for understanding and describing the mystery of God himself, for in the Christian vision of the Trinity, God is contemplated as Father, Son, and Spirit of love. The triune God is a communion of love, and the family is its living reflection. Saint John Paul II shed light on this when he said, "Our God in his deepest mystery is not solitude, but a family, for he has within himself fatherhood, sonship, and the essence of the family, which is love. That love, in the divine family, is the Holy Spirit."[6] The family is thus not unrelated to God's very being.[7] This Trinitarian dimension

finds expression in the theology of Saint Paul, who relates the couple to the "mystery" of the union of Christ and the Church (cf. Eph 5:21–33).

12. In speaking of marriage, Jesus refers us to yet another page of Genesis, which, in its second chapter, paints a splendid and detailed portrait of the couple. First, we see the man, who anxiously seeks "a helper fit for him" (vv. 18, 20), capable of alleviating the solitude which he feels amid the animals and the world around him. The original Hebrew suggests a direct encounter, face to face, eye to eye, in a kind of silent dialogue, for where love is concerned, silence is always more eloquent than words. It is an encounter with a face, a "thou," who reflects God's own love and is man's "best possession, a helper fit for him and a pillar of support," in the words of the biblical sage (Sir 36:24). Or again, as the woman of the Song of Solomon will sing in a magnificent profession of love and mutual self-bestowal: "My beloved is mine and I am his. . . . I am my beloved's and my beloved is mine" (2:16; 6:3).

13. This encounter, which relieves man's solitude, gives rise to new birth and to the family. Significantly, Adam, who is also the man of every time and place, together with his wife, starts a new family. Jesus speaks of this by quoting the passage from Genesis: "The man shall be joined to his wife, and the two shall become one" (Mt 19:5; cf. Gn 2:24). The very word "to be joined" or "to cleave," in the original Hebrew, bespeaks a profound harmony, a closeness both physical and interior, to such an extent that the word is used to describe our union with God: "My soul clings to you" (Ps 63:8). The marital union is thus evoked not only in its sexual and corporal dimension, but also in its voluntary self-giving in love. The result of this union is that the two "become one flesh," both physically and in the union of their hearts and lives, and, eventually, in a child, who will share not only genetically but also spiritually in the "flesh" of both parents.

Your children are as the shoots of an olive tree

14. Let us once more take up the song of the Psalmist. In the home where husband and wife are seated at table, children appear at their side "like olive shoots" (Ps 128:3), that is, full of energy and vitality. If the parents

are in some sense the foundations of the home, the children are like the "living stones" of the family (cf. 1 Pt 2:5). Significantly, the word which appears most frequently in the Old Testament after the name of God (*YHWH*, "the Lord"), is "child" (*ben*, "son"), which is itself related to the verb "to build" (*banah*). Hence, Psalm 128, in speaking of the gift of children, uses imagery drawn from the building of a house and the social life of cities: "Unless the Lord builds the house, those who build it labor in vain. . . . Lo, sons are a heritage from the Lord, the fruit of the womb, a reward. Like arrows in the hand of a warrior are the sons of one's youth. Happy is the man who has his quiver full of them! He shall not be put to shame when he speaks with his enemies in the gate" (Ps 127:1, 3–5). These images reflect the culture of an ancient society, yet the presence of children is a sign of the continuity of the family throughout salvation history, from generation to generation.

15. Here too, we can see another aspect of the family. We know that the New Testament speaks of "churches that meet in homes" (cf. 1 Cor 16:19; Rom 16:5; Col 4:15; Phlm 2). A family's living space could turn into a domestic church, a setting for the Eucharist, the presence of Christ seated at its table. We can never forget the image found in the Book of Revelation, where the Lord says: "Behold, I stand at the door and knock; if any one hears my voice and opens the door, I will come in to him and eat with him, and he with me" (Rv 3:20). Here we see a home filled with the presence of God, common prayer, and every blessing. This is the meaning of the conclusion of Psalm 128, which we cited above: "Thus shall the man be blessed who fears the Lord. The Lord bless you from Zion!" (Ps 128:4–5).

16. The Bible also presents the family as the place where children are brought up in the faith. This is evident from the description of the Passover celebration (cf. Ex 12:26–27; Dt 6:20–25) and it later appears explicitly in the Jewish *haggadah*, the dialogue accompanying the rite of the Passover meal. One of the Psalms celebrates the proclamation of faith within families: "All that we have heard and known, that our fathers have told us, we will not hide from their children, but tell to the coming generation the glorious deeds of the Lord, and his might, and the

wonders which he has wrought. He established a testimony in Jacob, and appointed a law in Israel, which he commanded our fathers to teach to their children; that the next generation might know them, the children yet unborn, and arise and tell them to their children" (Ps 78:3–6). The family is thus the place where parents become their children's first teachers in the faith. They learn this "trade," passing it down from one person to another: "When in time to come your son asks you . . . you shall say to him . . ." (Ex 13:14). Thus succeeding generations can raise their song to the Lord: "young men and maidens together, old and young together!" (Ps 148:12).

17. Parents have a serious responsibility for this work of education, as the biblical sages often remind us (cf. Prv 3:11–12; 6:20–22; 13:1; 22:15; 23:13–14; 29:17). Children, for their part, are called to accept and practice the commandment: "Honor your father and your mother" (Ex 20:12). Here the verb "to honor" has to do with the fulfillment of family and social commitments; these are not to be disregarded under the pretense of religious motives (cf. Mk 7:11–13). "Whoever honors his father atones for sins, and whoever glorifies his mother is like one who lays up treasure" (Sir 3:3–4).

18. The Gospel goes on to remind us that children are not the property of a family, but have their own lives to lead. Jesus is a model of obedience to his earthly parents, placing himself under their charge (cf. Lk 2:51), but he also shows that children's life decisions and their Christian vocation may demand a parting for the sake of the kingdom of God (cf. Mt 10:34–37; Lk 9:59–62). Jesus himself, at twelve years of age, tells Mary and Joseph that he has a greater mission to accomplish apart from his earthly family (cf. Lk 2:48–50). In this way, he shows the need for other, deeper bonds even within the family: "My mother and my brethren are those who hear the word of God and do it" (Lk 8:21). All the same, in the concern he shows for children—whom the societies of the ancient Near East viewed as subjects without particular rights and even as family property—Jesus goes so far as to present them as teachers, on account of their simple trust and spontaneity toward others. "Truly I say to you, unless you turn and become like children, you will never enter the kingdom of heaven.

Whoever humbles himself like this child, he is the greatest in the kingdom of heaven" (Mt 18:3–4).

A path of suffering and blood

19. The idyllic picture presented in Psalm 128 is not at odds with a bitter truth found throughout sacred Scripture, that is, the presence of pain, evil, and violence that break up families and their communion of life and love. For good reason Christ's teaching on marriage (cf. Mt 19:3–9) is inserted within a dispute about divorce. The word of God constantly testifies to that somber dimension already present at the beginning, when, through sin, the relationship of love and purity between man and woman turns into domination: "Your desire shall be for your husband, and he shall rule over you" (Gn 3:16).

20. This thread of suffering and bloodshed runs through numerous pages of the Bible, beginning with Cain's murder of his brother Abel. We read of the disputes between the sons and the wives of the Patriarchs Abraham, Isaac, and Jacob, the tragedies and violence marking the family of David, the family problems reflected in the story of Tobias, and the bitter complaint of Job: "He has put my brethren far from me . . . my kinsfolk and my close friends have failed me. . . . I am repulsive to my wife, loathsome to the sons of my own mother" (Jb 19:13–14, 17).

21. Jesus himself was born into a modest family that soon had to flee to a foreign land. He visits the home of Peter, whose mother-in-law is ill (cf. Mk 1:30–31) and shows sympathy upon hearing of deaths in the homes of Jairus and Lazarus (cf. Mk 5:22–24, 35–43; Jn 11:1–44). He hears the desperate wailing of the widow of Nain for her dead son (cf. Lk 7:11–15) and heeds the plea of the father of an epileptic child in a small country town (cf. Mk 9:17–27). He goes to the homes of tax collectors like Matthew and Zacchaeus (cf. Mt 9:9–13; Lk 19:1–10), and speaks to sinners like the woman in the house of Simon the Pharisee (cf. Lk 7:36–50). Jesus knows the anxieties and tensions experienced by families and he weaves them into his parables: children who leave home to seek adventure (cf. Lk 15:11–32), or who prove troublesome (Mt 21:28–31) or fall prey to violence (Mk 12:1–9). He is also sensitive to the embarrassment caused

by the lack of wine at a wedding feast (Jn 2:1–10), the failure of guests to come to a banquet (Mt 22:1–10), and the anxiety of a poor family over the loss of a coin (Lk 15:8–10).

22. In this brief review, we can see that the word of God is not a series of abstract ideas but rather a source of comfort and companionship for every family that experiences difficulties or suffering. For it shows them the goal of their journey, when God "will wipe away every tear from their eyes, and death shall be no more, neither shall there be mourning nor crying nor pain any more" (Rv 21:4).

The work of your hands

23. At the beginning of Psalm 128, the father appears as a laborer who by the work of his hands sustains the physical well-being and tranquility of his family: "You shall eat the fruit of the labor of your hands; you shall be happy, and it shall be well with you" (Ps 128:2). It is clear from the very first pages of the Bible that work is an essential part of human dignity; there we read that "the Lord God took the man and put him in the garden of Eden to till it and keep it" (Gn 2:15). Man is presented as a laborer who works the earth, harnesses the forces of nature, and produces "the bread of anxious toil" (Ps 127:2), in addition to cultivating his own gifts and talents.

24. Labor also makes possible the development of society and provides for the sustenance, stability, and fruitfulness of one's family: "May you see the prosperity of Jerusalem all the days of your life! May you see your children's children!" (Ps 128:5–6). The Book of Proverbs also presents the labor of mothers within the family; their daily work is described in detail as winning the praise of their husbands and children (cf. 31:10–31). The Apostle Paul was proud not to live as a burden to others, since he worked with his own hands and assured his own livelihood (cf. Acts 18:3; 1 Cor 4:12; 9:12). Paul was so convinced of the necessity of work that he laid down a strict rule for his communities: "If anyone will not work, let him not eat" (2 Thes 3:10; cf. 1 Thes 4:11).

25. This having been said, we can appreciate the suffering created by unemployment and the lack of steady work, as reflected in the Book of Ruth, Jesus' own parable of the laborers forced to stand idly in the town square (Mt 20:1–16), and his personal experience of meeting people suffering from poverty and hunger. Sadly, these realities are present in many countries today, where the lack of employment opportunities takes its toll on the serenity of family life.

26. Nor can we overlook the social degeneration brought about by sin, as, for example, when human beings tyrannize nature, selfishly and even brutally ravaging it. This leads to the desertification of the earth (cf. Gn 3:17–19) and those social and economic imbalances denounced by the prophets, beginning with Elijah (cf. 1 Kgs 21) and culminating in Jesus' own words against injustice (cf. Lk 12:13; 16:1–31).

The tenderness of an embrace

27. Christ proposed as the distinctive sign of his disciples the law of love and the gift of self for others (cf. Mt 22:39; Jn 13:34). He did so in stating a principle that fathers and mothers tend to embody in their own lives: "No one has greater love than this, to lay down one's life for one's friends" (Jn 15:13). Love also bears fruit in mercy and forgiveness. We see this in a particular way in the scene of the woman caught in adultery; in front of the Temple, the woman is surrounded by her accusers, but later, alone with Jesus, she meets not condemnation but the admonition to lead a more worthy life (cf. Jn 8:1–11).

28. Against this backdrop of love so central to the Christian experience of marriage and the family, another virtue stands out, one often overlooked in our world of frenetic and superficial relationships. It is tenderness. Let us consider the moving words of Psalm 131. As in other biblical texts (e.g., Ex 4:22; Is 49:15; Ps 27:10), the union between the Lord and his faithful ones is expressed in terms of parental love. Here we see a delicate and tender intimacy between mother and child: the image is that of a babe sleeping in his mother's arms after being nursed. As the Hebrew word *gamûl* suggests, the infant is now fed and clings to his mother, who takes him to her bosom. There is a closeness that is conscious and not simply

biological. Drawing on this image, the Psalmist sings: "I have calmed and quieted my soul, like a child quieted at its mother's breast" (Ps 131:2). We can also think of the touching words that the prophet Hosea puts on God's lips: "When Israel was a child, I loved him. . . . I took them up in my arms. . . . I led them with cords of compassion, with the bands of love, and I became to them as one who eases the yoke on their jaws, and I bent down to them and fed them" (Hos 11:1, 3–4).

29. With a gaze of faith and love, grace and fidelity, we have contemplated the relationship between human families and the divine Trinity. The word of God tells us that the family is entrusted to a man, a woman, and their children, so that they may become a communion of persons in the image of the union of the Father, the Son, and the Holy Spirit. Begetting and raising children, for its part, mirrors God's creative work. The family is called to join in daily prayer, to read the word of God, and to share in Eucharistic communion, and thus to grow in love and become ever more fully a temple in which the Spirit dwells.

30. Every family should look to the icon of the Holy Family of Nazareth. Its daily life had its share of burdens and even nightmares, as when they met with Herod's implacable violence. This last was an experience that, sad to say, continues to afflict the many refugee families who in our day feel rejected and helpless. Like the Magi, our families are invited to contemplate the Child and his Mother, to bow down and worship him (cf. Mt 2:11). Like Mary, they are asked to face their family's challenges with courage and serenity, in good times and bad, and to keep in their heart the great things which God has done (cf. Lk 2:19, 51). The treasury of Mary's heart also contains the experiences of every family, which she cherishes. For this reason, she can help us understand the meaning of these experiences and to hear the message God wishes to communicate through the life of our families.

CHAPTER TWO

THE EXPERIENCES AND CHALLENGES OF FAMILIES

31. The welfare of the family is decisive for the future of the world and that of the Church. Countless studies have been made of marriage and the family, their current problems and challenges. We do well to focus on concrete realities, since "the call and the demands of the Spirit resound in the events of history," and through these "the Church can also be guided to a more profound understanding of the inexhaustible mystery of marriage and the family."[8] I will not attempt here to present all that might be said about the family today. Nonetheless, because the Synod Fathers examined the situation of families worldwide, I consider it fitting to take up some of their pastoral insights, along with concerns derived from my own experience.

The current reality of the family

32. "Faithful to Christ's teaching we look to the reality of the family today in all its complexity, with both its lights and shadows. . . . Anthropological and cultural changes in our times influence all aspects of life and call for an analytic and diversified approach."[9] Several decades ago, the Spanish bishops noted that families have come to enjoy greater freedom "through an equitable distribution of duties, responsibilities and tasks"; indeed, "a greater emphasis on personal communication between the spouses helps to make family life more humane," while "neither today's society nor that to which we are progressing allow an uncritical survival of older forms and models."[10] It is also evident that "the principal tendencies in anthropological-cultural changes" are leading "individuals, in personal and family life, to receive less and less support from social structures than in the past."[11]

33. On the other hand, "equal consideration needs to be given to the growing danger represented by an extreme individualism which weakens family bonds and ends up considering each member of the family as an isolated unit, leading in some cases to the idea that one's personality

is shaped by his or her desires, which are considered absolute."[12] "The tensions created by an overly individualistic culture, caught up with possessions and pleasures, leads to intolerance and hostility in families."[13] Here I would also include today's fast pace of life, stress, and the organization of society and labor, since all these are cultural factors which militate against permanent decisions. We also encounter widespread uncertainty and ambiguity. For example, we rightly value a personalism that opts for authenticity as opposed to mere conformity. While this can favor spontaneity and a better use of people's talents, if misdirected it can foster attitudes of constant suspicion, fear of commitment, self-centeredness, and arrogance. Freedom of choice makes it possible to plan our lives and to make the most of ourselves. Yet if this freedom lacks noble goals or personal discipline, it degenerates into an inability to give oneself generously to others. Indeed, in many countries where the number of marriages is decreasing, more and more people are choosing to live alone or simply to spend time together without cohabiting. We can also point to a praiseworthy concern for justice; but if misunderstood, this can turn citizens into clients interested solely in the provision of services.

34. When these factors affect our understanding of the family, it can come to be seen as a way station, helpful when convenient, or a setting in which rights can be asserted while relationships are left to the changing winds of personal desire and circumstances. Ultimately, it is easy nowadays to confuse genuine freedom with the idea that each individual can act arbitrarily, as if there were no truths, values, and principles to provide guidance, and everything were possible and permissible. The ideal of marriage, marked by a commitment to exclusivity and stability, is swept aside whenever it proves inconvenient or tiresome. The fear of loneliness and the desire for stability and fidelity exist side by side with a growing fear of entrapment in a relationship that could hamper the achievement of one's personal goals.

35. As Christians, we can hardly stop advocating marriage simply to avoid countering contemporary sensibilities, or out of a desire to be fashionable or a sense of helplessness in the face of human and moral failings. We would be depriving the world of values that we can and must offer.

It is true that there is no sense in simply decrying present-day evils, as if this could change things. Nor it is helpful to try to impose rules by sheer authority. What we need is a more responsible and generous effort to present the reasons and motivations for choosing marriage and the family, and in this way to help men and women better to respond to the grace that God offers them.

36. We also need to be humble and realistic, acknowledging that at times the way we present our Christian beliefs and treat other people has helped contribute to today's problematic situation. We need a healthy dose of self-criticism. Then too, we often present marriage in such a way that its unitive meaning, its call to grow in love, and its ideal of mutual assistance are overshadowed by an almost exclusive insistence on the duty of procreation. Nor have we always provided solid guidance to young married couples, understanding their timetables, their way of thinking, and their concrete concerns. At times we have also proposed a far too abstract and almost artificial theological ideal of marriage, far removed from the concrete situations and practical possibilities of real families. This excessive idealization, especially when we have failed to inspire trust in God's grace, has not helped to make marriage more desirable and attractive, but quite the opposite.

37. We have long thought that simply by stressing doctrinal, bioethical, and moral issues, without encouraging openness to grace, we were providing sufficient support to families, strengthening the marriage bond and giving meaning to marital life. We find it difficult to present marriage more as a dynamic path to personal development and fulfillment than as a lifelong burden. We also find it hard to make room for the consciences of the faithful, who very often respond as best they can to the Gospel amid their limitations, and are capable of carrying out their own discernment in complex situations. We have been called to form consciences, not to replace them.

38. We must be grateful that most people do value family relationships that are permanent and marked by mutual respect. They appreciate the Church's efforts to offer guidance and counseling in areas related

to growth in love, overcoming conflict, and raising children. Many are touched by the power of grace experienced in sacramental Reconciliation and in the Eucharist, grace that helps them face the challenges of marriage and the family. In some countries, especially in various parts of Africa, secularism has not weakened certain traditional values, and marriages forge a strong bond between two wider families, with clearly defined structures for dealing with problems and conflicts. Nowadays we are grateful too for the witness of marriages that have not only proved lasting, but also fruitful and loving. All these factors can inspire a positive and welcoming pastoral approach capable of helping couples to grow in appreciation of the demands of the Gospel. Yet we have often been on the defensive, wasting pastoral energy on denouncing a decadent world without being proactive in proposing ways of finding true happiness. Many people feel that the Church's message on marriage and the family does not clearly reflect the preaching and attitudes of Jesus, who set forth a demanding ideal yet never failed to show compassion and closeness to the frailty of individuals like the Samaritan woman or the woman caught in adultery.

39. This is hardly to suggest that we cease warning against a cultural decline that fails to promote love or self-giving. The consultation that took place prior to the last two Synods pointed to the various symptoms of a "culture of the ephemeral." Here I think, for example, of the speed with which people move from one affective relationship to another. They believe, along the lines of social networks, that love can be connected or disconnected at the whim of the consumer, and the relationship quickly "blocked." I think too of the fears associated with permanent commitment, the obsession with free time, and those relationships that weigh costs and benefits for the sake of remedying loneliness, providing protection, or offering some service. We treat affective relationships the way we treat material objects and the environment: everything is disposable; everyone uses and throws away, takes and breaks, exploits and squeezes to the last drop. Then, goodbye. Narcissism makes people incapable of looking beyond themselves, beyond their own desires and needs. Yet sooner or later, those who use others end up being used themselves,

manipulated and discarded by that same mind-set. It is also worth noting that breakups often occur among older adults who seek a kind of "independence" and reject the ideal of growing old together, looking after and supporting one another.

40. "At the risk of oversimplifying, we might say that we live in a culture which pressures young people not to start a family, because they lack possibilities for the future. Yet this same culture presents others with so many options that they too are dissuaded from starting a family."[14] In some countries, many young persons "postpone a wedding for economic reasons, work or study. Some do so for other reasons, such as the influence of ideologies which devalue marriage and family, the desire to avoid the failures of other couples, the fear of something they consider too important and sacred, the social opportunities and economic benefits associated with simply living together, a purely emotional and romantic conception of love, the fear of losing their freedom and independence, and the rejection of something conceived as purely institutional and bureaucratic."[15] We need to find the right language, arguments, and forms of witness that can help us reach the hearts of young people, appealing to their capacity for generosity, commitment, love, and even heroism, and in this way inviting them to take up the challenge of marriage with enthusiasm and courage.

41. The Synod Fathers noted that "cultural tendencies in today's world seem to set no limits on a person's affectivity"; indeed, "a narcissistic, unstable, or changeable affectivity does not always allow a person to grow to maturity." They also expressed concern about the current "spread of pornography and the commercialization of the body, fostered also by a misuse of the internet," and about those "reprehensible situations where people are forced into prostitution." In this context, "couples are often uncertain, hesitant, and struggling to find ways to grow. Many tend to remain in the early stages of their affective and sexual life. A crisis in a couple's relationship destabilizes the family and may lead, through separation and divorce, to serious consequences for adults, children, and society as a whole, weakening its individual and social bonds."[16] Marital problems are "often confronted in haste and without the courage to

have patience and reflect, to make sacrifices and to forgive one another. Failures give rise to new relationships, new couples, new civil unions, and new marriages, creating family situations which are complex and problematic for the Christian life."[17]

42. Furthermore, "the decline in population, due to a mentality against having children and promoted by the world politics of reproductive health, creates not only a situation in which the relationship between generations is no longer ensured but also the danger that, over time, this decline will lead to economic impoverishment and a loss of hope in the future. The development of bio-technology has also had a major impact on the birth rate."[18] Added to this are other factors such as "industrialization, the sexual revolution, the fear of overpopulation, and economic problems. . . . Consumerism may also deter people from having children, simply so they can maintain a certain freedom and life-style."[19] The upright consciences of spouses who have been generous in transmitting life may lead them, for sufficiently serious reasons, to limit the number of their children, yet precisely "for the sake of this dignity of conscience, the Church strongly rejects the forced State intervention in favor of contraception, sterilization, and even abortion."[20] Such measures are unacceptable even in places with high birth rates, yet also in countries with disturbingly low birth rates we see politicians encouraging them. As the bishops of Korea have said, this is "to act in a way that is self-contradictory and to neglect one's duty."[21]

43. The weakening of faith and religious practice in some societies has an effect on families, leaving them more isolated amid their difficulties. The Synod Fathers noted that "one symptom of the great poverty of contemporary culture is loneliness, arising from the absence of God in a person's life and the fragility of relationships. There is also a general feeling of powerlessness in the face of socio-cultural realities that oftentimes end up crushing families. . . . Families often feel abandoned due to a lack of interest and attention on the part of institutions. The negative impact on the social order is clear, as seen in the demographic crisis, in the difficulty of raising children, in a hesitancy to welcome new life, in a tendency to see older persons as a burden, and in an increase of emotional problems

and outbreaks of violence. The State has the responsibility to pass laws and create work to ensure the future of young people and help them realize their plan of forming a family."[22]

44. The lack of dignified or affordable housing often leads to the postponement of formal relationships. It should be kept in mind that "the family has the right to decent housing, fitting for family life and commensurate to the number of the members, in a physical environment that provides the basic services for the life of the family and the community."[23] Families and homes go together. This makes us see how important it is to insist on the rights of the family and not only those of individuals. The family is a good which society cannot do without, and it ought to be protected.[24] "The Church has always held it part of her mission to promote marriage and the family and to defend them against those who attack them,"[25] especially today, when they are given scarce attention in political agendas. Families have the right to "to be able to count on an adequate family policy on the part of public authorities in the juridical, economic, social, and fiscal domains."[26] At times families suffer terribly when, faced with the illness of a loved one, they lack access to adequate health care, or struggle to find dignified employment. "Economic constraints prohibit a family's access to education, cultural activities, and involvement in the life of society. In many ways, the present-day economic situation is keeping people from participating in society. Families, in particular, suffer from problems related to work, where young people have few possibilities and job offers are very selective and insecure. Workdays are long and oftentimes made more burdensome by extended periods away from home. This situation does not help family members to gather together or parents to be with their children in such a way as to nurture their relationships each day."[27]

45. "A great number of children are born outside of wedlock, many of whom subsequently grow up with just one of their parents or in a blended or reconstituted family. . . . The sexual exploitation of children is yet another scandalous and perverse reality in present-day society. Societies experiencing violence due to war, terrorism, or the presence of organized crime are witnessing the deterioration of the family, above

all in large cities, where, on their outskirts, the so-called phenomenon of 'street-children' is on the rise."[28] The sexual abuse of children is all the more scandalous when it occurs in places where they ought to be most safe, particularly in families, schools, communities, and Christian institutions.[29]

46. "Migration is another sign of the times to be faced and understood in terms of its negative effects on family life."[30] The recent Synod drew attention to this issue, noting that "in various ways, migration affects whole populations in different parts of the world. The Church has exercised a major role in this area. Maintaining and expanding this witness to the Gospel (cf. Mt 25:35) is urgently needed today more than ever. . . . Human mobility, which corresponds to the natural historical movement of peoples, can prove to be a genuine enrichment for both families that migrate and countries that welcome them. Furthermore, forced migration of families, resulting from situations of war, persecution, poverty, and injustice, and marked by the vicissitudes of a journey that often puts lives at risk, traumatizes people and destabilizes families. In accompanying migrants, the Church needs a specific pastoral program addressed not only to families that migrate but also to those family members who remain behind. This pastoral activity must be implemented with due respect for their cultures, for the human and religious formation from which they come, and for the spiritual richness of their rites and traditions, even by means of a specific pastoral care. . . . Migration is particularly dramatic and devastating to families and individuals when it takes place illegally and is supported by international networks of human trafficking. This is equally true when it involves women or unaccompanied children who are forced to endure long periods of time in temporary facilities and refugee camps, where it is impossible to start a process of integration. Extreme poverty and other situations of family breakdown sometimes even lead families to sell their children for prostitution or for organ trafficking."[31] "The persecution of Christians and ethnic and religious minorities in many parts of the world, especially in the Middle East, are a great trial not only for the Church but also the entire international community. Every effort should be encouraged, even

in a practical way, to assist families and Christian communities to remain in their native lands."[32]

47. The Fathers also called particular attention to "families of persons with special needs, where the unexpected challenge of dealing with a disability can upset a family's equilibrium, desires, and expectations. . . . Families who lovingly accept the difficult trial of a child with special needs are greatly to be admired. They render the Church and society an invaluable witness of faithfulness to the gift of life. In these situations, the family can discover, together with the Christian community, new approaches, new ways of acting, a different way of understanding and identifying with others, by welcoming and caring for the mystery of the frailty of human life. People with disabilities are a gift for the family and an opportunity to grow in love, mutual aid, and unity. . . . If the family, in the light of the faith, accepts the presence of persons with special needs, they will be able to recognize and ensure the quality and value of every human life, with its proper needs, rights, and opportunities. This approach will promote care and services on behalf of these disadvantaged persons and will encourage people to draw near to them and provide affection at every stage of their life."[33] Here I would stress that dedication and concern shown to migrants and to persons with special needs alike is a sign of the Spirit. Both situations are paradigmatic: they serve as a test of our commitment to show mercy in welcoming others and to help the vulnerable to be fully a part of our communities.

48. "Most families have great respect for the elderly, surrounding them with affection and considering them a blessing. A special word of appreciation is due to those associations and family movements committed to serving the elderly, both spiritually and socially. . . . In highly industrialized societies, where the number of elderly persons is growing even as the birth rate declines, they can be regarded as a burden. On the other hand, the care that they require often puts a strain on their loved ones."[34] "Care and concern for the final stages of life is all the more necessary today, when contemporary society attempts to remove every trace of death and dying. The elderly who are vulnerable and dependent are at times unfairly exploited simply for economic advantage. Many families

show us that it is possible to approach the last stages of life by emphasizing the importance of a person's sense of fulfillment and participation in the Lord's paschal mystery. A great number of elderly people are cared for in Church institutions, where, materially and spiritually, they can live in a peaceful, family atmosphere. Euthanasia and assisted suicide are serious threats to families worldwide; in many countries, they have been legalized. The Church, while firmly opposing these practices, feels the need to assist families who take care of their elderly and infirm members."[35]

49. Here I would also like to mention the situation of families living in dire poverty and great limitations. The problems faced by poor households are often all the more trying.[36] For example, if a single mother has to raise a child by herself and needs to leave the child alone at home while she goes to work, the child can grow up exposed to all kind of risks and obstacles to personal growth. In such difficult situations of need, the Church must be particularly concerned to offer understanding, comfort, and acceptance, rather than imposing straightaway a set of rules that only lead people to feel judged and abandoned by the very Mother called to show them God's mercy. Rather than offering the healing power of grace and the light of the Gospel message, some would "indoctrinate" that message, turning it into "dead stones to be hurled at others."[37]

Some challenges

50. The responses given to the two pre-synodal consultations spoke of a great variety of situations and the new challenges that they pose. In addition to those already mentioned, many of the respondents pointed to the problems families face in raising children. In many cases, parents come home exhausted, not wanting to talk, and many families no longer even share a common meal. Distractions abound, including an addiction to television. This makes it all the more difficult for parents to hand on the faith to their children. Other responses pointed to the effect of severe stress on families, who often seem more caught up with securing their future than with enjoying the present. This is a broader cultural

problem, aggravated by fears about steady employment, finances, and the future of children.

51. Drug use was also mentioned as one of the scourges of our time, causing immense suffering and even breakup for many families. The same is true of alcoholism, gambling, and other addictions. The family could be the place where these are prevented and overcome, but society and politics fail to see that families at risk "lose the ability to act to help their members. . . . We see the serious effects of this breakdown in families torn apart, the young uprooted and the elderly abandoned, children who are orphans of living parents, adolescents and young adults confused and unsupported."[38] As the bishops of Mexico have pointed out, violence within families breeds new forms of social aggression, since "family relationships can also explain the tendency to a violent personality. This is often the case with families where communication is lacking, defensive attitudes predominate, the members are not supportive of one another, family activities that encourage participation are absent, the parental relationship is frequently conflictual and violent, and relationships between parents and children are marked by hostility. Violence within the family is a breeding-ground of resentment and hatred in the most basic human relationships."[39]

52. No one can think that the weakening of the family as that natural society founded on marriage will prove beneficial to society as a whole. The contrary is true: it poses a threat to the mature growth of individuals, the cultivation of community values, and the moral progress of cities and countries. There is a failure to realize that only the exclusive and indissoluble union between a man and a woman has a plenary role to play in society as a stable commitment that bears fruit in new life. We need to acknowledge the great variety of family situations that can offer a certain stability, but de facto or same-sex unions, for example, may not simply be equated with marriage. No union that is temporary or closed to the transmission of life can ensure the future of society. But nowadays who is making an effort to strengthen marriages, to help married couples overcome their problems, to assist them in the work of raising children, and, in general, to encourage the stability of the marriage bond?

53. "Some societies still maintain the practice of polygamy; in other places, arranged marriages are an enduring practice. . . . In many places, not only in the West, the practice of living together before marriage is widespread, as well as a type of cohabitation which totally excludes any intention to marry."[40] In various countries, legislation facilitates a growing variety of alternatives to marriage, with the result that marriage, with its characteristics of exclusivity, indissolubility, and openness to life, comes to appear as an old-fashioned and outdated option. Many countries are witnessing a legal deconstruction of the family, tending to adopt models based almost exclusively on the autonomy of the individual will. Surely it is legitimate and right to reject older forms of the traditional family marked by authoritarianism and even violence, yet this should not lead to a disparagement of marriage itself, but rather to the rediscovery of its authentic meaning and its renewal. The strength of the family "lies in its capacity to love and to teach how to love. For all a family's problems, it can always grow, beginning with love."[41]

54. In this brief overview, I would like to stress the fact that, even though significant advances have been made in the recognition of women's rights and their participation in public life, in some countries much remains to be done to promote these rights. Unacceptable customs still need to be eliminated. I think particularly of the shameful ill-treatment to which women are sometimes subjected, domestic violence and various forms of enslavement which, rather than a show of masculine power, are craven acts of cowardice. The verbal, physical, and sexual violence that women endure in some marriages contradicts the very nature of the conjugal union. I think of the reprehensible genital mutilation of women practiced in some cultures, but also of their lack of equal access to dignified work and roles of decision-making. History is burdened by the excesses of patriarchal cultures that considered women inferior, yet in our own day, we cannot overlook the use of surrogate mothers and "the exploitation and commercialization of the female body in the current media culture."[42] There are those who believe that many of today's problems have arisen because of feminine emancipation. This argument, however, is not valid, "it is false, untrue, a form of male chauvinism."[43] The equal dignity of

men and women makes us rejoice to see old forms of discrimination disappear, and within families there is a growing reciprocity. If certain forms of feminism have arisen which we must consider inadequate, we must nonetheless see in the women's movement the working of the Spirit for a clearer recognition of the dignity and rights of women.

55. Men "play an equally decisive role in family life, particularly with regard to the protection and support of their wives and children. . . . Many men are conscious of the importance of their role in the family and live their masculinity accordingly. The absence of a father gravely affects family life and the upbringing of children and their integration into society. This absence, which may be physical, emotional, psychological, and spiritual, deprives children of a suitable father figure."[44]

56. Yet another challenge is posed by the various forms of an ideology of gender that "denies the difference and reciprocity in nature of a man and a woman and envisages a society without sexual differences, thereby eliminating the anthropological basis of the family. This ideology leads to educational programs and legislative enactments that promote a personal identity and emotional intimacy radically separated from the biological difference between male and female. Consequently, human identity becomes the choice of the individual, one which can also change over time."[45] It is a source of concern that some ideologies of this sort, which seek to respond to what are at times understandable aspirations, manage to assert themselves as absolute and unquestionable, even dictating how children should be raised. It needs to be emphasized that "biological sex and the socio-cultural role of sex (gender) can be distinguished but not separated."[46] On the other hand, "the technological revolution in the field of human procreation has introduced the ability to manipulate the reproductive act, making it independent of the sexual relationship between a man and a woman. In this way, human life and parenthood have become modular and separable realities, subject mainly to the wishes of individuals or couples."[47] It is one thing to be understanding of human weakness and the complexities of life, and another to accept ideologies that attempt to sunder what are inseparable aspects of reality. Let us not fall into the sin of trying to replace the Creator. We are creatures, and not omnipotent.

Creation is prior to us and must be received as a gift. At the same time, we are called to protect our humanity, and this means, in the first place, accepting it and respecting it as it was created.

57. I thank God that many families, which are far from considering themselves perfect, live in love, fulfill their calling, and keep moving forward, even if they fall many times along the way. The Synod's reflections show us that there is no stereotype of the ideal family, but rather a challenging mosaic made up of many different realities, with all their joys, hopes, and problems. The situations that concern us are challenges. We should not be trapped into wasting our energy in doleful laments, but rather seek new forms of missionary creativity. In every situation that presents itself, "the Church is conscious of the need to offer a word of truth and hope. . . . The great values of marriage and the Christian family correspond to a yearning that is part and parcel of human existence."[48] If we see any number of problems, these should be, as the bishops of Colombia have said, a summons to "revive our hope and to make it the source of prophetic visions, transformative actions, and creative forms of charity."[49]

CHAPTER THREE

LOOKING TO JESUS: THE VOCATION OF THE FAMILY

58. In and among families, the Gospel message should always resound; the core of that message, the kerygma, is what is "most beautiful, most excellent, most appealing, and at the same time most necessary."[50] This message "has to occupy the center of all evangelizing activity."[51] It is the first and most important proclamation, "which we must hear again and again in different ways, and which we must always announce in one form or another."[52] Indeed, "nothing is more solid, profound, secure, meaningful, and wise than that message." In effect, "all Christian formation consists of entering more deeply into the kerygma."[53]

59. Our teaching on marriage and the family cannot fail to be inspired and transformed by this message of love and tenderness; otherwise, it becomes nothing more than the defense of a dry and lifeless doctrine. The mystery of the Christian family can be fully understood only in the light of the Father's infinite love revealed in Christ, who gave himself up for our sake and who continues to dwell in our midst. I now wish to turn my gaze to the living Christ, who is at the heart of so many love stories, and to invoke the fire of the Spirit upon all the world's families.

60. This brief chapter, then, will summarize the Church's teaching on marriage and the family. Here too I will mention what the Synod Fathers had to say about the light offered by our faith. They began with the gaze of Jesus and they spoke of how he "looked upon the women and men whom he met with love and tenderness, accompanying their steps in truth, patience and mercy as he proclaimed the demands of the kingdom of God."[54] The Lord is also with us today, as we seek to practice and pass on the Gospel of the family.

Jesus restores and fulfills God's plan

61. Contrary to those who rejected marriage as evil, the New Testament teaches that "everything created by God is good and nothing is to be rejected" (1 Tm 4:4). Marriage is "a gift" from the Lord (1 Cor 7:7). At

the same time, precisely because of this positive understanding, the New Testament strongly emphasizes the need to safeguard God's gift: "Let marriage be held in honor among all, and let the marriage bed be undefiled" (Heb 13:4). This divine gift includes sexuality: "Do not refuse one another" (1 Cor 7:5).

62. The Synod Fathers noted that Jesus, "in speaking of God's original plan for man and woman, reaffirmed the indissoluble union between them, even stating that 'it was for your hardness of heart that Moses allowed you to divorce your wives, but from the beginning it was not so' (Mt 19:8). The indissolubility of marriage—'what God has joined together, let no man put asunder' (Mt 19:6)—should not be viewed as a 'yoke' imposed on humanity, but as a 'gift' granted to those who are joined in marriage. . . . God's indulgent love always accompanies our human journey; through grace, it heals and transforms hardened hearts, leading them back to the beginning through the way of the cross. The Gospels clearly present the example of Jesus who . . . proclaimed the meaning of marriage as the fullness of revelation that restores God's original plan (cf. Mt 19:3)."[55]

63. "Jesus, who reconciled all things in himself, restored marriage and the family to their original form (cf. Mt 10:1–12). Marriage and the family have been redeemed by Christ (cf. Eph 5:21–32) and restored in the image of the Holy Trinity, the mystery from which all true love flows. The spousal covenant, originating in creation and revealed in the history of salvation, takes on its full meaning in Christ and his Church. Through his Church, Christ bestows on marriage and the family the grace necessary to bear witness to the love of God and to live the life of communion. The Gospel of the family spans the history of the world, from the creation of man and woman in the image and likeness of God (cf. Gn 1:26–27), to the fulfillment of the mystery of the covenant in Christ at the end of time with the marriage of the Lamb (cf. Rv 19:9)."[56]

64. "The example of Jesus is a paradigm for the Church. . . . He began his public ministry with the miracle at the wedding feast of Cana (cf. Jn 2:1–11). He shared in everyday moments of friendship with the family

of Lazarus and his sisters (cf. Lk 10:38) and with the family of Peter (cf. Mk 8:14). He sympathized with grieving parents and restored their children to life (cf. Mk 5:41; Lk 7:14–15). In this way he demonstrated the true meaning of mercy, which entails the restoration of the covenant (cf. John Paul II, *Dives in Misericordia,* 4). This is clear from his conversations with the Samaritan woman (cf. Jn 1:4–30) and with the woman found in adultery (cf. Jn 8:1–11), where the consciousness of sin is awakened by an encounter with Jesus' gratuitous love."[57]

65. The incarnation of the Word in a human family, in Nazareth, by its very newness changed the history of the world. We need to enter into the mystery of Jesus' birth, into that "yes" given by Mary to the message of the angel, when the Word was conceived in her womb, as well as the "yes" of Joseph, who gave a name to Jesus and watched over Mary. We need to contemplate the joy of the shepherds before the manger, the adoration of the Magi, and the flight into Egypt, in which Jesus shares his people's experience of exile, persecution, and humiliation. We need to contemplate the religious expectation of Zechariah and his joy at the birth of John the Baptist, the fulfillment of the promise made known to Simeon and Anna in the Temple, and the marvel of the teachers of the Law who listened to the wisdom of the child Jesus. We then need to peer into those thirty long years when Jesus earned his keep by the work of his hands, reciting the traditional prayers and expressions of his people's faith and coming to know that ancestral faith until he made it bear fruit in the mystery of the kingdom. This is the mystery of Christmas and the secret of Nazareth, exuding the beauty of family life! It was this that so fascinated Francis of Assisi, Thérèse of the Child Jesus, and Charles de Foucauld, and continues to fill Christian families with hope and joy.

66. "The covenant of love and fidelity lived by the Holy Family of Nazareth illuminates the principle which gives shape to every family, and enables it better to face the vicissitudes of life and history. On this basis, every family, despite its weaknesses, can become a light in the darkness of the world. 'Nazareth teaches us the meaning of family life, its loving communion, its simple and austere beauty, its sacred and inviolable character. May it teach how sweet and irreplaceable is its training, how

fundamental and incomparable its role in the social order' (Paul VI, *Address in Nazareth,* 5 January 1964)."[58]

The family in the documents of the Church

67. The Second Vatican Council, in its Pastoral Constitution *Gaudium et Spes,* was concerned "to promote the dignity of marriage and the family (cf. Nos. 47–52)." The Constitution "defined marriage as a community of life and love (cf. 48), placing love at the center of the family. . . . 'True love between husband and wife' (49) involves mutual self-giving, includes and integrates the sexual and affective dimensions, in accordance with God's plan (cf. 48–49)." The conciliar document also emphasizes "the grounding of the spouses in Christ. Christ the Lord 'makes himself present to the Christian spouses in the sacrament of Marriage' (48) and remains with them. In the incarnation, he assumes human love, purifies it, and brings it to fulfillment. By his Spirit, he gives spouses the capacity to live that love, permeating every part of their lives of faith, hope, and charity. In this way, the spouses are consecrated and by means of a special grace build up the Body of Christ and form a domestic church (cf. *Lumen Gentium,* 11), so that the Church, in order fully to understand her mystery, looks to the Christian family, which manifests her in a real way."[59]

68. "Blessed Paul VI, in the wake of the Second Vatican Council, further developed the Church's teaching on marriage and the family. In a particular way, with the Encyclical *Humanae Vitae* he brought out the intrinsic bond between conjugal love and the generation of life: 'Married love requires of husband and wife the full awareness of their obligations in the matter of responsible parenthood, which today, rightly enough, is much insisted upon, but which at the same time must be rightly understood. . . . The exercise of responsible parenthood requires that husband and wife, keeping a right order of priorities, recognize their own duties toward God, themselves, their families, and human society' (No. 10). In the Apostolic Exhortation *Evangelii Nuntiandi,* Paul VI highlighted the relationship between the family and the Church."[60]

69. "Saint John Paul II devoted special attention to the family in his catecheses on human love, in his Letter to Families *Gratissimam Sane* and

particularly in his Apostolic Exhortation *Familiaris Consortio*. In these documents, the Pope defined the family as 'the way of the Church.' He also offered a general vision of the vocation of men and women to love, and proposed basic guidelines for the pastoral care of the family and for the role of the family in society. In particular, by treating conjugal love (cf. No. 13), he described how spouses, in their mutual love, receive the gift of the Spirit of Christ and live their call to holiness."[61]

70. "Pope Benedict XVI, in his Encyclical *Deus Caritas Est*, returned to the topic of the truth of the love of man and woman, which is fully illuminated only in the love of the crucified Christ (cf. No. 2). He stressed that 'marriage based on an exclusive and definitive love becomes an icon of the relationship between God and his people, and vice versa. God's way of loving becomes the measure of human love' (11). Moreover, in the Encyclical *Caritas in Veritate*, he highlighted the importance of love as a principle of life in society (cf. 44), a place where we learn the experience of the common good."[62]

The sacrament of Matrimony

71. "Scripture and Tradition give us access to a knowledge of the Trinity, which is revealed with the features of a family. The family is the image of God, who is a communion of persons. At Christ's baptism, the Father's voice was heard, calling Jesus his beloved Son, and in this love we can recognize the Holy Spirit (cf. Mk 1:10–11). Jesus, who reconciled all things in himself and redeemed us from sin, not only returned marriage and the family to their original form, but also raised marriage to the sacramental sign of his love for the Church (cf. Mt 19:1–12; Mk 10:1–12; Eph 5:21–32). In the human family, gathered by Christ, 'the image and likeness' of the Most Holy Trinity (cf. Gn 1:26) has been restored, the mystery from which all true love flows. Through the Church, marriage and the family receive the grace of the Holy Spirit from Christ, in order to bear witness to the Gospel of God's love."[63]

72. The sacrament of Marriage is not a social convention, an empty ritual, or merely the outward sign of a commitment. The sacrament is a gift given for the sanctification and salvation of the spouses, since "their

mutual belonging is a real representation, through the sacramental sign, of the same relationship between Christ and the Church. The married couple are therefore a permanent reminder for the Church of what took place on the cross; they are for one another and for their children witnesses of the salvation in which they share through the sacrament."[64] Marriage is a vocation, inasmuch as it is a response to a specific call to experience conjugal love as an imperfect sign of the love between Christ and the Church. Consequently, the decision to marry and to have a family ought to be the fruit of a process of vocational discernment.

73. "Mutual self-giving in the sacrament of Matrimony is grounded in the grace of baptism, which establishes the foundational covenant of every person with Christ in the Church. In accepting each other, and with Christ's grace, the engaged couple promise each other total self-giving, faithfulness, and openness to new life. The couple recognizes these elements as constitutive of marriage, gifts offered to them by God, and take seriously their mutual commitment, in God's name and in the presence of the Church. Faith thus makes it possible for them to assume the goods of marriage as commitments that can be better kept through the help of the grace of the sacrament. . . . Consequently, the Church looks to married couples as the heart of the entire family, which, in turn, looks to Jesus."[65] The sacrament is not a "thing" or a "power," for in it Christ himself "now encounters Christian spouses. . . . He dwells with them, gives them the strength to take up their crosses and so follow him, to rise again after they have fallen, to forgive one another, to bear one another's burdens."[66] Christian marriage is a sign of how much Christ loved his Church in the covenant sealed on the cross, yet it also makes that love present in the communion of the spouses. By becoming one flesh, they embody the espousal of our human nature by the Son of God. That is why "in the joys of their love and family life, he gives them here on earth a foretaste of the wedding feast of the Lamb."[67] Even though the analogy between the human couple of husband and wife, and that of Christ and his Church, is "imperfect,"[68] it inspires us to beg the Lord to bestow on every married couple an outpouring of his divine love.

74. Sexual union, lovingly experienced and sanctified by the sacrament, is in turn a path of growth in the life of grace for the couple. It is the "nuptial mystery."[69] The meaning and value of their physical union is expressed in the words of consent, in which they accepted and offered themselves each to the other, in order to share their lives completely. Those words give meaning to the sexual relationship and free it from ambiguity. More generally, the common life of husband and wife, the entire network of relations that they build with their children and the world around them, will be steeped in and strengthened by the grace of the sacrament. For the sacrament of Marriage flows from the incarnation and the paschal mystery, whereby God showed the fullness of his love for humanity by becoming one with us. Neither of the spouses will be alone in facing whatever challenges may come their way. Both are called to respond to God's gift with commitment, creativity, perseverance, and daily effort. They can always invoke the assistance of the Holy Spirit who consecrated their union, so that his grace may be felt in every new situation that they encounter.

75. In the Church's Latin tradition, the ministers of the sacrament of Marriage are the man and the woman who marry;[70] by manifesting their consent and expressing it physically, they receive a great gift. Their consent and their bodily union are the divinely appointed means whereby they become "one flesh." By their baptismal consecration, they were enabled to join in marriage as the Lord's ministers and thus to respond to God's call. Hence, when two non-Christian spouses receive baptism, they need not renew their marriage vows; they need simply not reject them, since by the reception of baptism their union automatically becomes sacramental. Canon Law also recognizes the validity of certain unions celebrated without the presence of an ordained minister.[71] The natural order has been so imbued with the redemptive grace of Jesus that "a valid matrimonial contract cannot exist between the baptized without it being by that fact a sacrament."[72] The Church can require that the wedding be celebrated publicly, with the presence of witnesses and other conditions that have varied over the course of time, but this does not detract from the fact that the couple who marry are the ministers of the sacrament.

Nor does it affect the centrality of the consent given by the man and the woman, which of itself establishes the sacramental bond. This having been said, there is a need for further reflection on God's action in the marriage rite; this is clearly manifested in the Oriental Churches through the importance of the blessing that the couple receive as a sign of the gift of the Spirit.

Seeds of the Word and imperfect situations

76. "The Gospel of the family also nourishes seeds that are still waiting to grow, and serves as the basis for caring for those plants that are wilting and must not be neglected."[73] Thus, building on the gift of Christ in the sacrament, married couples "may be led patiently further on in order to achieve a deeper grasp and a fuller integration of this mystery in their lives."[74]

77. Appealing to the Bible's teaching that all was created through Christ and for Christ (cf. Col 1:16), the Synod Fathers noted that "the order of redemption illuminates and fulfills that of creation. Natural marriage, therefore, is fully understood in the light of its fulfillment in the sacrament of Matrimony: only in contemplating Christ does a person come to know the deepest truth about human relationships. 'Only in the mystery of the Incarnate Word does the mystery of man take on light. . . . Christ, the new Adam, by the revelation of the mystery of the Father and his love, fully reveals man to himself and makes his supreme calling clear' (*Gaudium et Spes*, 22). It is particularly helpful to understand in a Christocentric key . . . the good of the spouses (*bonum coniugum*),"[75] which includes unity, openness to life, fidelity, indissolubility, and, within Christian marriage, mutual support on the path toward complete friendship with the Lord. "Discernment of the presence of 'seeds of the Word' in other cultures (cf. *Ad Gentes* 11) can also apply to the reality of marriage and the family. In addition to true natural marriage, positive elements exist in the forms of marriage found in other religious traditions,"[76] even if, at times, obscurely. We can readily say that "anyone who wants to bring into this world a family which teaches children to be excited by every gesture aimed at overcoming evil—a family which shows that the

Spirit is alive and at work—will encounter our gratitude and our appreciation. Whatever the people, religion, or region to which they belong!"[77]

78. "The light of Christ enlightens every person (cf. Jn 1:9; *Gaudium et Spes*, 22). Seeing things with the eyes of Christ inspires the Church's pastoral care for the faithful who are living together, or are only married civilly, or are divorced and remarried. Following this divine pedagogy, the Church turns with love to those who participate in her life in an imperfect manner: she seeks the grace of conversion for them; she encourages them to do good, to take loving care of each other and to serve the community in which they live and work. . . . When a couple in an irregular union attains a noteworthy stability through a public bond—and is characterized by deep affection, responsibility toward the children, and the ability to overcome trials—this can be seen as an opportunity, where possible, to lead them to celebrate the sacrament of Matrimony."[78]

79. "When faced with difficult situations and wounded families, it is always necessary to recall this general principle: 'Pastors must know that, for the sake of truth, they are obliged to exercise careful discernment of situations' (*Familiaris Consortio*, 84). The degree of responsibility is not equal in all cases and factors may exist which limit the ability to make a decision. Therefore, while clearly stating the Church's teaching, pastors are to avoid judgments that do not take into account the complexity of various situations, and they are to be attentive, by necessity, to how people experience and endure distress because of their condition."[79]

The transmission of life and the rearing of children

80. Marriage is firstly an "intimate partnership of life and love"[80] which is a good for the spouses themselves,[81] while sexuality is "ordered to the conjugal love of man and woman."[82] It follows that "spouses to whom God has not granted children can have a conjugal life full of meaning, in both human and Christian terms."[83] Nonetheless, the conjugal union is ordered to procreation "by its very nature."[84] The child who is born "does not come from outside as something added on to the mutual love of the spouses, but springs from the very heart of that mutual giving, as its fruit and fulfillment."[85] He or she does not appear at the end of a

process, but is present from the beginning of love as an essential feature, one that cannot be denied without disfiguring that love itself. From the outset, love refuses every impulse to close in on itself; it is open to a fruitfulness that draws it beyond itself. Hence no genital act of husband and wife can refuse this meaning,[86] even when for various reasons it may not always in fact beget a new life.

81. A child deserves to be born of that love, and not by any other means, for "he or she is not something owed to one, but is a gift,"[87] which is "the fruit of the specific act of the conjugal love of the parents."[88] This is the case because, "according to the order of creation, conjugal love between a man and a woman, and the transmission of life are ordered to each other (cf. Gn 1:27–28). Thus the Creator made man and woman share in the work of his creation and, at the same time, made them instruments of his love, entrusting to them the responsibility for the future of mankind, through the transmission of human life."[89]

82. The Synod Fathers stated that "the growth of a mentality that would reduce the generation of human life to one variable of an individual's or a couple's plans is clearly evident."[90] The Church's teaching is meant to "help couples to experience in a complete, harmonious, and conscious way their communion as husband and wife, together with their responsibility for procreating life. We need to return to the message of the Encyclical *Humanae Vitae* of Blessed Pope Paul VI, which highlights the need to respect the dignity of the person in morally assessing methods of regulating birth. . . . The choice of adoption or foster parenting can also express that fruitfulness which is a characteristic of married life."[91] With special gratitude the Church "supports families who accept, raise, and surround with affection children with various disabilities."[92]

83. Here I feel it urgent to state that, if the family is the sanctuary of life, the place where life is conceived and cared for, it is a horrendous contradiction when it becomes a place where life is rejected and destroyed. So great is the value of a human life, and so inalienable the right to life of an innocent child growing in the mother's womb, that no alleged right to one's own body can justify a decision to terminate that life, which is

an end in itself and which can never be considered the "property" of another human being. The family protects human life in all its stages, including its last. Consequently, "those who work in healthcare facilities are reminded of the moral duty of conscientious objection. Similarly, the Church not only feels the urgency to assert the right to a natural death, without aggressive treatment and euthanasia," but likewise "firmly rejects the death penalty."[93]

84. The Synod Fathers also wished to emphasize that "one of the fundamental challenges facing families today is undoubtedly that of raising children, made all the more difficult and complex by today's cultural reality and the powerful influence of the media."[94] "The Church assumes a valuable role in supporting families, starting with Christian initiation, through welcoming communities."[95] At the same time I feel it important to reiterate that the overall education of children is a "most serious duty" and at the same time a "primary right" of parents.[96] This is not just a task or a burden, but an essential and inalienable right that parents are called to defend and of which no one may claim to deprive them. The State offers educational programs in a subsidiary way, supporting the parents in their indeclinable role; parents themselves enjoy the right to choose freely the kind of education—accessible and of good quality—which they wish to give their children in accordance with their convictions. Schools do not replace parents, but complement them. This is a basic principle: "all other participants in the process of education are only able to carry out their responsibilities in the name of the parents, with their consent and, to a certain degree, with their authorization."[97] Still, "a rift has opened up between the family and society, between family and the school; the educational pact today has been broken and thus the educational alliance between society and the family is in crisis."[98]

85. The Church is called to cooperate with parents through suitable pastoral initiatives, assisting them in the fulfillment of their educational mission. She must always do this by helping them to appreciate their proper role and to realize that by their reception of the sacrament of Marriage they become ministers of their children's education. In educating

them, they build up the Church,[99] and in so doing, they accept a God-given vocation.[100]

The family and the Church

86. "With inner joy and deep comfort, the Church looks to the families who remain faithful to the teachings of the Gospel, encouraging them and thanking them for the testimony they offer. For they bear witness, in a credible way, to the beauty of marriage as indissoluble and perpetually faithful. Within the family 'which could be called a domestic church' (*Lumen Gentium*, 11), individuals enter upon an ecclesial experience of communion among persons, which reflects, through grace, the mystery of the Holy Trinity. 'Here one learns endurance and the joy of work, fraternal love, generous—even repeated—forgiveness, and above all divine worship in prayer and the offering of one's life' (*Catechism of the Catholic Church*, 1657)."[101]

87. The Church is a family of families, constantly enriched by the lives of all those domestic churches. "In virtue of the sacrament of Matrimony, every family becomes, in effect, a good for the Church. From this standpoint, reflecting on the interplay between the family and the Church will prove a precious gift for the Church in our time. The Church is good for the family, and the family is good for the Church. The safeguarding of the Lord's gift in the sacrament of Matrimony is a concern not only of individual families but of the entire Christian community."[102]

88. The experience of love in families is a perennial source of strength for the life of the Church. "The unitive end of marriage is a constant summons to make this love grow and deepen. Through their union in love, the couple experiences the beauty of fatherhood and motherhood, and shares plans, trials, expectations, and concerns; they learn care for one another and mutual forgiveness. In this love, they celebrate their happy moments and support each other in the difficult passages of their life together. . . . The beauty of this mutual, gratuitous gift, the joy which comes from a life that is born and the loving care of all family members—from toddlers to seniors—are just a few of the fruits which make

the response to the vocation of the family unique and irreplaceable,"[103] both for the Church and for society as a whole.

CHAPTER FOUR

LOVE IN MARRIAGE

89. All that has been said so far would be insufficient to express the Gospel of marriage and the family, were we not also to *speak of love*. For we cannot encourage a path of fidelity and mutual self-giving without encouraging the growth, strengthening, and deepening of conjugal and family love. Indeed, the grace of the sacrament of Marriage is intended before all else "to perfect the couple's love."[104] Here too we can say that, "even if I have faith so as to remove mountains, but have not love, I am nothing. If I give all I have, and if I deliver my body to be burned, but have not love, I gain nothing" (1 Cor 13:2–3). The word "love," however, is commonly used and often misused.[105]

Our daily love

90. In a lyrical passage of Saint Paul, we see some of the features of true love:

> Love is patient,
> love is kind;
> love is not jealous or boastful;
> it is not arrogant or rude.
> Love does not insist on its own way,
> it is not irritable or resentful;
> it does not rejoice at wrong,
> but rejoices in the right.
> Love bears all things,
> believes all things,
> hopes all things,
> endures all things. (1 Cor 13:4–7)

Love is experienced and nurtured in the daily life of couples and their children. It is helpful to think more deeply about the meaning of this Pauline text and its relevance for the concrete situation of every family.

Love is patient

91. The first word used is *makrothyméi*. This does not simply have to do with "enduring all things," because we find that idea expressed at the end of the seventh verse. Its meaning is clarified by the Greek translation of the Old Testament, where we read that God is "slow to anger" (Ex 34:6; Nm 14:18). It refers, then, to the quality of one who does not act on impulse and avoids giving offense. We find this quality in the God of the Covenant, who calls us to imitate him also within the life of the family. Saint Paul's texts using this word need to be read in the light of the Book of Wisdom (cf. 11:23; 12:2, 15–18), which extols God's restraint, as leaving open the possibility of repentance, yet insists on his power, as revealed in his acts of mercy. God's "patience," shown in his mercy toward sinners, is a sign of his real power.

92. Being patient does not mean letting ourselves be constantly mistreated, tolerating physical aggression, or allowing other people to use us. We encounter problems whenever we think that relationships or people ought to be perfect, or when we put ourselves at the center and expect things to turn out our way. Then everything makes us impatient, everything makes us react aggressively. Unless we cultivate patience, we will always find excuses for responding angrily. We will end up incapable of living together, antisocial, unable to control our impulses, and our families will become battlegrounds. That is why the word of God tells us: "Let all bitterness and wrath and anger and clamor and slander be put away from you, with all malice" (Eph 4:31). Patience takes root when I recognize that other people also have a right to live in this world, just as they are. It does not matter if they hold me back, if they unsettle my plans, or annoy me by the way they act or think, or if they are not everything I want them to be. Love always has an aspect of deep compassion that leads to accepting the other person as part of this world, even when he or she acts differently than I would like.

Love is at the service of others

93. The next word that Paul uses is *chrestéuetai*. The word is used only here in the entire Bible. It is derived from *chrestós*: a good person, one

who shows his goodness by his deeds. Here, in strict parallelism with the preceding verb, it serves as a complement. Paul wants to make it clear that "patience" is not a completely passive attitude, but one accompanied by activity, by a dynamic and creative interaction with others. The word indicates that love benefits and helps others. For this reason it is translated as "kind"; love is ever ready to be of assistance.

94. Throughout the text, it is clear that Paul wants to stress that love is more than a mere feeling. Rather, it should be understood along the lines of the Hebrew verb "to love"; it is "to do good." As Saint Ignatius of Loyola said, "Love is shown more by deeds than by words."[106] It thus shows its fruitfulness and allows us to experience the happiness of giving, the nobility and grandeur of spending ourselves unstintingly, without asking to be repaid, purely for the pleasure of giving and serving.

Love is not jealous

95. Saint Paul goes on to reject as contrary to love an attitude expressed by the verb *zelói*—to be jealous or envious. This means that love has no room for discomfiture at another person's good fortune (cf. Acts 7:9; 17:5). Envy is a form of sadness provoked by another's prosperity; it shows that we are not concerned for the happiness of others but only with our own well-being. Whereas love makes us rise above ourselves, envy closes us in on ourselves. True love values the other person's achievements. It does not see him or her as a threat. It frees us from the sour taste of envy. It recognizes that everyone has different gifts and a unique path in life. So it strives to discover its own road to happiness, while allowing others to find theirs.

96. In a word, love means fulfilling the last two commandments of God's Law: "You shall not covet your neighbor's house; you shall not covet your neighbor's wife, or his manservant, or his maidservant, or his ox, or his donkey, or anything that is your neighbor's" (Ex 20:17). Love inspires a sincere esteem for every human being and the recognition of his or her own right to happiness. I love this person, and I see him or her with the eyes of God, who gives us everything "for our enjoyment" (1 Tm 6:17). As a result, I feel a deep sense of happiness and peace. This

same deeply rooted love also leads me to reject the injustice whereby some possess too much and others too little. It moves me to find ways of helping society's outcasts to find a modicum of joy. That is not envy, but the desire for equality.

Love is not boastful

97. The following word, *perpereúetai*, denotes vainglory, the need to be haughty, pedantic, and somewhat pushy. Those who love not only refrain from speaking too much about themselves, but are focused on others; they do not need to be the center of attention. The word that comes next—*physioútai*—is similar, indicating that love is not arrogant. Literally, it means that we do not become "puffed up" before others. It also points to something more subtle: an obsession with showing off and a loss of a sense of reality. Such people think that, because they are more "spiritual" or "wise," they are more important than they really are. Paul uses this verb on other occasions, as when he says that "knowledge puffs up," whereas "love builds up" (1 Cor 8:1). Some think that they are important because they are more knowledgeable than others; they want to lord it over them. Yet what really makes us important is a love that understands, shows concern, and embraces the weak. Elsewhere the word is used to criticize those who are "inflated" with their own importance (cf. 1 Cor 4:18) but in fact are filled more with empty words than the real "power" of the Spirit (cf. 1 Cor 4:19).

98. It is important for Christians to show their love by the way they treat family members who are less knowledgeable about the faith, weak or less sure in their convictions. At times the opposite occurs: the supposedly mature believers within the family become unbearably arrogant. Love, on the other hand, is marked by humility; if we are to understand, forgive, and serve others from the heart, our pride has to be healed and our humility must increase. Jesus told his disciples that in a world where power prevails, each tries to dominate the other, but "it shall not be so among you" (Mt 20:26). The inner logic of Christian love is not about importance and power; rather, "whoever would be first among you must be your slave" (Mt 20:27). In family life, the logic of domination and

competition about who is the most intelligent or powerful destroys love. Saint Peter's admonition also applies to the family: "Clothe yourselves, all of you, with humility toward one another, for 'God opposes the proud, but gives grace to the humble'" (1 Pt 5:5).

Love is not rude

99. To love is also to be gentle and thoughtful, and this is conveyed by the next word, *aschemonéi*. It indicates that love is not rude or impolite; it is not harsh. Its actions, words, and gestures are pleasing and not abrasive or rigid. Love abhors making others suffer. Courtesy "is a school of sensitivity and disinterestedness" which requires a person "to develop his or her mind and feelings, learning how to listen, to speak, and, at certain times, to keep quiet."[107] It is not something that a Christian may accept or reject. As an essential requirement of love, "every human being is bound to live agreeably with those around him."[108] Every day, "entering into the life of another, even when that person already has a part to play in our life, demands the sensitivity and restraint which can renew trust and respect. Indeed, the deeper love is, the more it calls for respect for the other's freedom and the ability to wait until the other opens the door to his or her heart."[109]

100. To be open to a genuine encounter with others, "a kind look" is essential. This is incompatible with a negative attitude that readily points out other people's shortcomings while overlooking one's own. A kind look helps us to see beyond our own limitations, to be patient, and to cooperate with others, despite our differences. Loving kindness builds bonds, cultivates relationships, creates new networks of integration, and knits a firm social fabric. In this way, it grows ever stronger, for without a sense of belonging we cannot sustain a commitment to others; we end up seeking our convenience alone and life in common becomes impossible. Antisocial persons think that others exist only for the satisfaction of their own needs. Consequently, there is no room for the gentleness of love and its expression. Those who love are capable of speaking words of comfort, strength, consolation, and encouragement. These were the words that Jesus himself spoke: "Take heart, my son!" (Mt 9:2); "Great

is your faith!" (Mt 15:28); "Arise!" (Mk 5:41); "Go in peace" (Lk 7:50); "Be not afraid" (Mt 14:27). These are not words that demean, sadden, anger, or show scorn. In our families, we must learn to imitate Jesus' own gentleness in our way of speaking to one another.

Love is generous

101. We have repeatedly said that to love another we must first love ourselves. Paul's hymn to love, however, states that love "does not seek its own interest," nor "seek what is its own." This same idea is expressed in another text: "Let each of you look not only to his own interests, but also to the interests of others" (Phil 2:4). The Bible makes it clear that generously serving others is far more noble than loving ourselves. Loving ourselves is only important as a psychological prerequisite for being able to love others: "If a man is mean to himself, to whom will he be generous? No one is meaner than the man who is grudging to himself" (Sir 14:5–6).

102. Saint Thomas Aquinas explains that "it is more proper to charity to desire to love than to desire to be loved";[110] indeed, "mothers, who are those who love the most, seek to love more than to be loved."[111] Consequently, love can transcend and overflow the demands of justice, "expecting nothing in return" (Lk 6:35), and the greatest of loves can lead to "laying down one's life" for another (cf. Jn 15:13). Can such generosity, which enables us to give freely and fully, really be possible? Yes, because it is demanded by the Gospel: "You received without pay, give without pay" (Mt 10:8).

Love is not irritable or resentful

103. If the first word of Paul's hymn spoke of the need for a patience that does not immediately react harshly to the weaknesses and faults of others, the word he uses next—*paroxýnetai*—has to do more with an interior indignation provoked by something from without. It refers to a violent reaction within, a hidden irritation that sets us on edge where others are concerned, as if they were troublesome or threatening and thus to be avoided. To nurture such interior hostility helps no one. It only causes hurt and alienation. Indignation is only healthy when it makes

us react to a grave injustice; when it permeates our attitude toward others it is harmful.

104. The Gospel tells us to look to the log in our own eye (cf. Mt 7:5). Christians cannot ignore the persistent admonition of God's word not to nurture anger: "Do not be overcome by evil" (Rom 12:21). "Let us not grow weary in doing good" (Gal 6:9). It is one thing to sense a sudden surge of hostility and another to give into it, letting it take root in our hearts: "Be angry but do not sin; do not let the sun go down on your anger" (Eph 4:26). My advice is never to let the day end without making peace in the family. "And how am I going to make peace? By getting down on my knees? No! Just by a small gesture, a little something, and harmony within your family will be restored. Just a little caress, no words are necessary. But do not let the day end without making peace in your family."[112] Our first reaction when we are annoyed should be one of heartfelt blessing, asking God to bless, free, and heal that person. "On the contrary bless, for to this you have been called, that you may obtain a blessing" (1 Pt 3:9). If we must fight evil, so be it; but we must always say "no" to violence in the home.

Love forgives

105. Once we allow ill will to take root in our hearts, it leads to deep resentment. The phrase *ou logízetai to kakón* means that love "takes no account of evil"; "it is not resentful." The opposite of resentment is forgiveness, which is rooted in a positive attitude that seeks to understand other people's weaknesses and to excuse them. As Jesus said, "Father, forgive them; for they know not what they do" (Lk 23:34). Yet we keep looking for more and more faults, imagining greater evils, presuming all kinds of bad intentions, and so resentment grows and deepens. Thus, every mistake or lapse on the part of a spouse can harm the bond of love and the stability of the family. Something is wrong when we see every problem as equally serious; in this way, we risk being unduly harsh with the failings of others. The just desire to see our rights respected turns into a thirst for vengeance rather than a reasoned defense of our dignity.

106. When we have been offended or let down, forgiveness is possible and desirable, but no one can say that it is easy. The truth is that "family communion can only be preserved and perfected through a great spirit of sacrifice. It requires, in fact, a ready and generous openness of each and all to understanding, to forbearance, to pardon, to reconciliation. There is no family that does not know how selfishness, discord, tension, and conflict violently attack and at times mortally wound its own communion: hence there arise the many and varied forms of division in family life."[113]

107. Today we recognize that being able to forgive others implies the liberating experience of understanding and forgiving ourselves. Often our mistakes, or criticism we have received from loved ones, can lead to a loss of self-esteem. We become distant from others, avoiding affection and fearful in our interpersonal relationships. Blaming others becomes falsely reassuring. We need to learn to pray over our past history, to accept ourselves, to learn how to live with our limitations, and even to forgive ourselves, in order to have this same attitude toward others.

108. All this assumes that we ourselves have had the experience of being forgiven by God, justified by his grace and not by our own merits. We have known a love that is prior to any of our own efforts, a love that constantly opens doors, promotes, and encourages. If we accept that God's love is unconditional, that the Father's love cannot be bought or sold, then we will become capable of showing boundless love and forgiving others even if they have wronged us. Otherwise, our family life will no longer be a place of understanding, support, and encouragement, but rather one of constant tension and mutual criticism.

Love rejoices with others

109. The expression *chaírei epì te adikía* has to do with a negativity lurking deep within a person's heart. It is the toxic attitude of those who rejoice at seeing an injustice done to others. The following phrase expresses its opposite: *sygchaírei te aletheía*: "it rejoices in the right." In other words, we rejoice at the good of others when we see their dignity and value their abilities and good works. This is impossible for those who must

always be comparing and competing, even with their spouse, so that they secretly rejoice in their failures.

110. When a loving person can do good for others, or sees that others are happy, they themselves live happily and in this way give glory to God, for "God loves a cheerful giver" (2 Cor 9:7). Our Lord especially appreciates those who find joy in the happiness of others. If we fail to learn how to rejoice in the well-being of others, and focus primarily on our own needs, we condemn ourselves to a joyless existence, for, as Jesus said, "it is more blessed to give than to receive" (Acts 20:35). The family must always be a place where, when something good happens to one of its members, they know that others will be there to celebrate it with them.

Love bears all things

111. Paul's list ends with four phrases containing the words "all things." Love bears all things, believes all things, hopes all things, endures all things. Here we see clearly the countercultural power of a love that is able to face whatever might threaten it.

112. First, Paul says that love "bears all things" (*panta stégei*). This is about more than simply putting up with evil; it has to do with *the use of the tongue*. The verb can mean "holding one's peace" about what may be wrong with another person. It implies limiting judgment, checking the impulse to issue a firm and ruthless condemnation: "Judge not and you will not be judged" (Lk 6:37). Although it runs contrary to the way we normally use our tongues, God's word tells us: "Do not speak evil against one another, brothers and sisters" (Jas 4:11). Being willing to speak ill of another person is a way of asserting ourselves, venting resentment and envy without concern for the harm we may do. We often forget that slander can be quite sinful; it is a grave offense against God when it seriously harms another person's good name and causes damage that is hard to repair. Hence God's word forthrightly states that the tongue "is a world of iniquity" that "stains the whole body" (Jas 3:6); it is a "restless evil, full of deadly poison" (3:8). Whereas the tongue can be used to "curse those who are made in the likeness of God" (3:9), love cherishes the good

name of others, even one's enemies. In seeking to uphold God's law we must never forget this specific requirement of love.

113. Married couples joined by love speak well of each other; they try to show their spouse's good side, not their weakness and faults. In any event, they keep silent rather than speak ill of them. This is not merely a way of acting in front of others; it springs from an interior attitude. Far from ingenuously claiming not to see the problems and weaknesses of others, it sees those weaknesses and faults in a wider context. It recognizes that these failings are a part of a bigger picture. We have to realize that all of us are a complex mixture of light and shadows. The other person is much more than the sum of the little things that annoy me. Love does not have to be perfect for us to value it. The other person loves me as best they can, with all their limits, but the fact that love is imperfect does not mean that it is untrue or unreal. It is real, albeit limited and earthly. If I expect too much, the other person will let me know, for he or she can neither play God nor serve all my needs. Love coexists with imperfection. It "bears all things" and can hold its peace before the limitations of the loved one.

Love believes all things

114. *Panta pisteúei.* Love believes all things. Here "belief" is not to be taken in its strict theological meaning, but more in the sense of what we mean by "trust." This goes beyond simply presuming that the other is not lying or cheating. Such basic trust recognizes God's light shining beyond the darkness, like an ember glowing beneath the ash.

115. This trust enables a relationship to be free. It means we do not have to control the other person, to follow their every step lest they escape our grip. Love trusts, it sets free, it does not try to control, possess, and dominate everything. This freedom, which fosters independence, an openness to the world around us and to new experiences, can only enrich and expand relationships. The spouses then share with one another the joy of all they have received and learned outside the family circle. At the same time, this freedom makes for sincerity and transparency, for those who know that they are trusted and appreciated can be open and

hide nothing. Those who know that their spouse is always suspicious, judgmental, and lacking unconditional love, will tend to keep secrets, conceal their failings and weaknesses, and pretend to be someone other than who they are. On the other hand, a family marked by loving trust, come what may, helps its members to be themselves and spontaneously to reject deceit, falsehood, and lies.

Love hopes all things

116. *Panta elpízei*. Love does not despair of the future. Following upon what has just been said, this phrase speaks of the hope of one who knows that others can change, mature, and radiate unexpected beauty and untold potential. This does not mean that everything will change in this life. It does involve realizing that, though things may not always turn out as we wish, God may well make crooked lines straight and draw some good from the evil we endure in this world.

117. Here hope comes most fully into its own, for it embraces the certainty of life after death. Each person, with all his or her failings, is called to the fullness of life in heaven. There, fully transformed by Christ's resurrection, every weakness, darkness, and infirmity will pass away. There the person's true being will shine forth in all its goodness and beauty. This realization helps us, amid the aggravations of this present life, to see each person from a supernatural perspective, in the light of hope, and await the fullness that he or she will receive in the heavenly kingdom, even if it is not yet visible.

Love endures all things

118. *Panta hypoménei*. This means that love bears every trial with a positive attitude. It stands firm in hostile surroundings. This "endurance" involves not only the ability to tolerate certain aggravations, but something greater: a constant readiness to confront any challenge. It is a love that *never gives up*, even in the darkest hour. It shows a certain dogged heroism, a power to resist every negative current, an irrepressible commitment to goodness. Here I think of the words of Martin Luther King Jr., who met every kind of trial and tribulation with fraternal love: "The

person who hates you most has some good in him; even the nation that hates you most has some good in it; even the race that hates you most has some good in it. And when you come to the point that you look in the face of every man and see deep down within him what religion calls 'the image of God,' you begin to love him in spite of [everything]. No matter what he does, you see God's image there. There is an element of goodness that he can never sluff off. . . . Another way that you love your enemy is this: when the opportunity presents itself for you to defeat your enemy, that is the time which you must not do it. . . . When you rise to the level of love, of its great beauty and power, you seek only to defeat evil systems. Individuals who happen to be caught up in that system, you love, but you seek to defeat the system. . . . Hate for hate only intensifies the existence of hate and evil in the universe. If I hit you and you hit me and I hit you back and you hit me back and so on, you see, that goes on ad infinitum. It just never ends. Somewhere somebody must have a little sense, and that's the strong person. The strong person is the person who can cut off the chain of hate, the chain of evil. . . . Somebody must have religion enough and morality enough to cut it off and inject within the very structure of the universe that strong and powerful element of love."[114]

119. In family life, we need to cultivate that strength of love which can help us fight every evil threatening it. Love does not yield to resentment, scorn for others, or the desire to hurt or to gain some advantage. The Christian ideal, especially in families, is a love that never gives up. I am sometimes amazed to see men or women who have had to separate from their spouse for their own protection, yet, because of their enduring conjugal love, still try to help them, even by enlisting others, in their moments of illness, suffering, or trial. Here too we see a love that never gives up.

Growing in conjugal love

120. Our reflection on Saint Paul's hymn to love has prepared us to discuss conjugal love. This is the love between husband and wife,[115] a love sanctified, enriched, and illuminated by the grace of the sacrament of

Marriage. It is an "affective union,"[116] spiritual and sacrificial, which combines the warmth of friendship and erotic passion, and endures long after emotions and passion subside. Pope Pius XI taught that this love permeates the duties of married life and enjoys pride of place.[117] Infused by the Holy Spirit, this powerful love is a reflection of the unbroken covenant between Christ and humanity that culminated in his self-sacrifice on the cross. "The Spirit which the Lord pours forth gives a new heart and renders man and woman capable of loving one another as Christ loved us. Conjugal love reaches that fullness to which it is interiorly ordained: conjugal charity."[118]

121. Marriage is a precious sign, for "when a man and a woman celebrate the sacrament of Marriage, God is, as it were, 'mirrored' in them; he impresses in them his own features and the indelible character of his love. Marriage is the icon of God's love for us. Indeed, God is also communion: the three Persons of the Father, the Son, and the Holy Spirit live eternally in perfect unity. And this is precisely the mystery of marriage: God makes of the two spouses one single existence."[119] This has concrete daily consequences, because the spouses, "in virtue of the sacrament, are invested with a true and proper mission, so that, starting with the simple ordinary things of life they can make visible the love with which Christ loves his Church and continues to give his life for her."[120]

122. We should not however confuse different levels: there is no need to lay upon two limited persons the tremendous burden of having to reproduce perfectly the union existing between Christ and his Church, for marriage as a sign entails "a dynamic process, . . . one which advances gradually with the progressive integration of the gifts of God."[121]

Lifelong sharing

123. After the love that unites us to God, conjugal love is the "greatest form of friendship."[122] It is a union possessing all the traits of a good friendship: concern for the good of the other, reciprocity, intimacy, warmth, stability, and the resemblance born of a shared life. Marriage joins to all this an indissoluble exclusivity expressed in the stable commitment to share and shape together the whole of life. Let us be honest

and acknowledge the signs that this is the case. Lovers do not see their relationship as merely temporary. Those who marry do not expect their excitement to fade. Those who witness the celebration of a loving union, however fragile, trust that it will pass the test of time. Children not only want their parents to love one another, but also to be faithful and remain together. These and similar signs show that it is in the very nature of conjugal love to be definitive. The lasting union expressed by the marriage vows is more than a formality or a traditional formula; it is rooted in the natural inclinations of the human person. For believers, it is also a covenant before God that calls for fidelity: "The Lord was witness to the covenant between you and the wife of your youth, to whom you have been faithless, though she is your companion and your wife by covenant. . . . Let none be faithless to the wife of his youth. For I hate divorce, says the Lord" (Mal 2:14–16).

124. A love that is weak or infirm, incapable of accepting marriage as a challenge to be taken up and fought for, reborn, renewed, and reinvented until death, cannot sustain a great commitment. It will succumb to the culture of the ephemeral that prevents a constant process of growth. Yet "promising love forever is possible when we perceive a plan bigger than our own ideas and undertakings, a plan which sustains us and enables us to surrender our future entirely to the one we love."[123] If this love is to overcome all trials and remain faithful in the face of everything, it needs the gift of grace to strengthen and elevate it. In the words of Saint Robert Bellarmine, "the fact that one man unites with one woman in an indissoluble bond, and that they remain inseparable despite every kind of difficulty, even when there is no longer hope for children, can only be the sign of a great mystery."[124]

125. Marriage is likewise a friendship marked by passion, but a passion always directed to an ever more stable and intense union. This is because "marriage was not instituted solely for the procreation of children" but also that mutual love "might be properly expressed, that it should grow and mature."[125] This unique friendship between a man and a woman acquires an all-encompassing character only within the conjugal union. Precisely as all-encompassing, this union is also exclusive, faithful, and

open to new life. It shares everything in constant mutual respect. The Second Vatican Council echoed this by stating that "such a love, bringing together the human and the divine, leads the partners to a free and mutual self-giving, experienced in tenderness and action, and permeating their entire lives."[126]

Joy and beauty

126. In marriage, the joy of love needs to be cultivated. When the search for pleasure becomes obsessive, it holds us in thrall and keeps us from experiencing other satisfactions. Joy, on the other hand, increases our pleasure and helps us find fulfillment in any number of things, even at those times of life when physical pleasure has ebbed. Saint Thomas Aquinas said that the word "joy" refers to an expansion of the heart.[127] Marital joy can be experienced even amid sorrow; it involves accepting that marriage is an inevitable mixture of enjoyment and struggles, tensions and repose, pain and relief, satisfactions and longings, annoyances and pleasures, but always on the path of friendship, which inspires married couples to care for one another: "they help and serve each other."[128]

127. The love of friendship is called "charity" when it perceives and esteems the "great worth" of another person.[129] Beauty—that "great worth" which is other than physical or psychological appeal—enables us to appreciate the sacredness of a person, without feeling the need to possess it. In a consumerist society, the sense of beauty is impoverished and so joy fades. Everything is there to be purchased, possessed, or consumed, including people. Tenderness, on the other hand, is a sign of a love free of selfish possessiveness. It makes us approach a person with immense respect and a certain dread of causing them harm or taking away their freedom. Loving another person involves the joy of contemplating and appreciating their innate beauty and sacredness, which is greater than my needs. This enables me to seek their good even when they cannot belong to me, or when they are no longer physically appealing but intrusive and annoying. For "the love by which one person is pleasing to another depends on his or her giving something freely."[130]

128. The aesthetic experience of love is expressed in that "gaze" which contemplates other persons as ends in themselves, even if they are infirm, elderly, or physically unattractive. A look of appreciation has enormous importance, and to begrudge it is usually hurtful. How many things do spouses and children sometimes do in order to be noticed! Much hurt and many problems result when we stop looking at one another. This lies behind the complaints and grievances we often hear in families: "My husband does not look at me; he acts as if I were invisible." "Please look at me when I am talking to you!" "My wife no longer looks at me, she only has eyes for our children." "In my own home nobody cares about me; they do not even see me; it is as if I did not exist." Love opens our eyes and enables us to see, beyond all else, the great worth of a human being.

129. The joy of this contemplative love needs to be cultivated. Since we were made for love, we know that there is no greater joy than that of sharing good things: "Give, take, and treat yourself well" (Sir 14:16). The most intense joys in life arise when we are able to elicit joy in others, as a foretaste of heaven. We can think of the lovely scene in the film *Babette's Feast*, when the generous cook receives a grateful hug and praise: "*Ah, how you will delight the angels!*" It is a joy and a great consolation to bring delight to others, to see them enjoying themselves. This joy, the fruit of fraternal love, is not that of the vain and self-centered, but of lovers who delight in the good of those whom they love, who give freely to them and thus bear good fruit.

130. On the other hand, joy also grows through pain and sorrow. In the words of Saint Augustine, "the greater the danger in battle the greater is the joy of victory."[131] After suffering and struggling together, spouses are able to experience that it was worth it, because they achieved some good, learned something as a couple, or came to appreciate what they have. Few human joys are as deep and thrilling as those experienced by two people who love one another and have achieved something as the result of a great, shared effort.

Marrying for love

131. I would like to say to young people that none of this is jeopardized when their love finds expression in marriage. Their union encounters in this institution the means to ensure that their love truly will endure and grow. Naturally, love is much more than an outward consent or a contract, yet it is nonetheless true that choosing to give marriage a visible form in society by undertaking certain commitments shows how important it is. It manifests the seriousness of each person's identification with the other and their firm decision to leave adolescent individualism behind and to belong to one another. Marriage is a means of expressing that we have truly left the security of the home in which we grew up in order to build other strong ties and to take on a new responsibility for another person. This is much more meaningful than a mere spontaneous association for mutual gratification, which would turn marriage into a purely private affair. As a social institution, marriage protects and shapes a shared commitment to deeper growth in love and commitment to one another, for the good of society as a whole. That is why marriage is more than a fleeting fashion; it is of enduring importance. Its essence derives from our human nature and social character. It involves a series of obligations born of love itself, a love so serious and generous that it is ready to face any risk.

132. To opt for marriage in this way expresses a genuine and firm decision to join paths, come what may. Given its seriousness, this public commitment of love cannot be the fruit of a hasty decision, but neither can it be postponed indefinitely. Committing oneself exclusively and definitively to another person always involves a risk and a bold gamble. Unwillingness to make such a commitment is selfish, calculating, and petty. It fails to recognize the rights of another person and to present him or her to society as someone worthy of unconditional love. If two persons are truly in love, they naturally show this to others. When love is expressed before others in the marriage contract, with all its public commitments, it clearly indicates and protects the "yes" which those persons speak freely and unreservedly to each other. This "yes" tells them that they can always trust one another, and that they will never be

abandoned when difficulties arise or new attractions or selfish interests present themselves.

A love that reveals itself and increases

133. The love of friendship unifies all aspects of marital life and helps family members to grow constantly. This love must be freely and generously expressed in words and acts. In the family, "three words need to be used. I want to repeat this! Three words: 'Please,' 'Thank you,' 'Sorry.' Three essential words!"[132] "In our families when we are not overbearing and ask: 'May I?'; in our families when we are not selfish and can say: 'Thank you!'; and in our families when someone realizes that he or she did something wrong and is able to say 'Sorry!' our family experiences peace and joy."[133] Let us not be stingy about using these words, but keep repeating them, day after day. For "certain silences are oppressive, even at times within families, between husbands and wives, between parents and children, among siblings."[134] The right words, spoken at the right time, daily protect and nurture love.

134. All this occurs through a process of constant growth. The very special form of love that is marriage is called to embody what Saint Thomas Aquinas said about charity in general. "Charity," he says, "by its very nature, has no limit to its increase, for it is a participation in that infinite charity which is the Holy Spirit. . . . Nor on the part of the subject can its limit be fixed, because as charity grows, so too does its capacity for an even greater increase."[135] Saint Paul also prays: "May the Lord make you increase and abound in love to one another" (1 Thes 3:12), and again, "concerning fraternal love . . . we urge you, beloved, to do so more and more" (1 Thes 4:9–10). More and more! Marital love is not defended primarily by presenting indissolubility as a duty, or by repeating doctrine, but by helping it to grow ever stronger under the impulse of grace. A love that fails to grow is at risk. Growth can only occur if we respond to God's grace through constant acts of love, acts of kindness that become ever more frequent, intense, generous, tender, and cheerful. Husbands and wives "become conscious of their unity and experience it more deeply

from day to day."[136] The gift of God's love poured out upon the spouses is also a summons to constant growth in grace.

135. It is not helpful to dream of an idyllic and perfect love needing no stimulus to grow. A celestial notion of earthly love forgets that the best is yet to come, that fine wine matures with age. As the bishops of Chile have pointed out, "the perfect families proposed by deceptive consumerist propaganda do not exist. In those families, no one grows old, there is no sickness, sorrow, or death. . . . Consumerist propaganda presents a fantasy that has nothing to do with the reality which must daily be faced by the heads of families."[137] It is much healthier to be realistic about our limits, defects, and imperfections, and to respond to the call to grow together, to bring love to maturity, and to strengthen the union, come what may.

Dialogue

136. Dialogue is essential for experiencing, expressing, and fostering love in marriage and family life. Yet it can only be the fruit of a long and demanding apprenticeship. Men and women, young people and adults, communicate differently. They speak different languages and they act in different ways. Our way of asking and responding to questions, the tone we use, our timing, and any number of other factors condition how well we communicate. We need to develop certain attitudes that express love and encourage authentic dialogue.

137. Take time, quality time. This means being ready to listen patiently and attentively to everything the other person wants to say. It requires the self-discipline of not speaking until the time is right. Instead of offering an opinion or advice, we need to be sure that we have heard everything the other person has to say. This means cultivating an interior silence that makes it possible to listen to the other person without mental or emotional distractions. Do not be rushed, put aside all of your own needs and worries, and make space. Often the other spouse does not need a solution to his or her problems, but simply to be heard, to feel that someone has acknowledged their pain, their disappointment, their fear, their anger, their hopes, and their dreams. How often we hear complaints like: "He

does not listen to me." "Even when you seem to, you are really doing something else." "I talk to her and I feel like she can't wait for me to finish." "When I speak to her, she tries to change the subject, or she gives me curt responses to end the conversation."

138. Develop the habit of giving real importance to the other person. This means appreciating them and recognizing their right to exist, to think as they do, and to be happy. Never downplay what they say or think, even if you need to express your own point of view. Everyone has something to contribute, because they have their life experiences, they look at things from a different standpoint, and they have their own concerns, abilities, and insights. We ought to be able to acknowledge the other person's truth, the value of his or her deepest concerns, and what it is that they are trying to communicate, however aggressively. We have to put ourselves in their shoes and try to peer into their hearts, to perceive their deepest concerns, and to take them as a point of departure for further dialogue.

139. Keep an open mind. Don't get bogged down in your own limited ideas and opinions, but be prepared to change or expand them. The combination of two different ways of thinking can lead to a synthesis that enriches both. The unity that we seek is not uniformity, but a "unity in diversity," or "reconciled diversity." Fraternal communion is enriched by respect and appreciation for differences within an overall perspective that advances the common good. We need to free ourselves from feeling that we all have to be alike. A certain astuteness is also needed to prevent the appearance of "static" that can interfere with the process of dialogue. For example, if hard feelings start to emerge, they should be dealt with sensitively, lest they interrupt the dynamic of dialogue. The ability to say what one is thinking without offending the other person is important. Words should be carefully chosen so as not to offend, especially when discussing difficult issues. Making a point should never involve venting anger and inflicting hurt. A patronizing tone only serves to hurt, ridicule, accuse, and offend others. Many disagreements between couples are not about important things. Mostly they are about trivial matters. What alters the mood, however, is the way things are said or the attitude with which they are said.

140. Show affection and concern for the other person. Love surmounts even the worst barriers. When we love someone, or when we feel loved by them, we can better understand what they are trying to communicate. Fearing the other person as a kind of "rival" is a sign of weakness and needs to be overcome. It is very important to base one's position on solid choices, beliefs, or values, and not on the need to win an argument or to be proved right.

141. Finally, let us acknowledge that for a worthwhile dialogue we have to have something to say. This can only be the fruit of an interior richness nourished by reading, personal reflection, prayer, and openness to the world around us. Otherwise, conversations become boring and trivial. When neither of the spouses works at this, and has little real contact with other people, family life becomes stifling and dialogue impoverished.

Passionate love

142. The Second Vatican Council teaches that this conjugal love "embraces the good of the whole person; it can enrich the sentiments of the spirit and their physical expression with a unique dignity and ennoble them as the special features and manifestation of the friendship proper to marriage."[138] For this reason, a love lacking either pleasure or passion is insufficient to symbolize the union of the human heart with God: "All the mystics have affirmed that supernatural love and heavenly love find the symbols which they seek in marital love, rather than in friendship, filial devotion or devotion to a cause. And the reason is to be found precisely in its totality."[139] Why then should we not pause to speak of feelings and sexuality in marriage?

The world of emotions

143. Desires, feelings, emotions, what the ancients called "the passions," all have an important place in married life. They are awakened whenever "another" becomes present and part of a person's life. It is characteristic of all living beings to reach out to other things, and this tendency always has basic affective signs: pleasure or pain, joy or sadness, tenderness or fear. They ground the most elementary psychological

activity. Human beings live on this earth, and all that they do and seek is fraught with passion.

144. As true man, Jesus showed his emotions. He was hurt by the rejection of Jerusalem (cf. Mt 23:27) and this moved him to tears (cf. Lk 19:41). He was also deeply moved by the sufferings of others (cf. Mk 6:34). He felt deeply their grief (cf. Jn 11:33), and he wept at the death of a friend (cf. Jn 11:35). These examples of his sensitivity showed how much his human heart was open to others.

145. Experiencing an emotion is not, in itself, morally good or evil.[140] The stirring of desire or repugnance is neither sinful nor blameworthy. What is morally good or evil is what we do on the basis of, or under the influence of, a given passion. But when passions are aroused or sought, and as a result we perform evil acts, the evil lies in the decision to fuel them and in the evil acts that result. Along the same lines, my being attracted to someone is not automatically good. If my attraction to that person makes me try to dominate him or her, then my feeling only serves my selfishness. To believe that we are good simply because "we feel good" is a tremendous illusion. There are those who feel themselves capable of great love only because they have a great need for affection, yet they prove incapable of the effort needed to bring happiness to others. They remain caught up in their own needs and desires. In such cases, emotions distract from the highest values and conceal a self-centeredness that makes it impossible to develop a healthy and happy family life.

146. This being said, if passion accompanies a free act, it can manifest the depth of that act. Marital love strives to ensure that one's entire emotional life benefits the family as a whole and stands at the service of its common life. A family is mature when the emotional life of its members becomes a form of sensitivity that neither stifles nor obscures great decisions and values, but rather follows each one's freedom,[141] springs from it, enriches, perfects, and harmonizes it in the service of all.

God loves the joy of his children

147. This calls for a pedagogical process that involves renunciation. This conviction on the part of the Church has often been rejected as opposed to human happiness. Benedict XVI summed up this charge with great clarity: "Doesn't the Church, with all her commandments and prohibitions, turn to bitterness the most precious thing in life? Doesn't she blow the whistle just when the joy which is the Creator's gift offers us a happiness which is itself a certain foretaste of the Divine?"[142] He responded that, although there have been exaggerations and deviant forms of asceticism in Christianity, the Church's official teaching, in fidelity to the Scriptures, did not reject "*eros* as such, but rather declared war on a warped and destructive form of it, because this counterfeit divinization of *eros* . . . actually strips it of divine dignity and dehumanizes it."[143]

148. Training in the areas of emotion and instinct is necessary, and at times this requires setting limits. Excess, lack of control, or obsession with a single form of pleasure can end up weakening and tainting that very pleasure[144] and damaging family life. A person can certainly channel his passions in a beautiful and healthy way, increasingly pointing them toward altruism and an integrated self-fulfillment that can only enrich interpersonal relationships in the heart of the family. This does not mean renouncing moments of intense enjoyment,[145] but rather integrating them with other moments of generous commitment, patient hope, inevitable weariness, and struggle to achieve an ideal. Family life is all this, and it deserves to be lived to the fullest.

149. Some currents of spirituality teach that desire has to be eliminated as a path to liberation from pain. Yet we believe that God loves the enjoyment felt by human beings: he created us and "richly furnishes us with everything to enjoy" (1 Tm 6:17). Let us be glad when with great love he tells us: "My son, treat yourself well. . . . Do not deprive yourself of a happy day" (Sir 14:11–14). Married couples likewise respond to God's will when they take up the biblical injunction: "Be joyful in the day of prosperity" (Eccl 7:14). What is important is to have the freedom to realize that pleasure can find different expressions at different times of life,

in accordance with the needs of mutual love. In this sense, we can appreciate the teachings of some Eastern masters who urge us to expand our consciousness, lest we be imprisoned by one limited experience that can blinker us. This expansion of consciousness is not the denial or destruction of desire so much as its broadening and perfection.

The erotic dimension of love

150. All this brings us to the sexual dimension of marriage. God himself created sexuality, which is a marvelous gift to his creatures. If this gift needs to be cultivated and directed, it is to prevent the "impoverishment of an authentic value."[146] Saint John Paul II rejected the claim that the Church's teaching is "a negation of the value of human sexuality," or that the Church simply tolerates sexuality "because it is necessary for procreation."[147] Sexual desire is not something to be looked down upon, "and there can be no attempt whatsoever to call into question its necessity."[148]

151. To those who fear that the training of the passions and of sexuality detracts from the spontaneity of sexual love, Saint John Paul II replied that human persons are "called to full and mature spontaneity in their relationships," a maturity that "is the gradual fruit of a discernment of the impulses of one's own heart."[149] This calls for discipline and self-mastery, since every human person "must learn, with perseverance and consistency, the meaning of his or her body."[150] Sexuality is not a means of gratification or entertainment; it is an interpersonal language wherein the other is taken seriously, in his or her sacred and inviolable dignity. As such, "the human heart comes to participate, so to speak, in another kind of spontaneity."[151] In this context, the erotic appears as a specifically human manifestation of sexuality. It enables us to discover "the nuptial meaning of the body and the authentic dignity of the gift."[152] In his catecheses on the theology of the body, Saint John Paul II taught that sexual differentiation not only is "a source of fruitfulness and procreation," but also possesses "the capacity of expressing love: that love precisely in which the human person becomes a gift."[153] A healthy sexual desire, albeit closely joined to a pursuit of pleasure, always involves a sense of wonder, and for that very reason can humanize the impulses.

152. In no way, then, can we consider the erotic dimension of love simply as a permissible evil or a burden to be tolerated for the good of the family. Rather, it must be seen as gift from God that enriches the relationship of the spouses. As a passion sublimated by a love respectful of the dignity of the other, it becomes a "pure, unadulterated affirmation" revealing the marvels of which the human heart is capable. In this way, even momentarily, we can feel that "life has turned out good and happy."[154]

Violence and manipulation

153. On the basis of this positive vision of sexuality, we can approach the entire subject with a healthy realism. It is, after all, a fact that sex often becomes depersonalized and unhealthy; as a result, "it becomes the occasion and instrument for self-assertion and the selfish satisfaction of personal desires and instincts."[155] In our own day, sexuality risks being poisoned by the mentality of "use and discard." The body of the other is often viewed as an object to be used as long as it offers satisfaction, and rejected once it is no longer appealing. Can we really ignore or overlook the continuing forms of domination, arrogance, abuse, sexual perversion, and violence that are the product of a warped understanding of sexuality? Or the fact that the dignity of others and our human vocation to love thus end up being less important than an obscure need to "find oneself"?

154. We also know that, within marriage itself, sex can become a source of suffering and manipulation. Hence it must be clearly reaffirmed that "a conjugal act imposed on one's spouse without regard to his or her condition, or personal and reasonable wishes in the matter, is no true act of love, and therefore offends the moral order in its particular application to the intimate relationship of husband and wife."[156] The acts proper to the sexual union of husband and wife correspond to the nature of sexuality as willed by God when they take place in "a manner which is truly human."[157] Saint Paul insists: "Let no one transgress and wrong his brother or sister in this matter" (1 Thes 4:6). Even though Paul was writing in the context of a patriarchal culture in which women were considered completely subordinate to men, he nonetheless taught that sex must involve communication between the spouses: he brings up the

possibility of postponing sexual relations for a period, but "by agreement" (1 Cor 7:5).

155. Saint John Paul II very subtly warned that a couple can be "threatened by insatiability."[158] In other words, while called to an increasingly profound union, they can risk effacing their differences and the rightful distance between the two. For each possesses his or her own proper and inalienable dignity. When reciprocal belonging turns into domination, "the structure of communion in interpersonal relations is essentially changed."[159] It is part of the mentality of domination that those who dominate end up negating their own dignity.[160] Ultimately, they no longer "identify themselves subjectively with their own body,"[161] because they take away its deepest meaning. They end up using sex as a form of escapism and renounce the beauty of conjugal union.

156. Every form of sexual submission must be clearly rejected. This includes all improper interpretations of the passage in the Letter to the Ephesians where Paul tells women to "be subject to your husbands" (Eph 5:22). This passage mirrors the cultural categories of the time, but our concern is not with its cultural matrix but with the revealed message that it conveys. As Saint John Paul II wisely observed: "Love excludes every kind of subjection whereby the wife might become a servant or a slave of the husband. . . . The community or unity which they should establish through marriage is constituted by a reciprocal donation of self, which is also a mutual subjection."[162] Hence Paul goes on to say that "husbands should love their wives as their own bodies" (Eph 5:28). The biblical text is actually concerned with encouraging everyone to overcome a complacent individualism and to be constantly mindful of others: "Be subject to one another" (Eph 5:21). In marriage, this reciprocal "submission" takes on a special meaning, and is seen as a freely chosen mutual belonging marked by fidelity, respect, and care. Sexuality is inseparably at the service of this conjugal friendship, for it is meant to aid the fulfillment of the other.

157. All the same, the rejection of distortions of sexuality and eroticism should never lead us to a disparagement or neglect of sexuality and eros

in themselves. The ideal of marriage cannot be seen purely as generous donation and self-sacrifice, where each spouse renounces all personal needs and seeks only the other's good without concern for personal satisfaction. We need to remember that authentic love also needs to be able to receive the other, to accept one's own vulnerability and needs, and to welcome with sincere and joyful gratitude the physical expressions of love found in a caress, an embrace, a kiss, and sexual union. Benedict XVI stated this very clearly: "Should man aspire to be pure spirit and to reject the flesh as pertaining to his animal nature alone, then spirit and body would both lose their dignity."[163] For this reason, "man cannot live by oblative, descending love alone. He cannot always give, he must also receive. Anyone who wishes to give love must also receive love as a gift."[164] Still, we must never forget that our human equilibrium is fragile; there is a part of us that resists real human growth, and any moment it can unleash the most primitive and selfish tendencies.

Marriage and virginity

158. "Many people who are unmarried are not only devoted to their own family but often render great service in their group of friends, in the Church community, and in their professional lives. Sometimes their presence and contributions are overlooked, causing in them a sense of isolation. Many put their talents at the service of the Christian community through charity and volunteer work. Others remain unmarried because they consecrate their lives to the love of Christ and neighbor. Their dedication greatly enriches the family, the Church, and society."[165]

159. Virginity is a form of love. As a sign, it speaks to us of the coming of the kingdom and the need for complete devotion to the cause of the Gospel (cf. 1 Cor 7:32). It is also a reflection of the fullness of heaven, where "they neither marry nor are given in marriage" (Mt 22:30). Saint Paul recommended virginity because he expected Jesus' imminent return and he wanted everyone to concentrate only on spreading the Gospel: "the appointed time has grown very short" (1 Cor 7:29). Nonetheless, he made it clear that this was his personal opinion and preference (cf. 1 Cor 7:6–9), not something demanded by Christ: "I have no command in the

Lord" (1 Cor 7:25). All the same, he recognized the value of the different callings: "Each has his or her own special gift from God, one of one kind and one of another" (1 Cor 7:7). Reflecting on this, Saint John Paul II noted that the biblical texts "give no reason to assert the 'inferiority' of marriage, nor the 'superiority' of virginity or celibacy"[166] based on sexual abstinence. Rather than speak absolutely of the superiority of virginity, it should be enough to point out that the different states of life complement one another, and consequently that some can be more perfect in one way and others in another. Alexander of Hales, for example, stated that in one sense marriage may be considered superior to the other sacraments, inasmuch as it symbolizes the great reality of "Christ's union with the Church, or the union of his divine and human natures."[167]

160. Consequently, "it is not a matter of diminishing the value of matrimony in favor of continence."[168] "There is no basis for playing one off against the other. . . . If, following a certain theological tradition, one speaks of a 'state of perfection' (*status perfectionis*), this has to do not with continence in itself, but with the entirety of a life based on the evangelical counsels."[169] A married person can experience the highest degree of charity and thus "reach the perfection which flows from charity, through fidelity to the spirit of those counsels. Such perfection is possible and accessible to every man and woman."[170]

161. The value of virginity lies in its symbolizing a love that has no need to possess the other; in this way it reflects the freedom of the Kingdom of Heaven. Virginity encourages married couples to live their own conjugal love against the backdrop of Christ's definitive love, journeying together toward the fullness of the Kingdom. For its part, conjugal love symbolizes other values. On the one hand, it is a particular reflection of that full unity in distinction found in the Trinity. The family is also a sign of Christ. It manifests the closeness of God who is a part of every human life, since he became one with us through his incarnation, death, and resurrection. Each spouse becomes "one flesh" with the other as a sign of willingness to share everything with him or her until death. Whereas virginity is an "eschatological" sign of the risen Christ, marriage is a "historical" sign for us living in this world, a sign of the earthly Christ

who chose to become one with us and gave himself up for us even to shedding his blood. Virginity and marriage are, and must be, different ways of loving. For "man cannot live without love. He remains a being that is incomprehensible for himself, his life is senseless, if love is not revealed to him."[171]

162. Celibacy can risk becoming a comfortable single life that provides the freedom to be independent, to move from one residence, work, or option to another, to spend money as one sees fit, and to spend time with others as one wants. In such cases, the witness of married people becomes especially eloquent. Those called to virginity can encounter in some marriages a clear sign of God's generous and steadfast fidelity to his covenant, and this can move them to a more concrete and generous availability to others. Many married couples remain faithful when one of them has become physically unattractive, or fails to satisfy the other's needs, despite the voices in our society that might encourage them to be unfaithful or to leave the other. A wife can care for her sick husband and thus, in drawing near to the Cross, renew her commitment to love unto death. In such love, the dignity of the true lover shines forth, inasmuch as it is more proper to charity to love than to be loved.[172] We could also point to the presence in many families of a capacity for selfless and loving service when children prove troublesome and even ungrateful. This makes those parents a sign of the free and selfless love of Jesus. Cases like these encourage celibate persons to live their commitment to the kingdom with greater generosity and openness. Today, secularization has obscured the value of a lifelong union and the beauty of the vocation to marriage. For this reason, it is "necessary to deepen an understanding of the *positive* aspects of conjugal love."[173]

The transformation of love

163. Longer life spans now mean that close and exclusive relationships must last for four, five, or even six decades; consequently, the initial decision has to be frequently renewed. While one of the spouses may no longer experience an intense sexual desire for the other, he or she may still experience the pleasure of mutual belonging and the knowledge that

neither of them is alone but has a "partner" with whom everything in life is shared. He or she is a companion on life's journey, one with whom to face life's difficulties and enjoy its pleasures. This satisfaction is part of the affection proper to conjugal love. There is no guarantee that we will feel the same way all through life. Yet if a couple can come up with a shared and lasting life project, they can love one another and live as one until death do them part, enjoying an enriching intimacy. The love they pledge is greater than any emotion, feeling, or state of mind, although it may include all of these. It is a deeper love, a lifelong decision of the heart. Even amid unresolved conflicts and confused emotional situations, they daily reaffirm their decision to love, to belong to one another, to share their lives, and to continue loving and forgiving. Each progresses along the path of personal growth and development. On this journey, love rejoices at every step and in every new stage.

164. In the course of every marriage physical appearances change, but this hardly means that love and attraction need fade. We love the other person for who they are, not simply for their body. Although the body ages, it still expresses that personal identity that first won our heart. Even if others can no longer see the beauty of that identity, a spouse continues to see it with the eyes of love and so his or her affection does not diminish. He or she reaffirms the decision to belong to the other and expresses that choice in faithful and loving closeness. The nobility of this decision, by its intensity and depth, gives rise to a new kind of emotion as they fulfill their marital mission. For "emotion, caused by another human being as a person . . . does not *per se* tend toward the conjugal act."[174] It finds other sensible expressions. Indeed, love "is a single reality, but with different dimensions; at different times, one or other dimension may emerge more clearly."[175] The marriage bond finds new forms of expression and constantly seeks new ways to grow in strength. These both preserve and strengthen the bond. They call for daily effort. None of this, however, is possible without praying to the Holy Spirit for an outpouring of his grace, his supernatural strength and his spiritual fire, to confirm, direct, and transform our love in every new situation.

CHAPTER FIVE

LOVE MADE FRUITFUL

165. Love always gives life. Conjugal love "does not end with the couple. . . . The couple, in giving themselves to one another, give not just themselves but also the reality of children, who are a living reflection of their love, a permanent sign of their conjugal unity and a living and inseparable synthesis of their being a father and a mother."[176]

Welcoming a new life

166. The family is the setting in which a new life is not only born but also welcomed as a gift of God. Each new life "allows us to appreciate the utterly gratuitous dimension of love, which never ceases to amaze us. It is the beauty of being loved first: children are loved even before they arrive."[177] Here we see a reflection of the primacy of the love of God, who always takes the initiative, for children "are loved before having done anything to deserve it."[178] And yet, "from the first moments of their lives, many children are rejected, abandoned, and robbed of their childhood and future. There are those who dare to say, as if to justify themselves, that it was a mistake to bring these children into the world. This is shameful! . . . How can we issue solemn declarations on human rights and the rights of children, if we then punish children for the errors of adults?"[179] If a child comes into this world in unwanted circumstances, the parents and other members of the family must do everything possible to accept that child as a gift from God and assume the responsibility of accepting him or her with openness and affection. For "when speaking of children who come into the world, no sacrifice made by adults will be considered too costly or too great, if it means the child never has to feel that he or she is a mistake, or worthless or abandoned to the four winds and the arrogance of man."[180] The gift of a new child, entrusted by the Lord to a father and a mother, begins with acceptance, continues with lifelong protection, and has as its final goal the joy of eternal life. By serenely contemplating the ultimate fulfillment of each human person,

parents will be even more aware of the precious gift entrusted to them. For God allows parents to choose the name by which he himself will call their child for all eternity.[181]

167. Large families are a joy for the Church. They are an expression of the fruitfulness of love. At the same time, Saint John Paul II rightly explained that responsible parenthood does not mean "unlimited procreation or lack of awareness of what is involved in rearing children, but rather the empowerment of couples to use their inviolable liberty wisely and responsibly, taking into account social and demographic realities, as well as their own situation and legitimate desires."[182]

Love and pregnancy

168. Pregnancy is a difficult but wonderful time. A mother joins with God to bring forth the miracle of a new life. Motherhood is the fruit of a "particular creative potential of the female body, directed to the conception and birth of a new human being."[183] Each woman shares in "the mystery of creation, which is renewed with each birth."[184] The Psalmist says: "You knit me together in my mother's womb" (Ps 139:13). Every child growing within the mother's womb is part of the eternal loving plan of God the Father: "Before I formed you in the womb I knew you, and before you were born I consecrated you" (Jer 1:5). Each child has a place in God's heart from all eternity; once he or she is conceived, the Creator's eternal dream comes true. Let us pause to think of the great value of that embryo from the moment of conception. We need to see it with the eyes of God, who always looks beyond mere appearances.

169. A pregnant woman can participate in God's plan by dreaming of her child. "For nine months every mother and father dreams about their child. . . . You can't have a family without dreams. Once a family loses the ability to dream, children do not grow, love does not grow, life shrivels up and dies."[185] For Christian married couples, baptism necessarily appears as a part of that dream. With their prayers, parents prepare for baptism, entrusting their baby to Jesus even before he or she is born.

170. Scientific advances today allow us to know beforehand what color a child's hair will be or what illnesses they may one day suffer, because all the somatic traits of the person are written in his or her genetic code already in the embryonic stage. Yet only the Father, the Creator, fully knows the child; he alone knows his or her deepest identity and worth. Expectant mothers need to ask God for the wisdom fully to know their children and to accept them as they are. Some parents feel that their child is not coming at the best time. They should ask the Lord to heal and strengthen them to accept their child fully and wholeheartedly. It is important for that child to feel wanted. He or she is not an accessory or a solution to some personal need. A child is a human being of immense worth and may never be used for one's own benefit. So it matters little whether this new life is convenient for you, whether it has features that please you, or whether it fits into your plans and aspirations. For "children are a gift. Each one is unique and irreplaceable. . . . We love our children because they are children, not because they are beautiful, or look or think as we do, or embody our dreams. We love them because they are children. A child is a child."[186] The love of parents is the means by which God our Father shows his own love. He awaits the birth of each child, accepts that child unconditionally, and welcomes him or her freely.

171. With great affection I urge all future mothers: keep happy and let nothing rob you of the interior joy of motherhood. Your child deserves your happiness. Don't let fears, worries, other people's comments or problems lessen your joy at being God's means of bringing a new life to the world. Prepare yourself for the birth of your child, but without obsessing, and join in Mary's song of joy: "My soul proclaims the greatness of the Lord and my spirit exults in God my Savior, for he has looked with favor on the lowliness of his servant" (Lk 1:46–48). Try to experience this serene excitement amid all your many concerns, and ask the Lord to preserve your joy, so that you can pass it on to your child.

The love of a mother and a father

172. "Children, once born, begin to receive, along with nourishment and care, the spiritual gift of knowing with certainty that they are loved.

This love is shown to them through the gift of their personal name, the sharing of language, looks of love, and the brightness of a smile. In this way, they learn that the beauty of human relationships touches our soul, seeks our freedom, accepts the difference of others, recognizes and respects them as a partner in dialogue. . . . Such is love, and it contains a spark of God's love!"[187] Every child has a right to receive love from a mother and a father; both are necessary for a child's integral and harmonious development. As the Australian bishops have observed, each of the spouses "contributes in a distinct way to the upbringing of a child. Respecting a child's dignity means affirming his or her need and natural right to have a mother and a father."[188] We are speaking not simply of the love of father and mother as individuals, but also of their mutual love, perceived as the source of one's life and the solid foundation of the family. Without this, a child could become a mere plaything. Husband and wife, father and mother, both "cooperate with the love of God the Creator, and are, in a certain sense, his interpreters."[189] They show their children the maternal and paternal face of the Lord. Together they teach the value of reciprocity, of respect for differences, and of being able to give and take. If for some inevitable reason one parent should be lacking, it is important to compensate for this loss, for the sake of the child's healthy growth to maturity.

173. The sense of being orphaned that affects many children and young people today is much deeper than we think. Nowadays we acknowledge as legitimate and indeed desirable that women wish to study, work, develop their skills, and have personal goals. At the same time, we cannot ignore the need that children have for a mother's presence, especially in the first months of life. Indeed, "the woman stands before the man as a mother, the subject of the new human life that is conceived and develops in her, and from her is born into the world."[190] The weakening of this maternal presence with its feminine qualities poses a grave risk to our world. I certainly value feminism, but one that does not demand uniformity or negate motherhood. For the grandeur of women includes all the rights derived from their inalienable human dignity but also from their feminine genius, which is essential to society. Their specifically

feminine abilities—motherhood in particular—also grant duties, because womanhood also entails a specific mission in this world, a mission that society needs to protect and preserve for the good of all.[191]

174. "Mothers are the strongest antidote to the spread of self-centered individualism. . . . It is they who testify to the beauty of life."[192] Certainly, "a society without mothers would be dehumanized, for mothers are always, even in the worst of times, witnesses to tenderness, dedication, and moral strength. Mothers often communicate the deepest meaning of religious practice in the first prayers and acts of devotion that their children learn. . . . Without mothers, not only would there be no new faithful, but the faith itself would lose a good part of its simple and profound warmth. . . . Dear mothers: thank you! Thank you for what you are in your family and for what you give to the Church and the world."[193]

175. A mother who watches over her child with tenderness and compassion helps him or her to grow in confidence and to experience that the world is a good and welcoming place. This helps the child to grow in self-esteem and, in turn, to develop a capacity for intimacy and empathy. A father, for his part, helps the child to perceive the limits of life, to be open to the challenges of the wider world, and to see the need for hard work and strenuous effort. A father possessed of a clear and serene masculine identity who demonstrates affection and concern for his wife is just as necessary as a caring mother. There can be a certain flexibility of roles and responsibilities, depending on the concrete circumstances of each particular family. But the clear and well-defined presence of both figures, female and male, creates the environment best suited to the growth of the child.

176. We often hear that ours is "a society without fathers." In Western culture, the father figure is said to be symbolically absent, missing, or vanished. Manhood itself seems to be called into question. The result has been an understandable confusion. "At first, this was perceived as a liberation: liberation from the father as master, from the father as the representative of a law imposed from without, from the father as the arbiter of his children's happiness and an obstacle to the emancipation

and autonomy of young people. In some homes authoritarianism once reigned and, at times, even oppression."[194] Yet, "as often happens, one goes from one extreme to the other. In our day, the problem no longer seems to be the overbearing presence of the father so much as his absence, his not being there. Fathers are often so caught up in themselves and their work, and at times in their own self-fulfillment, that they neglect their families. They leave the little ones and the young to themselves."[195] The presence of the father, and hence his authority, is also impacted by the amount of time given over to the communications and entertainment media. Nowadays authority is often considered suspect and adults treated with impertinence. They themselves become uncertain and so fail to offer sure and solid guidance to their children. A reversal of the roles of parents and children is unhealthy, since it hinders the proper process of development that children need to experience, and it denies them the love and guidance needed to mature.[196]

177. God sets the father in the family so that by the gifts of his masculinity he can be "close to his wife and share everything, joy and sorrow, hope and hardship. And to be close to his children as they grow—when they play and when they work, when they are carefree and when they are distressed, when they are talkative and when they are silent, when they are daring and when they are afraid, when they stray and when they get back on the right path. To be a father who is always present. When I say 'present,' I do not mean 'controlling.' Fathers who are too controlling overshadow their children, they don't let them develop."[197] Some fathers feel they are useless or unnecessary, but the fact is that "children need to find a father waiting for them when they return home with their problems. They may try hard not to admit it, not to show it, but they need it."[198] It is not good for children to lack a father and to grow up before they are ready.

An expanding fruitfulness

178. Some couples are unable to have children. We know that this can be a cause of real suffering for them. At the same time, we know that "marriage was not instituted solely for the procreation of children. . . .

Even in cases where, despite the intense desire of the spouses, there are no children, marriage still retains its character of being a whole manner and communion of life, and preserves its value and indissolubility."[199] So too, "motherhood is not a solely biological reality, but is expressed in diverse ways."[200]

179. Adoption is a very generous way to become parents. I encourage those who cannot have children to expand their marital love to embrace those who lack a proper family situation. They will never regret having been generous. Adopting a child is an act of love, offering the gift of a family to someone who has none. It is important to insist that legislation help facilitate the adoption process, above all in the case of unwanted children, in order to prevent their abortion or abandonment. Those who accept the challenge of adopting and accepting someone unconditionally and gratuitously become channels of God's love. For he says, "Even if your mother forgets you, I will not forget you" (Is 49:15).

180. "The choice of adoption and foster care expresses a particular kind of fruitfulness in the marriage experience, and not only in cases of infertility. In the light of those situations where a child is desired at any cost, as a right for one's self-fulfillment, adoption and foster care, correctly understood, manifest an important aspect of parenting and the raising of children. They make people aware that children, whether natural, adoptive, or taken in foster care, are persons in their own right who need to be accepted, loved and cared for, and not just brought into this world. The best interests of the child should always underlie any decision in adoption and foster care."[201] On the other hand, "the trafficking of children between countries and continents needs to be prevented by appropriate legislative action and state control."[202]

181. We also do well to remember that procreation and adoption are not the only ways of experiencing the fruitfulness of love. Even large families are called to make their mark on society, finding other expressions of fruitfulness that in some way prolong the love that sustains them. Christian families should never forget that "faith does not remove us from the world, but draws us more deeply into it. . . . Each of us, in fact,

has a special role in preparing for the coming of God's kingdom in our world."[203] Families should not see themselves as a refuge from society, but instead go forth from their homes in a spirit of solidarity with others. In this way, they become a hub for integrating persons into society and a point of contact between the public and private spheres. Married couples should have a clear awareness of their social obligations. With this, their affection does not diminish but is flooded with new light. As the poet says:

> Your hands are my caress,
> The harmony that fills my days.
> I love you because your hands
> Work for justice.
>
> If I love you, it is because you are
> My love, my companion and my all,
> And on the street, side by side,
> We are much more than just two.[204]

182. No family can be fruitful if it sees itself as overly different or "set apart." To avoid this risk, we should remember that Jesus' own family, so full of grace and wisdom, did not appear unusual or different from others. That is why people found it hard to acknowledge Jesus' wisdom: "Where did this man get all this? Is not this the carpenter, the son of Mary?" (Mk 6:2–3). "Is this not the carpenter's son?" (Mt 13:55). These questions make it clear that theirs was an ordinary family, close to others, a normal part of the community. Jesus did not grow up in a narrow and stifling relationship with Mary and Joseph, but readily interacted with the wider family, the relatives of his parents and their friends. This explains how, on returning from Jerusalem, Mary and Joseph could imagine for a whole day that the twelve-year-old Jesus was somewhere in the caravan, listening to people's stories and sharing their concerns: "Supposing him to be in the group of travelers, they went a day's journey" (Lk 2:44). Still, some Christian families, whether because of the language they use, the way they act or treat others, or their constant harping on the same two or three issues, end up being seen as remote and not really

a part of the community. Even their relatives feel looked down upon or judged by them.

183. A married couple who experience the power of love know that this love is called to bind the wounds of the outcast, to foster a culture of encounter, and to fight for justice. God has given the family the job of "domesticating" the world[205] and helping each person to see fellow human beings as brothers and sisters. "An attentive look at the everyday life of today's men and women immediately shows the omnipresent need for a healthy injection of family spirit. . . . Not only is the organization of ordinary life increasingly thwarted by a bureaucracy completely removed from fundamental human bonds, but even social and political mores show signs of degradation."[206] For their part, open and caring families find a place for the poor and build friendships with those less fortunate than themselves. In their efforts to live according to the Gospel, they are mindful of Jesus' words: "As you did it to one of the least of these my brethren, you did it to me" (Mt 25:40). In a very real way, their lives express what is asked of us all: "When you give a dinner or a banquet, do not invite your friends or your brothers or your kinsmen or rich neighbors, lest they also invite you in return, and you be repaid. But when you give a feast, invite the poor, the maimed, the lame, the blind, and you will be blessed" (Lk 14:12–14). You will be blessed! Here is the secret to a happy family.

184. By their witness as well as their words, families speak to others of Jesus. They pass on the faith, they arouse a desire for God and they reflect the beauty of the Gospel and its way of life. Christian marriages thus enliven society by their witness of fraternity, their social concern, their outspokenness on behalf of the underprivileged, their luminous faith, and their active hope. Their fruitfulness expands and in countless ways makes God's love present in society.

Discerning the body

185. Along these same lines, we do well to take seriously a biblical text usually interpreted outside of its context or in a generic sense, with the risk of overlooking its immediate and direct meaning, which is markedly

social. I am speaking of 1 Corinthians 11:17–34, where Saint Paul faces a shameful situation in the community. The wealthier members tended to discriminate against the poorer ones, and this carried over even to the *agape* meal that accompanied the celebration of the Eucharist. While the rich enjoyed their food, the poor looked on and went hungry: "One is hungry and another is drunk. Do you not have houses to eat and drink in? Or do you despise the Church of God and humiliate those who have nothing?" (vv. 21–22).

186. The Eucharist demands that we be members of the one body of the Church. Those who approach the Body and Blood of Christ may not wound that same Body by creating scandalous distinctions and divisions among its members. This is what it means to "discern" the body of the Lord, to acknowledge it with faith and charity both in the sacramental signs and in the community; those who fail to do so eat and drink judgment against themselves (cf. v. 29). The celebration of the Eucharist thus becomes a constant summons for everyone "to examine himself or herself" (v. 28), to open the doors of the family to greater fellowship with the underprivileged, and in this way to receive the sacrament of that eucharistic love which makes us one body. We must not forget that "the 'mysticism' of the sacrament has a social character."[207] When those who receive it turn a blind eye to the poor and suffering, or consent to various forms of division, contempt, and inequality, the Eucharist is received unworthily. On the other hand, families who are properly disposed and receive the Eucharist regularly, reinforce their desire for fraternity, their social consciousness, and their commitment to those in need.

Life in the wider family

187. The nuclear family needs to interact with the wider family made up of parents, aunts and uncles, cousins, and even neighbors. This greater family may have members who require assistance, or at least companionship and affection, or consolation amid suffering.[208] The individualism so prevalent today can lead to creating small nests of security, where others are perceived as bothersome or a threat. Such isolation, however, cannot

offer greater peace or happiness; rather, it straitens the heart of a family and makes its life all the more narrow.

Being sons and daughters

188. First, let us think of our parents. Jesus told the Pharisees that abandoning one's parents is contrary to God's law (cf. Mk 7:8–13). We do well to remember that each of us is a son or daughter. "Even if one becomes an adult, or an elderly person, even if one becomes a parent, if one occupies a position of responsibility, underneath all of this is still the identity of a child. We are all sons and daughters. And this always brings us back to the fact that we did not give ourselves life but that we received it. The great gift of life is the first gift that we received."[209]

189. Hence, "the fourth commandment asks children . . . to honor their father and mother (cf. Ex 20:12). This commandment comes immediately after those dealing with God himself. Indeed, it has to do with something sacred, something divine, something at the basis of every other kind of human respect. The biblical formulation of the fourth commandment goes on to say: 'that your days may be long in the land which the Lord your God gives you.' The virtuous bond between generations is the guarantee of the future, and is the guarantee of a truly humane society. A society with children who do not honor parents is a society without honor. . . . It is a society destined to be filled with surly and greedy young people."[210]

190. There is, however, another side to the coin. As the word of God tells us, "a man leaves his father and his mother" (Gn 2:24). This does not always happen, and a marriage is hampered by the failure to make this necessary sacrifice and surrender. Parents must not be abandoned or ignored, but marriage itself demands that they be "left," so that the new home will be a true hearth, a place of security, hope, and future plans, and the couple can truly become "one flesh" (ibid.). In some marriages, one spouse keeps secrets from the other, confiding them instead to his or her parents. As a result, the opinions of their parents become more important than the feelings and opinions of their spouse. This situation cannot go on for long, and even if it takes time, both spouses need to

make the effort to grow in trust and communication. Marriage challenges husbands and wives to find new ways of being sons and daughters.

The elderly

191. "Do not cast me off in the time of old age; forsake me not when my strength is spent" (Ps 71:9). This is the plea of the elderly, who fear being forgotten and rejected. Just as God asks us to be his means of hearing the cry of the poor, so too he wants us to hear the cry of the elderly.[211] This represents a challenge to families and communities, since "the Church cannot and does not want to conform to a mentality of impatience, and much less of indifference and contempt, toward old age. We must reawaken the collective sense of gratitude, of appreciation, of hospitality, which makes the elderly feel like a living part of the community. Our elderly are men and women, fathers and mothers, who came before us on our own road, in our own house, in our daily battle for a worthy life."[212] Indeed, "how I would like a Church that challenges the throw-away culture by the overflowing joy of a new embrace between young and old!"[213]

192. Saint John Paul II asked us to be attentive to the role of the elderly in our families, because there are cultures which, "especially in the wake of disordered industrial and urban development, have both in the past and in the present set the elderly aside in unacceptable ways."[214] The elderly help us to appreciate "the continuity of the generations," by their "charism of bridging the gap."[215] Very often it is grandparents who ensure that the most important values are passed down to their grandchildren, and "many people can testify that they owe their initiation into the Christian life to their grandparents."[216] Their words, their affection, or simply their presence help children to realize that history did not begin with them, that they are now part of an age-old pilgrimage, and that they need to respect all that came before them. Those who would break all ties with the past will surely find it difficult to build stable relationships and to realize that reality is bigger than they are. "Attention to the elderly makes the difference in a society. Does a society show concern for the

elderly? Does it make room for the elderly? Such a society will move forward if it respects the wisdom of the elderly."[217]

193. The lack of historical memory is a serious shortcoming in our society. A mentality that can only say, "Then was then, now is now," is ultimately immature. Knowing and judging past events is the only way to build a meaningful future. Memory is necessary for growth: "Recall the former days" (Heb 10:32). Listening to the elderly tell their stories is good for children and young people; it makes them feel connected to the living history of their families, their neighborhoods, and their country. A family that fails to respect and cherish its grandparents, who are its living memory, is already in decline, whereas a family that remembers has a future. "A society that has no room for the elderly or discards them because they create problems, has a deadly virus";[218] "it is torn from its roots."[219] Our contemporary experience of being orphans as a result of cultural discontinuity, uprootedness, and the collapse of the certainties that shape our lives, challenges us to make our families places where children can sink roots in the rich soil of a collective history.

Being brothers and sisters

194. Relationships between brothers and sisters deepen with the passing of time, and "the bond of fraternity that forms in the family between children, if consolidated by an educational atmosphere of openness to others, is a great school of freedom and peace. In the family, we learn how to live as one. Perhaps we do not always think about this, but the family itself introduces fraternity into the world. From this initial experience of fraternity, nourished by affection and education at home, the style of fraternity radiates like a promise upon the whole of society."[220]

195. Growing up with brothers and sisters makes for a beautiful experience of caring for and helping one another. For "fraternity in families is especially radiant when we see the care, the patience, the affection that surround the little brother or sister who is frail, sick, or disabled."[221] It must be acknowledged that "having a brother or a sister who loves you is a profound, precious, and unique experience."[222] Children do need to be patiently taught to treat one another as brothers and sisters. This

training, at times quite demanding, is a true school of socialization. In some countries, where it has become quite common to have only one child, the experience of being a brother or sister is less and less common. When it has been possible to have only one child, ways have to be found to ensure that he or she does not grow up alone or isolated.

A big heart

196. In addition to the small circle of the couple and their children, there is the larger family, which cannot be overlooked. Indeed, "the love between husband and wife and, in a derivative and broader way, the love between members of the same family—between parents and children, brothers and sisters, and relatives and members of the household—is given life and sustenance by an unceasing inner dynamism leading the family to ever deeper and more intense communion, which is the foundation and soul of the community of marriage and the family."[223] Friends and other families are part of this larger family, as well as communities of families who support one another in their difficulties, their social commitments, and their faith.

197. This larger family should provide love and support to teenage mothers, children without parents, single mothers left to raise children, persons with disabilities needing particular affection and closeness, young people struggling with addiction, the unmarried, separated, or widowed who are alone, and the elderly and infirm who lack the support of their children. It should also embrace "even those who have made shipwreck of their lives."[224] This wider family can help make up for the shortcomings of parents, detect and report possible situations in which children suffer violence and even abuse, and provide wholesome love and family stability in cases when parents prove incapable of this.

198. Finally, we cannot forget that this larger family includes fathers-in-law, mothers-in-law, and all the relatives of the couple. One particularly delicate aspect of love is learning not to view these relatives as somehow competitors, threats, or intruders. The conjugal union demands respect for their traditions and customs, an effort to understand their language and to refrain from criticism, caring for them and cherishing them while

maintaining the legitimate privacy and independence of the couple. Being willing to do so is also an exquisite expression of generous love for one's spouse.

CHAPTER SIX

SOME PASTORAL PERSPECTIVES

199. The dialogue that took place during the Synod raised the need for new pastoral methods. I will attempt to mention some of these in a very general way. Different communities will have to devise more practical and effective initiatives that respect both the Church's teaching and local problems and needs. Without claiming to present a pastoral plan for the family, I would now like to reflect on some more significant pastoral challenges.

Proclaiming the Gospel of the family today

200. The Synod Fathers emphasized that Christian families, by the grace of the sacrament of Matrimony, are the principal agents of the family apostolate, above all through "their joy-filled witness as domestic churches."[225] Consequently, "it is important that people experience the Gospel of the family as a joy that 'fills hearts and lives,' because in Christ we have been 'set free from sin, sorrow, inner emptiness, and loneliness' (*Evangelii Gaudium*, 1). As in the parable of the sower (cf. Mt 13:3–9), we are called to help sow seeds; the rest is God's work. Nor must we forget that, in her teaching on the family, the Church is a sign of contradiction."[226] Married couples are grateful that their pastors uphold the high ideal of a love that is strong, solid, enduring, and capable of sustaining them through whatever trials they may have to face. The Church wishes, with humility and compassion, to reach out to families and "to help each family to discover the best way to overcome any obstacles it encounters."[227] It is not enough to show generic concern for the family in pastoral planning. Enabling families to take up their role as active agents of the family apostolate calls for "an effort at evangelization and catechesis inside the family."[228]

201. "This effort calls for missionary conversion by everyone in the Church, that is, one that is not content to proclaim a merely theoretical message without connection to people's real problems."[229] Pastoral

care for families "needs to make it clear that the Gospel of the family responds to the deepest expectations of the human person: a response to each one's dignity and fulfillment in reciprocity, communion, and fruitfulness. This consists not merely in presenting a set of rules, but in proposing values that are clearly needed today, even in the most secularized of countries."[230] The Synod Fathers also "highlighted the fact that evangelization needs unambiguously to denounce cultural, social, political, and economic factors—such as the excessive importance given to market logic—that prevent authentic family life and lead to discrimination, poverty, exclusion, and violence. Consequently, dialogue and cooperation need to be fostered with societal structures and encouragement given to lay people who are involved, as Christians, in the cultural and socio-political fields."[231]

202. "The main contribution to the pastoral care of families is offered by the parish, which is the family of families, where small communities, ecclesial movements, and associations live in harmony."[232] Along with a pastoral outreach aimed specifically at families, this shows the need for "a more adequate formation . . . of priests, deacons, men and women religious, catechists, and other pastoral workers."[233] In the replies given to the worldwide consultation, it became clear that ordained ministers often lack the training needed to deal with the complex problems currently facing families. The experience of the broad oriental tradition of a married clergy could also be drawn upon.

203. Seminarians should receive a more extensive interdisciplinary, and not merely doctrinal, formation in the areas of engagement and marriage. Their training does not always allow them to explore their own psychological and affective background and experiences. Some come from troubled families, with absent parents and a lack of emotional stability. There is a need to ensure that the formation process can enable them to attain the maturity and psychological balance needed for their future ministry. Family bonds are essential for reinforcing healthy self-esteem. It is important for families to be part of the seminary process and priestly life, since they help to reaffirm these and to keep them well grounded in reality. It is helpful for seminarians to combine time in the seminary

with time spent in parishes. There they can have greater contact with the concrete realities of family life, since in their future ministry they will largely be dealing with families. "The presence of lay people, families, and especially the presence of women in priestly formation, promotes an appreciation of the diversity and complementarity of the different vocations in the Church."[234]

204. The response to the consultation also insisted on the need for training lay leaders who can assist in the pastoral care of families, with the help of teachers and counselors, family and community physicians, social workers, juvenile and family advocates, and drawing upon the contributions of psychology, sociology, marital therapy, and counseling. Professionals, especially those with practical experience, help keep pastoral initiatives grounded in the real situations and concrete concerns of families. "Courses and programs, planned specifically for pastoral workers, can be of assistance by integrating the premarital preparation program into the broader dynamic of ecclesial life."[235] Good pastoral training is important "especially in light of particular emergency situations arising from cases of domestic violence and sexual abuse."[236] All this in no way diminishes, but rather complements, the fundamental value of spiritual direction, the rich spiritual treasures of the Church, and the sacramental Reconciliation.

Preparing engaged couples for marriage

205. The Synod Fathers stated in a number of ways that we need to help young people discover the dignity and beauty of marriage.[237] They should be helped to perceive the attraction of a complete union that elevates and perfects the social dimension of existence, gives sexuality its deepest meaning, and benefits children by offering them the best context for their growth and development.

206. "The complexity of today's society and the challenges faced by the family require a greater effort on the part of the whole Christian community in preparing those who are about to be married. The importance of the virtues needs to be included. Among these, chastity proves invaluable for the genuine growth of love between persons. In this regard,

the Synod Fathers agreed on the need to involve the entire community more extensively by stressing the witness of families themselves and by grounding marriage preparation in the process of Christian initiation by bringing out the connection between marriage, baptism, and the other sacraments. The Fathers also spoke of the need for specific programs of marriage preparation aimed at giving couples a genuine experience of participation in ecclesial life and a complete introduction to various aspects of family life."[238]

207. I encourage Christian communities to recognize the great benefit that they themselves receive from supporting engaged couples as they grow in love. As the Italian bishops have observed, those couples are "a valuable resource because, as they sincerely commit themselves to grow in love and self-giving, they can help renew the fabric of the whole ecclesial body. Their special form of friendship can prove contagious and foster the growth of friendship and fraternity in the Christian community of which they are a part."[239] There are a number of legitimate ways to structure programs of marriage preparation, and each local Church will discern how best to provide a suitable formation without distancing young people from the sacrament. They do not need to be taught the entire *Catechism* or overwhelmed with too much information. Here too, "it is not great knowledge, but rather the ability to feel and relish things interiorly that contents and satisfies the soul."[240] Quality is more important than quantity, and priority should be given—along with a renewed proclamation of the kerygma—to an attractive and helpful presentation of information that can help couples to live the rest of their lives together "with great courage and generosity."[241] Marriage preparation should be a kind of "initiation" to the sacrament of Matrimony, providing couples with the help they need to receive the sacrament worthily and to make a solid beginning of life as a family.

208. With the help of missionary families, the couple's own families, and a variety of pastoral resources, ways should also be found to offer a remote preparation that, by example and good advice, can help their love to grow and mature. Discussion groups and optional talks on a variety of topics of genuine interest to young people can also prove helpful. All

the same, some individual meetings remain essential, since the primary objective is to help each to learn how to love this very real person with whom he or she plans to share his or her whole life. Learning to love someone does not happen automatically, nor can it be taught in a workshop just prior to the celebration of marriage. For every couple, marriage preparation begins at birth. What they received from their family should prepare them to know themselves and to make a full and definitive commitment. Those best prepared for marriage are probably those who learned what Christian marriage is from their own parents, who chose each other unconditionally and daily renew this decision. In this sense, pastoral initiatives aimed at helping married couples to grow in love and in the Gospel of the family also help their children, by preparing them for their future married life. Nor should we underestimate the pastoral value of traditional religious practices. To give just one example: I think of Saint Valentine's Day; in some countries, commercial interests are quicker to see the potential of this celebration than are we in the Church.

209. The timely preparation of engaged couples by the parish community should also assist them to recognize eventual problems and risks. In this way, they can come to realize the wisdom of breaking off a relationship whose failure and painful aftermath can be foreseen. In their initial enchantment with one another, couples can attempt to conceal or relativize certain things and to avoid disagreements; only later do problems surface. For this reason, they should be strongly encouraged to discuss what each expects from marriage, what they understand by love and commitment, what each wants from the other, and what kind of life they would like to build together. Such discussions would help them to see if they in fact have little in common and to realize that mutual attraction alone will not suffice to keep them together. Nothing is more volatile, precarious, and unpredictable than desire. The decision to marry should never be encouraged unless the couple has discerned deeper reasons that will ensure a genuine and stable commitment.

210. In any event, if one partner clearly recognizes the other's weak points, he or she needs to have a realistic trust in the possibility of helping to develop the good points that counterbalance them, and in this way

to foster their human growth. This entails a willingness to face eventual sacrifices, problems, and situations of conflict; it demands a firm resolve to be ready for this. Couples need to be able to detect danger signals in their relationship and to find, before the wedding, effective ways of responding to them. Sadly, many couples marry without really knowing one another. They have enjoyed each other's company and done things together, but without facing the challenge of revealing themselves and coming to know who the other person truly is.

211. Both short-term and long-term marriage preparation should ensure that the couple do not view the wedding ceremony as the end of the road, but instead embark upon marriage as a lifelong calling based on a firm and realistic decision to face all trials and difficult moments together. The pastoral care of engaged and married couples should be centered on the marriage bond, assisting couples not only to deepen their love but also to overcome problems and difficulties. This involves not only helping them to accept the Church's teaching and to have recourse to her valuable resources, but also offering practical programs, sound advice, proven strategies, and psychological guidance. All this calls for a pedagogy of love, attuned to the feelings and needs of young people and capable of helping them to grow interiorly. Marriage preparation should also provide couples with the names of places, people, and services to which they can turn for help when problems arise. It is also important to remind them of the availability of the sacrament of Reconciliation, which allows them to bring their sins and past mistakes, and their relationship itself, before God, and to receive in turn his merciful forgiveness and healing strength.

The preparation of the celebration

212. Short-term preparations for marriage tend to be concentrated on invitations, clothes, the party, and any number of other details that tend to drain not only the budget but energy and joy as well. The spouses come to the wedding ceremony exhausted and harried, rather than focused and ready for the great step that they are about to take. The same kind of preoccupation with a big celebration also affects certain *de facto*

unions; because of the expenses involved, the couple, instead of being concerned above all with their love and solemnizing it in the presence of others, never get married. Here let me say a word to fiancés. Have the courage to be different. Don't let yourselves get swallowed up by a society of consumption and empty appearances. What is important is the love you share, strengthened and sanctified by grace. You are capable of opting for a more modest and simple celebration in which love takes precedence over everything else. Pastoral workers and the entire community can help make this priority the norm rather than the exception.

213. In their preparation for marriage, the couple should be encouraged to make the liturgical celebration a profound personal experience and to appreciate the meaning of each of its signs. In the case of two baptized persons, the commitment expressed by the words of consent and the bodily union that consummates the marriage can only be seen as signs of the covenantal love and union between the incarnate Son of God and his Church. In the baptized, words and signs become an eloquent language of faith. The body, created with a God-given meaning, "becomes the language of the ministers of the sacrament, aware that in the conjugal pact there is expressed and realized the mystery that has its origin in God himself."[242]

214. At times, the couple does not grasp the theological and spiritual import of the words of consent, which illuminate the meaning of all the signs that follow. It needs to be stressed that these words cannot be reduced to the present; they involve a totality that includes the future: "until death do us part." The content of the words of consent makes it clear that "freedom and fidelity are not opposed to one another; rather, they are mutually supportive, both in interpersonal and social relationships. Indeed, let us consider the damage caused, in our culture of global communication, by the escalation of unkept promises. . . . Honoring one's word, fidelity to one's promises: these are things that cannot be bought and sold. They cannot be compelled by force or maintained without sacrifice."[243]

215. The Kenyan bishops have observed that "many [young people] concentrate on their wedding day and forget the lifelong commitment they are about to enter into."[244] They need to be encouraged to see the sacrament not as a single moment that then becomes a part of the past and its memories, but rather as a reality that permanently influences the whole of married life.[245] The procreative meaning of sexuality, the language of the body, and the signs of love shown throughout married life, all become an "uninterrupted continuity of liturgical language" and "conjugal life becomes in a certain sense liturgical."[246]

216. The couple can also meditate on the biblical readings and the meaningfulness of the rings they will exchange and the other signs that are part of the rite. Nor would it be good for them to arrive at the wedding without ever having prayed together, one for the other, to seek God's help in remaining faithful and generous, to ask the Lord together what he wants of them, and to consecrate their love before an image of the Virgin Mary. Those who help prepare them for marriage should help them experience these moments of prayer that can prove so beneficial. "The marriage liturgy is a unique event, which is both a family and a community celebration. The first signs of Jesus were performed at the wedding feast of Cana. The good wine, resulting from the Lord's miracle that brought joy to the beginning of a new family, is the new wine of Christ's covenant with the men and women of every age. . . . Frequently, the celebrant speaks to a congregation that includes people who seldom participate in the life of the Church, or who are members of other Christian denominations or religious communities. The occasion thus provides a valuable opportunity to proclaim the Gospel of Christ."[247]

Accompanying the first years of married life

217. It is important that marriage be seen as a matter of love, that only those who freely choose and love one another may marry. When love is merely physical attraction or a vague affection, spouses become particularly vulnerable once this affection wanes or physical attraction diminishes. Given the frequency with which this happens, it is all the more essential that couples be helped during the first years of their married

life to enrich and deepen their conscious and free decision to have, hold, and love one another for life. Often the engagement period is not long enough, the decision is precipitated for various reasons, and, what is even more problematic, the couple themselves are insufficiently mature. As a result, the newly married couple need to complete a process that should have taken place during their engagement.

218. Another great challenge of marriage preparation is to help couples realize that marriage is not something that happens once for all. Their union is real and irrevocable, confirmed and consecrated by the sacrament of Matrimony. Yet in joining their lives, the spouses assume an active and creative role in a lifelong project. Their gaze now has to be directed to the future that, with the help of God's grace, they are daily called to build. For this very reason, neither spouse can expect the other to be perfect. Each must set aside all illusions and accept the other as he or she actually is: an unfinished product, needing to grow, a work in progress. A persistently critical attitude toward one's partner is a sign that marriage was not entered into as a project to be worked on together, with patience, understanding, tolerance, and generosity. Slowly but surely, love will then give way to constant questioning and criticism, dwelling on each other's good and bad points, issuing ultimatums, and engaging in competition and self-justification. The couple then prove incapable of helping one another to build a mature union. This fact needs to be realistically presented to newly married couples from the outset, so that they can grasp that the wedding is "just the beginning." By saying "I do," they embark on a journey that requires them to overcome all obstacles standing in the way of their reaching the goal. The nuptial blessing that they receive is a grace and an incentive for this journey. They can only benefit from sitting down and talking to one another about how, concretely, they plan to achieve their goal.

219. I recall an old saying: still water becomes stagnant and good for nothing. If, in the first years of marriage, a couple's experience of love grows stagnant, it loses the very excitement that should be its propelling force. Young love needs to keep dancing toward the future with immense hope. Hope is the leaven that, in those first years of engagement and

marriage, makes it possible to look beyond arguments, conflicts, and problems and to see things in a broader perspective. It harnesses our uncertainties and concerns so that growth can take place. Hope also bids us live fully in the present, giving our all to the life of the family, for the best way to prepare a solid future is to live well in the present.

220. This process occurs in various stages that call for generosity and sacrifice. The first powerful feelings of attraction give way to the realization that the other is now a part of my life. The pleasure of belonging to one another leads to seeing life as a common project, putting the other's happiness ahead of my own, and realizing with joy that this marriage enriches society. As love matures, it also learns to "negotiate." Far from anything selfish or calculating, such negotiation is an exercise of mutual love, an interplay of give and take, for the good of the family. At each new stage of married life, there is a need to sit down and renegotiate agreements, so that there will be no winners and losers, but rather two winners. In the home, decisions cannot be made unilaterally, since each spouse shares responsibility for the family; yet each home is unique and each marriage will find an arrangement that works best.

221. Among the causes of broken marriages are unduly high expectations about conjugal life. Once it becomes apparent that the reality is more limited and challenging than one imagined, the solution is not to think quickly and irresponsibly about separation, but to come to the sober realization that married life is a process of growth, in which each spouse is God's means of helping the other to mature. Change, improvement, the flowering of the good qualities present in each person—all these are possible. Each marriage is a kind of "salvation history," which from fragile beginnings—thanks to God's gift and a creative and generous response on our part—grows over time into something precious and enduring. Might we say that the greatest mission of two people in love is to help one another become, respectively, more a man and more a woman? Fostering growth means helping a person to shape his or her own identity. Love is thus a kind of craftsmanship. When we read in the Bible about the creation of man and woman, we see God first forming Adam (cf. Gn 2:7); he realizes that something essential is lacking and so

he forms Eve and then hears the man exclaim in amazement, "Yes, this one is just right for me!" We can almost hear the amazing dialogue that must have taken place when the man and the woman first encountered one another. In the life of married couples, even at difficult moments, one person can always surprise the other, and new doors can open for their relationship, as if they were meeting for the first time. At every new stage, they can keep "forming" one another. Love makes each wait for the other with the patience of a craftsman, a patience which comes from God.

222. The pastoral care of newly married couples must also involve encouraging them to be generous in bestowing life. "In accord with the personal and fully human character of conjugal love, family planning fittingly takes place as the result a consensual dialogue between the spouses, respect for times and consideration of the dignity of the partner. In this sense, the teaching of the Encyclical *Humanae Vitae* (cf. 1014) and the Apostolic Exhortation *Familiaris Consortio* (cf. 14; 2835) ought to be taken up anew, in order to counter a mentality that is often hostile to life. . . . Decisions involving responsible parenthood presupposes the formation of conscience, which is 'the most secret core and sanctuary of a person. There each one is alone with God, whose voice echoes in the depths of the heart' (*Gaudium et Spes*, 16). The more the couple tries to listen in conscience to God and his commandments (cf. Rom 2:15), and is accompanied spiritually, the more their decision will be profoundly free of subjective caprice and accommodation to prevailing social mores."[248] The clear teaching of the Second Vatican Council still holds: "[The couple] will make decisions by common counsel and effort. Let them thoughtfully take into account both their own welfare and that of their children, those already born and those which the future may bring. For this accounting they need to reckon with both the material and the spiritual conditions of the times as well as of their state in life. Finally, they should consult the interests of the family group, of temporal society, and of the Church herself. The parents themselves and no one else should ultimately make this judgment in the sight of God."[249] Moreover, "the use of methods based on the 'laws of nature and the incidence of fertility' (*Humanae Vitae*, 11) are to be promoted, since 'these methods respect the

bodies of the spouses, encourage tenderness between them and favor the education of an authentic freedom' (*Catechism of the Catholic Church*, 2370). Greater emphasis needs to be placed on the fact that children are a wonderful gift from God and a joy for parents and the Church. Through them, the Lord renews the world."[250]

Some resources

223. The Synod Fathers observed that "the initial years of marriage are a vital and sensitive period during which couples become more aware of the challenges and meaning of married life. Consequently, pastoral accompaniment needs to go beyond the actual celebration of the sacrament (*Familiaris Consortio*, Part III). In this regard, experienced couples have an important role to play. The parish is a place where such experienced couples can help younger couples, with the eventual cooperation of associations, ecclesial movements, and new communities. Young couples need to be encouraged to be essentially open to the great gift of children. Emphasis should also be given to the importance of family spirituality, prayer, and participation in the Sunday Eucharist, and couples encouraged to meet regularly to promote growth in their spiritual life and solidarity in the concrete demands of life. Liturgies, devotional practices, and the Eucharist celebrated for families, especially on the wedding anniversary, were mentioned as vital factors in fostering evangelization through the family."[251]

224. This process takes time. Love needs time and space; everything else is secondary. Time is needed to talk things over, to embrace leisurely, to share plans, to listen to one other and gaze in each other's eyes, to appreciate one another, and to build a stronger relationship. Sometimes the frenetic pace of our society and the pressures of the workplace create problems. At other times, the problem is the lack of quality time together, sharing the same room without one even noticing the other. Pastoral workers and groups of married people should think of ways to help young or vulnerable couples to make the most of those moments, to be present to one another, even by sharing moments of meaningful silence.

225. Couples who have learned how to do this well can share some practical suggestions which they have found useful: planning free time together, moments of recreation with the children, different ways of celebrating important events, shared opportunities for spiritual growth. They can also provide resources that help young married couples to make those moments meaningful and loving, and thus to improve their communication. This is extremely important for the stage when the novelty of marriage has worn off. Once a couple no longer knows how to spend time together, one or both of them will end up taking refuge in gadgets, finding other commitments, seeking the embrace of another, or simply looking for ways to flee what has become an uncomfortable closeness.

226. Young married couples should be encouraged to develop a routine that gives a healthy sense of closeness and stability through shared daily rituals. These could include a morning kiss, an evening blessing, waiting at the door to welcome each other home, taking trips together, and sharing household chores. Yet it also helps to break the routine with a party, and to enjoy family celebrations of anniversaries and special events. We need these moments of cherishing God's gifts and renewing our zest for life. As long as we can celebrate, we are able to rekindle our love, to free it from monotony, and to color our daily routine with hope.

227. We pastors have to encourage families to grow in faith. This means encouraging frequent confession, spiritual direction, and occasional retreats. It also means encouraging family prayer during the week, since "the family that prays together stays together." When visiting our people's homes, we should gather all the members of the family and briefly pray for one another, placing the family in the Lord's hands. It is also helpful to encourage each of the spouses to find time for prayer alone with God, since each has his or her secret crosses to bear. Why shouldn't we tell God our troubles and ask him to grant us the healing and help we need to remain faithful? The Synod Fathers noted that "the word of God is the source of life and spirituality for the family. All pastoral work on behalf of the family must allow people to be interiorly fashioned and formed as members of the domestic church through the Church's prayerful reading of sacred Scripture. The word of God is not only good

news in a person's private life but also a criterion of judgment and a light in discerning the various challenges that married couples and families encounter."[252]

228. In some cases, one of the spouses is not baptized or does not want to practice the faith. This can make the other's desire to live and grow in the Christian life difficult and at times painful. Still, some common values can be found and these can be shared and relished. In any event, showing love for a spouse who is not a believer, bestowing happiness, soothing hurts, and sharing life together represents a true path of sanctification. Love is always a gift of God. Wherever it is poured out, it makes its transforming presence felt, often in mysterious ways, even to the point that "the unbelieving husband is consecrated through his wife, and the unbelieving wife is consecrated through her husband" (1 Cor 7:14).

229. Parishes, movements, schools, and other Church institutions can help in a variety of ways to support families and help them grow. These might include: meetings of couples living in the same neighborhood, brief retreats for couples, talks by experts on concrete issues facing families, marriage counseling, home missionaries who help couples discuss their difficulties and desires, social services dealing with family problems like addiction, infidelity, and domestic violence, programs of spiritual growth, workshops for parents with troubled children, and family meetings. The parish office should be prepared to deal helpfully and sensitively with family needs and be able to make referrals, when necessary, to those who can help. There is also the contribution made by groups of married couples that provide assistance as part of their commitment to service, prayer, formation, and mutual support. Such groups enable couples to be generous, to assist other families, and to share the faith; at the same time they strengthen marriages and help them to grow.

230. It is true that many couples, once married, drop out of the Christian community. Often, however, we ourselves do not take advantage of those occasions when they do return, to remind them of the beautiful ideal of Christian marriage and the support that our parishes can offer them. I think, for example, of the Baptism and First Holy Communion of their

children, or the funerals or weddings of their relatives or friends. Almost all married couples reappear on these occasions, and we should take greater advantage of this. Another way of growing closer is by blessing homes or by bringing a pilgrim image of Our Lady to houses in the neighborhood; this provides an opportunity for a pastoral conversation about the family's situation. It could also be helpful to ask older married couples to help younger couples in the neighborhood by visiting them and offering guidance in the early years of marriage. Given the pace of life today, most couples cannot attend frequent meetings; still, we cannot restrict our pastoral outreach to small and select groups. Nowadays, pastoral care for families has to be fundamentally missionary, going out to where people are. We can no longer be like a factory, churning out courses that for the most part are poorly attended.

Casting light on crises, worries, and difficulties

231. A word should also be said about those whose love, like a fine wine, has come into its own. Just as a good wine begins to "breathe" with time, so too the daily experience of fidelity gives married life richness and "body." Fidelity has to do with patience and expectation. Its joys and sacrifices bear fruit as the years go by and the couple rejoices to see their children's children. The love present from the beginning becomes more conscious, settled, and mature as the couple discover each other anew day after day, year after year. Saint John of the Cross tells us that "old lovers are tried and true." They "are outwardly no longer afire with powerful emotions and impulses, but now taste the sweetness of the wine of love, well-aged and stored deep within their hearts."[253] Such couples have successfully overcome crises and hardships without fleeing from challenges or concealing problems.

The challenge of crises

232. The life of every family is marked by all kinds of crises, yet these are also part of its dramatic beauty. Couples should be helped to realize that surmounting a crisis need not weaken their relationship; instead, it can improve, settle, and mature the wine of their union. Life together should

not diminish but increase their contentment; every new step along the way can help couples find new ways to happiness. Each crisis becomes an apprenticeship in growing closer together or learning a little more about what it means to be married. There is no need for couples to resign themselves to an inevitable downward spiral or a tolerable mediocrity. On the contrary, when marriage is seen as a challenge that involves overcoming obstacles, each crisis becomes an opportunity to let the wine of their relationship age and improve. Couples will gain from receiving help in facing crises, meeting challenges, and acknowledging them as part of family life. Experienced and trained couples should be open to offering guidance, so the couples will not be unnerved by these crises or tempted to hasty decisions. Each crisis has a lesson to teach us; we need to learn how to listen for it with the ear of the heart.

233. Faced with a crisis, we tend first to react defensively, since we feel that we are losing control, or are somehow at fault, and this makes us uneasy. We resort to denying the problem, hiding or downplaying it, and hoping that it will go away. But this does not help; it only makes things worse, wastes energy, and delays a solution. Couples grow apart and lose their ability to communicate. When problems are not dealt with, communication is the first thing to go. Little by little, the "the person I love" slowly becomes "my mate," then just "the father or mother of my children," and finally a stranger.

234. Crises need to be faced together. This is hard, since persons sometimes withdraw in order to avoid saying what they feel; they retreat into a craven silence. At these times, it becomes all the more important to create opportunities for speaking heart to heart. Unless a couple learns to do this, they will find it harder and harder as time passes. Communication is an art learned in moments of peace in order to be practiced in moments of difficulty. Spouses need help in discovering their deepest thoughts and feelings and expressing them. Like childbirth, this is a painful process that brings forth a new treasure. The answers given to the pre-synodal consultation showed that most people in difficult or critical situations do not seek pastoral assistance, since they do not find it sympathetic, realistic, or concerned for individual cases. This should spur us to try

to approach marriage crises with greater sensitivity to their burden of hurt and anxiety.

235. Some crises are typical of almost every marriage. Newly married couples need to learn how to accept their differences and to disengage from their parents. The arrival of a child presents new emotional challenges. Raising small children necessitates a change of lifestyle, while the onset of adolescence causes strain, frustration, and even tension between parents. An "empty nest" obliges a couple to redefine their relationship, while the need to care for aging parents involves making difficult decisions in their regard. All these are demanding situations that can cause apprehension, feelings of guilt, depression, and fatigue, with serious repercussions on a marriage.

236. Then there are those personal crises that affect the life of couples, often involving finances, problems in the workplace, emotional, social, and spiritual difficulties. Unexpected situations present themselves, disrupting family life and requiring a process of forgiveness and reconciliation. In resolving sincerely to forgive the other, each has to ask quietly and humbly if he or she has not somehow created the conditions that led to the other's mistakes. Some families break up when spouses engage in mutual recrimination, but "experience shows that with proper assistance and acts of reconciliation, through grace, a great percentage of troubled marriages find a solution in a satisfying manner. To know how to forgive and to feel forgiven is a basic experience in family life."[254] "The arduous art of reconciliation, which requires the support of grace, needs the generous cooperation of relatives and friends, and sometimes even outside help and professional assistance."[255]

237. It is becoming more and more common to think that, when one or both partners no longer feel fulfilled, or things have not turned out the way they wanted, sufficient reason exists to end the marriage. Were this the case, no marriage would last. At times, all it takes to decide that everything is over is a single instance of dissatisfaction, the absence of the other when he or she was most needed, wounded pride, or a vague fear. Inevitably, situations will arise involving human weakness and

these can prove emotionally overwhelming. One spouse may not feel fully appreciated, or may be attracted to another person. Jealousy and tensions may emerge, or new interests that consume the other's time and attention. Physical changes naturally occur in everyone. These, and so many other things, rather than threatening love, are so many occasions for reviving and renewing it.

238. In such situations, some have the maturity needed to reaffirm their choice of the other as their partner on life's journey, despite the limitations of the relationship. They realistically accept that the other cannot fulfill all their cherished dreams. Persons like this avoid thinking of themselves as martyrs; they make the most of whatever possibilities family life gives them and they work patiently at strengthening the marriage bond. They realize, after all, that every crisis can be a new "yes," enabling love to be renewed, deepened, and inwardly strengthened. When crises come, they are unafraid to get to the root of it, to renegotiate basic terms, to achieve a new equilibrium, and to move forward together. With this kind of constant openness they are able to face any number of difficult situations. In any event, while realizing that reconciliation is a possibility, we also see that "what is urgently needed today is a ministry to care for those whose marital relationship has broken down."[256]

Old wounds

239. Understandably, families often experience problems when one of their members is emotionally immature because he or she still bears the scars of earlier experiences. An unhappy childhood or adolescence can breed personal crises that affect one's marriage. Were everyone mature and normal, crises would be less frequent or less painful. Yet the fact is that only in their forties do some people achieve a maturity that should have come at the end of adolescence. Some love with the selfish, capricious, and self-centered love of a child: an insatiable love that screams or cries when it fails to get what it wants. Others love with an adolescent love marked by hostility, bitter criticism, and the need to blame others; caught up in their own emotions and fantasies, such persons expect others to fill their emptiness and to satisfy their every desire.

240. Many people leave childhood without ever having felt unconditional love. This affects their ability to be trusting and open with others. A poor relationship with one's parents and siblings, if left unhealed, can re-emerge and hurt a marriage. Unresolved issues need to be dealt with and a process of liberation must take place. When problems emerge in a marriage, before important decisions are made it is important to ensure that each spouse has come to grips with his or her own history. This involves recognizing a need for healing, insistent prayer for the grace to forgive and be forgiven, a willingness to accept help, and the determination not to give up but to keep trying. A sincere self-examination will make it possible to see how one's own shortcomings and immaturity affect the relationship. Even if it seems clear that the other person is at fault, a crisis will never be overcome simply by expecting him or her to change. We also have to ask what in our own life needs to grow or heal if the conflict is to be resolved.

Accompaniment after breakdown and divorce

241. In some cases, respect for one's own dignity and the good of the children requires not giving in to excessive demands or preventing a grave injustice, violence, or chronic ill-treatment. In such cases, "separation becomes inevitable. At times it even becomes morally necessary, precisely when it is a matter of removing the more vulnerable spouse or young children from serious injury due to abuse and violence, from humiliation and exploitation, and from disregard and indifference."[257] Even so, "separation must be considered as a last resort, after all other reasonable attempts at reconciliation have proved vain."[258]

242. The Synod Fathers noted that "special discernment is indispensable for the pastoral care of those who are separated, divorced, or abandoned. Respect needs to be shown especially for the sufferings of those who have unjustly endured separation, divorce, or abandonment, or those who have been forced by maltreatment from a husband or a wife to interrupt their life together. To forgive such an injustice that has been suffered is not easy, but grace makes this journey possible. Pastoral care must necessarily include efforts at reconciliation and mediation, through

the establishment of specialized counseling centers in dioceses."[259] At the same time, "divorced people who have not remarried, and often bear witness to marital fidelity, ought to be encouraged to find in the Eucharist the nourishment they need to sustain them in their present state of life. The local community and pastors should accompany these people with solicitude, particularly when children are involved or when they are in serious financial difficulty."[260] Family breakdown becomes even more traumatic and painful in the case of the poor, since they have far fewer resources at hand for starting a new life. A poor person, once removed from a secure family environment, is doubly vulnerable to abandonment and possible harm.

243. It is important that the divorced who have entered a new union should be made to feel part of the Church. "They are not excommunicated" and they should not be treated as such, since they remain part of the ecclesial community.[261] These situations "require careful discernment and respectful accompaniment. Language or conduct that might lead them to feel discriminated against should be avoided, and they should be encouraged to participate in the life of the community. The Christian community's care of such persons is not to be considered a weakening of its faith and testimony to the indissolubility of marriage; rather, such care is a particular expression of its charity."[262]

244. A large number of Synod Fathers also "emphasized the need to make the procedure in cases of nullity more accessible and less time consuming, and, if possible, free of charge."[263] The slowness of the process causes distress and strain on the parties. My two recent documents dealing with this issue[264] have simplified the procedures for the declarations of matrimonial nullity. With these, I wished "to make clear that the bishop himself, in the Church over which he has been appointed shepherd and head, is by that very fact the judge of those faithful entrusted to his care."[265] "The implementation of these documents is therefore a great responsibility for Ordinaries in dioceses, who are called upon to judge some cases themselves and, in every case, to ensure the faithful an easier access to justice. This involves preparing a sufficient staff, composed of clerics and lay persons who are primarily deputed to this ecclesial

service. Information, counseling, and mediation services associated with the family apostolate should also be made available to individuals who are separated or couples in crisis. These services could also include meeting with individuals in view of the preliminary inquiry of a matrimonial process (cf. *Mitis Iudex*, art. 2–3)."[266]

245. The Synod Fathers also pointed to "the consequences of separation or divorce on children, in every case the innocent victims of the situation."[267] Apart from every other consideration, the good of children should be the primary concern, and not overshadowed by any ulterior interest or objective. I make this appeal to parents who are separated: "Never ever, take your child hostage! You separated for many problems and reasons. Life gave you this trial, but your children should not have to bear the burden of this separation or be used as hostages against the other spouse. They should grow up hearing their mother speak well of their father, even though they are not together, and their father speak well of their mother."[268] It is irresponsible to disparage the other parent as a means of winning a child's affection, or out of revenge or self-justification. Doing so will affect the child's interior tranquility and cause wounds hard to heal.

246. The Church, while appreciating the situations of conflict that are part of marriage, cannot fail to speak out on behalf of those who are most vulnerable: the children who often suffer in silence. Today, "despite our seemingly evolved sensibilities and all our refined psychological analyses, I ask myself if we are not becoming numb to the hurt in children's souls. . . . Do we feel the immense psychological burden borne by children in families where the members mistreat and hurt one another, to the point of breaking the bonds of marital fidelity?"[269] Such harmful experiences do not help children to grow in the maturity needed to make definitive commitments. For this reason, Christian communities must not abandon divorced parents who have entered a new union, but should include and support them in their efforts to bring up their children. "How can we encourage those parents to do everything possible to raise their children in the Christian life, to give them an example of committed and practical faith, if we keep them at arm's length from the

life of the community, as if they were somehow excommunicated? We must keep from acting in a way that adds even more to the burdens that children in these situations already have to bear!"[270] Helping heal the wounds of parents and supporting them spiritually is also beneficial for children, who need the familiar face of the Church to see them through this traumatic experience. Divorce is an evil and the increasing number of divorces is very troubling. Hence, our most important pastoral task with regard to families is to strengthen their love, helping to heal wounds and working to prevent the spread of this drama of our times.

Certain complex situations

247. "Issues involving mixed marriages require particular attention. Marriages between Catholics and other baptized persons 'have their own particular nature, but they contain numerous elements that could well be made good use of and developed, both for their intrinsic value and for the contribution that they can make to the ecumenical movement.' For this purpose, 'an effort should be made to establish cordial cooperation between the Catholic and the non-Catholic ministers from the time that preparations begin for the marriage and the wedding ceremony' (*Familiaris Consortio*, 78). With regard to sharing in the Eucharist, 'the decision as to whether the non-Catholic party of the marriage may be admitted to Eucharistic communion is to be made in keeping with the general norms existing in the matter, both for Eastern Christians and for other Christians, taking into account the particular situation of the reception of the sacrament of Matrimony by two baptized Christians. Although the spouses in a mixed marriage share the sacraments of Baptism and Matrimony, eucharistic sharing can only be exceptional and in each case according to the stated norms' (Pontifical Council for Promoting Christian Unity, *Directory for the Application of Principles and Norms on Ecumenism*, 25 March 1993, 159–160)."[271]

248. "Marriages involving disparity of cult represent a privileged place for interreligious dialogue in everyday life. . . . They involve special difficulties regarding both the Christian identity of the family and the religious upbringing of the children. . . . The number of households with

married couples with disparity of cult, on the rise in mission territories, and even in countries of long Christian tradition, urgently requires providing a differentiated pastoral care according to various social and cultural contexts. In some countries where freedom of religion does not exist, the Christian spouse is obliged to convert to another religion in order to marry, and, therefore, cannot celebrate a canonical marriage involving disparity of cult or baptize the children. We must therefore reiterate the necessity that the religious freedom of all be respected."[272] "Attention needs to be given to the persons who enter such marriages, not only in the period before the wedding. Unique challenges face couples and families in which one partner is Catholic and the other is a non-believer. In such cases, bearing witness to the ability of the Gospel to immerse itself in these situations will make possible the upbringing of their children in the Christian faith."[273]

249. "Particular problems arise when persons in a complex marital situation wish to be baptized. These persons contracted a stable marriage at a time when at least one of them did not know the Christian faith. In such cases, bishops are called to exercise a pastoral discernment which is commensurate with their spiritual good."[274]

250. The Church makes her own the attitude of the Lord Jesus, who offers his boundless love to each person without exception.[275] During the Synod, we discussed the situation of families whose members include persons who experience same-sex attraction, a situation not easy either for parents or for children. We would like before all else to reaffirm that every person, regardless of sexual orientation, ought to be respected in his or her dignity and treated with consideration, while "every sign of unjust discrimination" is to be carefully avoided,[276] particularly any form of aggression and violence. Such families should be given respectful pastoral guidance, so that those who manifest a homosexual orientation can receive the assistance they need to understand and fully carry out God's will in their lives.[277]

251. In discussing the dignity and mission of the family, the Synod Fathers observed that, "as for proposals to place unions between homosexual

persons on the same level as marriage, there are absolutely no grounds for considering homosexual unions to be in any way similar or even remotely analogous to God's plan for marriage and family." It is unacceptable "that local Churches should be subjected to pressure in this matter and that international bodies should make financial aid to poor countries dependent on the introduction of laws to establish 'marriage' between persons of the same sex."[278]

252. Single-parent families often result from "the unwillingness of biological mothers or fathers to be part of a family; situations of violence, where one parent is forced to flee with the children; the death of one of the parents; the abandonment of the family by one parent, and other situations. Whatever the cause, single parents must receive encouragement and support from other families in the Christian community, and from the parish's pastoral outreach. Often these families endure other hardships, such as economic difficulties, uncertain employment prospects, problems with child support, and lack of housing."[279]

When death makes us feel its sting

253. At times family life is challenged by the death of a loved one. We cannot fail to offer the light of faith as a support to families going through this experience.[280] To turn our backs on a grieving family would show a lack of mercy, mean the loss of a pastoral opportunity, and close the door to other efforts at evangelization.

254. I can understand the anguish felt by those who have lost a much-loved person, a spouse with whom they have shared so much. Jesus himself was deeply moved and began to weep at the death of a friend (cf. Jn 11:33, 35). And how can we even begin to understand the grief of parents who have lost a child? "It is as if time stops altogether: a chasm opens to engulf both past and future," and "at times we even go so far as to lay the blame on God. How many people—I can understand them—get angry with God."[281] "Losing one's spouse is particularly difficult. . . . From the moment of enduring a loss, some display an ability to concentrate their energies in a greater dedication to their children and grandchildren, finding in this experience of love a renewed sense of mission in raising their

children. . . . Those who do not have relatives to spend time with and to receive affection from, should be aided by the Christian community with particular attention and availability, especially if they are poor."[282]

255. Ordinarily, the grieving process takes a fair amount of time, and when a pastor must accompany that process, he has to adapt to the demands of each of its stages. The entire process is filled with questions: about the reasons why the loved one had to die, about all the things that might have been done, about what a person experiences at the moment of death. With a sincere and patient process of prayer and interior liberation, peace returns. At particular times, we have to help the grieving person to realize that, after the loss of a loved one, we still have a mission to carry out, and that it does us no good to prolong the suffering, as if it were a form of tribute. Our loved ones have no need of our suffering, nor does it flatter them that we should ruin our lives. Nor is it the best expression of love to dwell on them and keep bringing up their name, because this is to be dependent on the past instead of continuing to love them now that they are elsewhere. They can no longer be physically present to us, yet for all death's power, "love is strong as death" (Sg 8:6). Love involves an intuition that can enable us to hear without sounds and to see the unseen. This does not mean imagining our loved ones as they were, but being able to accept them changed as they now are. The risen Jesus, when his friend Mary tried to embrace him, told her not to hold on to him (cf. Jn 20:17), in order to lead her to a different kind of encounter.

256. It consoles us to know that those who die do not completely pass away, and faith assures us that the risen Lord will never abandon us. Thus we can "prevent death from poisoning life, from rendering vain our love, from pushing us into the darkest chasm."[283] The Bible tells us that God created us out of love and made us in such a way that our life does not end with death (cf. Ws 3:2–3). Saint Paul speaks to us of an encounter with Christ immediately after death: "My desire is to depart and be with Christ" (Phil 1:23). With Christ, after death, there awaits us "what God has prepared for those who love him" (1 Cor 2:9). The Preface of the Liturgy of the Dead puts it nicely: "Although the certainty of death saddens us, we are consoled by the promise of future immortality. For

the life of those who believe in you, Lord, is not ended but changed." Indeed, "our loved ones are not lost in the shades of nothingness; hope assures us that they are in the good strong hands of God."[284]

257. One way of maintaining fellowship with our loved ones is to pray for them.[285] The Bible tells us that "to pray for the dead" is "holy and pious" (2 Mc 12:44–45). "Our prayer for them is capable not only of helping them, but also of making their intercession for us effective."[286] The Book of Revelation portrays the martyrs interceding for those who suffer injustice on earth (cf. Rv 6:9–11), in solidarity with this world and its history. Some saints, before dying, consoled their loved ones by promising them that they would be near to help them. Saint Thérèse of Lisieux wished to continue doing good from heaven.[287] Saint Dominic stated that "he would be more helpful after death . . . more powerful in obtaining graces."[288] These are truly "bonds of love,"[289] because "the union of the wayfarers with the brethren who sleep in the Lord is in no way interrupted . . . [but] reinforced by an exchange of spiritual goods."[290]

258. If we accept death, we can prepare ourselves for it. The way is to grow in our love for those who walk at our side, until that day when "death will be no more, mourning and crying and pain will be no more" (Rv 21:4). We will thus prepare ourselves to meet once more our loved ones who have died. Just as Jesus "gave back to his mother" (cf. Lk 7:15) her son who had died, so it will be with us. Let us not waste energy by dwelling on the distant past. The better we live on this earth, the greater the happiness we will be able to share with our loved ones in heaven. The more we are able to mature and develop in this world, the more gifts will we be able to bring to the heavenly banquet.

CHAPTER SEVEN

TOWARD A BETTER EDUCATION OF CHILDREN

259. Parents always influence the moral development of their children, for better or for worse. It follows that they should take up this essential role and carry it out consciously, enthusiastically, reasonably, and appropriately. Since the educational role of families is so important, and increasingly complex, I would like to discuss it in detail.

Where are our children?

260. Families cannot help but be places of support, guidance, and direction, however much they may have to rethink their methods and discover new resources. Parents need to consider what they want their children to be exposed to, and this necessarily means being concerned about who is providing their entertainment, who is entering their rooms through television and electronic devices, and with whom they are spending their free time. Only if we devote time to our children, speaking of important things with simplicity and concern, and finding healthy ways for them to spend their time, will we be able to shield them from harm. Vigilance is always necessary and neglect is never beneficial. Parents have to help prepare children and adolescents to confront the risk, for example, of aggression, abuse, or drug addiction.

261. Obsession, however, is not education. We cannot control every situation that a child may experience. Here it remains true that "time is greater than space."[291] In other words, it is more important to start processes than to dominate spaces. If parents are obsessed with always knowing where their children are and controlling all their movements, they will seek only to dominate space. But this is no way to educate, strengthen, and prepare their children to face challenges. What is most important is the ability lovingly to help them grow in freedom, maturity, overall discipline, and real autonomy. Only in this way will children come to possess the wherewithal needed to fend for themselves and to act intelligently and prudently whenever they meet with difficulties. The real

question, then, is not where our children are physically, or whom they are with at any given time, but rather where they are existentially, where they stand in terms of their convictions, goals, desires, and dreams. The questions I would put to parents are these: "Do we seek to understand 'where' our children really are in their journey? Where is their soul, do we really know? And above all, do we want to know?"[292]

262. Were maturity merely the development of something already present in our genetic code, not much would have to be done. But prudence, good judgment, and common sense are dependent not on purely quantitative growth factors, but rather on a whole series of things that come together deep within each person, or better, at the very core of our freedom. Inevitably, each child will surprise us with ideas and projects born of that freedom, which challenge us to rethink our own ideas. This is a good thing. Education includes encouraging the responsible use of freedom to face issues with good sense and intelligence. It involves forming persons who readily understand that their own lives, and the life of the community, are in their hands, and that freedom is itself a great gift.

The ethical formation of children

263. Parents rely on schools to ensure the basic instruction of their children, but can never completely delegate the moral formation of their children to others. A person's affective and ethical development is ultimately grounded in a particular experience, namely, that his or her parents can be trusted. This means that parents, as educators, are responsible, by their affection and example, for instilling in their children trust and loving respect. When children no longer feel that, for all their faults, they are important to their parents, or that their parents are sincerely concerned about them, this causes deep hurt and many difficulties along their path to maturity. This physical or emotional absence creates greater hurt than any scolding which a child may receive for doing something wrong.

264. Parents are also responsible for shaping the will of their children, fostering good habits and a natural inclination to goodness. This entails presenting certain ways of thinking and acting as desirable and worthwhile, as part of a gradual process of growth. The desire to fit into society,

or the habit of foregoing an immediate pleasure for the sake of a better and more orderly life in common, is itself a value that can then inspire openness to greater values. Moral formation should always take place with active methods and a dialogue that teaches through sensitivity and by using a language children can understand. It should also take place inductively, so that children can learn for themselves the importance of certain values, principles, and norms, rather than by imposing these as absolute and unquestionable truths.

265. Doing what is right means more than "judging what seems best" or knowing clearly what needs to be done, as important as this is. Often we prove inconsistent in our own convictions, however firm they may be; even when our conscience dictates a clear moral decision, other factors sometimes prove more attractive and powerful. We have to arrive at the point where the good that the intellect grasps can take root in us as a profound affective inclination, as a thirst for the good that outweighs other attractions and helps us to realize that what we consider objectively good is also good "for us" here and now. A good ethical education includes showing a person that it is in his own interest to do what is right. Today, it is less and less effective to demand something that calls for effort and sacrifice, without clearly pointing to the benefits which it can bring.

266. Good habits need to be developed. Even childhood habits can help to translate important interiorized values into sound and steady ways of acting. A person may be sociable and open to others, but if over a long period of time he has not been trained by his elders to say "Please," "Thank you," and "Sorry," his good interior disposition will not easily come to the fore. The strengthening of the will and the repetition of specific actions are the building blocks of moral conduct; without the conscious, free, and valued repetition of certain patterns of good behavior, moral education does not take place. Mere desire, or an attraction to a certain value, is not enough to instill a virtue in the absence of those properly motivated acts.

267. Freedom is something magnificent, yet it can also be dissipated and lost. Moral education has to do with cultivating freedom through

ideas, incentives, practical applications, stimuli, rewards, examples, models, symbols, reflections, encouragement, dialogue, and a constant rethinking of our way of doing things; all these can help develop those stable interior principles that lead us spontaneously to do good. Virtue is a conviction that has become a steadfast inner principle of operation. The virtuous life thus builds, strengthens, and shapes freedom, lest we become slaves of dehumanizing and antisocial inclinations. For human dignity itself demands that each of us "act out of conscious and free choice, as moved and drawn in a personal way from within."[293]

The value of correction as an incentive

268. It is also essential to help children and adolescents to realize that misbehavior has consequences. They need to be encouraged to put themselves in other people's shoes and to acknowledge the hurt they have caused. Some punishments—those for aggressive, antisocial conduct—can partially serve this purpose. It is important to train children firmly to ask forgiveness and to repair the harm done to others. As the educational process bears fruit in the growth of personal freedom, children come to appreciate that it was good to grow up in a family and even to put up with the demands that every process of formation makes.

269. Correction is also an incentive whenever children's efforts are appreciated and acknowledged, and they sense their parents' constant, patient trust. Children who are lovingly corrected feel cared for; they perceive that they are individuals whose potential is recognized. This does not require parents to be perfect, but to be able humbly to acknowledge their own limitations and make efforts to improve. Still, one of the things children need to learn from their parents is not to get carried away by anger. A child who does something wrong must be corrected, but never treated as an enemy or an object on which to take out one's own frustrations. Adults also need to realize that some kinds of misbehavior have to do with the frailty and limitations typical of youth. An attitude constantly prone to punishment would be harmful and not help children to realize that some actions are more serious than others. It would lead

to discouragement and resentment: "Parents, do not provoke your children" (Eph 6:4; cf. Col 3:21).

270. It is important that discipline not lead to discouragement, but be instead a stimulus to further progress. How can discipline be best interiorized? How do we ensure that discipline is a constructive limit placed on a child's actions and not a barrier standing in the way of his or her growth? A balance has to be found between two equally harmful extremes. One would be to try to make everything revolve around the child's desires; such children will grow up with a sense of their rights but not their responsibilities. The other would be to deprive the child of an awareness of his or her dignity, personal identity, and rights; such children end up overwhelmed by their duties and a need to carry out other people's wishes.

Patient realism

271. Moral education entails asking of a child or a young person only those things that do not involve a disproportionate sacrifice, and demanding only a degree of effort that will not lead to resentment or coercion. Ordinarily this is done by proposing small steps that can be understood, accepted, and appreciated, while including a proportionate sacrifice. Otherwise, by demanding too much, we gain nothing. Once the child is free of our authority, he or she may possibly cease to do good.

272. Ethical formation is at times frowned upon, due to experiences of neglect, disappointment, lack of affection, or poor models of parenting. Ethical values are associated with negative images of parental figures or the shortcomings of adults. For this reason, adolescents should be helped to draw analogies: to appreciate that values are best embodied in a few exemplary persons, but also realized imperfectly and to different degrees in others. At the same time, since their hesitation can be tied to bad experiences, they need help in the process of inner healing and in this way to grow in the ability to understand and live in peace with others and the larger community.

273. In proposing values, we have to proceed slowly, taking into consideration the child's age and abilities, without presuming to apply rigid and inflexible methods. The valuable contributions of psychology and the educational sciences have shown that changing a child's behavior involves a gradual process, but also that freedom needs to be channeled and stimulated, since by itself it does not ensure growth in maturity. Situated freedom, real freedom, is limited and conditioned. It is not simply the ability to choose what is good with complete spontaneity. A distinction is not always adequately drawn between "voluntary" and "free" acts. A person may clearly and willingly desire something evil, but do so as the result of an irresistible passion or a poor upbringing. In such cases, while the decision is voluntary, inasmuch as it does not run counter to the inclination of their desire, it is not free, since it is practically impossible for them not to choose that evil. We see this in the case of compulsive drug addicts. When they want a fix, they want it completely, yet they are so conditioned that at that moment no other decision is possible. Their decision is voluntary but not free. It makes no sense to "let them freely choose," since in fact they cannot choose, and exposing them to drugs only increases their addiction. They need the help of others and a process of rehabilitation.

Family life as an educational setting

274. The family is the first school of human values, where we learn the wise use of freedom. Certain inclinations develop in childhood and become so deeply rooted that they remain throughout life, either as attractions to a particular value or a natural repugnance to certain ways of acting. Many people think and act in a certain way because they deem it to be right on the basis of what they learned, as if by osmosis, from their earliest years: "That's how I was taught." "That's what I learned to do." In the family we can also learn to be critical about certain messages sent by the various media. Sad to say, some television programs or forms of advertising often negatively influence and undercut the values inculcated in family life.

275. In our own day, dominated by stress and rapid technological advances, one of the most important tasks of families is to provide an education in hope. This does not mean preventing children from playing with electronic devices, but rather finding ways to help them develop their critical abilities and not to think that digital speed can apply to everything in life. Postponing desires does not mean denying them but simply deferring their fulfillment. When children or adolescents are not helped to realize that some things have to be waited for, they can become obsessed with satisfying their immediate needs and develop the vice of "wanting it all now." This is a grand illusion which does not favor freedom but weakens it. On the other hand, when we are taught to postpone some things until the right moment, we learn self-mastery and detachment from our impulses. When children realize that they have to be responsible for themselves, their self-esteem is enriched. This in turn teaches them to respect the freedom of others. Obviously this does not mean expecting children to act like adults, but neither does it mean underestimating their ability to grow in responsible freedom. In a healthy family, this learning process usually takes place through the demands made by life in common.

276. The family is the primary setting for socialization, since it is where we first learn to relate to others, to listen and share, to be patient and show respect, to help one another and live as one. The task of education is to make us sense that the world and society are also our home; it trains us how to live together in this greater home. In the family, we learn closeness, care, and respect for others. We break out of our fatal self-absorption and come to realize that we are living with and alongside others who are worthy of our concern, our kindness, and our affection. There is no social bond without this primary, everyday, almost microscopic aspect of living side by side, crossing paths at different times of the day, being concerned about everything that affects us, helping one another with ordinary little things. Every day the family has to come up with new ways of appreciating and acknowledging its members.

277. In the family too, we can rethink our habits of consumption and join in caring for the environment as our common home. "The family

is the principal agent of an integral ecology, because it is the primary social subject which contains within it the two fundamental principles of human civilization on earth: the principle of communion and the principle of fruitfulness."[294] In the same way, times of difficulty and trouble in the lives of family life can teach important lessons. This happens, for example, when illness strikes, since "in the face of illness, even in families, difficulties arise due to human weakness. But in general, times of illness enable family bonds to grow stronger. . . . An education that fails to encourage sensitivity to human illness makes the heart grow cold; it makes young people 'anesthetized' to the suffering of others, incapable of facing suffering and of living the experience of limitation."[295]

278. The educational process that occurs between parents and children can be helped or hindered by the increasing sophistication of the communications and entertainment media. When well used, these media can be helpful for connecting family members who live apart from one another. Frequent contacts help to overcome difficulties.[296] Still, it is clear that these media cannot replace the need for more personal and direct dialogue, which requires physical presence or at least hearing the voice of the other person. We know that sometimes they can keep people apart rather than together, as when at dinnertime everyone is surfing on a mobile phone, or when one spouse falls asleep waiting for the other who spends hours playing with an electronic device. This is also something that families have to discuss and resolve in ways which encourage interaction without imposing unrealistic prohibitions. In any event, we cannot ignore the risks that these new forms of communication pose for children and adolescents; at times they can foster apathy and disconnect from the real world. This "technological disconnect" exposes them more easily to manipulation by those who would invade their private space with selfish interests.

279. Nor is it good for parents to be domineering. When children are made to feel that only their parents can be trusted, this hinders an adequate process of socialization and growth in affective maturity. To help expand the parental relationship to broader realities, "Christian communities are called to offer support to the educational mission of

families,"[297] particularly through the catechesis associated with Christian initiation. To foster an integral education, we need to "renew the covenant between the family and the Christian community."[298] The Synod wanted to emphasize the importance of Catholic schools which "play a vital role in assisting parents in their duty to raise their children. . . . Catholic schools should be encouraged in their mission to help pupils grow into mature adults who can view the world with the love of Jesus and who can understand life as a call to serve God."[299] For this reason, "the Church strongly affirms her freedom to set forth her teaching and the right of conscientious objection on the part of educators."[300]

The need for sex education

280. The Second Vatican Council spoke of the need for "a positive and prudent sex education" to be imparted to children and adolescents "as they grow older," with "due weight being given to the advances in the psychological, pedagogical, and didactic sciences."[301] We may well ask ourselves if our educational institutions have taken up this challenge. It is not easy to approach the issue of sex education in an age when sexuality tends to be trivialized and impoverished. It can only be seen within the broader framework of an education for love, for mutual self-giving. In such a way, the language of sexuality would not be sadly impoverished but illuminated and enriched. The sexual urge can be directed through a process of growth in self-knowledge and self-control capable of nurturing valuable capacities for joy and for loving encounter.

281. Sex education should provide information while keeping in mind that children and young people have not yet attained full maturity. The information has to come at a proper time and in a way suited to their age. It is not helpful to overwhelm them with data without also helping them to develop a critical sense in dealing with the onslaught of new ideas and suggestions, the flood of pornography, and the overload of stimuli that can deform sexuality. Young people need to realize that they are bombarded by messages that are not beneficial for their growth toward maturity. They should be helped to recognize and to seek out positive influences, while shunning the things that cripple their capacity

for love. We also have to realize that "a new and more appropriate language" is needed "in introducing children and adolescents to the topic of sexuality."[302]

282. A sexual education that fosters a healthy sense of modesty has immense value, however much some people nowadays consider modesty a relic of a bygone era. Modesty is a natural means whereby we defend our personal privacy and prevent ourselves from being turned into objects to be used. Without a sense of modesty, affection and sexuality can be reduced to an obsession with genitality and unhealthy behaviors that distort our capacity for love, and with forms of sexual violence that lead to inhuman treatment or cause hurt to others.

283. Frequently, sex education deals primarily with "protection" through the practice of "safe sex." Such expressions convey a negative attitude toward the natural procreative finality of sexuality, as if an eventual child were an enemy to be protected against. This way of thinking promotes narcissism and aggressivity in place of acceptance. It is always irresponsible to invite adolescents to toy with their bodies and their desires, as if they possessed the maturity, values, mutual commitment, and goals proper to marriage. They end up being blithely encouraged to use other persons as a means of fulfilling their needs or limitations. The important thing is to teach them sensitivity to different expressions of love, mutual concern and care, loving respect, and deeply meaningful communication. All of these prepare them for an integral and generous gift of self that will be expressed, following a public commitment, in the gift of their bodies. Sexual union in marriage will thus appear as a sign of an all-inclusive commitment, enriched by everything that has preceded it.

284. Young people should not be deceived into confusing two levels of reality: "sexual attraction creates, for the moment, the illusion of union, yet, without love, this 'union' leaves strangers as far apart as they were before."[303] The language of the body calls for a patient apprenticeship in learning to interpret and channel desires in view of authentic self-giving. When we presume to give everything all at once, it may well be that we give nothing. It is one thing to understand how fragile and bewildered

young people can be, but another thing entirely to encourage them to prolong their immaturity in the way they show love. But who speaks of these things today? Who is capable of taking young people seriously? Who helps them to prepare seriously for a great and generous love? Where sex education is concerned, much is at stake.

285. Sex education should also include respect and appreciation for differences, as a way of helping the young to overcome their self-absorption and to be open and accepting of others. Beyond the understandable difficulties which individuals may experience, the young need to be helped to accept their own body as it was created, for "thinking that we enjoy absolute power over our own bodies turns, often subtly, into thinking that we enjoy absolute power over creation. . . . An appreciation of our body as male or female is also necessary for our own self-awareness in an encounter with others different from ourselves. In this way we can joyfully accept the specific gifts of another man or woman, the work of God the Creator, and find mutual enrichment."[304] Only by losing the fear of being different, can we be freed of self-centeredness and self-absorption. Sex education should help young people to accept their own bodies and to avoid the pretension "to cancel out sexual difference because one no longer knows how to deal with it."[305]

286. Nor can we ignore the fact that the configuration of our own mode of being, whether as male or female, is not simply the result of biological or genetic factors, but of multiple elements having to do with temperament, family history, culture, experience, education, the influence of friends, family members, and respected persons, as well as other formative situations. It is true that we cannot separate the masculine and the feminine from God's work of creation, which is prior to all our decisions and experiences, and where biological elements exist which are impossible to ignore. But it is also true that masculinity and femininity are not rigid categories. It is possible, for example, that a husband's way of being masculine can be flexibly adapted to the wife's work schedule. Taking on domestic chores or some aspects of raising children does not make him any less masculine or imply failure, irresponsibility, or cause for shame. Children have to be helped to accept as normal such healthy "exchanges"

which do not diminish the dignity of the father figure. A rigid approach turns into an overaccentuation of the masculine or feminine, and does not help children and young people to appreciate the genuine reciprocity incarnate in the real conditions of matrimony. Such rigidity, in turn, can hinder the development of an individual's abilities, to the point of leading him or her to think, for example, that it is not really masculine to cultivate art or dance, or not very feminine to exercise leadership. This, thank God, has changed, but in some places deficient notions still condition the legitimate freedom and hamper the authentic development of children's specific identity and potential.

Passing on the faith

287. Raising children calls for an orderly process of handing on the faith. This is made difficult by current lifestyles, work schedules, and the complexity of today's world, where many people keep up a frenetic pace just to survive.[306] Even so, the home must continue to be the place where we learn to appreciate the meaning and beauty of the faith, to pray and to serve our neighbor. This begins with baptism, in which, as Saint Augustine said, mothers who bring their children "cooperate in the sacred birthing."[307] Thus begins the journey of growth in that new life. Faith is God's gift, received in baptism, and not our own work, yet parents are the means that God uses for it to grow and develop. Hence "it is beautiful when mothers teach their little children to blow a kiss to Jesus or to Our Lady. How much love there is in that! At that moment the child's heart becomes a place of prayer."[308] Handing on the faith presumes that parents themselves genuinely trust God, seek him, and sense their need for him, for only in this way does "one generation laud your works to another, and declare your mighty acts" (Ps 144:4) and "fathers make known to children your faithfulness" (Is 38:19). This means that we need to ask God to act in their hearts, in places where we ourselves cannot reach. A mustard seed, small as it is, becomes a great tree (cf. Mt 13:31–32); this teaches us to see the disproportion between our actions and their effects. We know that we do not own the gift, but that its care is entrusted to us. Yet our creative commitment is itself an offering which

enables us to cooperate with God's plan. For this reason, "couples and parents should be properly appreciated as active agents in catechesis. . . . Family catechesis is of great assistance as an effective method in training young parents to be aware of their mission as the evangelizers of their own family."[309]

288. Education in the faith has to adapt to each child, since older resources and recipes do not always work. Children need symbols, actions, and stories. Since adolescents usually have issues with authority and rules, it is best to encourage their own experience of faith and to provide them with attractive testimonies that win them over by their sheer beauty. Parents desirous of nurturing the faith of their children are sensitive to their patterns of growth, for they know that spiritual experience is not imposed but freely proposed. It is essential that children actually see that, for their parents, prayer is something truly important. Hence moments of family prayer and acts of devotion can be more powerful for evangelization than any catechism class or sermon. Here I would like to express my particular gratitude to all those mothers who continue to pray, like Saint Monica, for their children who have strayed from Christ.

289. The work of handing on the faith to children, in the sense of facilitating its expression and growth, helps the whole family in its evangelizing mission. It naturally begins to spread the faith to all around them, even outside of the family circle. Children who grew up in missionary families often become missionaries themselves; growing up in warm and friendly families, they learn to relate to the world in this way, without giving up their faith or their convictions. We know that Jesus himself ate and drank with sinners (cf. Mk 2:16; Mt 11:19), conversed with a Samaritan woman (cf. Jn 4:7–26), received Nicodemus by night (cf. Jn 3:1–21), allowed his feet to be anointed by a prostitute (cf. Lk 7:36–50), and did not hesitate to lay his hands on those who were sick (cf. Mk 1:40–45; 7:33). The same was true of his apostles, who did not look down on others, or cluster together in small and elite groups, cut off from the life of their people. Although the authorities harassed them, they nonetheless enjoyed the favor "of all the people" (Acts 2:47; cf. 4:21, 33; 5:13).

290. "The family is thus an agent of pastoral activity through its explicit proclamation of the Gospel and its legacy of varied forms of witness, namely solidarity with the poor, openness to a diversity of people, the protection of creation, moral and material solidarity with other families, including those most in need, commitment to the promotion of the common good and the transformation of unjust social structures, beginning in the territory in which the family lives, through the practice of the corporal and spiritual works of mercy."[310] All this is an expression of our profound Christian belief in the love of the Father who guides and sustains us, a love manifested in the total self-gift of Jesus Christ, who even now lives in our midst and enables us to face together the storms of life at every stage. In all families the Good News needs to resound, in good times and in bad, as a source of light along the way. All of us should be able to say, thanks to the experience of our life in the family: "We come to believe in the love that God has for us" (1 Jn 4:16). Only on the basis of this experience will the Church's pastoral care for families enable them to be both domestic churches and a leaven of evangelization in society.

CHAPTER EIGHT

ACCOMPANYING, DISCERNING, AND INTEGRATING WEAKNESS

291. The Synod Fathers stated that, although the Church realizes that any breach of the marriage bond "is against the will of God," she is also "conscious of the frailty of many of her children."[311] Illumined by the gaze of Jesus Christ, "she turns with love to those who participate in her life in an incomplete manner, recognizing that the grace of God works also in their lives by giving them the courage to do good, to care for one another in love, and to be of service to the community in which they live and work."[312] This approach is also confirmed by our celebration of this Jubilee Year devoted to mercy. Although she constantly holds up the call to perfection and asks for a fuller response to God, "the Church must accompany with attention and care the weakest of her children, who show signs of a wounded and troubled love, by restoring in them hope and confidence, like the beacon of a lighthouse in a port or a torch carried among the people to enlighten those who have lost their way or who are in the midst of a storm."[313] Let us not forget that the Church's task is often like that of a field hospital.

292. Christian marriage, as a reflection of the union between Christ and his Church, is fully realized in the union between a man and a woman who give themselves to each other in a free, faithful, and exclusive love, who belong to each other until death and are open to the transmission of life, and are consecrated by the sacrament, which grants them the grace to become a domestic church and a leaven of new life for society. Some forms of union radically contradict this ideal, while others realize it in at least a partial and analogous way. The Synod Fathers stated that the Church does not disregard the constructive elements in those situations which do not yet or no longer correspond to her teaching on marriage.[314]

Gradualness in pastoral care

293. The Fathers also considered the specific situation of a merely civil marriage or, with due distinction, even simple cohabitation, noting that "when such unions attain a particular stability, legally recognized, are characterized by deep affection and responsibility for their offspring, and demonstrate an ability to overcome trials, they can provide occasions for pastoral care with a view to the eventual celebration of the sacrament of Marriage."[315] On the other hand, it is a source of concern that many young people today distrust marriage and live together, putting off indefinitely the commitment of marriage, while yet others break a commitment already made and immediately assume a new one. "As members of the Church, they too need pastoral care that is merciful and helpful."[316] For the Church's pastors are not only responsible for promoting Christian marriage, but also the "pastoral discernment of the situations of a great many who no longer live this reality. Entering into pastoral dialogue with these persons is needed to distinguish elements in their lives that can lead to a greater openness to the Gospel of marriage in its fullness."[317] In this pastoral discernment, there is a need "to identify elements that can foster evangelization and human and spiritual growth."[318]

294. "The choice of a civil marriage or, in many cases, of simple cohabitation, is often not motivated by prejudice or resistance to a sacramental union, but by cultural or contingent situations."[319] In such cases, respect also can be shown for those signs of love which in some way reflect God's own love.[320] We know that there is "a continual increase in the number of those who, after having lived together for a long period, request the celebration of marriage in Church. Simply to live together is often a choice based on a general attitude opposed to anything institutional or definitive; it can also be done while awaiting more security in life (a steady job and steady income). In some countries, *de facto* unions are very numerous, not only because of a rejection of values concerning the family and matrimony, but primarily because celebrating a marriage is considered too expensive in the social circumstances. As a result, material poverty drives people into *de facto* unions."[321] Whatever the case, "all these situations require a constructive response seeking to transform

them into opportunities that can lead to the full reality of marriage and family in conformity with the Gospel. These couples need to be welcomed and guided patiently and discreetly."[322] That is how Jesus treated the Samaritan woman (cf. Jn 4:1–26): he addressed her desire for true love, in order to free her from the darkness in her life and to bring her to the full joy of the Gospel.

295. Along these lines, Saint John Paul II proposed the so-called "law of gradualness" in the knowledge that the human being "knows, loves, and accomplishes moral good by different stages of growth."[323] This is not a "gradualness of law" but rather a gradualness in the prudential exercise of free acts on the part of subjects who are not in a position to understand, appreciate, or fully carry out the objective demands of the law. For the law is itself a gift of God which points out the way, a gift for everyone without exception; it can be followed with the help of grace, even though each human being "advances gradually with the progressive integration of the gifts of God and the demands of God's definitive and absolute love in his or her entire personal and social life."[324]

The discernment of "irregular" situations[325]

296. The Synod addressed various situations of weakness or imperfection. Here I would like to reiterate something I sought to make clear to the whole Church, lest we take the wrong path: "There are two ways of thinking which recur throughout the Church's history: casting off and reinstating. The Church's way, from the time of the Council of Jerusalem, has always been the way of Jesus, the way of mercy and reinstatement. . . . The way of the Church is not to condemn anyone forever; it is to pour out the balm of God's mercy on all those who ask for it with a sincere heart. . . . For true charity is always unmerited, unconditional and gratuitous."[326] Consequently, there is a need "to avoid judgments which do not take into account the complexity of various situations" and "to be attentive, by necessity, to how people experience distress because of their condition."[327]

297. It is a matter of reaching out to everyone, of needing to help each person find his or her proper way of participating in the ecclesial

community and thus to experience being touched by an "unmerited, unconditional, and gratuitous" mercy. No one can be condemned forever, because that is not the logic of the Gospel! Here I am not speaking only of the divorced and remarried, but of everyone, in whatever situation they find themselves. Naturally, if someone flaunts an objective sin as if it were part of the Christian ideal, or wants to impose something other than what the Church teaches, he or she can in no way presume to teach or preach to others; this is a case of something which separates from the community (cf. Mt 18:17). Such a person needs to listen once more to the Gospel message and its call to conversion. Yet even for that person there can be some way of taking part in the life of community, whether in social service, prayer meetings, or another way that his or her own initiative, together with the discernment of the parish priest, may suggest. As for the way of dealing with different "irregular" situations, the Synod Fathers reached a general consensus, which I support: "In considering a pastoral approach toward people who have contracted a civil marriage, who are divorced and remarried, or simply living together, the Church has the responsibility of helping them understand the divine pedagogy of grace in their lives and offering them assistance so they can reach the fullness of God's plan for them,"[328] something which is always possible by the power of the Holy Spirit.

298. The divorced who have entered a new union, for example, can find themselves in a variety of situations, which should not be pigeonholed or fit into overly rigid classifications leaving no room for a suitable personal and pastoral discernment. One thing is a second union consolidated over time, with new children, proven fidelity, generous self giving, Christian commitment, a consciousness of its irregularity and of the great difficulty of going back without feeling in conscience that one would fall into new sins. The Church acknowledges situations "where, for serious reasons, such as the children's upbringing, a man and woman cannot satisfy the obligation to separate."[329] There are also the cases of those who made every effort to save their first marriage and were unjustly abandoned, or of "those who have entered into a second union for the sake of the children's upbringing, and are sometimes subjectively certain

in conscience that their previous and irreparably broken marriage had never been valid."[330] Another thing is a new union arising from a recent divorce, with all the suffering and confusion which this entails for children and entire families, or the case of someone who has consistently failed in his obligations to the family. It must remain clear that this is not the ideal which the Gospel proposes for marriage and the family. The Synod Fathers stated that the discernment of pastors must always take place "by adequately distinguishing,"[331] with an approach which "carefully discerns situations."[332] We know that no "easy recipes" exist.[333]

299. I am in agreement with the many Synod Fathers who observed that "the baptized who are divorced and civilly remarried need to be more fully integrated into Christian communities in the variety of ways possible, while avoiding any occasion of scandal. The logic of integration is the key to their pastoral care, a care which would allow them not only to realize that they belong to the Church as the body of Christ, but also to know that they can have a joyful and fruitful experience in it. They are baptized; they are brothers and sisters; the Holy Spirit pours into their hearts gifts and talents for the good of all. Their participation can be expressed in different ecclesial services, which necessarily requires discerning which of the various forms of exclusion currently practiced in the liturgical, pastoral, educational, and institutional framework, can be surmounted. Such persons need to feel not as excommunicated members of the Church, but instead as living members, able to live and grow in the Church and experience her as a mother who welcomes them always, who takes care of them with affection and encourages them along the path of life and the Gospel. This integration is also needed in the care and Christian upbringing of their children, who ought to be considered most important."[334]

300. If we consider the immense variety of concrete situations such as those I have mentioned, it is understandable that neither the Synod nor this Exhortation could be expected to provide a new set of general rules, canonical in nature and applicable to all cases. What is possible is simply a renewed encouragement to undertake a responsible personal and pastoral discernment of particular cases, one which would recognize that,

since "the degree of responsibility is not equal in all cases,"[335] the consequences or effects of a rule need not necessarily always be the same.[336] Priests have the duty to "accompany [the divorced and remarried] in helping them to understand their situation according to the teaching of the Church and the guidelines of the bishop. Useful in this process is an examination of conscience through moments of reflection and repentance. The divorced and remarried should ask themselves: how did they act toward their children when the conjugal union entered into crisis; whether or not they made attempts at re-conciliation; what has become of the abandoned party; what consequences the new relationship has on the rest of the family and the community of the faithful; and what example is being set for young people who are preparing for marriage. A sincere reflection can strengthen trust in the mercy of God which is not denied anyone."[337] What we are speaking of is a process of accompaniment and discernment which "guides the faithful to an awareness of their situation before God. Conversation with the priest, in the internal forum, contributes to the formation of a correct judgment on what hinders the possibility of a fuller participation in the life of the Church and on what steps can foster it and make it grow. Given that gradualness is not in the law itself (cf. *Familiaris Consortio*, 34), this discernment can never prescind from the Gospel demands of truth and charity, as proposed by the Church. For this discernment to happen, the following conditions must necessarily be present: humility, discretion, and love for the Church and her teaching, in a sincere search for God's will and a desire to make a more perfect response to it."[338] These attitudes are essential for avoiding the grave danger of misunderstandings, such as the notion that any priest can quickly grant "exceptions," or that some people can obtain sacramental privileges in exchange for favors. When a responsible and tactful person, who does not presume to put his or her own desires ahead of the common good of the Church, meets with a pastor capable of acknowledging the seriousness of the matter before him, there can be no risk that a specific discernment may lead people to think that the Church maintains a double standard.

Mitigating factors in pastoral discernment

301. For an adequate understanding of the possibility and need of special discernment in certain "irregular" situations, one thing must always be taken into account, lest anyone think that the demands of the Gospel are in any way being compromised. The Church possesses a solid body of reflection concerning mitigating factors and situations. Hence it is can no longer simply be said that all those in any "irregular" situation are living in a state of mortal sin and are deprived of sanctifying grace. More is involved here than mere ignorance of the rule. A subject may know full well the rule, yet have great difficulty in understanding "its inherent values,"[339] or be in a concrete situation which does not allow him or her to act differently and decide otherwise without further sin. As the Synod Fathers put it, "factors may exist which limit the ability to make a decision."[340] Saint Thomas Aquinas himself recognized that someone may possess grace and charity, yet not be able to exercise any one of the virtues well;[341] in other words, although someone may possess all the infused moral virtues, he does not clearly manifest the existence of one of them, because the outward practice of that virtue is rendered difficult: "Certain saints are said not to possess certain virtues, in so far as they experience difficulty in the acts of those virtues, even though they have the habits of all the virtues."[342]

302. The *Catechism of the Catholic Church* clearly mentions these factors: "imputability and responsibility for an action can be diminished or even nullified by ignorance, inadvertence, duress, fear, habit, inordinate attachments, and other psychological or social factors."[343] In another paragraph, the *Catechism* refers once again to circumstances which mitigate moral responsibility, and mentions at length "affective immaturity, force of acquired habit, conditions of anxiety or other psychological or social factors that lessen or even extenuate moral culpability."[344] For this reason, a negative judgment about an objective situation does not imply a judgment about the imputability or culpability of the person involved.[345] On the basis of these convictions, I consider very fitting what many Synod Fathers wanted to affirm: "Under certain circumstances people find it very difficult to act differently. Therefore, while upholding a general

rule, it is necessary to recognize that responsibility with respect to certain actions or decisions is not the same in all cases. Pastoral discernment, while taking into account a person's properly formed conscience, must take responsibility for these situations. Even the consequences of actions taken are not necessarily the same in all cases."[346]

303. Recognizing the influence of such concrete factors, we can add that individual conscience needs to be better incorporated into the Church's praxis in certain situations which do not objectively embody our understanding of marriage. Naturally, every effort should be made to encourage the development of an enlightened conscience, formed and guided by the responsible and serious discernment of one's pastor, and to encourage an ever greater trust in God's grace. Yet conscience can do more than recognize that a given situation does not correspond objectively to the overall demands of the Gospel. It can also recognize with sincerity and honesty what for now is the most generous response which can be given to God, and come to see with a certain moral security that it is what God himself is asking amid the concrete complexity of one's limits, while yet not fully the objective ideal. In any event, let us recall that this discernment is dynamic; it must remain ever open to new stages of growth and to new decisions which can enable the ideal to be more fully realized.

Rules and discernment

304. It is reductive simply to consider whether or not an individual's actions correspond to a general law or rule, because that is not enough to discern and ensure full fidelity to God in the concrete life of a human being. I earnestly ask that we always recall a teaching of Saint Thomas Aquinas and learn to incorporate it in our pastoral discernment: "Although there is necessity in the general principles, the more we descend to matters of detail, the more frequently we encounter defects. . . . In matters of action, truth or practical rectitude is not the same for all, as to matters of detail, but only as to the general principles; and where there is the same rectitude in matters of detail, it is not equally known to all. . . . The principle will be found to fail, according as we descend

further into detail."[347] It is true that general rules set forth a good which can never be disregarded or neglected, but in their formulation they cannot provide absolutely for all particular situations. At the same time, it must be said that, precisely for that reason, what is part of a practical discernment in particular circumstances cannot be elevated to the level of a rule. That would not only lead to an intolerable casuistry, but would endanger the very values which must be preserved with special care.[348]

305. For this reason, a pastor cannot feel that it is enough simply to apply moral laws to those living in "irregular" situations, as if they were stones to throw at people's lives. This would bespeak the closed heart of one used to hiding behind the Church's teachings, "sitting on the chair of Moses and judging at times with superiority and superficiality difficult cases and wounded families."[349] Along these same lines, the International Theological Commission has noted that "natural law could not be presented as an already established set of rules that impose themselves *a priori* on the moral subject; rather, it is a source of objective inspiration for the deeply personal process of making decisions."[350] Because of forms of conditioning and mitigating factors, it is possible that in an objective situation of sin—which may not be subjectively culpable, or fully such—a person can be living in God's grace, can love, and can also grow in the life of grace and charity, while receiving the Church's help to this end.[351] Discernment must help to find possible ways of responding to God and growing in the midst of limits. By thinking that everything is black and white, we sometimes close off the way of grace and of growth, and discourage paths of sanctification which give glory to God. Let us remember that "a small step, in the midst of great human limitations, can be more pleasing to God than a life which appears outwardly in order, but moves through the day without confronting great difficulties."[352] The practical pastoral care of ministers and of communities must not fail to embrace this reality.

306. In every situation, when dealing with those who have difficulties in living God's law to the full, the invitation to pursue the *via caritatis* must be clearly heard. Fraternal charity is the first law of Christians (cf. Jn 15:12; Gal 5:14). Let us not forget the reassuring words of Scripture:

"Maintain constant love for one another, for love covers a multitude of sins" (1 Pt 4:8); "Atone for your sins with righteousness, and your iniquities with mercy to the oppressed, so that your prosperity may be prolonged" (Dn 4:27); "As water extinguishes a blazing fire, so almsgiving atones for sins" (Sir 3:30). This is also what Saint Augustine teaches: "Just as, at the threat of a fire, we would run for water to extinguish it . . . so too, if the flame of sin rises from our chaff and we are troubled, if the chance to perform a work of mercy is offered us, let us rejoice in it, as if it were a fountain offered us to extinguish the blaze."[353]

The logic of pastoral mercy

307. In order to avoid all misunderstanding, I would point out that in no way must the Church desist from proposing the full ideal of marriage, God's plan in all its grandeur: "Young people who are baptized should be encouraged to understand that the sacrament of Marriage can enrich their prospects of love and that they can be sustained by the grace of Christ in the sacrament and by the possibility of participating fully in the life of the Church."[354] A lukewarm attitude, any kind of relativism, or an undue reticence in proposing that ideal, would be a lack of fidelity to the Gospel and also of love on the part of the Church for young people themselves. To show understanding in the face of exceptional situations never implies dimming the light of the fuller ideal, or proposing less than what Jesus offers to the human being. Today, more important than the pastoral care of failures is the pastoral effort to strengthen marriages and thus to prevent their breakdown.

308. At the same time, from our awareness of the weight of mitigating circumstances—psychological, historical, and even biological—it follows that "without detracting from the evangelical ideal, there is a need to accompany with mercy and patience the eventual stages of personal growth as these progressively appear," making room for "the Lord's mercy, which spurs us on to do our best."[355] I understand those who prefer a more rigorous pastoral care which leaves no room for confusion. But I sincerely believe that Jesus wants a Church attentive to the goodness which the Holy Spirit sows in the midst of human weakness, a Mother

who, while clearly expressing her objective teaching, "always does what good she can, even if in the process, her shoes get soiled by the mud of the street."[356] The Church's pastors, in proposing to the faithful the full ideal of the Gospel and the Church's teaching, must also help them to treat the weak with compassion, avoiding aggravation or unduly harsh or hasty judgments. The Gospel itself tells us not to judge or condemn (cf. Mt 7:1; Lk 6:37). Jesus "expects us to stop looking for those personal or communal niches which shelter us from the maelstrom of human misfortune, and instead to enter into the reality of other people's lives and to know the power of tenderness. Whenever we do so, our lives become wonderfully complicated."[357]

309. It is providential that these reflections take place in the context of a Holy Year devoted to mercy, because also in the variety of situations affecting families "the Church is commissioned to proclaim the mercy of God, the beating heart of the Gospel, which in its own way must penetrate the mind and heart of every person. The Bride of Christ must pattern her behavior after the Son of God who goes out to everyone without exception."[358] She knows that Jesus himself is the shepherd of the hundred, not just of the ninety-nine. He loves them all. On the basis of this realization, it will become possible for "the balm of mercy to reach everyone, believers and those far away, as a sign that the kingdom of God is already present in our midst."[359]

310. We cannot forget that "mercy is not only the working of the Father; it becomes a criterion for knowing who his true children are. In a word, we are called to show mercy because mercy was first shown to us."[360] This is not sheer romanticism or a lukewarm response to God's love, which always seeks what is best for us, for "mercy is the very foundation of the Church's life. All of her pastoral activity should be caught up in the tenderness which she shows to believers; nothing in her preaching and her witness to the world can be lacking in mercy."[361] It is true that at times "we act as arbiters of grace rather than its facilitators. But the Church is not a tollhouse; it is the house of the Father, where there is a place for everyone, with all their problems."[362]

311. The teaching of moral theology should not fail to incorporate these considerations, for although it is quite true that concern must be shown for the integrity of the Church's moral teaching, special care should always be shown to emphasize and encourage the highest and most central values of the Gospel,[363] particularly the primacy of charity as a response to the completely gratuitous offer of God's love. At times we find it hard to make room for God's unconditional love in our pastoral activity.[364] We put so many conditions on mercy that we empty it of its concrete meaning and real significance. That is the worst way of watering down the Gospel. It is true, for example, that mercy does not exclude justice and truth, but first and foremost we have to say that mercy is the fullness of justice and the most radiant manifestation of God's truth. For this reason, we should always consider "inadequate any theological conception which in the end puts in doubt the omnipotence of God and, especially, his mercy."[365]

312. This offers us a framework and a setting which help us avoid a cold bureaucratic morality in dealing with more sensitive issues. Instead, it sets us in the context of a pastoral discernment filled with merciful love, which is ever ready to understand, forgive, accompany, hope, and above all integrate. That is the mindset which should prevail in the Church and lead us to "open our hearts to those living on the outermost fringes of society."[366] I encourage the faithful who find themselves in complicated situations to speak confidently with their pastors or with other lay people whose lives are committed to the Lord. They may not always encounter in them a confirmation of their own ideas or desires, but they will surely receive some light to help them better understand their situation and discover a path to personal growth. I also encourage the Church's pastors to listen to them with sensitivity and serenity, with a sincere desire to understand their plight and their point of view, in order to help them live better lives and to recognize their proper place in the Church.

CHAPTER NINE

THE SPIRITUALITY OF MARRIAGE AND THE FAMILY

313. Charity takes on different hues, depending on the state of life to which we have been called. Several decades ago, in speaking of the lay apostolate, the Second Vatican Council emphasized the spirituality born of family life. The Council stated that lay spirituality "will take its particular character from the circumstances of . . . married and family life,"[367] and that "family cares should not be foreign" to that spirituality.[368] It is worth pausing to describe certain basic characteristics of this specific spirituality that unfolds in family life and its relationships.

A spirituality of supernatural communion

314. We have always spoken of how God dwells in the hearts of those living in his grace. Today we can add that the Trinity is present in the temple of marital communion. Just as God dwells in the praises of his people (cf. Ps 22:3), so he dwells deep within the marital love that gives him glory.

315. The Lord's presence dwells in real and concrete families, with all their daily troubles and struggles, joys and hopes. Living in a family makes it hard for us to feign or lie; we cannot hide behind a mask. If that authenticity is inspired by love, then the Lord reigns there, with his joy and his peace. The spirituality of family love is made up of thousands of small but real gestures. In that variety of gifts and encounters which deepen communion, God has his dwelling place. This mutual concern "brings together the human and the divine,"[369] for it is filled with the love of God. In the end, marital spirituality is a spirituality of the bond, in which divine love dwells.

316. A positive experience of family communion is a true path to daily sanctification and mystical growth, a means for deeper union with God. The fraternal and communal demands of family life are an incentive to growth in openness of heart and thus to an ever fuller encounter with the Lord. The word of God tells us that "the one who hates his brother is in the darkness, and walks in the darkness" (1 Jn 2:11); such a

person "abides in death" (1 Jn 3:14) and "does not know God" (1 Jn 4:8). My predecessor Benedict XVI pointed out that "closing our eyes to our neighbor also blinds us to God,"[370] and that, in the end, love is the only light which can "constantly illuminate a world grown dim."[371] If only we "love one another, God abides in us and his love is perfected in us" (1 Jn 4:12). Since "the human person has an inherent social dimension,"[372] and "the first and basic expression of that social dimension of the person is the married couple and the family,"[373] spirituality becomes incarnate in the communion of the family. Hence, those who have deep spiritual aspirations should not feel that the family detracts from their growth in the life of the Spirit, but rather see it as a path which the Lord is using to lead them to the heights of mystical union.

Gathered in prayer in the light of Easter

317. If a family is centered on Christ, he will unify and illumine its entire life. Moments of pain and difficulty will be experienced in union with the Lord's cross, and his closeness will make it possible to surmount them. In the darkest hours of a family's life, union with Jesus in his abandonment can help avoid a breakup. Gradually, "with the grace of the Holy Spirit, [the spouses] grow in holiness through married life, also by sharing in the mystery of Christ's cross, which transforms difficulties and sufferings into an offering of love."[374] Moreover, moments of joy, relaxation, celebration, and even sexuality can be experienced as a sharing in the full life of the resurrection. Married couples shape with different daily gestures a "God-enlightened space in which to experience the hidden presence of the risen Lord."[375]

318. Family prayer is a special way of expressing and strengthening this paschal faith.[376] A few minutes can be found each day to come together before the living God, to tell him our worries, to ask for the needs of our family, to pray for someone experiencing difficulty, to ask for help in showing love, to give thanks for life and for its blessings, and to ask Our Lady to protect us beneath her maternal mantle. With a few simple words, this moment of prayer can do immense good for our families. The various expressions of popular piety are a treasure of spirituality

for many families. The family's communal journey of prayer culminates by sharing together in the Eucharist, especially in the context of the Sunday rest. Jesus knocks on the door of families, to share with them the Eucharistic supper (cf. Rv 3:20). There, spouses can always seal anew the paschal covenant which united them and which ought to reflect the covenant which God sealed with mankind in the cross.[377] The Eucharist is the sacrament of the new covenant, where Christ's redemptive work is carried out (cf. Lk 22:20). The close bond between married life and the Eucharist thus becomes all the more clear.[378] For the food of the Eucharist offers the spouses the strength and incentive needed to live the marriage covenant each day as a "domestic church."[379]

A spirituality of exclusive and free love

319. Marriage is also the experience of belonging completely to another person. Spouses accept the challenge and aspiration of supporting one another, growing old together, and in this way reflecting God's own faithfulness. This firm decision, which shapes a style of life, is an "interior requirement of the covenant of conjugal love,"[380] since "a person who cannot choose to love forever can hardly love for even a single day."[381] At the same time, such fidelity would be spiritually meaningless were it simply a matter of following a law with obedient resignation. Rather, it is a matter of the heart, into which God alone sees (cf. Mt 5:28). Every morning, on rising, we reaffirm before God our decision to be faithful, come what may in the course of the day. And all of us, before going to sleep, hope to wake up and continue this adventure, trusting in the Lord's help. In this way, each spouse is for the other a sign and instrument of the closeness of the Lord, who never abandons us: "Lo, I am with you always, to the close of the age" (Mt 28:20).

320. There comes a point where a couple's love attains the height of its freedom and becomes the basis of a healthy autonomy. This happens when each spouse realizes that the other is not his or her own, but has a much more important master, the one Lord. No one but God can presume to take over the deepest and most personal core of the loved one; he alone can be the ultimate center of their life. At the same time, the

principle of spiritual realism requires that one spouse not presume that the other can completely satisfy his or her needs. The spiritual journey of each—as Dietrich Bonhoeffer nicely put it—needs to help them to a certain "disillusionment" with regard to the other,[382] to stop expecting from that person something which is proper to the love of God alone. This demands an interior divestment. The space which each of the spouses makes exclusively for their personal relationship with God not only helps heal the hurts of life in common, but also enables the spouses to find in the love of God the deepest source of meaning in their own lives. Each day we have to invoke the help of the Holy Spirit to make this interior freedom possible.

A spirituality of care, consolation, and incentive

321. "Christian couples are, for each other, for their children, and for their relatives, cooperators of grace and witnesses of the faith."[383] God calls them to bestow life and to care for life. For this reason the family "has always been the nearest 'hospital.'"[384] So let us care for one another, guide and encourage one another, and experience this as a part of our family spirituality. Life as a couple is a daily sharing in God's creative work, and each person is for the other a constant challenge from the Holy Spirit. God's love is proclaimed "through the living and concrete word whereby a man and the woman express their conjugal love."[385] The two are thus mutual reflections of that divine love which comforts with a word, a look, a helping hand, a caress, an embrace. For this reason "to want to form a family is to resolve to be a part of God's dream, to choose to dream with him, to want to build with him, to join him in this saga of building a world where no one will feel alone."[386]

322. All family life is a "shepherding" in mercy. Each of us, by our love and care, leaves a mark on the life of others; with Paul, we can say: "You are our letter of recommendation, written on your hearts . . . not with ink, but with the Spirit of the living God" (2 Cor 3:2–3). Each of us is a "fisher of men" (Lk 5:10) who in Jesus' name "casts the nets" (cf. Lk 5:5) to others, or a farmer who tills the fresh soil of those whom he or she loves, seeking to bring out the best in them. Marital fruitfulness involves

helping others, for "to love anybody is to expect from him something which can neither be defined nor foreseen; it is at the same time in some way to make it possible for him to fulfill this expectation."[387] This is itself a way to worship God, who has sown so much good in others in the hope that we will help make it grow.

323. It is a profound spiritual experience to contemplate our loved ones with the eyes of God and to see Christ in them. This demands a freedom and openness which enable us to appreciate their dignity. We can be fully present to others only by giving fully of ourselves and forgetting all else. Our loved ones merit our complete attention. Jesus is our model in this, for whenever people approached to speak with him, he would meet their gaze, directly and lovingly (cf. Mk 10:21). No one felt overlooked in his presence, since his words and gestures conveyed the question: "What do you want me to do for you?" (Mk 10:51). This is what we experience in the daily life of the family. We are constantly reminded that each of those who live with us merits complete attention, since he or she possesses infinite dignity as an object of the Father's immense love. This gives rise to a tenderness which can "stir in the other the joy of being loved. Tenderness is expressed in a particular way by exercising loving care in treating the limitations of the other, especially when they are evident."[388]

324. Led by the Spirit, the family circle is not only open to life by generating it within itself, but also by going forth and spreading life by caring for others and seeking their happiness. This openness finds particular expression in hospitality,[389] which the word of God eloquently encourages: "Do not neglect to show hospitality to strangers, for thereby some have entertained angels unawares" (Heb 13:2). When a family is welcoming and reaches out to others, especially the poor and the neglected, it is "a symbol, witness and participant in the Church's motherhood."[390] Social love, as a reflection of the Trinity, is what truly unifies the spiritual meaning of the family and its mission to others, for it makes present the kerygma in all its communal imperatives. The family lives its spirituality precisely by being at one and the same time a domestic church and a vital cell for transforming the world.[391]

•••

325. The teaching of the Master (cf. Mt 22:30) and Saint Paul (cf. 1 Cor 7:29–31) on marriage is set—and not by chance—in the context of the ultimate and definitive dimension of our human existence. We urgently need to rediscover the richness of this teaching. By heeding it, married couples will come to see the deeper meaning of their journey through life. As this Exhortation has often noted, no family drops down from heaven perfectly formed; families need constantly to grow and mature in the ability to love. This is a never-ending vocation born of the full communion of the Trinity, the profound unity between Christ and his Church, the loving community which is the Holy Family of Nazareth, and the pure fraternity existing among the saints of heaven. Our contemplation of the fulfillment which we have yet to attain also allows us to see in proper perspective the historical journey which we make as families, and in this way to stop demanding of our interpersonal relationships a perfection, a purity of intentions, and a consistency which we will only encounter in the kingdom to come. It also keeps us from judging harshly those who live in situations of frailty. All of us are called to keep striving toward something greater than ourselves and our families, and every family must feel this constant impulse. Let us make this journey as families, let us keep walking together. What we have been promised is greater than we can imagine. May we never lose heart because of our limitations, or ever stop seeking that fullness of love and communion which God holds out before us.

Prayer to the Holy Family

Jesus, Mary, and Joseph,
in you we contemplate
the splendor of true love;
to you we turn with trust.

Holy Family of Nazareth,
grant that our families too
may be places of communion and prayer,

authentic schools of the Gospel
and small domestic churches.

Holy Family of Nazareth,
may families never again experience
violence, rejection, and division;
may all who have been hurt or scandalized
find ready comfort and healing.

Holy Family of Nazareth,
make us once more mindful
of the sacredness and inviolability of the family,
and its beauty in God's plan.

Jesus, Mary, and Joseph,
Graciously hear our prayer.

Amen.

Given in Rome, at Saint Peter's, during the Extraordinary Jubilee of Mercy, on 19 March, the Solemnity of Saint Joseph, in the year 2016, the fourth of my Pontificate.

FRANCISCUS

Notes

1. Third Extraordinary General Assembly of the Synod of Bishops, *Relatio Synodi* (18 October 2014), 2.

2. Fourteenth Ordinary General Assembly of the Synod of Bishops, *Relatio Finalis* (24 October 2015), 3.

3. *Concluding Address of the Fourteenth Ordinary General Assembly of the Synod of Bishops* (24 October 2015): *L'Osservatore Romano*, 26–27 October 2015, 13; cf. Pontifical Biblical Commission, *Fede e cultura alla luce della Bibbia. Atti della sessione plenaria 1979 della Pontificia Commissione Biblica*, Turin, 1981; Second Vatican Ecumenical Council, Pastoral Constitution on the Church in the Modern World *Gaudium et Spes*, 44; John Paul II, Encyclical Letter *Redemptoris Missio* (7 December 1990), 52: AAS 83 (1991), 300; Apostolic Exhortation *Evangelii Gaudium* (24 November 2013), 69, 117: AAS 105 (2013), 1049, 1068–1069.

4. *Address at the Meeting of Families in Santiago de Cuba* (22 September 2015): *L'Osservatore Romano*, 24 September 2015, 7.

5. Jorge Luis Borges, "Calle Desconocida," in *Fervor de Buenos Aires*, Buenos Aires, 2011, 23.

6. Homily at the Eucharistic Celebration in Puebla de los Ángeles (28 January 1979), 2: AAS 71 (1979), 184.

7. Cf. ibid.

8. John Paul II, Apostolic Exhortation *Familiaris Consortio* (22 November 1981), 4: AAS 74 (1982), 84.

9. *Relatio Synodi* 2014, 5.

10. Spanish Bishops' Conference, *Matrimonio y familia* (6 July 1979), 3, 16, 23.

11. *Relatio Finalis* 2015, 5.

12. *Relatio Synodi* 2014, 5.

13. *Relatio Finalis* 2015, 8.

14. *Address to the United States Congress* (24 September 2015): *L'Osservatore Romano*, 26 September 2015, 7.

15. *Relatio Finalis* 2015, 29.

16. *Relatio Synodi* 2014, 10.

17. Third Extraordinary General Assembly of the Synod of Bishops, *Message*, 18 October 2014.

18. *Relatio Synodi* 2014, 10.

19. *Relatio Finalis* 2015, 7.

20. Ibid., 63.

21. Catholic Bishops' Conference of Korea, *Towards a Culture of Life!* (15 March 2007), 2.

22. *Relatio Synodi* 2014, 6.

23. Pontifical Council for the Family, *Charter of the Rights of the Family* (22 October 1983), art. 11.

24. Cf. *Relatio Finalis* 2015, 11–12.

25. Pontifical Council for the Family, *Charter of the Rights of the Family* (22 October 1983), Introduction.

26. Ibid., 9.

27. *Relatio Finalis* 2015, 14.

28. *Relatio Synodi* 2014, 8.

29. Cf. *Relatio Finalis* 2015, 78.

30. *Relatio Synodi* 2014, 8.

31. *Relatio Finalis* 2015, 23; cf. *Message for the World Day of Migrants and Refugees* on 17 January 2016 (12 September 2015), *L'Osservatore Romano*, 2 October 2015, 8.

32. *Relatio Finalis* 2015, 24.

33. Ibid., 21.

34. Ibid., 17.

35. Ibid., 20.

36. Cf. ibid., 15.

37. *Concluding Address of the Fourteenth Ordinary General Assembly of the Synod of Bishops* (24 October 2015): *L'Osservatore Romano*, 26–27 October 2015, 13.

38. Argentinian Bishops' Conference, *Navega mar adentro* (31 May 2003), 42.

39. Mexican Bishops' Conference, *Que en Cristo Nuestra Paz México tenga vida digna* (15 February 2009), 67.

40. *Relatio Finalis* 2015, 25.

41. Ibid., 10.

42. *Catechesis* (22 April 2015): *L'Osservatore Romano*, 23 April 2015, 7.

43. *Catechesis* (29 April 2015): *L'Osservatore Romano*, 30 April 2015, 8.

44. *Relatio Finalis* 2015, 28.

45. Ibid., 8.

46. Ibid., 58.

47. Ibid., 33.

48. *Relatio Synodi* 2014, 11.

49. Colombian Bishops' Conference, *A tiempos dificiles, colombianos nuevos* (13 February 2003), 3.

50. Apostolic Exhortation *Evangelii Gaudium* (24 November 2013), 35: AAS 105 (2013), 1034.

51. Ibid., 164: AAS 105 (2013), 1088.

52. Ibid.

53. Ibid., 165: AAS 105 (2013), 1089.

54. *Relatio Synodi* 2014, 12.

55. Ibid., 14.

56. Ibid., 16.

57. *Relatio Finalis* 2015, 41.

58. Ibid., 38.

59. *Relatio Synodi* 2014, 17.

60. *Relatio Finalis* 2015, 43.

61. *Relatio Synodi* 2014, 18.

62. Ibid., 19.

63. *Relatio Finalis* 2015, 38.

64. John Paul II, Apostolic Exhortation *Familiaris Consortio* (22 November 1981), 13: AAS 74 (1982), 94.

65. *Relatio Synodi* 2014, 21.

66. *Catechism of the Catholic Church*, 1642.

67. Ibid.

68. *Catechesis* (6 May 2015): *L'Osservatore Romano*, 7 May 2015, 8.

69. Leo the Great, *Epistula Rustico Narbonensi Episcopo*, Inquis. IV: PL 54, 1205A; cf. Hincmar of Rheims, *Epist.* 22: PL 126, 142.

70. Cf. Pius XII, Encyclical Letter *Mystici Corporis Christi* (29 June 1943): AAS 35 (1943), 202: "*Matrimonio enim quo coniuges sibi invicem sunt ministri gratiae . . .*"

71. Cf. *Code of Canon Law*, cc. 1116; 1161–1165; *Code of Canons of the Eastern Churches*, 832; 848–852.

72. Ibid., c. 1055 §2.

73. *Relatio Synodi* 2014, 23.

74. John Paul II, Apostolic Exhortation *Familiaris Consortio* (22 November 1981), 9: AAS 74 (1982), 90.

75. *Relatio Finalis* 2015, 47.

76. Ibid.

77. Homily for the Concluding Mass of the Eighth World Meeting of Families in Philadelphia (27 September 2015): *L'Osservatore Romano*, 28–29 September 2015, 7.

78. *Relatio Finalis* 2015, 53–54.

79. Ibid., 51.

80. Second Vatican Ecumenical Council, Pastoral Constitution on the Church in the Modern World *Gaudium et Spes*, 48.

81. Cf. *Code of Canon Law*, c. 1055 § 1: "*ad bonum coniugum atque ad prolis generationem et educationem ordinatum.*"

82. *Catechism of the Catholic Church*, 2360.

83. Ibid., 1654.

84. Second Vatican Ecumenical Council, Pastoral Constitution on the Church in the Modern World *Gaudium et Spes*, 48.

85. *Catechism of the Catholic Church*, 2366.

86. Cf. Paul VI, Encyclical Letter *Humanae Vitae* (25 July 1968), 11–12: AAS 60 (1968), 488–489.

87. *Catechism of the Catholic Church*, 2378.

88. Congregation for the Doctrine of the Faith, Instruction *Donum Vitae* (22 February 1987), II, 8: AAS 80 (1988), 97.

89. *Relatio Finalis* 2015, 63.

90. *Relatio Synodi* 2014, 57.

91. Ibid., 58.

92. Ibid., 57.

93. *Relatio Finalis* 2015, 64.

94. *Relatio Synodi* 2014, 60.

95. Ibid., 61.

96. *Code of Canon Law*, c. 1136; cf. *Code of Canons of the Eastern Churches*, 627.

97. Pontifical Council for the Family, *The Truth and Meaning of Human Sexuality* (8 December 1995), 23.

98. *Catechesis* (20 May 2015): *L'Osservatore Romano*, 21 May 2015, 8.

99. John Paul II, Apostolic Exhortation *Familiaris Consortio* (28 November 1981) 38: AAS 74 (1982), 129.

100. Cf. *Address to the Diocesan Conference of Rome* (14 June 2015): *L'Osservatore Romano*, 15–16 June 2015, 8.

101. *Relatio Synodi* 2014, 23.

102. *Relatio Finalis* 2015, 52.

103. Ibid., 49–50.

104. *Catechism of the Catholic Church*, 1641.

105. Cf. Benedict XVI, Encyclical Letter *Deus Caritas Est* (25 December 2005), 2: AAS 98 (2006), 218.

106. *Spiritual Exercises*, Contemplation to Attain Love (230).

107. Octavio Paz, *La llama doble*, Barcelona, 1993, 35.

108. Thomas Aquinas, *Summa Theologiae* II–II, q. 114, art. 2, ad 1.

109. *Catechesis* (13 May 2005): *L'Osservatore Romano*, 14 May 2015, 8.

110. Thomas Aquinas, *Summa Theologiae*, II–II, q. 27, art. 1, ad 2.

111. Ibid., q. 27, art. 1.

112. *Catechesis* (13 May 2015): *L'Osservatore Romano*, 14 May 2015, 8.

113. John Paul II, Apostolic Exhortation *Familiaris Consortio* (22 November 1981), 21: AAS 74 (1982), 106.

114. Martin Luther King Jr., *Sermon Delivered at Dexter Avenue Baptist Church*, Montgomery, Alabama, 17 November 1957.

115. Thomas Aquinas calls love a *vis unitiva* (*Summa Theologiae* I, q. 20, art. 1, ad 3), echoing a phrase of Pseudo-Dionysius the Areopagite (*De Divinis Nominibus*, IV, 12: PG 3, 709).

116. Thomas Aquinas, *Summa Theologiae* II–II, q. 27, art. 2.

117. Encyclical Letter *Casti Connubii* (31 December 1930): AAS 22 (1930), 547–548.

118. John Paul II, Apostolic Exhortation *Familiaris Consortio* (22 November 1981) 13: AAS 74 (1982), 94.

119. *Catechesis* (2 April 2014): *L'Osservatore Romano*, 3 April 2014, 8.

120. Ibid.

121. John Paul II, Apostolic Exhortation *Familiaris Consortio* (22 November 1981), 9: AAS 75 (1982), 90.

122. Thomas Aquinas, *Summa Contra Gentiles* III, 123; cf. Aristotle, *Nicomachean Ethics*, 8, 12 (ed. Bywater, Oxford, 1984, 174).

123. Encyclical Letter *Lumen Fidei* (29 June 2013), 52: AAS 105 (2013), 590.

124. *De sacramento matrimonii*, I, 2; in id., *Disputationes*, III, 5, 3 (ed. Giuliano, Naples, 1858), 778.

125. Second Vatican Ecumenical Council, Pastoral Constitution on the Church in the Modern World *Gaudium et Spes*, 50.

126. Ibid., 49.

127. Cf. *Summa Theologiae* I–II, q. 31, art. 3., ad 3.

128. Second Vatican Ecumenical Council, Pastoral Constitution on the Church in the Modern World *Gaudium et Spes*, 48.

129. Cf. Thomas Aquinas, *Summa Theologiae* I–II, q. 26, art. 3.

130. Ibid., q. 110, art. 1.

131. Augustine, *Confessions*, VIII, III, 7: PL 32, 752.

132. *Address to the Pilgrimage of Families during the Year of Faith* (26 October 2013): AAS 105 (2013), 980.

133. Angelus Message (29 December 2013): *L'Osservatore Romano*, 30–31 December 2013, 7.

134. *Address to the Pilgrimage of Families during the Year of Faith* (26 October 2013): AAS 105 (2013), 978.

135. *Summa Theologiae* II–II, q. 24, art. 7.

136. Second Vatican Ecumenical Council, Pastoral Constitution on the Church in the Modern World *Gaudium et Spes*, 48.

137. Chilean Bishops' Conference, *La vida y la familia: regalos de Dios para cada uno de nosotros* (21 July 2014).

138. Second Vatican Ecumenical Council, Pastoral Constitution on the Church in the Modern World *Gaudium et Spes*, 49.

139. A. Sertillanges, *L'Amour chrétien*, Paris, 1920, 174.

140. Cf. Thomas Aquinas, *Summa Theologiae* I–II, q. 24, art. 1.

141. Cf. ibid., q. 59, art. 5.

142. Encyclical Letter *Deus Caritas Est* (25 December 2005), 3: AAS 98 (2006), 219–220.

143. Ibid., 4: AAS 98 (2006), 220.

144. Cf. Thomas Aquinas, *Summa Theologiae* I–II, q. 32, art. 7.

145. Cf. id., *Summa Theologiae* II–II, q. 153, art. 2, ad 2: "*Abundantia delectationis quae est in actu venereo secundum rationem ordinato, non contrariatur medio virtutis.*"

146. John Paul II, *Catechesis* (22 October 1980), 5: *Insegnamenti* III/2 (1980), 951.

147. Ibid., 3.

148. Id., *Catechesis* (24 September 1980), 4: *Insegnamenti* III/2 (1980), 719.

149. *Catechesis* (12 November 1980), 2: *Insegnamenti* III/2 (1980), 1133.

150. Ibid., 4.

151. Ibid., 5.

152. Ibid., 1:1132.

153. *Catechesis* (16 January 1980), 1: *Insegnamenti* III/1 (1980), 151.

154. Josef Pieper, *Über die Liebe*, Munich, 2014, 174. English: *On Love*, in *Faith, Hope, Love*, San Francisco, 1997, 256.

155. John Paul II, Encyclical Letter *Evangelium Vitae* (25 March 1995), 23: AAS 87 (1995), 427.

156. Paul VI, Encyclical Letter *Humanae Vitae* (25 July 1968), 13: AAS 60 (1968), 489.

157. Second Vatican Ecumenical Council, Pastoral Constitution on the Church in the Modern World *Gaudium et Spes*, 49.

158. *Catechesis* (18 June 1980), 5: *Insegnamenti* III / 1 (1980), 1778.

159. Ibid., 6.

160. Cf. *Catechesis* (30 July 1980), 1: *Insegnamenti* III / 2 (1980), 311.

161. *Catechesis* (8 April 1981), 3: *Insegnamenti* IV / 1 (1981), 904.

162. *Catechesis* (11 August 1982), 4: *Insegnamenti* V / 3 (1982), 205–206.

163. Encyclical Letter *Deus Caritas Est* (25 December 2005), 5: AAS 98 (2006), 221.

164. Ibid., 7.

165. *Relatio Finalis* 2015, 22.

166. *Catechesis* (14 April 1982), 1: *Insegnamenti* V / 1 (1982), 1176.

167. *Glossa in quatuor libros sententiarum Petri Lombardi*, IV, XXVI, 2 (Quaracchi, 1957, 446).

168. John Paul II, *Catechesis* (7 April 1982), 2: *Insegnamenti* V / 1 (1982), 1127.

169. Id., *Catechesis* (14 April 1982), 3: *Insegnamenti* V / 1 (1982), 1177.

170. Ibid.

171. Id., Encyclical Letter *Redemptor Hominis* (4 March 1979), 10: AAS 71 (1979), 274.

172. Cf. Thomas Aquinas, *Summa Theologiae*, II–II, q. 27, art. 1.

173. Pontifical Council for the Family, *Family, Marriage, and "De Facto" Unions* (26 July 2000), 40.

174. John Paul II, *Catechesis* (31 October 1984), 6: *Insegnamenti* VII / 2 (1984), 1072.

175. Benedict XVI, Encyclical Letter *Deus Caritas Est* (25 December 2005), 8: AAS 98 (2006), 224.

176. John Paul II, Apostolic Exhortation *Familiaris Consortio* (22 November 1981), 14: AAS 74 (1982), 96.

177. *Catechesis* (11 February 2015): *L'Osservatore Romano*, 12 February 2015, 8.

178. Ibid.

179. *Catechesis* (8 April 2015): *L'Osservatore Romano*, 9 April 2015, 8.

180. Ibid.

181. Cf. Second Vatican Ecumenical Council, Pastoral Constitution on the Church in the Modern World *Gaudium et Spes*, 51: "Let us all be convinced that human life and its transmission are realities whose meaning is not limited by the horizons of this life only: their true evaluation and full meaning can only be understood in reference to our eternal destiny."

182. *Letter to the Secretary General of the United Nations Organization on Population and Development* (18 March 1994): *Insegnamenti* XVII/1 (1994), 750–751.

183. John Paul II, *Catechesis* (12 March 1980), 3: *Insegnamenti* III/1 (1980), 543.

184. Ibid.

185. *Address at the Meeting with Families in Manila* (16 January 2015): AAS 107 (2015), 176.

186. *Catechesis* (11 February 2015): *L'Osservatore Romano*, 12 February 2015, 8.

187. *Catechesis* (14 October 2015): *L'Osservatore Romano*, 15 October 2015, 8.

188. Australian Catholic Bishops' Conference, Pastoral Letter *Don't Mess with Marriage* (24 November 2015), 13.

189. Second Vatican Ecumenical Council, Pastoral Constitution on the Church in the Modern World *Gaudium et Spes*, 50.

190. John Paul II, *Catechesis* (12 March 1980), 2: *Insegnamenti* III/1 (1980), 542.

191. Cf. id., Apostolic Letter *Mulieris Dignitatem* (15 August 1988), 30–31: AAS 80 (1988), 1726–1729.

192. *Catechesis* (7 January 2015): *L'Osservatore Romano*, 7–8 January 2015, 8.

193. Ibid.

194. *Catechesis* (28 January 2015): *L'Osservatore Romano*, 29 January 2015, 8.

195. Ibid.

196. Cf. *Relatio Finalis* 2015, 28.

197. *Catechesis* (4 February 2015): *L'Osservatore Romano*, 5 February 2015, 8.

198. Ibid.

199. Second Vatican Ecumenical Council, Pastoral Constitution on the Church in the Modern World *Gaudium et Spes*, 50.

200. Fifth General Conference of the Latin American and Caribbean Bishops, *Aparecida Document* (29 June 2007), No. 457.

201. *Relatio Finalis* 2015, 65.

202. Ibid.

203. *Address at the Meeting with Families in Manila* (16 January 2015): AAS 107 (2015), 178.

204. Mario Benedetti, "Te Quiero," *in Poemas de otros*, Buenos Aires 1993, 316: *"Tus manos son mi caricia / mis acordes cotidianos / te quiero porque tus manos / trabajan por la justicia. // Si te quiero es porque sos / mi amor mi cómplice y todo / y en la calle codo a codo / somos mucho más que dos."*

205. Cf. *Catechesis* (16 September 2015): *L'Osservatore Romano*, 17 September 2015, 8.

206. *Catechesis* (7 October 2015): *L'Osservatore Romano*, 9 October 2015, 8.

207. Benedict XVI, Encyclical Letter *Deus Caritas Est* (25 December 2005), 14: AAS 98 (2006), 228.

208. Cf. *Relatio Finalis* 2015, 11.

209. *Catechesis* (18 March 2015): *L'Osservatore Romano*, 19 March 2015, 8.

210. *Catechesis* (11 February 2015): *L'Osservatore Romano*, 12 February 2015, 8.

211. Cf. *Relatio Finalis* 2015, 17–18.

212. *Catechesis* (4 March 2015): *L'Osservatore Romano*, 5 March 2015, 8.

213. *Catechesis* (11 March 2015): *L'Osservatore Romano*, 12 March 2015, 8.

214. Apostolic Exhortation *Familiaris Consortio*, 27 (22 November 1981): AAS 74 (1982), 113.

215. Id., *Address to Participants in the "International Forum on Active Aging"* (5 September 1980), 5: *Insegnamenti* III/2 (1980), 539.

216. *Relatio Finalis* 2015, 18.

217. *Catechesis* (4 March 2015): *L'Osservatore Romano*, 5 March 2015, 8.

218. Ibid.

219. *Address at the Meeting with the Elderly* (28 September 2014): *L'Osservatore Romano*, 29-30 September 2014, 7.

220. *Catechesis* (18 February 2015): *L'Osservatore Romano*, 19 February 2015, 8.

221. Ibid.

222. Ibid.

223. John Paul II, Apostolic Exhortation *Familiaris Consortio* (22 November 1981), 18: AAS 74 (1982), 101.

224. *Catechesis* (7 October 2015): *L'Osservatore Romano*, 8 October 2015, 8.

225. *Relatio Synodi* 2014, 30.

226. Ibid., 31.

227. *Relatio Finalis* 2015, 56.

228. Ibid., 89.

229. *Relatio Synodi* 2014, 32.

230. Ibid., 33.

231. Ibid., 38.

232. *Relatio Finalis* 2015, 77.

233. Ibid., 61.

234. Ibid.

235. Ibid.

236. Ibid.

237. Cf. *Relatio Synodi* 2014, 26.

238. Ibid., 39.

239. Italian Bishops' Conference, Episcopal Commission on Family and Life, *Orientamenti pastorali sulla preparazione al matrimonio e alla famiglia* (22 October 2012), 1.

240. Ignatius of Loyola, *Spiritual Exercises*, Annotation 2.

241. Ibid., Annotation 5.

242. John Paul II, *Catechesis* (27 June 1984), 4: *Insegnamenti* VII/1 (1984), 1941.

243. *Catechesis* (21 October 2015): *L'Osservatore Romano*, 22 October 2015, 12.

244. Kenya Conference of Catholic Bishops, *Lenten Message* (18 February 2015).

245. Cf. Pius XI, Encyclical Letter *Casti Connubii* (31 December 1930): AAS 22 (1930), 583.

246. John Paul II, *Catechesis* (4 July 1984), 3, 6: *Insegnamenti* VII/2 (1984), 9, 10.

247. *Relatio Finalis* 2015, 59.

248. Ibid., 63.

249. Second Vatican Ecumenical Council, Pastoral Constitution on the Church in the Modern World *Gaudium et Spes*, 50.

250. *Relatio Finalis* 2015, 63.

251. *Relatio Synodi* 2014, 40.

252. Ibid., 34.

253. *Cántico Espiritual* B, XXV, 11.

254. *Relatio Synodi* 2014, 44.

255. *Relatio Finalis* 2015, 81.

256. Ibid., 78.

257. *Catechesis* (24 June 2015): *L'Osservatore Romano*, 25 June 2015, 8.

258. John Paul II, Apostolic Exhortation *Familiaris Consortio* (22 November 1981), 83: AAS 74 (1982), 184.

259. *Relatio Synodi* 2014, 47.

260. Ibid., 50.

261. *Catechesis* (5 August 2015): *L'Osservatore Romano*, 6 August 2015, 7.

262. *Relatio Synodi* 2014, 51; cf. *Relatio Finalis* 2015, 84.

263. Ibid., 48.

264. Motu Proprio *Mitis Iudex Dominus Iesus* (15 August 2015): *L'Osservatore Romano*, 9 September 2015, 3–4; cf. Motu Proprio *Mitis et Misericors Iesus* (15 August 2015): *L'Osservatore Romano*, 9 September 2015, 5–6.

265. Motu Proprio *Mitis Iudex Dominus Iesus* (15 August 2015), Preamble, III: *L'Osservatore Romano*, 9 September 2015, 3.

266. *Relatio Finalis* 2015, 82.

267. *Relatio Synodi* 2014, 47.

268. *Catechesis* (20 May 2015): *L'Osservatore Romano*, 21 May 2015, 8.

269. *Catechesis* (24 June 2015): *L'Osservatore Romano*, 25 June 2015, 8.

270. *Catechesis* (5 August 2015): *L'Osservatore Romano*, 6 August 2015, 7.

271. *Relatio Finalis* 2015, 72.

272. Ibid., 73.

273. Ibid., 74.

274. Ibid., 75.

275. Cf. Bull *Misericordiae Vultus*, 12: AAS 107 (2015), 407.

276. *Catechism of the Catholic Church*, 2358; cf. *Relatio Finalis* 2015, 76.

277. Ibid.

278. *Relatio Finalis* 2015, 76; cf. Congregation for the Doctrine of the Faith, *Considerations Regarding Proposals to Give Legal Recognition to Unions between Homosexual Persons* (3 June 2003), 4.

279. Ibid., 80.

280. Cf. ibid., 20.

281. *Catechesis* (17 June 2015): *L'Osservatore Romano*, 18 June 2015, 8.

282. *Relatio Finalis* 2015, 19.
283. *Catechesis* (17 June 2015): *L'Osservatore Romano*, 18 June 2015, 8.
284. Ibid.
285. Cf. *Catechism of the Catholic Church*, 958.
286. Ibid.
287. Cf. Thérèse of Lisieux, *Derniers Entretiens: Le "carnet jaune" de Mère Agnès*, 17 July 1897, in *Oeuvres Complètes*, Paris, 1996, 1050. Her Carmelite sisters spoke of a promise made by Saint Thérèse that her departure from this world would be "like a shower of roses" (ibid., 9 June 1897, 1013).
288. Jordan of Saxony, *Libellus de principiis Ordinis Praedicatorum*, 93: *Monumenta Historica Sancti Patris Nostri Dominici*, XVI, Rome, 1935, 69.
289. Cf. *Catechism of the Catholic Church*, 957.
290. Second Vatican Ecumenical Council, Dogmatic Constitution on the Church *Lumen Gentium*, 49.
291. Apostolic Exhortation *Evangelii Gaudium* (24 November 2013), 222: AAS 105 (2013), 1111.
292. *Catechesis* (20 May 2015): *L'Osservatore Romano*, 21 May 2015, 8.
293. Second Vatican Ecumenical Council, Pastoral Constitution on the Church in the Modern World *Gaudium et Spes*, 17.
294. *Catechesis* (30 September 2015): *L'Osservatore Romano*, 1 October 2015, 8.
295. *Catechesis* (10 June 2015): *L'Osservatore Romano*, 11 June 2015, 8.
296. Cf. *Relatio Finalis* 2015, 67.
297. *Catechesis* (20 May 2015): *L'Osservatore Romano*, 21 May 2015, 8.
298. *Catechesis* (9 September 2015): *L'Osservatore Romano*, 10 September 2015, 8.
299. *Relatio Finalis* 2015, 68.
300. Ibid., 58.
301. Second Vatican Ecumenical Council, Declaration on Christian Education *Gravissimum Educationis*, 1.
302. *Relatio Finalis* 2015, 56.
303. Erich Fromm, *The Art of Loving*, New York, 1956, 54.
304. Encyclical Letter *Laudato Si'* (24 May 2015), 155.
305. *Catechesis* (15 April 2015): *L'Osservatore Romano*, 16 April 2015, 8.
306. Cf. *Relatio Finalis* 2015, 13–14.
307. Augustine, *De sancta virginitate* 7, 7: PL 40, 400.
308. *Catechesis* (26 August 2015): *L'Osservatore Romano*, 27 August 2015, 8.
309. *Relatio Finalis* 2015, 89.
310. Ibid., 93.
311. *Relatio Synodi* 2014, 24.
312. Ibid., 25.
313. Ibid., 28.
314. Cf. ibid., 41, 43; *Relatio Finalis* 2015, 70.
315. Ibid., 27.

316. Ibid., 26.

317. Ibid., 41.

318. Ibid.

319. *Relatio Finalis* 2015, 71.

320. Cf. ibid.

321. *Relatio Synodi* 2014, 42.

322. Ibid., 43.

323. Apostolic Exhortation *Familiaris Consortio* (22 November 1981), 34: AAS 74 (1982), 123.

324. Ibid., 9: AAS 74 (1982), 90.

325. Cf. *Catechesis* (24 June 2015): *L'Osservatore Romano*, 25 June 2015, 8.

326. Homily at Mass Celebrated with the New Cardinals (15 February 2015): AAS 107 (2015), 257.

327. *Relatio Finalis* 2015, 51.

328. *Relatio Synodi* 2014, 25.

329. John Paul II, Apostolic Exhortation *Familiaris Consortio* (22 November 1981), 84: AAS 74 (1982), 186. In such situations, many people, knowing and accepting the possibility of living "as brothers and sisters" which the Church offers them, point out that if certain expressions of intimacy are lacking, "it often happens that faithfulness is endangered and the good of the children suffers" (Second Vatican Ecumenical Council, Pastoral Constitution on the Church in the Modern World *Gaudium et Spes*, 51).

330. Ibid.

331. *Relatio Synodi* 2014, 26.

332. Ibid., 45.

333. Benedict XVI, *Address to the Seventh World Meeting of Families* in Milan (2 June 2012), Response n. 5: *Insegnamenti* VIII/1 (2012), 691.

334. *Relatio Finalis* 2015, 84.

335. Ibid., 51.

336. This is also the case with regard to sacramental discipline, since discernment can recognize that in a particular situation no grave fault exists. In such cases, what is found in another document applies: cf. *Evangelii Gaudium* (24 November 2013), 44 and 47: AAS 105 (2013), 1038–1040.

337. *Relatio Finalis* 2015, 85.

338. Ibid., 86.

339. John Paul II, Apostolic Exhortation *Familiaris Consortio* (22 November 1981), 33: AAS 74 (1982), 121.

340. *Relatio Finalis* 2015, 51.

341. Cf. *Summa Theologiae* I–II, q. 65, art. 3, ad 2; *De Malo*, q. 2, art. 2.

342. Ibid., ad 3.

343. No. 1735.

344. Ibid., 2352; Congregation for the Doctrine of the Faith, Declaration on Euthanasia *Iura et Bona* (5 May 1980), II: AAS 72 (1980), 546; John Paul II, in his critique of the category of "fundamental option," recognized that "doubtless there can occur situations which are very complex and obscure from a psychological viewpoint, and which have an influence on the sinner's subjective culpability" (Apostolic Exhortation *Reconciliatio et Paenitentia* [2 December 1984], 17: AAS 77 [1985], 223).

345. Cf. Pontifical Council for Legislative Texts, *Declaration Concerning the Admission to Holy Communion of Faithful Who Are Divorced and Remarried* (24 June 2000), 2.

346. *Relatio Finalis* 2015, 85.

347. *Summa Theologiae*, I–II, q. 94, art. 4.

348. In another text, referring to the general knowledge of the rule and the particular knowledge of practical discernment, Saint Thomas states that "if only one of the two is present, it is preferable that it be the knowledge of the particular reality, which is closer to the act": *Sententia libri Ethicorum*, VI, 6 (ed. Leonina, t. XLVII, 354).

349. *Address for the Conclusion of the Fourteenth Ordinary General Assembly of the Synod of Bishops* (24 October 2015): *L'Osservatore Romano*, 26–27 October 2015, 13.

350. International Theological Commission, *In Search of a Universal Ethic: A New Look at Natural Law* (2009), 59.

351. In certain cases, this can include the help of the sacraments. Hence, "I want to remind priests that the confessional must not be a torture chamber, but rather an encounter with the Lord's mercy" (Apostolic Exhortation *Evangelii Gaudium* [24 November 2013], 44: AAS 105 [2013], 1038). I would also point out that the Eucharist "is not a prize for the perfect, but a powerful medicine and nourishment for the weak" (ibid., 47: 1039).

352. Apostolic Exhortation *Evangelii Gaudium* (24 November 2013), 44: AAS 105 (2013), 1038–1039.

353. *De Catechizandis Rudibus*, I, 14, 22: PL 40, 327; cf. Apostolic Exhortation *Evangelii Gaudium* (24 November 2013), 194: AAS 105 (2013), 1101.

354. *Relatio Synodi* 2014, 26.

355. Apostolic Exhortation *Evangelii Gaudium* (24 November 2013), 44: AAS 105 (2013), 1038.

356. Ibid., 45.

357. Ibid., 270.

358. Bull *Misericordiae Vultus* (11 April 2015), 12: AAS 107 (2015), 407.

359. Ibid., 5:402.

360. Ibid., 9:405.

361. Ibid., 10:406.

362. Apostolic Exhortation *Evangelii Gaudium* (24 November 2013), 47: AAS 105 (2013), 1040.

363. Cf. ibid., 36–37: AAS 105 (2013), 1035.

364. Perhaps out of a certain scrupulosity, concealed beneath a zeal for fidelity to the truth, some priests demand of penitents a purpose of amendment so lacking

in nuance that it causes mercy to be obscured by the pursuit of a supposedly pure justice. For this reason, it is helpful to recall the teaching of Saint John Paul II, who stated that the possibility of a new fall "should not prejudice the authenticity of the resolution" (*Letter to Cardinal William W. Baum on the Occasion of the Course on the Internal Forum Organized by the Apostolic Penitentiary* [22 March 1996], 5: *Insegnamenti* XIX/1 [1996], 589).

365. International Theological Commission, *The Hope of Salvation for Infants Who Die Without Being Baptized* (19 April 2007), 2.

366. Bull *Misericordiae Vultus* (11 April 2015), 15: AAS 107 (2015), 409.

367. Decree on the Apostolate of the Laity *Apostolicam Actuositatem*, 4.

368. Cf. ibid.

369. Second Vatican Ecumenical Council, Pastoral Constitution on the Church in the Modern World *Gaudium et Spes*, 49.

370. Encyclical Letter *Deus Caritas Est* (25 December 2015), 16: AAS 98 (2006), 230.

371. Ibid., 39: AAS 98 (2006), 250.

372. John Paul II, Post-Synodal Apostolic Exhortation *Christifideles Laici* (30 December 1988), 40: AAS 81 (1989), 468.

373. Ibid.

374. *Relatio Finalis* 2015, 87.

375. John Paul II, Post-Synodal Apostolic Exhortation *Vita Consecrata* (25 March 1996), 42: AAS 88 (1996), 416.

376. Cf. *Relatio Finalis* 2015, 87.

377. Cf. John Paul II, Apostolic Exhortation *Familiaris Consortio* (22 November 1981), 57: AAS 74 (1982), 150.

378. Nor should we forget that God's covenant with his people is expressed as an espousal (cf. Ez 16:8, 60; Is 62:5; Hos 2:21–22), and that the new covenant is also presented as a betrothal (cf. Rv 19:7; 21:2; Eph 5:25).

379. Second Vatican Ecumenical Council, Dogmatic Constitution on the Church *Lumen Gentium*, 11.

380. John Paul II, Apostolic Exhortation *Familiaris Consortio* (22 November 1981), 11: AAS 74 (1982), 93.

381. Id., Homily at Mass with Families, Cordoba, Argentina (8 April 1987), 4: *Insegnamenti* X/1 (1987), 1161–1162.

382. Cf. *Gemeinsames Leben*, Munich, 1973, 18. English: *Life Together*, New York, 1954, 27.

383. Second Vatican Ecumenical Council, Decree on the Apostolate of the Laity *Apostolicam Actuositatem*, 11.

384. *Catechesis* (10 June 2015): *L'Osservatore Romano*, 11 June 2015, 8.

385. John Paul II, Apostolic Exhortation *Familiaris Consortio* (22 November 1981), 12: AAS 74 (1982), 93.

386. *Address at the Prayer Vigil of the Festival of Families*, Philadelphia (26 September 2015): *L'Osservatore Romano*, 28–29 September 2015, 6.

387. Gabriel Marcel, *Homo Viator: prolégomènes à une métaphysique de l'espérance,* Paris, 1944, 66. English: *Homo Viator: An Introduction to a Metaphysics of Hope,* London, 1951, 49.

388. *Relatio Finalis* 2015, 88.

389. Cf. John Paul II, Apostolic Exhortation *Familiaris Consortio* (22 November 1981), 44: AAS 74 (1982), 136.

390. Ibid., 49: AAS 74 (1982), 141.

391. For the social aspects of the family, cf. Pontifical Council for Justice and Peace, *Compendium of the Social Doctrine of the Church,* 248–254.

Pope Francis was born Jorge Mario Bergoglio in Buenos Aires, Argentina, to parents of Italian descent. He was ordained a Jesuit priest in 1969, ordained auxiliary bishop of Buenos Aires in 1992, installed as bishop in 1998, and elevated to cardinal in 2001. He was elected by the College of Cardinals in March 2013 as the 266th pontiff of the Roman Catholic Church and took the name Francis for St. Francis of Assisi. He is the first Jesuit pope, the first pope from the Americas, and the first non-European pope in more than twelve centuries.